CONSUMERISM IN THE UNITED STATES

CONSUMERISM IN THE UNITED STATES

An Inter-Industry Analysis

edited by

JOEL R. EVANS

PRAEGER

PRAEGER SPECIAL STUDIES • PRAEGER SCIENTIFIC

Library of Congress Cataloging in Publication Data

Main entry under title:

Consumerism in the United States.

    Includes bibliographies.
    1. Consumer protection--United States.   I. Evans,
Joel R.
HC110.C63C6435   381'.34'0973   79-25341
ISBN 0-03-056846-3

Published in 1980 by Praeger Publishers
CBS Educational and Professional Publishing
A Division of CBS, Inc.
521 Fifth Avenue, New York, New York 10017 U.S.A.

0123456789   038   987654321

Printed in the United States of America

PREFACE

This book examines consumerism in an empirical manner for a wide variety of industries. In each of ten industries consumerism is described historically and the roles of consumer groups, government, the industry, and individual companies are explored. A balanced presentation is offered, since industry and company viewpoints are included as well as government and consumerism perspectives.

It is intended that this book detail the state of consumerism in the United States in a broad, comprehensive, empirical, objective, and analytical manner. All parties under investigation—consumer groups, government, industry, and companies—as well as educators and students, should learn from the findings of this study. They also should find certain statements controversial and thought provoking. All of these reactions are sought.

Eleven people worked almost two years to produce this finished volume. The study began with the development of a research proposal by the editor. Ten graduating MBA students agreed to participate in the research, with their finished projects representing master theses. All of the researchers did exhaustive literature searches, primary data collection, and thorough analyses for the industries they assessed. Their work is contained in Chapters 2 through 11, which were tightly edited and shortened by the editor.

The entire study was sponsored by the School of Business at Hofstra University. Special thanks are due to Harold Lazarus, Barry Berman, John Ullmann, the late Fred Stuart, Adelaide Berg, and Florence Schwanemann (all of Hofstra) for their help and support. Thank you to Phyllis Knauf for her fine typing job, "rushed" as usual.

To my wife, Linda, and daughter, Jennifer, thank you again for letting me barricade myself in my office in pursuit of many dreams.

One last note: any errors of omission or commission rest with the editor.

CONTENTS

Chapter

LIST OF TABLES AND FIGURES

CONSUMERISM IN THE UNITED STATES

1

A NEW APPROACH TO
THE STUDY OF CONSUMERISM

Joel R. Evans

INTRODUCTION

Consumerism may be defined as:

A social force within the environment designed to aid
and protect the consumer by exerting legal, moral, and
economic pressure on business [1, p. 24].

And:

the widening range of activities of government, business,
and independent organizations that are designed to protect
individuals from practices that infringe upon their rights
as consumers [2, p. 12].

In the United States, consumerism has evolved through three
distinct eras: the early 1900s, the 1930s to the 1950s, and the 1960s
to the present. The first era concentrated on unsafe and unhealthy
business practices. The second era centered on preserving competition. The third era has focused on a wide range of activities.

Two major events ushered in the modern era of consumerism.
First, President John F. Kennedy enunciated the consumer's bill of
rights in 1962. Kennedy said consumers had the right to safety, to
information, to choose, and to be heard. Second, Ralph Nader published Unsafe at Any Speed in 1965. The book was an indictment of the
automobile industry, particularly the Corvair. Since the mid-1960s,
a number of consumer laws and regulations have been enacted.

The current consumer movement has grown in importance for
several reasons, including:

The increased sophistication and demands of consumers.

The continuation of unfair, unsafe, and misleading business practices.

Publicity of poor business practices by the media.

Heightened government intervention.

Insensitivity of some business people to consumer needs.

High inflation rates.

Shortages of essential products and services.

Unsatisfactory processing of complaints.

Excessive expectations by consumers.

The emergence of consumer advocates.

The desire of many companies to please consumers by understanding and reacting to their wants and behavior.

Demands of citizens for perfection.

There are several elements in the consumerism process besides individual consumers and companies. The most important of these are trade associations (which function as representatives of member companies and present their views), consumer groups, government agencies, and government legislation. To show their scope, a detailed, but not all-inclusive, listing of these elements is presented in Tables 1.1 through 1.4. The listing covers ten industries: appliances, banking, clothing, household products, lead, asbestos, and fluorocarbons, mail order, petroleum, pharmaceuticals, professions, and retailing. From these tables, it should be clear that the modern era of consumerism is complex and extensive. Industries have generated a large amount of trade associations to cope with the effects of consumerism. These associations far outnumber consumer groups and government agencies.

THE PURPOSE OF THE STUDY

Thousands of articles, books, and research reports have been written on consumerism. Many of these works are cited in the bibliographies following Chapters 2 through 11. Previous discussions of consumerism frequently have been issue- or industry-specific. That is, each project centered on one consumer topic, such as product safety or deceptive advertising, or one industry, such as major appliances or banking. A number of other works have been theoretical, without empirical evidence to support conclusions. In addition, some authors have been biased against business, all but ignoring the perspectives of trade associations and companies.

Since the analysis of consumerism is now reaching a stage of maturity, it is important to undertake a broad, comprehensive, and

TABLE 1.1

Major Trade Associations

Aerosol Education Bureau
Air Conditioning and Refrigeration Institute
Aluminum Foil Container Manufacturers Association
American Academy of Family Physicians
American Apparel Manufacturers Association
American Bankers Association
American Bar Association
American Brush Manufacturers Association
American College of Obstetricians and Gynecologists
American College of Physicians
American Medical Association
American Pet Products Manufacturers Association
American Petroleum Institute
American Research Merchandising Institute
American Retail Association of Executives
American Retail Federation
American Savings and Loan Association
Appliance Parts Distributors Association
Asbestos Textile Institute
Associated Fur Manufacturers
Associated Third-Class Mail Users
Association of Home Appliance Manufacturers
Association of Second-Class Mail Publishers
Bank Marketing Association
Better Business Bureau
Can Manufacturers Institute
Chemical Specialties Manufacturers Association
Clothing Manufacturers Association
Composite Can and Tube Institute
Consumer Bankers Association
Cosmetic, Toiletry, and Fragrance Association
Council of Mutual Savings Associations
Direct Mail/Marketing Association
Direct Selling Association
Drug Wholesalers Association
Electronic Industries Association
Gas Appliance Manufacturers Association
Glass Packaging Institute
Greater Blouse, Shirt, and Undergarment Association
Independent Bankers Association of America
Independent Refiners Association of America
Independent Retail Businessman's Association
Lead Industries Association

(continued)

Table 1.1 (continued)

Lead-Zinc Producers Committee
Legal Services Corporation
Mail Order Association of America
Mail Advertising Service Association International
Men's Fashion Association
Mid-Continent Oil and Gas Association
National Appliance and Radio-TV Dealers Association
National Appliance Service Association
National Association of Chain Drug Stores
National Association of Drug & Allied Sales Organizations
National Association of Glue Manufacturers
National Association of Mutual Savings Banks
National Association of Retail Druggists
National Association of Television and Electronic Servicers of America
National Broom and Mop Council
National Dress Manufacturers Association
National Drug Trade Conference
National Electrical Manufacturers Association
National Energy Producers Council
National Legal Aid and Defender Association
National Mass Retailing Institute
National Outerwear and Sportswear Association
National Paint & Coatings Association
National Petroleum Refiners Association
National Pharmaceutical Council
National Retail Merchants Association
National Soft Drink Association
National Star Route Carriers Association
National Wholesale Druggists Association
Oil Spill Control Association of America
Paperboard Packaging Council
Parcel Post Association
Pennsylvania Grade Crude Oil Association
Pesticide Formulators Association
Pharmaceutical Manufacturers Association
Pharmaceutical Proprietary Association
Plastic Containers Manufacturers Institute
Retail Advertising Conference
Soap and Detergent Association
Society of Cosmetic Chemists
Society of Independent Gasoline Marketers of America
Toiletry Merchandisers Association
United Infants' and Children's Wear Association

Source: Compiled by the author.

TABLE 1.2

Major Consumer Groups

Action for the Prevention of Burn Injuries to Children
American Council on Consumer Interests
American Farm Bureau Federation
Common Cause
Consumer Action
Consumer Federation of America
Consumers' Research
Consumers Union
Environmental Defense Fund
Federation of Homemakers
General Federation of Women's Clubs
Nader Organizations
National Consumers' League
National Fire Protection Association
National Home Economics Association
National Organization of Women
National Resources Defense Council
Petroleum Watchdog
Public Interest Research Group
Sierra Club
Truth in Advertising

Source: Compiled by the author.

objective investigation of the consumer movement. In this book, such an examination is described.

A systematic assessment of the effects of consumerism and business reactions to consumer issues is detailed for ten diverse industries: major appliances, banking, clothing, household products, lead, asbestos, and fluorocarbons, mail order, petroleum, pharmaceuticals, legal and medical professions, and retailing.

METHODOLOGY OF THE STUDY

The study was designed and supervised by the editor. A team of ten advanced graduate researchers was assembled. Each researcher was asked to generate data on and analyze one of the specific indus-

TABLE 1.3

Major Federal Government Agencies
Involved with Consumer Issues

Atomic Energy Commission
Comptroller of the Currency
Consumer Product Safety Commission
Department of Agriculture
Department of Commerce
Department of Energy
Department of Health, Education, and Welfare
Environmental Protection Agency
Federal Deposit Insurance Corporation
Federal Home Loan Bank Board
Federal Reserve System
Federal Savings and Loan Insurance Corporation
Federal Trade Commission
Food and Drug Administration
Interstate Commerce Commission
Justice Department
National Bureau of Standards
Occupational Safety and Health Administration
Office of Economic Opportunity
Post Office

Source: Compiled by the author.

tries noted above, and attended several group meetings to discuss
joint issues and problems. The researchers were skilled, objective
professionals, with experience in the industries they were examining.

For each industry, various components of consumerism were
reviewed: history of consumerism, era of consumerism, and major
issues; active consumer groups; government agencies, legislation,
and court cases; and industry and company responses. Data collection included an extensive secondary data search. A wide range of
consumer, business, government, general, trade, and company
publications were reviewed for every industry under investigation.
The search for several industries went back well into the 1800s.

To complement the secondary data search, two primary studies
were conducted. One mail questionnaire, Figure 1.1, was sent to
about 100 trade associations to determine their attitudes and responses

TABLE 1.4

Major Federal Legislation Affecting Consumer Issues

Air Pollution and Prevention and Control Act
Anti-Merger Act
Banking Act of 1933
Clayton Anti-Trust Act
Clean Air Act
Consumer Product Safety Act
Energy Conservation Act
Equal Credit Opportunity Act
Fair Credit Billing Act
Fair Credit Reporting Act
Fair Packaging and Labeling Act
Federal Reserve Act
Federal Trade Commission Act
Flammable Fabrics Act
Food, Drug, and Cosmetic Act
Fur Products Labeling Act
Hazardous Substances Labeling Act
Home Mortgage Disclosure Act
Home Owners Loan Corporation
Insecticide, Fungicide, and Rodenticide Act
Lead-Based Paint Poisoning Prevention Act
Magnuson-Moss Warranty Act
Medicaid
Medicare
Occupational Safety and Health Act
Permanent Care Labeling Rule
Poison Prevention Packaging Act
Postal Fraud Statute
Radiation Control for Safety Act
Real Estate Settlement Procedures Act
Robinson-Patman Act
Sherman Anti-Trust Act
Textile Fabric Identification Act
Toxic Substances Control Act
Truth-in-Lending Act
Unfair and Deceptive Practices by Banks Act
Wool Products Labeling Act

Source: Compiled by the author.

FIGURE 1.1

General Form of Mail Questionnaire to Trade Associations

HOFSTRA UNIVERSITY
HEMPSTEAD, NEW YORK 11550

Executive Director

Dear Mr.

The Hofstra University School of Business is undertaking a study of consumerism. We are very much interested in your participation. Information on how   has responded to the consumer movement will be quite helpful.

A short series of questions are presented below. Your thoughts and comments about them are sincerely appreciated.

1. Generally speaking, how does your association feel about the consumer movement?
2. How has the consumer movement affected the companies that belong to your association, in regard to   ?
3. Has the association created a position, panel or department to deal with the effects of the consumer movement? If so, please describe.
4. Does the association provide representatives to appear before government committees examining consumer issues? If so, please describe.
5. Does the association provide speakers to appear before national and/or local consumer organizations? If yes, please describe.
6. What do you perceive to be the long-term impact of consumerism on the industry you represent?

In addition to the above, could you please send us copies of any consumer-oriented publications issued by your association.

Also, perhaps there are other areas of concern not raised by this letter upon which you would like to comment. Any information you can provide will supplement what is obtained from governmental agencies, library research, consumer interest groups, and companies.

Thank you in advance for your cooperation.

Very truly yours,

Joel Evans, Ph.D.
School of Business

P.S. For your convenience, a stamped, self-addressed envelope is enclosed.

FIGURE 1.2

General Form of Mail Questionnaire to Individual Companies

HOFSTRA UNIVERSITY   HEMPSTEAD, NEW YORK 11550

President,   Company

Dear Mr.

The Hofstra University School of Business is undertaking a study
on consumerism. We are very much interested in your participation.   is well-known in the field of
and therefore, any information you could supply regarding your
approach to the consumer movement would be appreciated.

The information should pertain to your approach in three main
areas -- interacting with the consumer, product and/or service
development, and the effect of outside influences:

1. The Consumer:
    -What type of policy do you have for handling complaints?
    -Do you have a consumer complaint dept.? If so, how is it
     structured?
    -Is there a consumer advocate in-house? If so, where is
     he/she located within the organization structure?
    -Do you have an educational program or participate in
     educational programs for consumers? If yes, please describe.

2. The Product or Service:
    -What type of product-related information is made available
     to the public?
    -Are you modifying or changing your products in response to
     consumerism?
    -What procedure do you follow to ensure product and service
     quality?

3. Outside Influences:
    -What type of consumer regulations affect your operations?
    -How do you respond to outside consumer pressures?
    -How do you evaluate the effect of consumerism on your
     company?

Perhaps there are other areas of concern not raised by this
letter upon which you would like to comment. Any information
you can provide will supplement what is obtained from governmental agencies, library research, consumer interest groups,
and trade associations.

Your cooperation is sincerely appreciated.

                              Very truly yours,

                              Joel Evans, Ph.D.
                              School of Business

P.S. For your convenience, a stamped, self-addressed envelope
      is enclosed.

9

to consumerism. A second mail questionnaire, Figure 1.2, was
sent to more than 100 companies to obtain their views and reactions
to consumerism.

After all the material was collected and assessed, the overall
effects of consumerism, an evaluation of consumerism, the future
outlook for the consumer movement, and recommendations for all
the parties involved with consumerism were developed for each
industry.

FORMAT OF THE BOOK

Chapters 2 through 11 report on the role and impact of consumerism on the ten industries cited above. At the end of each of
these chapters, an extended bibliography is provided. In all, well
over 1,000 data sources are cited. Chapter 12 contains an inter-
industry analysis of consumerism. In this chapter, overall conclusions and recommendations are presented.

BIBLIOGRAPHY

1. Cravens, David W., and Hills, Gerald G. "Consumerism:
   A Perspective for Business." Business Horizons 18 (August
   1970), pp. 21-28.

2. Day, George S., and Aaker, David A. "A Guide to Consumerism."
   Journal of Marketing 34 (July 1970), pp. 12-19.

2

CONSUMERISM AND THE APPLIANCE INDUSTRY

Kevin E. Dembinski

INTRODUCTION

The average U.S. household has a large number of major appliances, from a refrigerator to a dishwasher to a washing machine. In total, more than one billion major appliances are owned by U.S. citizens.

Growing demand has led not only to a proliferation of appliances, but also to an increase in their complexity. This partly explains why many consumers are encountering difficulties with major appliances. During the last several years, consumers have made numerous and vehement complaints to government agencies concerning a variety of problems, such as unfulfilled warranties, inferior quality of products, and inadequate availability of facilities for repair and service.

The historical development of the consumer movement, active consumer groups, the role of the government, and industry and firm responses to consumerism in the major appliance industry are examined in this chapter.

THE HISTORY OF CONSUMERISM
IN THE MAJOR APPLIANCE INDUSTRY

The First Era: The Early 1900s

The manufacture of major appliances began in the early 1900s. The new devices received praise, without criticism, from consumers and manufacturers alike, due to their time-saving qualities [22].

The health hazards of mechanical refrigerators were not given much attention until the American Health Association began to warn users of the dangers of refrigerants. This was spurred on by ten deaths and 30 nonfatal injuries in 1925 in Chicago. The deaths and injuries were caused by the gases used in mechanical refrigerators [17].

Until this time, the general public believed that the cold in refrigerators was produced by electricity, when in actuality, toxic gases were employed as the coolants. Consumers bought refrigerators because they believed that manufacturers would not expose them to undue danger, and some manufacturers did substitute the less toxic methyl chloride for other gases [17].

The development of the wringer washing machine brought additional hazards for consumers. Moving parts of the motor and wringer were often unshielded and unprotected, making them dangerous to young children [22].

The Second Era: Development of Durable Goods

In the 1930s, discontent with new and unfamiliar durable goods increased. Consumers were concerned with safety, brand proliferation, and unwise spending [14]. These issues were important during the time period when money and jobs were scarce, and the maximization of buying power essential.

Home economists supported the National Recovery Administration's plan to establish specific industrial codes. The plan proposed price and quality relationships [47]. A Consumers Advisory Board was made part of the National Recovery Administration. More than one-half of the approved codes had references pertaining to the establishment of standards, grades, or labels. Slogans such as "Read the Label" became quite common.

In World War II, plastics were used in many appliances, especially washing machines and refrigerators, due to shortages of material. Plastic interiors and parts were not as sturdy or durable as the metal pieces they replaced. Therefore, the lifespan of the product was often reduced [4].

Consumer education was stressed during and after World War II. A national program, "The Consumer Speaks," was established that included group discussions on product characteristics of washing machines and refrigerators [4].

Television sales grew in the late 1940s and 1950s. Some of the televisions held risks of injury for consumers. Of particular concern was the possibility of electrical shock with small portable sets [27]. To maintain light weight and compactness, General Electric and other manufacturers built the portables with metal cabinets and metallic rectifiers. The only safeguard between the wiring and the metal cabinet was a resistor or condenser, which frequently broke down and resulted in a short circuit [52]. In 1956, Consumers' Research wrote a highly critical analysis of this problem [27, p. 17].

Another safety hazard involved certain oscillating-agitator-type washing machines. With some washing machines, such as the Easy and Philco models, the tub continued to spin for as long as one to two minutes after the machine was shut off [9]. Anyone who wished to remove clothes from the machine at the end of the spin cycle, before the tub came to a complete stop, risked bruising a hand, wrist, or arm.

The 1950s also saw increased consumer concern about the difficulty of repairing major appliances. Complaints were made about the time needed to complete a repair, high prices, and unsatisfactory repairs [14]. Consumer groups advised the public to carefully read and understand appliance warranties [55]. Most warranties were in effect for one year and included parts and labor (except when the purchase was made at a discount store).

Many companies seemed intent on eliminating do-it-yourself repairs. Lamps and fuses, especially on kitchen ranges, were inaccessible [3]. A representative of a major appliance manufacturer stated that several lawsuits were filed against his firm by people injured while doing their own repairs. The company did its best to discourage such activities [55].

Two types of service facilities evolved: the independent shop and the factory-authorized agency. At this time, the consumer benefited by patronizing the agency, which posted prices and had the manufacturer's backing. The independent shop was not endorsed or supervised by the manufacturer [55].

In recognition of the importance of servicing appliances, one large firm set up its own standards of performance and a distinct organizational division to enforce them. The company also bought a series of advertisements in several magazines to advise consumers about the performance they should expect from a major appliance [41].

The Third Era: 1960s and 1970s

During the 1960s and 1970s, there have been many specific issues of consumerism involving the major appliance industry. These include sales-push money, warranties, servicing, product information, planned obsolescence, product safety, and replacement parts availability.

Sales-Push Money

Sales-push money is a cash bonus given to sales representatives and distributors to stress merchandise a manufacturer or store is most interested in selling. The merchandise may be pushed because it is overstocked or provides a high profit margin. Sales-push money rewards a representative for convincing a customer to buy the model the manufacturer or store wants to sell rather than another brand or model.

Some manufacturers have continually offered sales incentives to retail appliance salespeople. These incentives range from men's shirts for the sale of laundry equipment to European vacations for the sale of a specified number of refrigerators. The most prevalent practice is the payment of cash bonuses [34].

Sales-push money is criticized by consumers because it causes higher prices, emphasizes specific brands, and pressures consumers into buying the salesperson's choice and not their own. When sales-push money is used as a bait-and-switch tactic, it is illegal.

Warranties

A product warranty is the manufacturer's (retailer's) assurance to the consumer that a product will perform as specified, provide true value, and be free from hidden defects or limitations [40]. However, there has been growing criticism that warranties are not being handled in this manner. In the opinion of Consumers Union:

> Most manufacturers, instead of standing behind the general fitness of what they sell, try to assume narrower obligations in a written warranty or guarantee (they amount to the same thing) by setting time limits, making exceptions to lists of parts covered, and being their own judge of warranty claims [19, p. 389].

In an examination of warranties and guarantees on major household appliances, the FTC has concluded that:

> . . . It is fair to state that it is not uncommon for the manufacturer to ignore the complaints altogether and make no response. Some do respond and advise the consumer to contact the dealer about whose conduct she complained. Others recommend contact with a distributor or area service representative. This often leads to what is described as the 'run around,' with a considerable exchange of correspondence, broken appointments, and nothing being done, with the manufacturer, distributor, and retailer all disclaiming any blame or liability to solve the problem [53, p. 61].

Many times the manufacturer only repairs or replaces parts that are proven, within a given period of time, to be defective in either workmanship or material [12]. The questions of how the parts are discovered to be faulty, who will return them to the factory, and who will install the replaced part, are not answered clearly in most warranties.

Extended warranty policies tend to be misleading to the consumer. When a consumer purchases a refrigerator, home freezer, or room air conditioner, he or she believes that everything inside the appliance is guaranteed (including parts and labor) for one year. Yet this is not the intention of the manufacturer, who does not warrant against defective light bulbs, breakage of plastic or porcelain parts, or leakages of refrigerant gas. With most extended parts warranties, the manufacturer incurs little risk, since the parts most likely to fail (timer, solenoids, heating elements, valves, and switches) are returned to the supplying vendor [34].

Factory-operated or authorized service agencies generally follow a strict interpretation of the terms expressed in the warranty. As a result, consumers often are charged for repairs during the warranty period that are the result of poor design or fabrication on the part of the manufacturer [53].

Even when the warranty is honored, the consumer may be adversely affected. If a refrigerator compressor fails within the first five years of ownership and the manufacturer replaces it, the consumer is not reimbursed for inconvenience, aggravation, or spoiled food [40].

All color and some black-and-white televisions have a one-year warranty on parts. Larger units normally require in-home servicing; however, manufacturers add an extra charge for this. Despite the charge, the manufacturer expects the dealer to make repairs during the usual 90-day labor warranty period immediately following the purchase [40].

Servicing

In the past, according to J. M. Juran, a consulting engineer and quality control expert, the consumer was tolerant of product failures because of an awareness of the limitations of mass production [13]. Now the appliance industry is faced with a "no tolerance era." The consumer expects prompt repair at a reasonable cost [52].

Consumers complain of:

exposure to repair rackets, in which repairmen conceal the simplicity of the work needed and charge for repair of nonexistent defects; lack of skill by repairmen, with

resultant failure to identify what is needed, to make
satisfactory repair when the need is identified, or to
make repairs in a reasonable time; and an inadequate
supply of repairmen and repair facilities, which results
in delays before repairs can be obtained and, in extreme
cases, in inability to get the product repaired [60, p. 68].

For example, in the early 1960s, all but a few manufacturers
produced televisions with copper-etched or printed circuits. The
circuit boards frequently cracked while being transported to dealers.
Service technicians were not trained to handle this problem, and
many refused to work on the damaged boards or worsened the situation [34].

A survey of television repairers was conducted in New York
City in 1974. Of the 20 repairers called to repair the sets, 17 were
reported to be dishonest or incompetent. Repair costs ranged from
$4 to $30 on what should have been a cost of $8.93, including parts
and labor [56, p. 257].

While the major appliance industry has been growing rapidly,
the recruitment and training of service personnel has fallen far behind. In response to this, a number of firms have expanded their
service-training programs. Maytag has trained about 19,000 service
technicians and provides instructional materials, speakers, and
equipment for almost 300 vocational schools [41, p. 26]. Others,
such as RCA, offer assistance to local independent service shops by
conducting workshops and providing factory service manuals. Trade
associations, including the Refrigeration Service Engineers Society
and the Electronics Industries Association, have instituted industrywide training programs [52].

Product Information

In some cases, manufacturers exaggerate the performance
capability of their products. For example, washer-dryers often
are sold with baskets that are larger than their recommended load
sizes. This confuses the consumer [60, p. 65].

Manufacturers have not exerted much control over appliance
dealers, who exhibit a wide range of competing brands and use persuasion, rather than information, to sell products. Since appliances
appear to be similar objects, sales personnel can be quite effective
[42]. Because of this, some manufacturers, trade associations,
retailers, consumer groups, and government agencies are empha-
sizing consumer information and education. In several instances,
company-sponsored programs have become too promotional [41].

An industry goal of education is to improve the satisfaction of
consumers with appliance purchases. As one manufacturing executive

has said: "Customer satisfaction with a product starts with knowing how to use it successfully" [41, p. 30]. Many see the improvement of written instructions for using and maintaining a new appliance as an essential point, particularly since companies want more complex options to be purchased [28, 53].

Planned Obsolescence

Critics assert that planned obsolescence is one objective of manufacturers. One type of planned obsolescence is the delicate underengineering of a product so that it has a short life span. Manufacturers assert that products are designed at the durability level that yields a competitive price; consumers get what they pay for. While critics call repeat purchases wasteful, manufacturers state that consumers do not and will not pay for higher-priced appliances that will last longer [56]. The desire for new styling and poor maintenance by consumers also affect the life span of appliances.

The rising costs of labor and materials force appliance manufacturers to use less costly components and more economical production methods. For example, plastic frequently is used in refrigerators and televisions [45, 52]. But plastic in refrigerator door liners is easily cracked; aluminum, now substituted for copper, is not as efficient a cold conductor; sprayed-on vinyl coatings inside of dishwashers may discolor; and enamel paint in the side panels of ranges may discolor and become scratched.

Manufacturers have not been able simultaneously to eliminate these problems, extend the life span of appliances, and keep costs down.

Product Safety

In a thorough study, the National Commission on Product Safety concluded that: "The exposure of consumers to unreasonable consumer product hazards is excessive by any standard of measurement" [56, p. 255]. Dangerously exposed electrical terminals were found on kitchen ranges, broilers, and dryers; and radiation hazards were found in televisions and microwave ovens.

In 1966, General Electric built and sold at least 90,000 large-screen televisions that emitted excessive X-rays through the bottoms of the sets because a new type of high-voltage regulator tube failed [2]. The function of the high-voltage regulator, used in all large color televisions, was to control the 25,000 volts of current needed to brighten the color screen [34]. When the tube failed, voltages went to 28,000 volts or higher [50]. During 1975, a survey of 5,000 color televisions in Suffolk County, New York, showed that 20 percent emitted X-rays above the danger level [28].

Nearly 250,000 Amana side-by-side refrigerator-freezers made between February 1969 and September 1974 had a design defect that could lead to a shock hazard [61]. According to Amana, frequent door openings could erode the insulation from the wiring and lead to contact between base wire and the doorshell. As of August 1977, 41 shock incidents had been reported to the Consumer Product Safety Commission. Amana notified owners of these models by mail and sent a field kit to correct the defect.

Replacement Parts Availability

Consumer surveys have shown that between 15 and 20 percent of all complaints involve the process of acquiring replacement parts [52]. Many complaints concern the time needed to obtain a part and the nonuse of an appliance during this time. The cost of a part is another area of criticism. For example, a replacement compressor for a two-year-old refrigerator may be half the original cost of the entire appliance.

One manufacturer undertook a consumer survey regarding customer tolerance in waiting for critical replacement parts. Owners of color televisions and automatic washers showed a mean tolerance of 2.2 days to 4.6 days, depending on the age of the appliance. These times were much shorter than the delivery that most manufacturers could provide [52, p. 41].

Access to parts has improved during the last few years, but not enough to satisfy the consumer. A presidential task force has requested that manufacturers supply parts lists and service manuals to parts depots and service agencies, even before new models are put on the market [53].

ACTIVE CONSUMER GROUPS

Consumers' Research, headquartered in Washington, New Jersey, has exposed anticonsumer trade practices in its monthly publication Consumers' Research Magazine (prior to 1972 known as Consumers' Research Bulletin). It has concentrated on exaggerated capacities of dishwashers, clothes dryers, washing machines, refrigerators, and freezers. Consumers' Research has been instrumental in promoting responsible action by trade associations and certification programs in the major appliance industry [29].

Through the years, in a section of its magazine called "Off the Editor's Chest," Consumers' Research has spoken out on many issues affecting the major appliance consumer, such as better service, improved warranty adherence, more informative labeling, and safeguards to reduce the dangers of radiation from color televisions. The editorials have requested action from industry, trade associations, and government [57]. An example is this 1976 editorial dealing with informative labeling:

> Voluntary attempts on the part of manufacturers and merchants to provide useful information about their products should be encouraged, although there is much room for improvement in the standards used for determination for various features. As indicated in our report of refrigerator-freezers currently tested, our system of measurement of capacity of these appliances and that adopted by the Association of Home Appliance Manufacturers (AHAM) differ considerably. We have previously had occasion to criticize industry standards which set up a certification program (accepted by the Federal Trade Commission) whereby all boxes are measured in the same way with the idea that rated capacities would be roughly comparable. As we have pointed out, however, the AHAM rated capacities, do not reflect actual usable refrigerated spaces, which CR's measurements take into account [48, p. 19].

Consumers Union, headquartered in Mount Vernon, New York, has also evaluated and tested major appliances, and reports its results in the monthly Consumer Reports. Consumers Union is now considered "the most significant private effort in the United States to evaluate products and pass this information on to consumers" [57, p. 100]. There have been key evaluations of refrigerators, color televisions, air conditioners, dishwashers, and other major appliances. The area of household equipment has been the second most discussed interest of Consumers Union, exceeded only by automobiles [1].

For many years, Consumers Union has campaigned for the alleviation of radiation exposure from color televisions and against appliances with electrical shock dangers. Consumer Reports investigated the possible shock hazards with some Amana refrigerator-freezers, and published an article in the September 1975 issue. Amana did not follow up until after a long period of time [61, p. 26].

Despite suggestions that they are vastly different in philosophy, point of view, and type of activity, both Consumers' Research and Consumers Union emphasize a practical guide for buyers, presenting suggestions for the best value for the dollar as well as potential hazards to the consumer [23].

At this time, there are no consumer groups that specialize in the appliance industry. Of the general consumer organizations, Consumers' Research and Consumers Union are by far the most influential.

GOVERNMENT

The government has been involved with setting minimum product standards for safety and performance. On the federal level, the major appliance industry is regulated by three agencies: Federal Trade Commission, Food and Drug Administration, and the Consumer Product Safety Commission.

Federal Trade Commission

Under the provisions of the Federal Trade Commission Act (1914) and the Wheeler-Lea Amendment (1938), the Federal Trade Commission (FTC) is empowered to eliminate unfair competition and deceptive acts or practices. This legislation also gives the FTC jurisdiction over advertising.

The FTC used its power under the Wheeler-Lea Amendment in a 1973 action against General Electric. The FTC charged that General Electric falsely advertised that independent surveys showed its sets required less service than all other U.S. color sets, continued the false advertisements after learning of contradictory evidence, and did not forward promised data to consumers who requested it [30, p. 346]. General Electric signed consent orders, promising not to use information in advertisements unless substantiated by tests. The orders covered audio equipment, household appliances, and other products in the company's line.

There are two recent acts that fall under the responsibility of the FTC and affect the major appliance industry: the Magnuson-Moss Warranty-Federal Trade Commission Improvement Act (1975) and the Energy Conservation Act (1975).

Magnuson-Moss Warranty-Federal Trade Commission Improvement Act

Warranties and guarantees have been the subject of congressional scrutiny since 1969, when a presidential task force concluded that unfair exclusions and exceptions were utilized [54, p. 30]. In 1974, a House committee examined 200 warranties from 51 major companies and found them to be confusing, ambiguous, and filled with disclaimers. As a result, the Magnuson-Moss Act was passed in 1975. Under it, the FTC can make rules regarding warranties.

The FTC has developed the following rules: a written warranty is not required; a written warranty must be clearly labeled as full or limited; a full warranty is all-inclusive; a full warranty may be passed on to a secondhand consumer; warranty terms must be available and easily read; a consumer may sue if injured by a deceptive warranty; and the FTC may sue in federal court on behalf of consumers [65, p. 1].

Energy Conservation Act

The Energy Conservation Act established the details for mandatory operating-cost labels for 13 major appliances listed in its Section 322. The appliances include refrigerators, freezers, dishwashers, clothes dryers, room air conditioners, televisions, kitchen ranges and ovens, and clothes washers [62].

The FTC prescribes test procedures for the determination of annual operating costs and the measurement of energy consumption [62, p. 919]. This information is made available to consumers via "operating cost" labels placed on appliances by manufacturers. Beginning in early 1978, many appliances contained these labels [61].

Food and Drug Administration

The Food and Drug Administration (FDA) has responsibility for one act that has an impact on the major appliance industry: the Radiation Control for Health and Safety Act (1968).

In 1967, a General Electric press release stated that 150,000 televisions were capable of emitting harmful levels of X-radiation [1]. As a result, the Radiation Control for Health and Safety Act was passed. This law set acceptable maximum levels of radiation for color televisions, microwave ovens, and X-ray machines [68]. It is enforced by the FDA's Bureau of Radiological Health.

Under the act, manufacturers must conform to specific standards, certify the compliance of their products, and maintain a written record of quality control and safety correspondence. Dealers must keep lists of purchasers of items costing more than $50 for at least five years. The FDA requires annual reports, accident reports, and notification of new products [31, 43].

Consumer Product Safety Commission

In 1967, the National Commission on Product Safety was established. It reported on the fragmented nature of product safety legislation and the high incidence of injuries in 1970 [11, 51]. The Consumer Product Safety Commission (CPSC) was created in 1972, and was empowered to force design changes, ban products, recall products, and so forth.

Early in its existence, the CPSC published a list of 400 product categories considered dangerous. Televisions (48 percent were cited as potential sources of radiation and fire) and major household appliances (56 percent were cited as potential electrical shock and fire hazards) were included in the list [11, p. 82].

The CPSC established a National Electronic Inquiry Surveillance System (NEISS) to analyze injury reports from hospitals. In 1974, NEISS reported that ranges and ovens were among the "Twenty Most Dangerous" consumer products [66]. Unfortunately, data were not provided about product age, design, and manufacturer.

NEISS reported that 12,000 television-related accidents were treated in hospital emergency rooms in a one-year period [64]. Most injuries were lacerations, contusions, or abrasions resulting from accidental contact with television sets. Fires, shocks, and explosions also were reported and investigated. By the end of February 1974, nine manufacturers indicated that they were aware of potential hazards.

To maintain continuity in the enforcement of product safety laws, Congress placed the Refrigerator Safety Act (1957) under the jurisdiction of the CPSC in 1972. The act states:

> It shall be unlawful for any person to introduce or
> deliver for introduction into interstate commerce any
> household refrigerator manufactured on or after the
> date this section takes effect unless it is equipped with
> a device enabling the door thereof to be opened from
> the inside [66, p. 1126].

INDUSTRY RESPONSES TO CONSUMERISM

The responses of the major appliance industry to consumerism are revealed by a review of the available literature and the participation of trade associations in a primary study.

Industry Responses as Reported in the Literature

Trade associations have been especially active in establishing programs to respond to consumerism in the major appliance industry. Many trade associations have addressed the consumer movement; a few others have made limited attempts to meet this challenge. Individual trade associations have established certification programs, organized complaint-resolution procedures and consumer action panels, supplied product information, and developed service personnel training programs.

Certification Programs

The Association of Home Appliance Manufacturers (AHAM) contains more than 100 members. It has developed a number of product standards and tests models for compliance, involving items like electric ranges, room air conditioners, dishwashers, dehumidifiers, and refrigerators [6, 7]. To communicate test results with consumers, AHAM administers a certification program indicating (through a certification seal) that a model's performance capabilities have been stated accurately and meet the standard. AHAM retains an independent testing laboratory to administer tests and verify results. Although the program is voluntary, usage is widespread. For instance, every room air conditioner sold in the United States is certified by AHAM.

AHAM certification for refrigerators and freezers tests net general refrigerated volume, net freezer volume, net refrigerated volume, and net shelf area. Uniform standards and independently verified measurements are available in advertising and at point-of-sale [5].

The National Electrical Manufacturers Association (NEMA) is the largest trade organization for electrical products manufacturers in the United States. NEMA advocates voluntary standards for safety, in cooperation with AHAM and the Electronic Industries Association [46].

Another type of certification involves service personnel. Some trade associations have initiated programs to certify service technicians. The National Electronic Association uses national examinations. The National Association of Television and Electronic Servicers of America tests a technician's ability to service sets with a variety of malfunctions within a specified time period [44].

Complaint Resolution and Consumer Action Panels

Some trade associations have developed programs to resolve business-consumer disputes. A major program is the Major Appliance Consumer Action Panel (MACAP), which was established by the Association of Home Appliance Manufacturers, the Gas Appliances Manufacturers Association, and the American Retail Federation [54]. MACAP has a voluntary board of experts, is completely autonomous, and sometimes differs with manufacturers in testifying for consumer legislation [40]. MACAP also provides advice for manufacturers and consumers alike, as it attempts to facilitate cooperation between the two [39].

The Electronic Industries Association has a consumer affairs office to handle complaints on televisions and other home entertainment products. When safety is involved, the office accepts collect telephone calls and refers the consumer to the appropriate company representative. In addition, educational material is sent to the consumer [24].

The Council of Better Business Bureaus has established a national system for handling consumer problems. Through local Better Business Bureaus, arbitration panels have been created. The program is voluntary, with private hearings, confidential results, and no fees. Postresolution inspection for compliance is available in the event of further contention [49, 54].

The National Association of Television and Electronic Servicers of America sends complaints regarding televisions and other electronic products directly to government agencies and manufacturers. This association insists on a strict code of ethics and fairness in advertising for its members [45].

Product Information

Trade associations provide product information, usually through the mail, if requested by the consumer. For example, the Better Business Bureau lists the comparative advantages and disadvantages of central and room air conditioning. It also publishes pamphlets, such as "Tips on Television Sets," which offer suggestions on how to shop for a set, how to compare values, and how to select a set [20].

The Electronics Industries Association provides "Tips for Consumers on Electronic Products Service," as well as warnings of potential hazards [25]. In its publication, "Television Safety Tips," the association offers help on avoiding personal injury [26].

The National Association of Television and Electronic Servicers of America distributes publications on servicing and offers a code of ethics for service technicians [44, 45].

The Association of Home Appliance Manufacturers publishes consumer pamphlets, available on request. For example, in "Consumer Recommendations on the Safe Use of Appliances," general safety precautions for gas and/or electric ranges, dishwashers, refrigerators, washers, and dryers are suggested [7].

Training Programs

Trade associations supply vocational schools with training information. As an illustration, the Association of Home Appliance

Manufacturers has a guide called "Training the Home Appliance
Service Technician." Many associations work with local boards of
education to aid in designing curricula. They sponsor advisors,
provide instructors, conduct workshops for instructions, and participate in cooperative programs [52].

The National Association of Television and Electronic Servicers
of America has publications, conventions, and meetings to keep
members technologically current. It also distributes films to organizations and schools, such as "So You Want to Be an Electronics
Technician" [44].

The National Appliance and Radio-TV Dealers Association is
not satisfied with its training program. According to Jules Steinberg,
executive vice-president, the association

> developed a sixty-hour training course in which it could
> take any man who knew the difference between a screw-
> driver and pliers and make him a washing-machine
> repairman. He could handle eighty-five percent of the
> problems on a washing machine. The other fifteen
> percent would be in the transmission, and even though
> he could not fix that, he could diagnose it [42, p. 183].

The program failed "because manufacturers collectively would not
admit there was a technician shortage" [42, p. 183]. Manufacturers
would not supply the most up-to-date technical information for service
training.

Despite these attempts by trade associations, most training
programs are company-sponsored.

Trade Association Responses to Primary Study

Nine trade associations were contacted and asked to respond
to specific questions and supply additional materials. Seven associa-
tions replied: Association of Home Appliance Manufacturers (AHAM),
Air Conditioning and Refrigeration Institute (ARI), Appliance Parts
Distributors Association (APDA), Gas Appliance Manufacturers
Association (GAMA), National Appliance Service Association (NASA),
National Electrical Manufacturers Association (NEMA), and National
Association of Television and Electronic Servicers of America
(NATESA). Two associations, Electronic Industries Association
and National Appliance and Radio-TV Dealers Association, did not
participate in the study, despite two requests.

The responses to the survey are quite diverse and difficult to
generalize, although two basic points do seem evident. First, con-

sumerism has had a positive but limited effect, because of increases in operating costs. Second, the associations feel overregulated and believe self-regulation is more cost-effective.

A question-by-question summary shows that most associations favor the consumer movement, and react with concern and not resentment toward its goals. Many feel there are negative effects, such as costs and unreasonable demands. The major impact has been to increase awareness about consumer issues. Companies are implementing quality control standards, establishing consumer affairs departments, and complying with government regulations. Most trade associations have a person or position to deal with consumerism. Representatives appear before governmental agencies. Speakers are available to speak before consumer groups. The long-run impact of consumerism is seen as increased prices. Reasonableness on the part of consumerists is requested.

Table 2.1 contains capsule responses to the survey for those responding trade associations. Each trade association did not answer every question. Some responses were open-ended and were interpreted by the author. All responses are condensed in this table and phrased by the author.

COMPANY RESPONSES TO CONSUMERISM

The responses of major appliance companies to consumerism are shown through a review of the literature and participation in a mail survey.

Company Responses as Reported in the Literature

The responses of individual appliance companies to consumerism have been mixed. Many companies, especially the larger ones, have established consumer affairs offices to "interpret the consumer point of view to the company and provide meaningful communications between the company and the consumer" [56, p. 259]. Companies such as Whirlpool, Motorola, General Electric, and RCA have become quite consumer-oriented.

Not all companies have responded positively to consumerism. According to a 1973 study, planned and coordinated reactions to consumerism were the exception, not the rule [67]. Some responses have been superficial since "most industrial manufacturers seem to regard consumerism erroneously as something that does not influence them" [67, p. 89].

TABLE 2.1

Major Appliance Trade Association Responses to Study

Question 1	Generally speaking, how does your association feel about the consumer movement?
AHAM	There is genuine concern about consumer problems; but the movement presents costly and technical problems.
ARI	It is not resented. There are constructive attempts to respond.
APDA	As a wholesalers' association, consumer problems are not addressed.
GAMA	The movement has had positive and detrimental effects. Extremists have taken advantage.
NASA	Service was stressed before the current movement; today's consumers seem unreasonable and demanding without cause.
NEMA	The movement is generally favored; but, additional bureaucratic agencies are counterproductive.
NATESA	What is good for the consumer is good for the association, as expressed in its code of ethics.
Question 2	How has the consumer movement affected the companies that belong to your association, in regard to the manufacture of televisions and appliances?
AHAM	Effects include: new quality control procedures, availability of authorized factory-trained service technicians, and consumer affairs departments. The Consumer Product Safety Commission and the Magnuson-Moss Act have caused extra work, confusion, and rewording of warranties.
ARI	New staff positions have been developed to respond to consumerism.
GAMA	Business is overregulated, with little incentive to invest in new plant and equipment.
NASA	The effect has been limited, since NASA members are consumer-oriented.
NEMA	Standards have been established to maximize the objectivity of definitions and improve safety parameters.
Question 3	Has the association created a position, panel, or department to deal with the effects of the consumer movement?
AHAM	Yes, AHAM is a cosponsor of the Major Appliance Consumer Action Panel (MACAP) and has a separate department to administer MACAP.

(continued)

Table 2.1 (continued)

ARI	Several years ago, ARI had a staff position; now, there is a Public Affairs Department.
GAMA	Yes, GAMA is a cosponsor of MACAP and has staff members to support it.
NASA	No, issues are followed and consumerism discussed at annual conventions.
Question 4	Does the association provide representatives to appear before government committees examining consumer issues?
AHAM	Yes, in 1976 an office was established in Washington, D.C., to act as liaison and testify before Congress. In 1977, there were 16 testimonies.
ARI	ARI members and staff appear before congressional, agency, and state legislative committees. Written statements are usually provided.
GAMA	Yes, there is testimony regarding consumer legislation.
NASA	Representatives have not been provided, although they would if invited or necessary. It cooperates with government inquiries.
Question 5	Does the association provide speakers to appear before national and/or local consumer organizations?
AHAM	Speakers are provided, but there is no organized bureau. Cooperation is always sought.
ARI	No.
GAMA	Speakers are provided when asked, which has been rare.
NASA	No.
Question 6	What do you perceive to be the long-term impact of consumerism on the industry you represent?
AHAM	The industry must strive to respond to consumer expectations; yet, consumers must be informed and responsible.
ARI	Prices will increase, without subsequent rises in sales. Costs will outweigh benefits.
GAMA	The free enterprise system may be destroyed and less variety offered at higher prices.
NASA	Consumerism will continue and prices will increase to cover costs.
NATESA	The pendulum may swing too far if extremists dominate consumerism and lose sight of cost effectiveness.

Source: Compiled by the author.

A number of companies have fought against consumer legislation [56, p. 260]. In those cases where laws have passed, some have sought to reduce their effectiveness by watering down the impact or limiting the funds to enforce the laws [8, p. 71]. On the other side, there have been companies who have asked for improved standards to protect the consumer [56].

Following are examples of specific company actions; omissions do not imply a negative performance. Areas of focus are: organizational departments for consumer affairs, servicing, warranties, complaint resolution and organization, training of service technicians, and product information.

Organizational Departments for Consumer Affairs

The placement of the consumer affairs function within the organizational structure of a company depends upon its size, nature, and diversity of operations. It also depends on the role and importance assigned by management [41].

In a large corporation, a single consumer affairs unit is often maintained and located at corporate headquarters. The unit acquires maximum status and visibility. For example, at RCA:

> Our new consumer affairs office at the corporate level is intended to give us an effective additional instrument for carrying out . . . a long-standing policy [of consumer satisfaction]. It will enable us to respond even more rapidly to customer requirements and suggestions, and to focus maximum attention on consumer needs in all of RCA's product planning, manufacturing, and servicing activities [33, p. 94].

Whirlpool has followed a similar strategy. A consumer services division was established in 1959, placing all product service information and programs under this division. Consumer services reports to a vice-president in the marketing area [16]. Zenith developed a customer relations department in 1968, formalizing actions begun in 1920 [41, p. 98]. At Zenith, the president and chairman of the board examine complaint letters from consumers [41].

In the Tappan Company, there is a corporate director of consumer relations who reports to a corporate vice-president. This director also serves as an in-house consumer advocate [10]. Motorola established an Office of Consumer Affairs in 1970. This office resides in the consumer products division [41].

Servicing

Several companies have instituted programs to deal more effectively with consumer-servicing problems. For example, in 1961 Maytag introduced Red Carpet Service to offer customers speedy, efficient, and personal responses to calls for appliance service [37, p. 52]. A Red Carpet Service license is given to dealers or service centers that react within 24 hours after a call, properly train and uniform service technicians, and use a vehicle that carries a complete stock of repair parts. Red carpets are placed around the area to be repaired and protect the appliance [37]. After the repair is finished, the technician polishes the appliance and gives the consumer an evaluation card to mail to the dealer [39].

In the early 1960s, Whirlpool established Tech-Care service programs. By 1977, 1,200 franchised repair and service outlets throughout the country participated. Service representatives agree to perform in-warranty and nonwarranty servicing on Whirlpool products using only authorized parts. Firms have to hire only trained technicians and maintain current records [69].

Zenith monitors service performance by evaluating a sample of complaint letters at random. Complainants are called and their levels of satisfaction noted. A mail survey supplements this [41]. White-Westinghouse offers a Sure Service program. This is a national program that provides prompt, complete, and professional service by company-trained personnel [71].

The Service Department at Frigidaire has a vigorous incentive plan, called the Award of Merit, for dealers and servicing units that annually meet rigid service standards. Technicians and other personnel participate in a nationwide accredited program. There also are continuing training sessions [18].

Warranties

Companies provided warranties prior to 1975, when the Magnuson-Moss Act was passed. But, as Stephen E. Upton of Whirlpool stated, it "has forced us, like every business affected by it, to examine our entire warranty program and related activities" [40, p. 8].

Whirlpool established a program entitled Warranty Service Central in the mid-1960s. Under the program, Whirlpool agreed to pay for parts and labor on in-warranty repairs. After an appliance was serviced, Whirlpool was billed by the dealer or service center. In 1967, Whirlpool began to simplify its warranties and adopted a letterstyle format to inform the consumer as to what was covered, who would provide repairs, and where to complain [40, 69]. Today, Whirlpool is "committed to providing our customers with the most complete warranty coverage we can provide" [40, p. 11].

Prior to 1966, Maytag had warranties that covered the replacement or repair of parts proven to be defective during the first year. These warranties had several exclusions [37]. Changes were made in 1966 and 1969 to simplify the language and extend coverage. By 1975, after Magnuson-Moss, the warranties included parts and labor for a year; during the second year, the consumer would pay for labor; certain major component parts were warranted for five years; and information on servicing was distributed [39].

Service Technician Training

A number of firms have expanded their service training programs in an effort to decrease the shortage of technicians and to keep them up-to-date on technological product changes. For example, RCA conducted over 11,500 training sessions for 158,000 independent service personnel during one five-year period. During this period, over 11,300 RCA service technicians spent more than 20,000 man-weeks in formal training [41, p. 27].

The service training program at Maytag consists of monthly service schools in company headquarters and classes throughout the United States. On the average, more than 18,000 technicians receive training at 1,900 service schools per year [16, p. 1]. Frigidaire owns and operates training facilities for dealer and company-sponsored service organizations. There are 30 centers all over the country. Each has a factory-trained instructor and modern facilities [18]. Zenith maintains a full-time staff of 16 field managers to help service outlets by training and assisting personnel. Audiovisual equipment is also utilized for on-the-job use [41, p. 101].

The Whirlpool training programs are year-round and include classroom and at-home courses. Program materials are available in English and Spanish. Trainees choose from hands-on repair seminars, computerized appliance breakdowns, and live and video-taped courses [60, p. 4]. Over 500 technicians attend the seminars each year and 4,000 enroll in home courses. Others are reached through field training and vocational schools [70, p. 1].

Complaint Resolution and Organization

Many companies have established complaint resolution systems. The Motorola system answers most complaints sent to headquarters within 24 hours. Regional service managers receive letters on each complaint and monthly status reports. Each manager is responsible for detailed field reports and follow-ups [41]. At General Electric, grievances are processed promptly, with actions and/or explanations provided. Consumers are encouraged to contact the nearest GE or Hotpoint office, the nearest product service center, or the Product Service Department in Louisville, Kentucky. Zenith attempts to handle complaints at the dealer or service organization level. Complaints received at headquarters are answered within 48 hours, though servicing and adjustments occur in the consumer's home area [41].

Perhaps the best known complaint resolution system is the Whirlpool Cool-Line, which was created in 1967 to expedite the servicing of products. The system was altered when Whirlpool learned that many consumers were interested in product-use or product-purchase information. Cool-Line is now a nationwide, toll-free, telephone service. It is open 24 hours a day, seven days a week, and is staffed by consumer consultants [41]. According to Whirlpool, over 90 percent of the cases are closed (the problem resolved or questions answered) over the telephone. The remaining 10 percent require further investigation and often repair by local service units. A central file remains open until the problem is resolved. Whirlpool states that consumers have given Cool-Line a 95-percent success rate [41, pp. 97-98].

Product Information

Many consumer complaints result because of misuse, improper maintenance, and other misunderstandings of products. As a result, a number of companies have developed procedures or programs to improve the availability of information about product purchases and use.

General Electric provides free materials to high-school home economics classes and shop instructors. The company also assists with filmstrips, textbooks, cooking demonstrations, and arranges for school discount purchases of GE appliances [41]. Tappan offers consumer education and information through sales training, demonstrations, and printed materials like owners' guides and fact tags [10]. Whirlpool attaches a "Consumer Buying Guide" to each appliance. After a purchase, the consumer uses a home care package, which contains operating instructions and tips for maximum performance [69].

Company Responses to Primary Study

Fifteen manufacturers of major appliances were contacted and requested to participate in this study. Five companies cooperated: Frigidaire, General Electric, Tappan, Whirlpool, and Zenith. Three firms (Admiral, Kelvinator, and Maytag) replied to the survey letter, but did not answer the questions. Seven firms did not respond at all: Gibson, Magic Chef, Magnavox, Motorola, North American Phillips, RCA, and SONY.

There are few areas in which responses seem fairly consistent. Companies are cognizant of the need for consumer complaint resolution panels; all participating firms have organizations within their structure. Most companies have a consumer relations department under the jurisdiction of a director or vice-president. There is consensus that the Magnuson-Moss Act and other legislation have had definite effects upon operations. Most feel that legislation has had a strong impact on costs.

A question-by-question analysis reveals that some firms stress the handling of complaints on the local level by dealers or service organizations, even though there are consumer complaint departments. The majority of companies have an in-house consumer advocate at the director or vice-president level. All the firms have some type of educational programs, including training and literature. Information is made available through many channels, including advertisements, demonstrations, fact tags, and care booklets. Many companies modify products in response to consumers. Product quality is assured by thorough inspection; service quality is insured by training service technicians. Government legislation has had an impact on company operations, while outside consumer pressures have had mixed results. Overall, the firms state that consumerism has had positive effects, but sometimes has added unnecessary costs.

Table 2.2 contains capsule responses to the specific questions asked of the companies. Each firm did not answer every question. Some responses were open-ended and interpreted by the author. All responses are condensed in the table and phrased by the author.

THE OVERALL EFFECTS OF CONSUMERISM

Consumerism has had a substantial impact upon the major appliance industry and the companies within it, particularly in the last ten to 20 years. This period has seen the establishment of complaint resolution departments, consumer action panels, service-training programs, certification programs, and consumer affairs departments. Product information has grown a great deal.

Consumer action panels, formed by trade associations and individual companies, have been helpful in opening lines of communication between consumers and the industry. These panels also have provided information to top management, through consumer affairs departments or directly. Whirlpool's Cool-Line and the Major Appliance Consumer Action Panel have accomplished this.

One of the major areas of consumer dissatisfaction has been the lack of adequate servicing. Trade associations as well as individual companies have expanded service and training programs to reduce

TABLE 2.2

Major Appliance Company Responses to Study

Question 1	The Consumer: What type of policy do you have for handling complaints? Do you have a consumer complaint department? Is there a consumer advocate in-house? Do you have an educational program or participate in educational programs for consumers?
Frigidaire	There is a well-organized consumer relations activity within the National Service Department. A woman supervisor has broad responsibility for handling complaints. She can deal with the consumer or through the national service organization. There is no in-house advocate.
GE	Every consumer complaint is handled promptly and fairly, with appropriate action taken. The consumer complaint structure is complex. It is desired that a complaint be processed at the first step, the nearest GE major appliance office or product service center. There is a vice-president who acts as an in-house consumer advocate. Most consumer education programs are the responsibility of the Consumer Institute, but individual areas provide literature.
Tappan	Most consumer complaints are received by mail or via the toll-free Sentinel Line. Complaints are processed promptly, usually by the division responsible for the product. Complaints go to the consumer relations department, which has a manager, nine consultants, and two clerk-typists. The corporate director of customer relations is the in-house consumer advocate. Educational programs, demonstrations, guides, and trade associations are supported.
Whirlpool	The main complaint resolution system is Cool-Line. Complaints needing field follow-up go to local managers. Cool-Line is under the control of the manager of customer relations. There is no in-house consumer advocate, but there is a vice-president of consumer and public affairs. Educational programs range from a series of newspaper features on how to buy, use, and care for appliances to a booklet on energy savings.
Zenith	Many complaints are processed locally; complaints received centrally are sent to the appropriate area. The complaint organization reports to a vice-president

(continued)

Table 2.2 (continued)

	of consumer affairs and managers of customer communications and warranty claims. The consumer affairs vice-president is the in-house consumer advocate. Educational programs consist of public relations material and product information.
Question 2	The Product: What type of product-related information is made available to the public? Are you modifying or changing your products in response to consumerism? What procedure do you follow to ensure product and service quality?
Frigidaire	Information is contained in a use-and-care booklet, with a discussion on the product, warranties, and service. There are continuing quality control programs as well as engineer design programs.
GE	Product information is distributed through advertisements, news releases, specification sheets, use-and-care books, demonstrations, fact tags, answers to questions, strip films, etc. Products are changed or modified as improvements become possible or necessary, or as consumers or government desires. Inspection is rigid and sophisticated, with intense testing and training of personnel.
Tappan	Product-related information is available through dealers in the form of specification sheets, fact tags, and warranties. Products are continuously modified or redesigned to serve consumers. The corporate director of Quality Control monitors product and service quality. Each division has a detailed inspection and audit program. Service personnel are well-trained.
Whirlpool	Products are constantly revised in response to consumer concerns; this is an economic fact of life. There are many programs and procedures to insure product and service quality, including service training, Tech-Care service, and warranty programs.
Zenith	Product information is made available through distributors and dealers. Product designs have not been subject to consumerism pressure, but product quality and reliability are primary company objectives. Product and service quality are maximized by attention to engineering design, product safety engineering,

(continued)

Table 2.2 (continued)

	factory quality control, service training, and technical publications.
Question 3	Outside influences: What type of consumer regulations affect your operations? How do you respond to outside consumer pressures? How do you evaluate the effect of consumerism on your company?
GE	Regulations having an impact include those pertaining to warranties, energy, labels, closures on refrigerators, brakes on washers, outlets on ranges, emission standards on microwave ovens, franchises, advertising, etc. The company is sensitive to consumer pressure, and tries to respond quickly and positively (where practical). Consumerism is vast, amorphous, and difficult to write about.
Tappan	There are numerous federal consumer regulations, such as Magnuson-Moss and others, that affect the company. In addition, many state regulations could eventually affect interstate commerce. Consumer pressures involving Tappan are handled in-house. Industry problems are covered by trade associations. Consumerism has not changed over the last ten years. It has caused increased work and costs, and heightened government regulations.
Whirlpool	Consumer Product Safety Commission regulations and Magnuson-Moss require additional paperwork, which is not always meaningful. Valid consumer concerns are pursued; emotionally-based pressures are usually without merit. Consumer interest has been and is good for the company, since it has given Whirlpool a chance to discuss many programs and personalize the buyer-seller relationship.
Zenith	Operations are affected by all government regulations relating to advertising, warranties, safety, labeling, etc. There is no substantial consumer pressure for product changes. The effect of consumerism has been favorable because of the company's long-standing reputation for quality.

Source: Compiled by the author.

36

this problem. Schools and service centers have been provided with a variety of training materials and monthly publications and seminars.

The lack of available product information has been a problem facing the industry. Trade associations and companies have introduced product information programs, increased point-of-purchase information, added new pamphlets, and have begun other ways of providing consumers with adequate information. Certification programs, which use independent testing agencies to verify minimum standards compliance, enable consumers to identify those products and service technicians who satisfy stated standards.

Several associations and companies have enacted consumer affairs departments or consumer advocate positions. These function as liaisons in acquiring information and solving problems, suggest improved design features, advocate tighter quality control, and interact with government agencies.

The industry has taken affirmative action in dealing with consumer problems. The attitude of many associations and companies has changed from tokenism to positive action.

Impact of Consumerism

Consumerism has evolved from a period of little concern or action to one where individual, dissatisfied consumers are demanding action by government, industry, and companies. Major issues include product safety, warranties, servicing, replacement part availability, and product information.

The oldest consumer issue has been safety, from the toxic gases used in early refrigerators to the electric shocks of portable televisions and the radiation hazards of color televisions and microwave ovens. Despite attempts to reduce dangers by industry, government, and consumers, new dangers constantly are emerging. For example, a recent General Accounting Office audit stated high levels of radiation were emanating from microwave ovens and televisions.

The area of warranties remains a vital concern to consumers, although it appears to be lessening due to the Magnuson-Moss Warranty Act. However, it took the Federal Trade Commission two years to develop rules for its implementation and enforcement. Test cases on warranty violations have not yet occurred.

Servicing still causes dissatisfaction among consumers. Some repairers continue to charge for unnecessary or uncompleted jobs. A shortage of technicians and facilities exists, despite industry and company attempts. Waits for service can be inordinate. In addition, technicians frequently lack adequate training and current knowledge. This leads to improper diagnosis, repair, and lengthy time to finish the job.

Availability of replacement parts is still a problem with high costs and time delays. Manufacturers are just beginning to view the replacement parts market as a profitable opportunity, rather than a customer obligation. Because of this, the situation should improve. Product information and its availability remain controversial because many industry and company programs are too promotional. Consumer groups such as Consumers Union and Consumers' Research provide valuable information. However, the audience and products tested are limited.

In summary, the industry and its companies are becoming more responsive to consumerism, and acknowledge that the movement has positive features. Dissatisfied consumers and government legislation require business to be more responsible. The industry has tried hard to regulate itself by implementing the programs mentioned previously.

Evaluation of Consumerism

Modern consumerism has exposed many problems that did not previously receive attention from major appliance manufacturers or trade associations. In a number of cases, the industry has initiated consumer-oriented policies. However, many responses to consumerism have been brought about by federal legislation. The fear of additional legislation also has led to some positive self-regulatory reactions, in areas like product information, consumer complaint resolution, service training, sales-push money, and product safety.

Much still needs to be done. Consumers should not have to pay for product information, wait to receive it, nor write to manufacturers. Technician training programs do not reach those in remote geographic regions. Independents are frequently undertrained. Manufacturers have little control at the retail level and have been unable to eliminate salespeople selling inappropriate items for specific customer needs. In the area of safety, government and industry have to reach agreement as to the relation of safety and cost.

FUTURE OUTLOOK

Consumerism, growing slowly and unevenly, will be an important force in the future. There will be no major changes in the composition of consumer groups, due in part to the economic limitations placed upon them (product testing being quite expensive). In order to support undertakings, the groups will continue to direct publications at middle- and upper-class consumers. The major role of these groups will still be to provide information and reveal hazards.

There will be a slowdown in the passage of new government regulations, due to complaints from business of overregulation and a general societal attitude about excessive government intervention. Federal agencies will be under close congressional scrutiny, and there may be major reorganizations. There will also be a closer relationship among the industry, companies, and government to resolve problems jointly without additional laws. The government will take a more active role in product testing.

The industry, through trade associations, will become further involved with upgrading product quality, performance standards, uniform warranties, training programs for service technicians, licensing programs, coordinating and disseminating technical information, and organizing consumer panels.

Many individual companies will pattern their consumer affairs departments after Whirlpool and Maytag, which employ action-lines and design consultation with consumer affairs. Most large companies will employ in-house consumer advocates at the vice-president level and position them to interact with other functional areas. Small companies will rely upon trade associations for help in responding to consumerism.

RECOMMENDATIONS

Recommendations are offered that will enable consumer groups, government, the industry, and companies to maximize the positive impact of consumerism in the major appliance industry.

Consumer Groups

Consumer groups should become more active in lobbying for consumer legislation and supporting consumer-oriented political candidates. The groups must go beyond providing information in order to counter the efforts of business.

Consumer groups should become more concerned with supplying information to lower-income consumers. Pamphlets and other forms of information must be distributed to various low-income community groups and organizations. Language must be simplified and more readable. Products important to the poor should be tested.

Government

The government should simplify regulation and enforcement procedures. Legislation should be easily understood and complied with by business. It is currently quite difficult to enforce legislation and fulfill the proper objectives. Governmental information-keeping requests must consider the costs to business.

The government should better enforce existing legislation rather than enact further regulations; manpower and budgets are limited. There should be an avoidance of trivial actions and a concentration on important issues.

The Industry

The industry, through trade associations, should improve the job status of service personnel. This will attract more people into the technician field. Career growth must be possible through a clearly defined career path.

The industry should establish performance guidelines. Consumer fraud would be reduced by tighter standards and stricter self-regulatory enforcement. Companies should be encouraged to provide estimated costs in advance of services, notify customers if appointments cannot be kept, perform only repairs authorized in writing by consumers, and display standard service charges.

The industry should work with government agencies and consumer groups to coordinate information and cooperatively resolve problems.

Companies

Manufacturers should increase the availability of key component parts at reasonable prices, particularly for expensive parts like refrigerator compressors and television picture tubes.

Companies should try to simplify their products to allow easier use and home repair by consumers. This also would help alleviate the shortage of service personnel. Detailed repair manuals should be more available for consumers.

Firms should develop better product information and training for retail sales personnel. This will allow consumers to make better purchasing decisions. Elimination of sales-push money will stop sales personnel from switching consumers to the wrong appliance models. Product-line information should be distributed to enable consumers to select the right item in a manufacturer's product line.

Manufacturers should establish direct relationships with government agencies and consumer groups to resolve problems in a cooperative manner. Communication channels must be kept open.

BIBLIOGRAPHY

1. Aaker, David A., and Day, George S. Consumerism: Search for Consumer Interest, 2d ed. New York: Macmillan, 1974.

2. ____. Consumerism: Search for Consumer Interest, 1st ed. New York: Free Press, 1971.

3. "A Conference on Consumer Problems." Consumer Reports (September 1955), p. 400.

4. "Appliance Policy: Production Cuts Will Start at High Levels; Many New Materials in Use." Business Week (August 2, 1941), p. 28.

5. Association of Home Appliance Manufacturers. 1978 Directory of Certified Refrigerators and Freezers. Chicago: The Association of Home Appliance Manufacturers, 1978.

6. ____. 1977 Directory of Certified Air Conditioners. Chicago: The Association of Home Appliance Manufacturers, 1977.

7. ____. AHAM Consumer Recommendations on the Safe Use of Appliances. Chicago: The Association of Home Appliance Manufacturers, 1973.

8. "A Successful Attack by the Business Lobby." Business Week (July 4, 1977), p. 71.

9. "Automatic Washing Machines and Washer-Dryer Combinations." Consumers' Research Bulletin 39 (January 1957), pp. 5-13.

10. Baumgart, Guenther. "Industrywide Cooperation for Consumer Affairs." California Management Review 16 (Spring 1974), pp. 52-57.

11. Benningson, Lawrence A., and Benningson, Arnold I. "Product Liability: Manufacturers Beware!" Harvard Business Review 52 (May-June 1974), pp. 122-32.

12. Berens, John S. "Consumer Costs in Product Failure." MSU Business Topics 19 (Spring 1971), pp. 27-30.

13. "Better Appliance Servicing Wanted." Consumer Bulletin 53 (October 1970), pp. 13-15.

14. Broffman, Morton H. "Is Consumerism Merely Another Marketing Concept?" MSU Business Topics 19 (Winter 1971), pp. 15-21.

15. Bruce, Ronald. The Consumer's Guide to Product Safety. New York: Awards Books, 1971.

16. "Business Response to Consumerism." Business Week (September 6, 1969), pp. 94-108.

17. Connolly, Joel J.; Claffy, Thomas J.; and Aeberly, John J. "Difficulties Encountered in the Control of Mechanical Refrigeration." American Journal of Public Health 20 (March 1930), pp. 252-56.

18. Consdorf, Arnold P. "What's Right with Service?" Appliance Manufacturer (October 1977), pp. 1-9.

19. Consumer Reports' Buying Guide. Mount Vernon, New York: Consumers Union, 1975.

20. Council of Better Business Bureaus. Tips on Television Sets. Washington, D.C.: Council of Better Business Bureaus, 1972.

21. Cravens, David W., and Hills, Gerald E. "Consumerism: A Perspective for Business." Business Horizons (August 1970), pp. 22-24.

22. Davison, Eloise. "Electrical Washers." Ladies Home Journal 60 (November 1932), p. 46.

23. Dickman, Irving R. Making Products Safer: What Consumers Can Do. Washington, D.C.: Public Affairs Committee, 1975.

24. Electronic Industries Association. Fact Sheet/Consumer Complaint Assistance. Washington, D.C.: Electronic Industries Association, 1976.

25. ____. Television Safety Tips. Washington, D.C.: Electronic Industries Association, 1976.

26. ____. Tips for Consumers on Electronic Products Service. Washington, D.C.: Electronic Industries Association, 1975.

27. "Fatal Accident Involving a TV Receiver." Consumer Bulletin 39 (September 1957), p. 17.

28. Feldman, Laurence P. Consumer Protection: Problems and Prospects. St. Paul, Minn.: West Publishing, 1976.

29. "50 Years of Faithful Service to the Consumer." Consumers' Research Magazine 52 (October 1977), pp. 1-3.

30. "FTC Raps Misleading Ads for G.E., Panasonic TV's." Consumer Reports 42 (June 1977), p. 346.

31. Gaedecke, Ralph M. "The Movement for Consumer Protection: A Century of Mixed Accomplishments." University of Washington Business Review (Spring 1970), pp. 31-40.

32. Gardiner, David Morgan, and Jones, Mary Gardiner. Consumerism, A New Force in Society. New York: D. C. Heath and Company, 1976.

33. Initiatives in Corporate Responsibility. A Report of the Committee on Commerce, U.S. Senate, 92d Congress, Second Session, Washington, D.C.: U.S. Government Printing Office (October 2, 1972).

34. Klamkin, Charles. If It Doesn't Work, Read the Instructions. New York: Stein and Day, 1970.

35. Kotler, Philip. "What Consumerism Means for Marketers." Harvard Business Review 50 (May–June 1972), pp. 44-52.

36. Krattenmaker, Thomas G. "The Federal Trade Commission and Consumer Protection." California Management Review 18 (Summer 1976), pp. 89-103.

37. Krumm, Daniel J. "Warranties: A Study of Marketplace Reactions in the Appliance Industry." In Consumerism, A New Force in Society. D. M. Gardiner and M. G. Jones, eds. Lexington, Mass.: D. C. Heath and Company, 1976.

38. Major Appliance Consumer Action Panel. MACAP: Representing Consumers at the Highest Level of Industry. Chicago: The Major Appliance Consumer Action Panel, 1976.

39. Maytag Company. Backgrounder: Maytag Consumer Service. Newton, Iowa: The Maytag Company, 1977.

40. McGuire, E. Patrick. Consumer Product Warranties. New York: The Conference Board, 1975.

41. ____. The Consumer Affairs Department: Organization and Functions. New York: The Conference Board, 1974.

42. McQuade, Walter. "Why Nobody's Happy About Appliances." Fortune 85 (May 1972), pp. 180-84ff.

43. Moss, Frank E. "The Manufacturer's Role in Product Safety." The Conference Board Record 11 (April 1974), pp. 30-37.

44. National Association of Television and Electronic Servicers of America (NATESA). NATESA Is the Only Answer to Greater Prestige and Prosperity for Ethical Professional Servicers. Chicago: The National Association of Television and Electronic Servicers of America, 1977.

45. ____. Joys of Electronic Living. Chicago: The National Association of Television and Electronic Servicers of America, 1977.

46. National Electrical Manufacturers Association. Standardization/ A Dynamic Process: NEMA's Approach. New York: The National Electrical Manufacturers Association, 1977.

47. O'Brien, Ruth. "Consumer Movement in the United States." Journal of Home Economics 40 (November 1949), pp. 505-08.

48. "Off the Editor's Chest: Informative Labeling for Effective Communication to Consumers." Consumer Bulletin 53 (July 1976), pp. 18-19.

49. Palmer, H. Bruce. "Consumerism: The Business of Business." Michigan Business Review (July 1971), pp. 60-62.

50. Paul, Jan S. "Radiation from Color TV Receivers, Where Lies the Danger?" Consumer Bulletin 53 (December 1970), pp. 43-44.

51. Pittle, R. David. "The Consumer Product Safety Commission." California Management Review 18 (Summer 1976), pp. 105-09.

52. Product Performance and Servicing: An Examination of Consumer Problems and Business Response. A Report of the Sub-Council on Performance and Service of the National Business Council for Consumer Affairs. Washington, D.C.: U.S. Government Printing Office, 1973.

53. Report of the Task Force on Appliance and Warranties and Service. Washington, D.C.: Superintendent of Documents, 1968.

54. Rosenbloom, Joseph. Consumer Complaint Guide 1977. New York: Macmillan, 1976.

55. Schlink, F. J., et al. "Off the Editor's Chest." Consumers' Research Bulletin 39 (January 1957), pp. 28-30.

56. Steiner, George A. Business and Society. New York: Random House, 1975.

57. Swagler, Roger M. Caveat Emptor! An Introductory Analysis of Consumer Problems. Lexington, Mass.: D. C. Heath and Company, 1975.

58. Taylor, Russell. "Action People." Marketing Communications 299 (February 1971), pp. 13-14.

59. "The Age of Television." New Yorker (July 27, 1940), pp. 22-23.

60. The Challenge of Consumerism: A Symposium. New York: The Conference Board, 1971.

61. "Top-Freezer Refrigerators." Consumer Reports 43 (January 1978), pp. 23-26.

62. United States Code: Congressional and Administrative News. St. Paul, Minn.: West Publishing, 1976.

63. United States Code: Congressional and Administrative News. Brooklyn, N.Y.: Edward Thompson, 1957.

64. U.S. Consumer Product Safety Commission. Hazard Analysis of Television Sets. Washington, D.C.: U.S. Government Printing Office, 1974.

65. Warranties: There Ought to Be a Law. Washington, D.C.: Federal Trade Commission, 1977.

66. Weaver, Paul H. "The Hazards of Trying to Make Consumer Products Safer." Fortune 92 (July 1975), pp. 133-36.

67. Webster, Frederick E., Jr. "Does Business Misunderstand Consumerism?" The Harvard Business Review 51 (September-October 1973), pp. 89-97.

68. We Want You to Know About the Laws Enforced by FDA. Washington, D.C.: U.S. Department of Health, Education, and Welfare, 1975.

69. Whirlpool Corporation. Whirlpool Corporation: Consumer Programs. Benton Harbor, Mich.: The Whirlpool Corporation, 1977.

70. ____. The Appliance Industry Assists Vocational Schools. Benton Harbor, Mich.: The Whirlpool Consumer Affairs Training Center, 1977.

71. White-Westinghouse Corporation. The New Generation Washer. Cleveland, Ohio: White-Westinghouse, 1977.

3

CONSUMERISM AND BANKING

Peter D. Hein

INTRODUCTION

The banking industry includes commercial banks, mutual savings banks, savings and loan associations, and credit unions. At their inception, these banking forms had specific roles. Commercial banks created money, issued notes, and financed business. Mutual savings banks were formed by philanthropists in seaboard cities interested in reducing poverty by encouraging saving habits. Savings and loan associations (or building and loan associations) financed the housing and building industry. Credit unions were formed to aid common workers, instill a desire for saving, and provide reasonably priced loans.

Today, the roles of banking types are different and the delineations among them are not clear-cut. Commercial banks are stock-owned and pay dividends. These banks offer checking accounts, savings accounts, certificates of deposit, personal loans, automobile loans, and business loans. Most have departments to purchase stocks and other investment transactions. Commercial banks play an important role in the creation of money and the growth of the economy. They have the right to invest in corporate stocks and bonds, government and municipal bonds, and mortgages [108].

Mutual savings banks are located mostly in New England and the middle Atlantic states. Their main business is to collect and channel the savings of small investors into mortages, government bonds, stocks, and other securities. Until recently, they did not provide checking accounts. In New York, Massachusetts, and Connecticut, these banks are permitted to issue low-cost life insurance. Mutual savings banks are state chartered and supervised, nonstock institutions, owned entirely by depositors. Policy is determined by self-perpetuating boards of trustees. Investments in federal government obligations, municipal bonds, utility bonds rated Baa and better, industrial bonds, and blue chip stocks are allowed [98, pp. 13–15]. The banks may extend first mortgage loans on improved real estate, purchase mortgages from other lenders, make loans to depositors against their savings accounts, and make several other types of loans.

Savings and loan associations limit business almost entirely to the channeling of savings into residential mortgages. The associations are mutual organizations, although many are state chartered; savers are owners, not creditors [98, p. 3]. Directors are elected by members, with one vote for every $100 of savings up to a maximum of 50 votes [98, p. 24]. Over four-fifths of mortgage loans are conventional, not guaranteed by the Veterans' Administration nor the Federal Housing Administration. Associations may invest in federal government obligations and general obligation municipal bonds, but not revenue bonds.

Credit unions are cooperative, self-help societies made up of individuals joined together through a common employer or membership in a labor union, church, or fraternal society. Members purchase ownership shares, which are like savings accounts, and may borrow from the union. Dividends are paid to members from income on loans and investments. Unions are state or federally chartered.

The asset size and loan and deposit figures for these institutions as of the end of 1977 are shown in Table 3.1.

In this chapter, the history of consumerism and banking is investigated from the early 1800s to the present. Active consumer groups, governmental intervention, and the attitudes and actions of bankers are examined.

THE HISTORY OF CONSUMERISM IN THE BANKING INDUSTRY

Early Issues

Consumerism during the beginning of the banking industry was negligible, since consumers had little discretionary income or education. Nonetheless, bank insolvencies, failures of bank notes, robberies, and losses of specie value were common in the nineteenth-century U.S. banking industry.

In the early 1800s, there was extensive speculation in bank charters, which led to oversubscription, bank failures, and suspension of note redemption [122]. There were general suspensions of specie payments in 1814, 1818, 1837, 1841, and 1857. In 1837, 40 wildcat banks went into operation; by 1839, 39 had failed [126]. The American Bankers Association was formed in 1875 to aid in the creation of a better banking system and prevent bank robberies [76].

TABLE 3.1

Asset Size and Loan and Deposit Figures by Banking Type, 1977
(billions of dollars)

	Commercial Banks	Savings and Loan Associations	Mutual Savings Banks	Credit Unions
Assets	$1071.8	$444.5	$143.8	$52.2
Loans	888.6	367.0	92.5	40.7
Deposits				
Demand	317.7	—	—	—
Time	534.1	377.3	130.4	44.9

Source: Federal Reserve Bulletin (November 1977).

The period between 1875 and 1900 was tumultuous, since workers had little discretionary income, savings were nil, personal loans were nonexistent, home mortgages were not available from commercial banks, and checking accounts were solely for business transactions. The main banking function was the creation and issuance of bank notes, and the money supply was quite inelastic. A major concern of citizens and legislators was the development of a sound banking system [126, p. 300].

Monetary unrest continued into the twentieth century. There were panics in 1893 and 1907. Banks failed and counterfeit money was circulated. On December 12, 1913, the Federal Reserve Act was passed. Its purpose was "to provide for the establishment of Federal Reserve Banks, to furnish elastic currency, to afford means of discounting commercial paper, to establish a more effective supervisor of banking in the United States and for other purposes" [24]. National banks were given trust powers, the ability to make direct loans on real estate security (mortgages) for up to five-year terms and 50 percent of the estimated land value, and the power to run savings departments. The consumer was given the ability to obtain mortgages and savings accounts at commercial banks (which previously were not available), although not allowed to receive install- ment loans. By 1915, mutual savings banks had savings deposits of $4 billion, savings and loan associations had $1 billion, and commer- cial banks had $3 billion [124]. Consumer unions, begun in 1909, were still in their infancy [90].

The period after World War I was difficult for commercial banks. Despite the Federal Reserve Act, 10,816 banks failed be- tween 1921 and 1932. In 1933, an estimated 1,783 commercial banks failed [126, p. 671]. On June 16, 1933, the Banking Act of 1933 was enacted to revitalize the banking system.

Before the 1930s, most installment loans were not permitted, due to small loan laws and usury laws. Individual loans were strictly regulated at unprofitable rates. Loan sharks and pawnbrokers flour- ished, with rates from 6 to 40 percent per month. In 1929, only $3,158 million in installment loans were outstanding at all lending agencies [79]. In the 1930s, when business loans were limited, installment loans grew. World War II brought new restrictions to installment lending, as Regulation W imposed maximum maturities and minimum down payments [91].

After World War II, installment purchases and savings in- creased, banks expanded, consumer unions flourished, and consumer credit lending increased substantially. By 1955, there were 16,201 credit unions, with $2.4 billion in deposits and $1.9 billion in out- standing loans [90, p. 359]. Commercial banks had $47.8 billion in deposits; savings banks had $27.2 billion [124, p. 77].

Modern Issues

Prior to the 1960s, the banking industry was insulated from direct consumer pressure because of structural and performance factors. The industry was not involved with product safety, public safety, or health. Advertising was relatively honest. There were steady improvements in service and customer orientation [83, p. 13]. However, consumer attitudes changed as banks became viewed as growing impersonal, their role in the economy expanded, and questionable banking practices came to light. These practices involved checking accounts, savings account loans, collections, and investments [83, p. 15].

In the 1960s, consumerism began to focus on banking practices such as disclosure and information about interest rates. Senator Douglas of Illinois, in a 1960 congressional hearing on a "Consumer Credit Labeling Act," stated that

> The benefits of effective competition cannot be realized if the buyers [borrowers] do not have adequate knowledge of the alternatives which are available to them. In my judgment S.2755 would invigorate competition in the consumer credit market by requiring a return to price competition. Extra normal profits earned through the ability to mislead borrowers [consumers] would be minimized [94, p. 502].

Financial institutions resisted truth-in-lending, asserting that costs were prohibitive and benefits few. It was not until 1968, after years of debate and delay, that the Consumer Credit Protection Act (Truth-in-Lending) was passed. Section 102 of the act explains its importance and purpose:

> The Congress finds that economic stabilization would be enhanced and the competition among various financial institutions and other firms engaged in the extension of consumer credit would be strengthened by the informed use of credit. The informed use of credit results from an awareness of the costs thereof by consumers. It is the purpose of this title to assure a meaningful disclosure of credit terms so that the consumer will be able to compare more readily the use of credit and to protect the consumer against inaccurate and unfair credit billing and credit card practices [24, p. 238].

At the same time, the Uniform Consumer Credit Codes (UCCC) were developed and promulgated by the National Conference of Com-

missioners on Uniform State Laws [56]. UCCC preceded the Credit
Act in origin, was deeper in scope, and contained similar disclosure
requirements. Its intent was to remove variations in state laws
pertaining to consumer credit. UCCC called for the elimination
and repeal of all existing general interest and usury statutes, small
loan and large loan acts, industrial loan laws, retail installment
sales, commercial bank laws, revolving credit, truth-in-lending,
second mortgages, and other provisions. As of the end of 1977,
UCCC had been accepted in only seven states [118].

Consumers have become concerned about the fairness of fees
charged on checking accounts and the hidden nature of some charges.
The charges include per-check fees, monthly service fees, stop-
payment fees, fees for legal procedures involving attachments or
garnishments, and overdraft charges. Consumers also are interested in how savings account interest is calculated, since various
institutions use day-of-deposit/day-of-withdrawal accounts, give
grace days for deposits and withdrawals, compound continuously,
compound daily, compound monthly, or compound quarterly. Some
pay 4 percent, 4.5 percent, 5 percent, 5.25 percent, or other interest rates.

California recently has taken action that requires banks to
disclose all normal business charges on demand savings or time
deposits [30, p. 2]. The law took effect July 1, 1977. In New York,
Governor Hugh Carey announced the consideration of a truth-in-
lending law, under which banks must disclose the annual rate of
simple interest, the formula for calculating interest, when deposits
earn interest, delays in posting interest, grace periods, minimum
balances, minimum time periods, fees for inactive accounts, and
withdrawal penalties [73].

Consumerists have been involved with abolishing discriminatory
credit practices based upon race, color, religion, national origin,
sex, marital status, and age. In 1974, the Equal Credit Opportunity
Act was enacted; it was expanded in 1976. As of June 1977, married
women were allowed to establish their own credit histories [88].
Other consumer interests have centered on billing procedures,
collection practices, allocation of mortgage money, credit reporting,
and disclosure of mortgage closing costs. A great deal of government legislation has been passed recently in these areas.

Credit unions have expanded into the mortgage market with
30-year loans, 12-year personal loans, and preauthorized lines of
credit (which should lead to a credit-card system). Unions are
expanding at the rate of 14 percent a year. A recent move to issue
interest-bearing share drafts has been thwarted by an American
Bankers Association lawsuit [54]. Mutual savings banks have added
NOW accounts, savings accounts with checking privileges that pay

interest and have liberal loan terms [100]. Federal legislation affecting accounts for all types of banks is pending.

New forms of banking are being developed via Electronic Funds Transfer (EFT) systems. Terminals offer immediate funds transfers from consumer to merchant accounts. However, consumers are concerned about privacy and fear this depersonalization of banking [60]. Ralph Nader has said that EFT "would result in McDonaldization of the banking industry" [59].

Another important issue involves redlining, the refusal of banks to grant mortgages in certain geographic areas. The Home Mortgage Disclosure Act was legislated in 1975 to provide the public with information about the geographic locations of banks' mortgage loans. Civil rights groups have claimed that banks employ policies to avoid granting mortgages to minorities, women, and those buying a house in an older neighborhood. At the urging of civil rights groups, the Federal Home Loan Bank Board is proposing, as of this date, regulations to monitor and weed out discriminatory practices [120]. Banks oppose the legislation as being too costly and prone to granting questionable loans.

ACTIVE CONSUMER GROUPS

The number of active consumer groups in the banking industry is limited. Yet, a recent Louis Harris poll showed that 41 percent of the respondents stated that more attention should be focused on the banking industry [47]. The few groups operating in this area have been quite effective.

The Consumer Federation of America, composed of 220 nonprofit organizations representing over 30 million consumers, testified in support of the Truth-in-Lending and the Equal Credit Opportunity bills. It consistently appears at meetings of the House Banking and Finance Committee [67, 77, 121]. In April 1977, the Federation chastised the Federal Reserve Bank for not enforcing the Equal Credit Act [67, p. 4]. Its most recent actions have been support of education for federal auditors, support of a national consumer bank, a losing fight for passage of new debt collection practices legislation, support of Fair Credit Reporting Act amendments, a fight to expand thrift institutions, opposition to a truth-in-lending provision weakening disclosure, and opposition to any efforts to hurt borrowers through variable mortgage rates [67, p. 11].

Consumer Action, a San Francisco-based group of 4,000 member families, has published Break the Banks (1974) and It's in Your Interest (1976). It's in Your Interest is a 95-page book that compares passbook rates of 47 institutions and advises against commercial bank savings accounts. Consumer Action successfully campaigned for a consumer disclosure law that requires banks to provide customers with complete breakdowns of charges, interest rates, and methods by which rates are computed. Consumer Action was able to force Bank of America to withdraw advertisements for automobile loans that it thought were misleading. After withdrawing the advertisements, the bank lowered its rates on three-year loans from 13.26 to 12.39 percent [25, 26]. Consumer Action surveyed 96 advertisements in 13 cities in March 1977. It reported the unsubstantiated use of superlatives, distorted use of the word free, and a failure to state clearly the conditions for receiving gifts [50, p. 19]. Consumer Action brought suit against the Federal Reserve to force it to release the data used in developing its monthly survey of consumer interest rates. The group also testified before Congress [119].

Ralph Nader has been active in confronting the banking industry. As early as 1970, Nader accused the banks of deceptive practices and stated that they were engaging in "the largest kind of organized crime in our country—economic crime" through "established practices" [92]. Among the practices were redlining and the use of trust funds to generate "compensating balances from brokerage houses" [92]. Nader has accused the Federal Reserve of being too secretive and failing to understand the general public [93]. In 1974, Nader criticized First National City Bank (now Citibank) in a book entitled <u>Citibank</u>. The bank's lending policies were labeled as too liberal; mortgage money was found to be too tight; there were interlocking directories; and the bank was determined not to have been thoroughly investigated by the Comptroller of the Currency [87]. In a speech to the Independent Bankers Association of America, Nader suggested a coalition to serve common banker–consumer interests [93].

Common Cause, with a membership of 200,000 citizens, frequently uses mass letter writing campaigns. It was active in pushing for Truth-in-Lending and Equal Credit Opportunity [77, 105].

GOVERNMENT

Banking is heavily regulated by government agencies, often with overlapping authorities. The myriad of agencies has evolved because of the different types of banking institutions. For purposes of continuity, the agencies are described in chronological order, not according to relative importance: Comptroller of the Currency, Federal Reserve System, Federal Trade Commission, Federal Deposit Insurance Corporation, Federal Home Loan Bank Board, and the National Credit Union Administration.

Comptroller of the Currency

The Office of Comptroller of the Currency was founded in 1863 and operates within the Treasury Department. The office considers applications for charters of new banks. These applications are investigated and approved or rejected. Only nationally chartered commercial banks are covered. The Comptroller also has control over bank mergers and consolidations and supervises operations of national banks [108]. The Comptroller enforces compliance with Regulation Z (Truth-in-Lending) and Regulation B (Equal Credit Opportunity) under the Federal Reserve Act.

Federal Reserve System

The Federal Reserve System, the central bank of the United States, administers and develops policy for credit and monetary affairs. The "Federal Reserve helps to maintain the banking industry in sound condition, capable of responding to the nation's domestic and international financial needs and objectives" [122, p. 535]. The Federal Reserve was formed on December 23, 1913.

The board of the Federal Reserve sets requirements for the reserves to be maintained against deposits and has the power to determine maximum rates paid on time and savings deposits. The board supervises member banks, 12 in number, and state member banks. It has the power to approve branching, mergers, and acquisitions. Under the Bank Holding Act of 1956, the board rules on acquisitions by bank holding companies. Under Truth-in-Lending, the board prescribes regulations to assure "meaningful disclosure by lenders of credit terms so that consumers will be able to compare more readily the various credit terms available and avoid the uniform use of credit" [122]. The board also establishes and supervises rules for the Equal Credit Opportunity Act, the Home Mortgage Disclosure Act, the Fair Credit Billing Act, and banking provisions of the Federal Trade Commission Act.

Federal Trade Commission

The Federal Trade Commission, founded in 1914, limits monopolies, restraints of trade, and unfair or deceptive trade practices [122, p. 540]. It uses cease-and-desist orders and court-imposed fines. The Federal Trade Commission is responsible for the Truth-in-Lending Act (1968) and the Fair Credit Reporting Act (1970). Under Truth-in-Lending, the commission seeks true credit disclosure by creditors, retailers, finance companies, nonfederal credit unions, and others. It also regulates the insurance and liability of credit cards to prevent fraudulent interstate use.

Federal Deposit Insurance Corporation

The Federal Deposit Insurance Corporation (FDIC) was organized in 1934 as part of the Banking Act of 1933. In 1950, the Federal Deposit Insurance Act made FDIC an independent agency [122, p. 509]. The FDIC insures deposits in national banks, state banks that are part of the Federal Reserve System, and state banks that apply for FDIC insurance. The corporation may aid mergers or protect depositors, and is authorized to terminate the insured status of a bank that engages in unsound practices. FDIC acts as a receiver for all national banks placed in receivership and for state banks, when appointed by state authorities.

Other FDIC functions include: periodic examination of banks that are not members of the Federal Reserve, approval of conversions and mergers, approval or disapproval of new branches, issuance of cease-and-desist orders for banks involved with personal dishonesty, suspension and release of personnel, regulation of interest payment and advertising, requirements for banks to maintain adequate security, and requirements for compliance with cost disclosure of consumer credit [122]. A special Office of Bank Customer Affairs has been created.

Federal Home Loan Bank Board

The Federal Home Loan Bank Board was established by the Federal Home Loan Bank Act in 1952 to encourage thrift and economical home ownership [122]. The board supervises and regulates savings and loan associations that specialize in lending for homes. The board operates the Federal Savings and Loan Insurance Corporation (FSLIC), which protects the savings of over 60 million people with accounts in insured savings and loans. The board directs the Federal Home Loan System, which is similar to the Federal Reserve. Twelve regional banks are authorized to perform debt marketing operations, liquidity portfolio management, and financial forecasting. The board also oversees truth-in-lending and credit opportunity laws.

National Credit Union Administration

The National Credit Union Administration was set up as an independent federal agency in 1970. It is responsible for chartering, insuring, supervising, and examining federal credit unions. The administration directs the National Credit Union Share Insurance Fund. It also investigates consumer complaints regarding violations of the Federal Credit Union Act or Truth-in-Lending [122].

Major Consumer Legislation

A number of federal laws, enforced by the preceding agencies, regulate the banking industry and have an impact on final consumers. Eleven acts are summarized in chronological order in Table 3.2. The major consumer-oriented acts are the Consumer Credit Protection Act, Fair Credit Reporting Act, Equal Opportunity Credit Act, Fair Credit Billing Act, Real Estate Settlement Procedures Act, Unfair and Deceptive Practices by Banks Act, and Home Mortgage Disclosure Act.

Recent Government Actions

In its December 1976 report to Congress, the Federal Reserve Board stated that it had received 3,585 complaints for the year. The board handled 2,216 complaints and referred 1,116 to other, more appropriate agencies. Of the board's complaints, 665 related to the Equal Credit Opportunity Act, 656 to Truth-in-Lending, 530 to unfair or deceptive practices, 264 to interest rates, 154 to the Fair Credit Reporting Act, and 15 to miscellaneous items [68].

The Federal Deposit Insurance Corporation, in its 1976 congressional report, noted that out of 7,700 bank examinations, 28.5 percent yielded violations, most of a technical nature [106].

The Federal Reserve Bank's 1976 report on enforcement of the Equal Credit Opportunity Act made no note of the number of complaints or actions taken [62]. The report was criticized by the Consumer Federation of America because of its lack of information and enforcement [67]. The consumer group also commented that examiners were neither educated nor qualified to investigate banks. The allegations caused federal agencies to improve the education of examiners and become more involved with enforcement.

In its 1977 report to Congress on Truth-in-Lending, the Federal Reserve Board mentioned increased enforcement and compliance. Most violations resulted from misunderstanding, inadvertence, or clerical error. However, regulatory agencies noted a significant increase in the number of banks found in error. For example, the Federal Deposit Insurance Corporation reported noncompliance at 25.6 percent in 1976 and 36.2 percent in 1977. It had to issue seven cease-and-desist orders involving Truth-in-Lending violations [118].

TABLE 3.2

Federal Legislation Affecting the Banking Industry

Legislation	Year Enacted	Key Provisions
Federal Reserve Act	1913	Establishes a Federal Reserve System, allows real estate loans and savings departments in national banks
McFadden–Pepper Act	1927	Alters Federal Reserve Act, increasing time deposits lent for real estate and raising mortgage terms to five years
Banking Act of 1933	1933	Shores up the collapsing bank system and changes the Federal Reserve Act, creates the Federal Deposit Insurance Corporation, enables national banks to have branches, prohibits member banks from paying interest on demand deposits, gives the Federal Reserve the power to limit rates on time deposits
Home Owners Loan Corporation	1933	Assists distressed homeowners who are unable to meet mortgage payments by refinancing the loans
Consumer Credit Protection Act (Truth–in–Lending)	1968	Covers disclosure of all aspects of consumer credit from bank loans to credit cards and leasing, requires that finance charges be computed in a pre–scribed manner and an annual percentage rate (APR) be computed in a specific manner, provides for civil and criminal penalties for violations

Fair Credit Reporting Act	1970	Requires consumer reporting agencies to adopt reasonable procedures for acquiring information about consumers while protecting their rights, that consumers be allowed to see and comment on their files, provides for liability of violators
Equal Credit Opportunity Act	1974	Insures that institutions are nondiscriminatory in making credit available, allows civil liability for violators
Fair Credit Billing Act	1974	Establishes a procedure for consumers to contest billing disputes, applies mostly to open-end bank credit lines and bank credit cards, specifies penalties
Real Estate Settlement Procedures Act	1974	Provides homebuyers with information regarding costs involved in the settlement of real estate transactions, makes mandatory the distribution of "Settlement Costs—A HUD Guide," specifies fines
Unfair and Deceptive Practices by Banks Act	1975	Prevents unfair or deceptive banking practices by establishing consumer affairs departments in the Office of Comptroller of the Currency, Federal Reserve Board, and the Federal Deposit Insurance Corporation to monitor banks
Home Mortgage Disclosure Act	1975	Requires banks to maintain records of all mortgages by census area in terms of numbers and dollar amounts, provides no specific penalties

Source: Compiled by the author.

During the same time period, the Comptroller of the Currency estimated that 88 percent of the national banks had not achieved full compliance; almost all violations were technical. The Federal Reserve Board estimated that 72 percent of state member banks had failed to comply fully due to technical errors. It was concluded that the increased number of violations was due to the intensified examination efforts [118].

Legal suits regarding Truth-in-Lending violations increased from 415 to 2,237 between 1972 and 1975, a 439 percent jump. But the results of the few class action suits in federal courts have gone against consumers in most of the cases [106]. No verdicts have resulted in substantial judgments, and the courts have been quite strict in allowing class action suits to be brought [94]. The most notable case was Ratner v. Chemical Bank, in which it was alleged that Chemical Bank failed to disclose the "nominal APR of interest" for credit cards. The case involved 132,233 cardholders and potential liability of $13,233,000. The court denied the class action suit and awarded a summary judgment of $20,000 to Ratner [94].

In 1976, the Library of Congress provided data on class action suits to a House subcommittee. This 1972-75 data showed that the suits had little effect. For example, in Eoualdi v. First National Bank of Chicago, the plaintiff won only actual damages and attorney's fees and the class action suit was disallowed. Legislation to correct the situation was proposed in the House, but it was never accepted [106]. According to Herbert Newberg, only 39 class action suits involving credit and truth-in-lending were brought between 1966 and 1976; only 11 cases were won by consumers. Of the 11, seven involved commercial banks and three were against savings and loans. These numbers seem to reflect the sizes of these two institutions [94, vol. 6].

A review of the government's enforcement role shows a subdued attitude. For instance, the Federal Deposit Insurance Corporation has defined its role as providing and ensuring soundness in the banking system [65]. Senator William Proxmire has commented that agencies "have done little consumer education, assigned only minimum personnel to process complaints and have failed to take action when banks are found violating federal laws" [105, p. 2]. The Consumer Federation has echoed these sentiments [67].

Federal agencies respond that they have become more active with violations being disclosed and enforcement action undertaken [118]. The Federal Deposit Insurance Corporation has set up a team of compliance officers to conduct special examinations once every 15 months. The Comptroller of the Currency has established a similar department with 250 experts to examine national banks [95].

INDUSTRY RESPONSES TO CONSUMERISM

This section offers a compendium of industry responses to consumerism, as found in the general and specialized literature and as disclosed in a primary survey involving major bank trade associations.

Industry Responses as Reported in the Literature

The American Bankers Association was founded in 1875. Its initial goals were to foster uniform action by banks, help prevent bank failures, and protect banks against robberies and crime [76, p. 21]. In 1913, the association voiced agreement with the proposed Federal Reserve Act's intent to "furnish an elastic currency, to afford means of rediscounting commercial paper and to establish a more effective supervision of banking in the United States" [24, p. 1]. However, it also criticized some elements of the proposal and made several recommendations [84, p. 2,244].

In 1924, the American Bankers Association Executive Council endorsed the McFadden Bill, saying "this bill is the most important banking bill which has come before the House since the passage of the Federal Reserve Act and its enactment into law is necessary to preserve and more firmly establish the benefit of that Act" [1, p. 2,619]. The bill ultimately increased national bank branching and mortgage powers, and offered consumers better services and greater alternatives.

From 1927 to 1933 the country had many banking failures, and there was great concern for the safety of money. The banking industry backed the Banking Act of 1933 in an effort to ensure a safer banking system [84, p. 2,619]. From this point until the 1950s, there were few consumer complaints and no significant bank responses to consumerism.

During the 1950s, there were expansion, branching, and mergers; trade associations had some disputes among themselves. In the late 1950s and early 1960s, consumers and legislators sought fuller disclosure of loan terms. Numerous industry responses were elicited by the Douglas hearings in the Senate.

In 1962, the American Bankers Association wrote to Senator Douglas and endorsed the primary objective of the bill, full disclosure of finance charges, but raised two major reservations: states should set and enforce laws, not the federal government, and simple annual rates are difficult and expensive to utilize [74, p. 68]. On June 4, 1963, the association reiterated its views and stated opposition to the Douglas Bill in an **American Banker** editorial.

The New York State Bankers Association indicated support for the bill, but wanted to use dollar payment terms, not annual percentage rates [74, p. 136]. The National Association of Mutual Savings Banks supported the law "as it relates to mortgage lending" [75, p. 926]. The United States Savings and Loan League stated that it "takes no position for or against any legislation dealing with interest rate disclosure" [75, p. 254]. Credit unions opposed the Douglas Bill, indicating that they were consumer-oriented and that any law would be costly and burdensome [75, p. 254]. Despite opposition by the industry, the 1968 Consumer Protection Act was passed in form close to the original Douglas Bill, although it took eight years for approval.

Senator Proxmire introduced a Fair Credit Reporting bill in 1969. At the hearings, the American Bankers Association stated: "those engaged in the consumer credit business are fully capable of policing their own operations" [28, p. 42]. The association felt the bill would restrict the free movement of credit information at a time when more than $1 trillion of consumer and real estate credit required more, not less information [20, p. 42].

The Independent Bankers Association of America also opposed the Fair Credit Reporting bill at hearings, saying: "thousands and thousands of cases handled to the mutual benefit of borrower and lender have been overlooked, overshadowed by the attention focused on the few inaccuracies that occur in the credit reporting industry" [88, p. 96]. The Fair Credit Reporting Act was passed in 1970.

In a 1976 meeting before Congress, the Consumer Bankers Association indicated that consumer legislation was often too technical, costly, and self-defeating. It suggested that Congress "place a moratorium on any legislation until some independent organization has an opportunity to evaluate the impact of the recently passed acts and regulations on the consumer credit market" [109, p. 2]. The American Bankers Association recommended that Congress require any new legislation to be accompanied by a cost-benefit analysis, estimating the costs to government and the industry. The National Association of Mutual Savings Banks concluded that Congress frequently passed legislation that was difficult to implement or ended up not being used. It concluded that the Real Estate Settlement Procedures Act was originally too burdensome and did not help the consumer [109]. Subsequently, the act was amended.

Trade associations have tried to communicate consumer problems, complaints, issues, and consumer group criticisms to member banks. The American Bankers Association has said banks must respond to consumerism to avoid excessive regulation:

Unless we bankers can demonstrate we are already
addressing the problems identified by the activists—

or unless we can demonstrate that these problems will not be solved solely through financial institutions—we face the very real threat of government attempts to find solutions for us [43, p. 2].

In the area of advertising, the Bank Marketing Association has enacted self-regulation through a Financial Advertising Code of Ethics (FACE). This guides banks in full disclosure and proper advertising: "Any features, any terms (including price) or any purchase benefits must be presented in a manner that does not mislead either by what is stated or by what is omitted" [89, p. 8]. According to FACE, consumers should be able to grasp essential information from the advertisement without reading every word or fine print.

During 1978, industry associations told federal agencies there was no need to regulate community lending practices of banks and savings institutions. Witnesses told Congress to avoid writing broad new regulations and to evaluate each lender's performance individually, taking into account varying markets and credit needs. Industry representatives were concerned that a proposed Community Reinvestment Act would be tantamount to credit allocation, and felt banks would operate more efficiently under self-regulation [2]. Many banks have cooperated with their associations' requests by instituting voluntary disclosure and consumer affairs departments and by taking other proconsumer actions.

Trade Association Responses to Primary Study

Ten banking trade associations were contacted and asked to participate in a study. Five cooperated: Consumer Bankers Association (CBA), Independent Bankers Association of America (IBAA), Long Island Bankers Association (LIBA), National Association of Mutual Savings Banks (NAMSB), and the New York State Bankers Association (NYSBA). One association, the Bank Marketing Association, sent a letter stating it is involved with internal bank training and has nothing to do with consumerism. Another association, the Council of Mutual Savings Associations, returned a letter saying it is dedicated to research, public education, and legislation concerning mutual savings institutions, and does not get involved with the consumer movement in any way. Three associations provided no responses, despite two requests: American Bankers Association, American Savings and Loan League, and Independent Bankers Association of New York.

The overall response of the associations is that the consumer movement is costly, and these costs must ultimately be borne by consumers. The movement is viewed as a powerful and pervasive force that has had positive effects. The impact of consumerism will continue in the future.

A question-by-question summary shows that many associations feel the consumer movement has had positive effects and they view it as a powerful force. Two associations are not involved with consumerism. Four of the associations believe that consumerism has caused higher costs. One states that members have become more aware of consumer demands. One association has established a formal panel to deal with consumerism while four have not. All the associations provide representatives to appear before government committees and speakers for consumer organizations. Each of the associations feels that consumerism will result in increased costs to consumers in the long run.

Table 3.3 contains condensed responses to the survey for those participating trade associations. Each association did not answer every question. Open-ended responses were interpreted by the author.

COMPANY RESPONSES TO CONSUMERISM

This section examines the responses of individual banks to consumerism, as found in the literature and revealed in a primary study of major commercial banks.

Company Responses as Reported in the Literature

In the early 1900s, national banks resisted the Federal Reserve Act, claiming it gave government too much power and was unfair to national banks as state banks did not have to join the system. A response by a representative of the First National Bank of Abingdon, Virginia, was typical:

> The national banks are in a less favorable position than
> the state banks on account of being compelled to either
> enter into the Federal Reserve System or give up their
> charters, for you know state banks have the option of
> either becoming members or remaining as they are. . . .
> It would seem that under the new law the banks might
> be placed in a position of having to consult the Federal
> Reserve Board before extending their customers a line
> of credit [84, p. 2,356].

Many national banks entered state banking systems. These included Wells-Fargo of San Francisco, First National Bank of Cleve-

TABLE 3.3

Banking Trade Association Responses to Study

Question 1	Generally speaking, how does your association feel about the consumer movement?
CBA	The consumer movement is a very powerful force affecting the banking industry, as evidenced by recent court cases and class action suits.
IBAA	Consumers are of prime concern, and the consumer movement is supported, since IBAA and the movement sprang from the same marketplace.
LIBA	The consumer movement has a positive effect in opening a dialogue between consumers and banks, enabling the banks to be more responsive to consumer needs and to educate them.
NAMSB	The consumer movement has and will continue to serve a useful purpose. Consumerism is most effective when a good climate for market forces to operate is created. The "adversary climate" created by consumer groups can lead to unnecessary legislation and result in higher costs.
NYSBA	There is concern about the consumer movement and its effects on member commercial banks. The association is active in issues like equal credit and truth-in-lending.
Question 2	How has the consumer movement affected the companies that belong to your association?
CBA	Some member banks have been the targets of class action suits. Overall, banks have become much more aware of policies and compliance procedures as a result of consumer pressures.
IBAA	Consumerism has sometimes been exploited politically, resulting in ends detrimental to association members and consumers. The Equal Credit Opportunity Act allows women to be "protected" from the ability to get credit.
LIBA	Compliance with consumer laws and regulations tends to erode profits from some services, resulting in higher prices for services or discontinuance by banks.

(continued)

Table 3.3 (continued)

NAMSB	The consumer movement has had a pervasive effect. "Financial consumerism" imposes costly and time-consuming disclosure and recordkeeping. Costs are absorbed by depositors and borrowers.
NYSBA	Member banks have frequently established a position of compliance officer, which is extremely costly.
Question 3	Has the association created a position, panel, or department to deal with the effects of the consumer movement?
CBA	No new panels or positions have been created. There is consideration for a joint meeting with consumer groups under the auspices of a federal agency.
IBAA	There is no panel or department.
LIBA	There is not and will not be a department created, and the association does not take positions on the effects of dealing with consumerism.
NAMSB	In 1977, a Special Committee on Consumer Affairs, comprised of 17 prominent savings banks, was formed. The committee mobilizes the expertise of individual banks in addressing the many aspects of "financial consumerism."
NYSBA	There is no formal committee, but the Consumer Credit Division holds compliance seminars, inviting regulatory agencies to send speakers.
Question 4	Does the association provide representatives to appear before government committees examining consumer issues?
CBA	The association testifies before many government committees.
IBAA	The association provides representatives to appear for testimony on request.
LIBA	The association appears before government bodies.
NAMSB	Representatives are provided to appear before federal committees; the new Special Committee on Consumer Affairs assists in this.
NYSBA	The association gives testimony at public hearings, such as those held on redlining by the Senate Banking Committee.

(continued)

Question 5	Does the association provide speakers to appear before national and/or local consumer organizations?
CBA	Speakers would be supplied upon request; no such request has been made.
IBA	Speakers are provided, but only by invitation.
LIBA	Speakers from member banks appear upon request.
NAMSB	There is no speakers bureau, but representatives do participate in meetings. Members of consumer groups also are invited to speak at NAMSB programs.
NYSBA	Speakers are supplied, but a speakers bureau is not maintained.

Question 6	What do you perceive to be the long-term impact of consumerism on the industry you represent?
CBA	As consumer groups challenge traditional practices, such as pricing or creditor remedies against delinquent debtors, banks will become more price conscious in marketing products. If income is reduced in one area, price increases must occur in others.
IBAA	Consumerism is oversimplified and will result in increased costs, which will be passed on to consumers. The availability of credit and service will decline; traditional providers of credit will leave the field. Complexities and liabilities in operations will become too great. IBAA will be more sophisticated in dealing with consumerism.
LIBA	Consumer knowledge will grow, making banking more competitive and efficient. In the transition to the "new banking mode," consumers will pay more.
NAMSB	Consumerism has the potential to provide real benefits, as well as the potential for counterproductive results. It is hoped that consumerism will have a constructive long-run impact. There is deep concern about future government policies.
NYSBA	Banks will have to live with consumerism and train personnel to cope with it. The movement will continue, but not be more intense.

Source: Compiled by the author.

land, Irving National of New York, and National Bank of North America [74, p. 2,620]. This action inspired the McFadden Act, which gave national banks greater branching power and the ability to make more liberal mortgages, and resulted in more housing and convenient branches for consumers. The national banks' approval of the McFadden Act was emphasized when 25 top bank executives met with the Comptroller of the Currency to support the bill [8, p. 41].

In 1950, banks hailed legislation allowing the expansion of services. Irving Trust indicated consumers would benefit by commercial banks gaining trust powers. The Bowery Savings Bank said that broadening investment powers of savings banks would increase housing for customers. Despite opposition from savings and commercial banks, savings and loan associations were allowed to rent safe deposit boxes and make larger home improvement loans [11, p. 1].

During the 1962 hearings on Truth-in-Lending, First National City Bank voiced the negative sentiments of many banks:

> The object—Truth-in-Lending—is assuredly reasonable. Every borrower should know what he is being charged for interest. Yet, as prolonged hearings on the bill have brought out, there are in fact some weighty objections to passage of a Federal law of the sort envisaged by Senator Douglas. For one thing, regulation of rates chargeable by lenders is a function performed by State governments and there is a question whether a Federal law in this area would be constitutional [74, p. 378].

The bank also criticized the requirement of a simple annual rate of interest, stating "this kind of calculation is one that stumps the experts" [74, p. 378]. Truth-in-Lending was fought for eight years.

In 1969, one year after the bill was passed, Banking conducted a study of chief executive officers to determine their problems with Regulation Z. An officer of a medium-sized Massachusetts bank replied that there were many complications in calculation and considerable time spent on required forms. The president of a medium-sized Tennessee bank said the drafting of a new form was time-consuming and expensive, and interpreting the law was difficult. The president of a small Arkansas bank remarked that his staff was not able to understand the original ruling or subsequent explanations from FDIC. The chairman of a medium-sized Arkansas bank felt the law was too complicated, time-consuming, and costly. Forty percent of the respondents said the law was explained to consumers when they applied for loans and was not publicized via brochures and advertisements [9].

The largest U.S. bank, Bank of America, expressed a consumer-oriented philosophy in 1971. It stated that banks could no longer think only of themselves. They had to ask: "Is it good for the consumer? Is it good for the community as a whole? Is it good for the bank?" [85, p. 23]. However, an article in Bank Marketing in 1976 concluded that much legislation was "capricious, pernicious, malicious and counter-productive to the consumer's best interest" [48, p. 15].

In the 1970s, Citibank (then First National City Bank) became prolific in its articles and comments about consumerism. James Farley, a Citibank spokesman and advocate for consumerism in banking, said at a national American Bankers Association conference: "The thrust of consumerism in banking and its impact on installment credit practices should be viewed as an opportunity for bankers to meet the service demands of consumers and not as a threat for banking" [80, p. 2].

Citibank expressed other thoughts about consumerism. Legislators had to be made aware of the relation between credit costs and availability. Bankers were not to respond negatively, but to contribute to positive consumer programs. Nondiscrimination laws made lending more liberal, restricted a bank's ability to collect, and were counterproductive since they made banks less willing to lend [123].

Edward Farash of Shawmut Corporation spoke to the Boston College Finance Academy in the early 1970s:

> Our awareness and responsiveness is far more effective
> than regulation in meeting consumerism. We must learn
> to think about our daily activities from the consumer
> point of view; to be self-critical; to change in advance of
> need. . . . Our greatest challenge is to set aside in-
> difference. Indifference to having to fight our battle
> in the legislative area. Indifference to our own cus-
> tomers and serving them and indifference to reflecting
> an open society [123, p. 15].

Recently, credit unions have labeled regulations as too ambiguous and costly, especially since the unions are consumer-operated. They also have criticized banks and thrift institutions for not using their expertise to shape the technical details of consumer credit laws [57]. However, some banks were active in responding to consumerism well before these 1976 comments.

In 1971, Ohio National Bank was one of the first banks to become involved with consumerism by establishing an "Action Center," a new Department of Consumer Affairs designed to improve communications. The Director of Consumer Affairs reported directly to the president and established a central source of assistance and information [103].

First National City Bank formed a Department of Consumer Affairs, headed by Bess Myerson, in 1973. The department was responsible for planning new customer services and improving the handling of customer complaints [21]. Shortly thereafter, Chase Manhattan Bank created a Consumer Affairs Department to improve communications [42]. Smaller banks, such as the First National Bank of Atlanta and United California Bank of Los Angeles, developed consumer-oriented positions in the mid-1970s [12, 115].

In 1976, Crocker National Bank in California accused competitors of being traditional, self-centered, and unconcerned about consumer needs. Crocker established "people hours" (8:30 A.M. to 4:30 P.M.), increased savings rates, offered free checking to the elderly, eliminated legalese, instituted simple documents, and credited savings interest on a monthly rather than a quarterly basis. These programs increased new deposits by $100 million in one year [55]. Other major banks, for example, Continental Illinois National Bank and Citibank, have also developed simple forms. Bank of America provides customers with full disclosure regarding their accounts [39].

An important 1974 study in Michigan examined banks' reactions to consumerism. Of those participating, approximately 91 percent of the institutions stated that consumerism had influenced policies and procedures. Thirty-nine percent disagreed with the statement that consumer groups helped bank customers, while just 13 percent of the credit unions disagreed. Only 11.44 percent employed a consumer compliance officer to handle complaints and inquiries [58].

Company Responses to Primary Study

A mail questionnaire was sent to 11 large commercial banks. The study was restricted to commercial banks in order to simplify and structure the analysis, since the objective was to assess qualitatively the attitudes of individual banks toward consumerism. This was readily accomplished by contacting one banking type.

Seven banks completed the survey: Bankers Trust, Bank of America, Chase Manhattan, Chemical Bank, Citibank, First National Bank of Chicago (FNBC), and Manufacturers Hanover Trust (MHT). One bank, Mellon National, sent a letter stating it did not wish to participate. Three banks did not respond at all, despite two requests: Crocker National Bank, European National Bank, and National Bank of North America.

Analysis of responses on a question-by-question basis indicates that four banks have established complaint departments, while three have not. Three banks have developed formal education programs; three have not. Two banks have in-house consumer advocates; of the other five banks, four mention they have no advocates. All banks feel brochures are the primary basis of service information. Two banks ensure service quality through special consumer departments. Four banks state that services often change in response to consumerism; the other three do not answer this question. All the banks are affected by numerous regulations. Four banks handle complaints on an individual basis. Three companies feel consumerism is costly, while two indicate it has had positive effects.

In addition to answering the survey questions, Bank of America, Citibank, and Manufacturers Hanover Trust submitted materials. Bank of America discussed its program of corporate responsibility and a pilot program called Public Awareness Communications Exchange (PACE). Citibank reported on a program to improve relations with consumer groups throughout the country. Manufacturers Hanover Trust describes an audiovisual package called "Economics for Young Americans," money management seminars for women, and the use of customer focus groups.

Table 3.4 contains condensed responses to the survey for participating banks. Each bank did not answer every question. Open-ended responses were interpreted by the author.

THE OVERALL EFFECTS OF CONSUMERISM

Following is a synopsis of the overall effects of consumerism in the banking industry and an evaluation of the effectiveness of the consumer movement.

Impact of Consumerism

In reviewing the history of consumerism in banking, it has been found that consumerism has had an impact on the industry and individual banks, as well as consumers. During the early 1900s, consumer pressure for better service and safer banks influenced the creation of the Federal Reserve System, which benefits consumers and banks. The McFadden Act in 1927 and the Banking Act of 1933 fulfilled consumer needs for convenience and safety, while strengthening the banking system and the economy.

The 1950s saw bank expansion, branching, mergers, and a dramatic increase in consumer credit. These activities aided con-

TABLE 3.4

Banking Company Responses to Study

Question 1	The Consumer: What type of policy do you have for handling complaints? Do you have an in-house consumer advocate? Do you have an educational program?
Bankers Trust	Complaints are handled by a regional vice-president or higher. There is no consumer complaint department, in-house consumer advocate, or formal consumer education program.
Bank of America	The complaint policy is to acknowledge and resolve complaints at the branch level when possible. Those not resolved locally are sent to regional district administrators. There is no formal consumer complaint department. The Consumer Affairs Officer in the Social Policy Department serves as the internal consumer advocate. Consumer information reports on money management and bank services and procedures are distributed.
Chase Manhattan	A consumer affairs division handles retail-oriented complaints and is headed by a second vice-president. Seminars on money management have been sponsored in many communities.
Chemical Bank	Each complaint is promptly resolved by an area officer. There is a Consumer Affairs unit, under the Public Relations Department, which deals with complaints sent to top management. No consumer advocate has been established. Consumer education seminars are offered from time to time.
Citibank	Complaints sent to top management are routed to the Public Affairs Department, which sends acknowledgment telegrams signed by the president; the appropriate vice-president must respond to the letters within two weeks. The letters are used as quarterly management tools. There is an in-house consumer advocate, who is special consultant to the president and chairman of the board. No staff is specifically involved with consumer education, but numerous brochures and newsletters are published.

(continued)

FNBC	Complaints are processed by the "Action Center," which consists of a director, manager, service manager, and service representative. They report to a senior vice-president. Action Center analyzes complaints and makes recommendations to meet consumer needs. There are no established education programs, but account executives are trained to provide necessary counseling.
MHT	There is a formalized complaint unit called "Customer Relations," staffed with four people and representing the Director of Consumer Affairs. The unit logs, investigates, and resolves all customer complaints. Educational programs are sponsored, including programs for high schools and women's workshops.
Question 2	The Service: What type of service-related information is made available to the public? What procedure do you follow to ensure service quality? Are you modifying or changing your services in response to consumerism?
Bankers Trust	Service-related information is made available to the public through brochures and mass media advertising.
Bank of America	Information is provided through Disclosure Information and Promotion materials. The Consumer Affairs Officer frequently has discussions with the marketing department in the design of new services. Consumer needs are evaluated and researched continuously.
Chase Manhattan	The bank must be responsive to consumer demands since competition is intense. Without good, high quality service, the bank will lose business.
Chemical Bank	Advertising brochures describe customer services. Management and marketing constantly research and implement services that effectively react to consumer needs and wishes. Management is layered to provide direct control over branches and their services.

(continued)

Table 3.4 (continued)

Citibank	Brochures are available for all services. Recently, consumer credit applications and contracts were reworded in simple language. A "Citibank Customer Handbook" is in distribution.
FNBC	Numerous brochures on services have been issued. Customer satisfaction is monitored, and problem areas referred to appropriate managers.
MHT	Descriptive brochures are provided for all services. A new quarterly letter, "Consumer Update," is published. The Consumer Relations Department reviews complaints and questionnaires.
Question 3	Outside Influences: What type of consumer regulations affect your operations? How do you respond to outside consumer pressure? How do you evaluate the effects of consumerism on your bank?
Bankers Trust	Operations are affected by legislation enforced by the Federal Reserve Bank, Federal Trade Commission, New York State Banking Department, and others. Responses to consumer pressure are made on an individual case basis. No formal evaluation of consumerism has been undertaken.
Bank of America	Many consumer regulations, both federal and state, have an impact on the bank. These include: Consumer Credit Protection Act, Truth-in-Lending, Equal Credit Opportunity Act, Rees-Levering Motor Vehicle Sales & Finance Act, Spanish Translation Requirements on Credit Contracts, and Song-Beverly Credit Card Act. The Consumer Affairs officer keeps a file on current concerns of consumer groups, which may be later incorporated in bank policy. Consumerism has led to costly paperwork, recordkeeping, and training. The bank attempts to go beyond the law and conducts voluntary efforts to educate and inform consumers.

(continued)

Chase Manhattan	Consumer regulations affecting the bank range from Truth-in-Lending to advertising. The bank is generally responsive to consumer pressure and prefers to hear from consumer groups before making decisions.
Chemical Bank	All federal and state banking laws and Federal Reserve regulations have a direct impact on the bank's operations. The only organized consumer pressure was a class action suit that was settled out of court.
Citibank	Consumer legislation has proliferated in the last decade. With the onset of electronic banking, legislation will not abate. The laws have proven costly and excessive, but must have benefited the consumer.
FNBC	Numberous consumer regulations affect operations. Management keeps abreast of consumer concerns and works with consumer groups.
MHT	Truth-in-Lending and the Equal Credit Opportunity Act have had the greatest impact. The bank has not felt outside pressure since it takes positive voluntary action to benefit consumers. Consumerism has caused the bank to improve its capabilities and responses to consumers.

Source: Compiled by the author.

sumers and raised bank profits. The 1960s saw continued expansion, growing competition, and increasing consumer credit. Consumerists sought more information about credit and rates, but the banks fought information bills until their passage. Truth-in-lending legislation required banks to incur costs through employee training and new forms. These costs were passed on to consumers. The Equal Credit Opportunity Act reduced discrimination, but again caused costs and paperwork for banks.

The current state of consumerism is dynamic. Consumerists have made demands for banks to disclose savings and checking information, so that customers may shop around. Many banks have responded positively, often before legislation is passed. Some banks, such as Bank of America, use consumer-oriented policies to draw new business. A number of banks now realize the importance of the consumer movement.

The costs of implementing consumer laws have had great impact on the banks. For example, lending costs (losses and collections) of the Equal Credit Opportunity Act were estimated at $61 million in 1976 by Dr. James Smith of the Federal Reserve Bank. Dr. Smith estimated the start-up and recurrent administrative costs of the act to be $293.3 million. Generating separate credit histories for husbands and wives would cost an additional $201.4 million [113].

Total cost estimates for other consumer laws have not been made available. However, a House committee has reported that the original Real Estate Settlement Procedures Act cost mortgage lenders $35 to $90 per mortgage for the 12-day advance disclosure provision. This provision was later removed.

Evaluation of Consumerism

Consumer activists have played an essential role in making the industry aware of consumer needs and passing legislation. They have been effective with Truth-in-Lending, Fair Credit Reporting, Equal Credit Opportunity, and state disclosure laws. The laws have been beneficial, but have also brought costs. Through various publications, the public has been educated about checking, savings, and other calculations and charges.

Government laws and regulations have been numerous, but there have been problems with the quality of agencies and the implementation of regulations. Consumerists have been critical of implementation, training of examiners, nonpublication of findings, and the lack of cease-and-desist orders.

Often, laws are enacted that are sound in principle, but too complex to implement. An example of this was the Real Estate

Settlement Procedures Act of 1974 (RESPA). In a 1975 hearing before the Committee on Banking, it was stated that:

> Since the implementation of RESPA on June 20 of this
> year this committee has received an enormous amount
> of complaints from all around the country from lenders,
> real estate agents, attorneys, and most importantly,
> from the home-buying public. . . . The subcommittee
> was told that processing delays were causing buyers
> to lose interest money and numerous transactions were
> terminated because of the complications caused by the
> Act. The presence of civil and criminal penalties
> caused lending institutions to be extremely wary of
> providing facts and figures of what must be disclosed.
> It was certainly not the intention of your committee in
> enacting RESPA last year to have caused these types
> of circumstances [40, p. 3].

RESPA was amended in 1976 to repeal all objectionable features.

A 1977 survey by Hiram Barksdale showed the public's support for industry self-regulation over government regulation. Those favoring government regulation dropped by 8 percent in the mid-1970s, while 58 percent agreed that self-regulation was desirable [17, p. 133].

The banking industry has been slow to realize the importance of consumerism, being shielded from it until the 1960s. At first, the industry fought against consumer bills because of their costs and implementation problems. Associations worked to defeat the bills, not to alter them and make them workable. More recently, industry and company responses have changed with the realization that consumerism is here to stay and can be used to the banks' advantage.

Many banks now have education programs, distribute brochures, interface with consumers, and acquire consumer input. The industry has come to understand that self-regulation is less costly and more effective than government intervention. An example of this is the Financial Advertisers Code of Ethics (FACE) developed by the Bank Marketing Association in 1976. On an individual basis, Bank of America, through its full disclosure and equal credit opportunity policies, is an illustration of a bank employing self-regulation.

FUTURE OUTLOOK

Consumerism will continue as a dynamic, pervasive force in the banking industry. The electronic funds system will be closely monitored by consumerists to ensure privacy and regulation of disclosure. While west coast banks have been most affected by consumer groups, consumer groups have been moving east. Consumerists will seek full disclosure for checking account charges and lending policies. They will try to reduce redlining, and require community reinvestment. Trust departments will come under consumer pressure and stock transactions will be questioned. Fuller truth-in-lending will be sought.

Government activity, complete with restrictive regulations, will continue unless banks offer input into the process instead of lobbying against all consumer legislation. The government will move more strongly toward credit allocation, in order to remove redlining and meet inner city and other social needs. There will be a trend toward enacting simpler and less expensive laws.

The banking industry will increase voluntary actions in response to consumer desires and to avoid government and consumer group criticism. More in-house consumer advocates, complaint departments, consumer affairs departments, and "personal bankers" will be utilized. Consumerism will have an impact on the competition among bank types, causing commercial banks, mutual savings banks, savings and loan associations, and credit unions to become more similar. Changes will include: elimination of Regulation Q ceilings, thus allowing all institutions to pay any interest on savings accounts that they choose; elimination of mortgage ceilings, thus making more mortgage money available; the equalization of all investment and loan powers; and interest on demand deposits. With these changes, customer satisfaction will increase in importance. Banks also will change their marketing policies because of electronic banking.

RECOMMENDATIONS

Recommendations are made for consumer groups, government, the industry, and individual banks.

Consumer Groups

Consumer groups must sustain their fight for consumer rights and legislation. They also must become better acquainted with the costs and technical problems of such legislation. Groups should take advantage of the forums and seminars offered by banks, and communicate with the associations and individual banks. Consumer groups should work with the banks to secure an acceptable electronic banking system. Consumer groups should be more interactive with one another and form a national federation to act as a clearinghouse for information.

Government

Government must not be overzealous and politically motivated when considering consumer laws. The costs and inconvenience of bills need to be evaluated before legislation is passed. Laws should be worded simply and minimize technical violations. Committees should assess the effectiveness of laws after their passage and amendments should be made as necessary. Prime consideration should be given to a dialogue with banks to encourage more self-regulation.

The Industry

Trade associations must communicate with the public, government, and consumer groups. The associations should enlighten legislators and consumer groups, enter on the side of legislation rather than lobby against it, and convert burdensome laws into meaningful, less costly ones. The industry must take the initiative toward self-regulation and establish voluntary codes that are beneficial to banks and consumers. Full disclosure must be supported, since consumers have the right to be informed. Consumer affairs departments should grow in importance, be used by each type of banking institution, and filter information to individual members.

Individual Banking Institutions

Each banking institution must strive for consumer satisfaction and communicate with customers. Banking must strive to be less impersonal. Complaint departments, in-house consumer advocates, and action centers should be expanded and given greater powers. Banks should provide speakers and be active in local communities. They should educate consumers about personal finance and inform them of all bank policies, functions, and charges. Banks should work with consumer groups, support self-regulation, and form voluntary bank coalitions to respond to consumer needs. Individual banks should prove that government regulation is not needed to protect consumers.

BIBLIOGRAPHY

1. Aaker, David A., and Day, George S. Consumerism: Search for the Consumer Interest, 2d ed. New York: Free Press, 1974.

2. "Agencies Get Conflicting Advice on How to Regulate Concerns' Lending Practices." Wall Street Journal (March 17, 1978), p. 22.

3. "Amendments to Reg. Z." Federal Reserve Bulletin 61 (October 1975), pp. 650-66.

4. Andreasen, R., and Best, Arthur. "Consumers Complain—Does Business Respond?" Harvard Business Review (July-August 1977), pp. 93-101.

5. "Announcements: Fair Credit Billing Regulations." Federal Reserve Bulletin 61 (Spring 1975), pp. 60-62.

6. "Announcements: Reg. AA Complaints Alleging Unfair or Deceptive Practices by Banks." Federal Reserve Bulletin 62 (October 1976), p. 879.

7. Anthony, W. P., and Haynes, J. B. "Consumerism: A Three Generation Paradigm." University of Michigan Business Review 27 (November 1975), pp. 21-26.

8. "Bankers Approve McFadden Bill to Amend Laws Regulating Banks' Operations Including Opening of Branches." New York Times (September 10, 1925), p. 41.

9. "Bankers Discuss Truth-in-Lending." Banking 61 (August 1968), pp. 51-52, 96-98.

10. "Bankers Discuss Truth-in-Lending." Banking 62 (December 1969), pp. 51-52.

11. "Bankers Hail Legislation Passed 1950 by NYS Legislation, Major Laws Revised." New York Times (May 14, 1950), p. C1.

12. "Banks Create Consumer Affairs Post." Burroughs Clearing House 59 (September 1975), pp. 8-9.

13. "Banks Reform Awaits a Carter Imprimatur." Business Week (January 17, 1977), p. 27.

14. "Banks Seek Consumer Business, Nat'l City, Chase Manhattan Open Branches from 6-8 P.M." New York Times (1955).

15. "Banks vs. Loan Assoc." Business Week (June 20, 1936), p. 30.

16. "Bank Urges Customer to Phone Ideas, Complaints and Questions." Ohio National Bank of Columbus Banking (September 1972), p. 50.

17. Barksdale, Hiram C. "Changes in Consumer Attitudes Toward Marketing, Consumerism and Government Regulations 1971-75." Journal of Consumer Affairs (Winter 1976), pp. 117-39.

18. Berry, Jeffrey. Lobbying for the People. Princeton, New Jersey: Princeton University Press, 1977.

19. Berry, Leonard. "Banking and Consumerism: Opportunity in the New Society." Bankers Monthly (November 1973), pp. 19-22.

20. ____. "Consumerism in Banking—How Banks Can Respond." Bank Marketing Association Conference (Change and the Public Relations Response) (1977), p. 61.

21. "Bess Meyerson Retained As Citibank Advisor." American Banker (November 9, 1973), p. 10.

22. "Best Banking Law, Glass Steagall Bill." Business Week (June 17, 1933).

23. Bloomstein, Morris J. Consumer's Guide to Fighting Back. New York: Dodd, Mead, 1976.

24. Board of Governors of Federal Reserve System. "Federal Reserve Act 1913 As Amended Thru 1976." Federal Reserve Publication (December 1976).

25. "B of A Denies Assertion Consumerists' Drive Forced Car-Rate Cut." American Banker (November 29, 1976), pp. 2, 16.

26. "B of A Withdraws Ads for Auto Loans After Consumerist Prodding." American Banker (November 15, 1976), pp. 1, 40.

27. Brandel, R. E. "New Dangers Arise in Point Scoring, But You Can't Afford to Be Without It." Banking 68 (March 1976), p. 86.

28. Bratler, H. "Hearings on Fair Credit Reporting (Proxmire Bill)." Banking 62 (July 1969), pp. 41-43.

29. Burke, J. "Credit Unions, Past, Present, Future." Banking 68 (Spring 1976), p. 42.

30. "California Banks, S & L's Required to Disclose All Charges on Demand, Savings Acts." American Banker (June 1, 1977), p. 2.

31. "California Consumer Action Book Urges Savings Switch from Banks to S & L's." American Banker (November 18, 1976), pp. 1, 10.

32. Cargill, T. F. "Recent Research on Credit Unions—A Survey." Journal of Economics & Business (Winter 1977), pp. 155-62.

33. Cartes, D. C. "Interest on Checking Accts: The Impact on Bigger Banks." Banker Magazine 159 (Summer 1976), pp. 112-14.

34. ____. "Paying Interest on Checking Accounts." Bankers Magazine 159 (Spring 1976), pp. 114-17.

35. "CBT Ruled Illegal If Off Premises." Chicago Illinois Banking (July 1976), p. 10.

36. "Class Actions Against Banks." Bankers Magazine (Winter 1971), p. 75.

37. Clontz, Ralph C., Jr. Equal Credit Opportunity Manual. Warren, Gorham & Lamont, 1977.

38. ____. Truth-in-Lending Manual. Warren, Gorham & Lamont, 1969.

39. "Comment on Plain Language Bill by Assemblyman Peter Sullivan. Citibank Had Been Able to Simplify Form, Bill Would Require Simplifying Forms." New York Times (August 8, 1977), p. 4.

40. "Committee on Banking, Currency and Housing, House of Representatives, Report." No. 94-667, 94th Congress, 1st Session (November 14, 1975), pp. 2-3.

41. "Comprehensive Compliance Manual, Regulation B of the Equal Credit Opportunity Act." American Bankers Association (1977).

42. "Conference Board Study Cites Chase Programs As a Model for Preserving Consumer Goodwill." American Banker (March 11, 1974), pp. 2, 14.

43. Conover, Lynn. "Banks Urged to Heed Consumer Criticisms Because They Could Signal Future Problems." American Banker (June 27, 1977), p. 2.

44. "Consumer Action Guide Boosts Savings At Associations." Savings & Loan News (April 1977), p. 73.

45. "Consumer Credit: Banks Will Offer Finance Companies Plenty of Competition." Business Week (December 2, 1944), pp. 70-72.

46. "Consumer Credit Protection Act to Prohibit Abusive Practices by Debt Collectors; Measure Passed 199-198." New York Times (April 10, 1977), p. 1.

47. "Consumerism At the Crossroad—A National Opinion Survey of Public, Activist, Business and Regulatory Attitudes Toward the Consumer Movement." Sentry Insurance (July 1976), pp. 6-7, 13.

48. "Consumer Legislation: Making It Meaningful for Today's Banking." Bank Marketing (January 1976), pp. 14-16.

49. "Consumer Movement Calls for Stiff New Bank Management Rules." American Banker (April 13, 1976), pp. 4, 10, 15.

50. "Consumers Group's 13-City Survey Calls Some Bank Ads Misleading." New York Times (March 29, 1977), p. 19.

51. "Cont. Illinois Rewrites Checking, Savings Terms to Make Them Easier to Understand." American Banker (July 13, 1976), p. 6.

52. "Controversy Over Truth-in-Lending Act Stemming from Congress Initiates to Simplify It, Consumer Advocates Fear Changes Urged Will Weaken Law." New York Times (July 4, 1977), p. 4.

53. "Credit Terms in Bigger Type." Business Week (April 2, 1977), p. 60.

54. "Credit Unions Move Deeper into Banking." Business Week (April 11, 1977), p. 52.

55. "Crocker Assault on Traditional Banking Brings $100 Mil. in Deposits in 12 Months." American Banker (March 2, 1976), pp. 3, 10.

56. Cursen, Barbara A. Trends in Consumer Credit Leg. Illinois: Chicago University Press, 1966.

57. "CU's Growl At Consumer Laws As Destructive to Their Business." American Banker (April 1976), pp. 4, 14.

58. "Dept. of Commerce." State of Michigan Consumer Survey (May 31, 1974).

59. "Electronic Banking, A Retreat from the Cashless Society." Business Week (April 18, 1977), p. 83.

60. "Electronic Funds Transfer Is Coming." Banking (September 1972), p. 42.

61. Elliot, R. H. "Consumerism and the Thrift Industry." Federal Home Loan Bank Board Journal 9 (December 1976), pp. 24-27.

62. "Enforcement of Equal Credit Opportunity—Annual Report to Congress for Year 1976." Commerce Clearing House Credit Guide (February 9, 1977).

63. "Facts About Installment Credit." Business Week (September 14, 1940), pp. 34-35.

64. Farley, James D. "Demands of Consumerism Advocates: How Should Bankers Respond?" NABW Journal (March-April 1972), p. 22.

65. "FDIC Examiners and Congress Are Unhappy Over Consumer Laws." American Banker (October 29, 1976), pp. 4, 18.

66. "FDIC News Release to Member and Non-member Banks." April 2, 1975.

67. "Fed Board Accused of Failing to Enforce Consumer Legislation." American Banker (April 8, 1977), p. 2.

68. "Fed Gives Consumer Complaint Breakdown." American Banker (March 18, 1977), p. 11.

69. "Fed Rules on Consumer Complaints." American Banker (October 4, 1976).

70. Feldman, Stephen. Credit Unions. New York: Hofstra University Yearbook of Business, series 10, volume 2, 1972.

71. "FTC Announces New Investigations to Determine If Women Etc. Are Being Unfairly Treated for Home Loans." New York Times (August 1977), p. 1.

72. "FTC Reviews Its Own Consumer Rules." Business Week (March 28, 1977), p. 92.

73. "Full Disclosure For Banks." Newsday (March 16, 1978), p. 9A.

74. Hearings before the Subcommittee of the Committee on Banking and Currency. United States Senate, 87th Congress, on S1740 (May 8-18, 1962).

75. Hearings before the Subcommittee of the Committee on Banking and Currency, United States Senate, 87th Congress, p. S750 (1963-64).

76. "History of the American Bankers Association, 1875-1924." American Bankers Association (November 10, 1926).

77. House of Representatives, 94th Congress, 2d Session. Federal Banking Agencies Enforcement of TIL. September 15-16, 1976.

78. "Independents, Consumer Groups, Should Unite in Consumer Interest." American Banker (April 2, 1974), p. 5.

79. Installment Credit. Washington, D.C.: American Institute of Banking, 1964.

80. "Instead of Threat, Consumerism Offers Guide to Serving Public, Farley of Citibank Says." American Banker (March 20, 1973), pp. 2, 12.

81. Keyes, Emerson W. A History of Savings Banks in the United States. New York: Rhodes, 1876.

82. Kotler, Philip. "How to Anticipate Consumerism's Coming Threat to Banking." Banking (January 1973).

83. ____. "Marketing's Role in the Age of Consumerism." 1973 National Marketing Conference (January 14-17, 1973).

84. Krooss, Herman E. Documentary History of Banking and Currency in the United States, vols. 3 & 4. New York: Chelsea House, 1969.

85. Larkin, Kenneth V. "How Banks Can Live with the New Consumerism." Banking (August 1971), p. 23.

86. "Law Against Unfair Credit, Ad Practices Signed in Michigan." American Banker (January 5, 1977), pp. 1, 12.

87. Leinsdorf, David. Citibank (Ralph Nader's Report on First National City Bank). New York: Grossman, 1973.

88. "Married Women Get a Credit Rating." Business Week (June 6, 1977), p. 28.

89. Mazuy, Kay. "Consumerism: We Must Respond." American Banker (February 9, 1977), pp. 4, 23.

90. Moody, Carroll J. The Credit Union Movement. Nebraska: University of Nebraska Press, 1971.

91. Moore, Geoffry H. The Quality of Consumer Credit. New York: Columbia University Press, 1967.

92. "Nader Accuses Banks of 'Economic Crime' Against the Consumer." American Banker (February 6, 1970), p. 2.

93. "Nader Suggests Independent Banks Join Consumer Groups in Common Interest." American Banker (March 26, 1976), pp. 1, 24.

94. Newberg, Herbert. Newberg on Class Actions, vols. 4, 5, & 6. New York: McGraw-Hill, 1977.

95. "New FDIC Exams to Check Consumer Law Compliance." American Banker (June 15, 1977), pp. 1, 8.

96. "New FTC Rule Irks the Banks—Elimination of Holder-in-Due-Course Rule Means Banks Will Have to Guarantee Products They Finance." Business Week (May 24, 1976), p. 52.

97. Nielsen, R. P. "Implications of Equal Credit Opportunity Act Amendment of 1976." Journal of Consumer Affairs (Summer 1977), pp. 167-70.

98. "Non-Bank Financial Institutions." Federal Reserve Board of Richmond (June 1968).

99. Norris, Frank. The Octopus. New York: Grossman, 1901.

100. "NOW Accounts Arrive At Capital Hill." Business Week (June 27, 1977), p. 96.

101. "NYS Bankers Association Recommends Comm'l Banks Pay Interest on Checking Accts. If Congress Authorizes." New York Times (May 25, 1977), pp. 1, 2.

102. "N.Y. Times Survey Finds Revolutionary Electronic Funds Transfer System Is Changing Way in Which People Handle Money . . . But May Be Outracing Willingness of Consumers to Change Their Habits." New York Times (May 31, 1977), p. 1.

103. "Ohio National Bank Establishes Action Center for Better Public, Management Communications." American Banker (April 18, 1972), p. 6.

104. Peterson, Mary. The Regulated Consumer. Nash Publishing, 1971.

105. "Proxmire Says Agencies Drag Feet on Consumers." American Banker (October 6, 1976), p. 2.

106. "Qui Tam & Federal Reserve Procedures, Hearing Before the Subcommittee on Consumer Affairs" (March 16, 1976).

107. "Retailing Lures the Bankers: Bankers Trust Co., N.Y. Is Latest to Go Over to Large-Scale Branch Banking." Business Week (December 1, 1951), pp. 124ff.

108. Robertson, Ross. The Comptroller and Bank Supervision. Washington, D.C.: Office of Comptroller of the Currency, 1968.

109. Rossmann, Laura W. "Bankers Tell Congress Impact of Consumer Laws Should Be Assessed Before Passage." American Banker (February 11, 1977), p. 2.

110. Schlink, F. J., and Chase, Stuart. Your Money's Worth. New York: Macmillan, 1927.

111. Schlink, F. J., and Mallet, A. 100,000,000 Guinea Pigs. New York: Vanguard Press, 1932.

112. Sinclair, Upton. The Jungle. New York: Doubleday, 1906.

113. Smith, James. "Equal Credit Opportunity Act of 1974—A Cost/Benefit Analysis." Address at Annual Meeting of the American Finance Association, September 17, 1976.

114. The Consumer Advocate Versus the Consumer. New York: 1977.

115. "The First National Bank of Atlanta Appoints Consumer Affairs Rep." Southern Banker (November 1975), p. 56.

116. "The Rebellion Against the 'Plain-English Law'." Business Week (January 23, 1978), p. 112.

117. "To an Alert Banker, Consumer Movement Offers Opportunity." American Banker (April 13, 1977), pp. 4-5, 8-9, 11.

118. "Truth-in-Lending Annual Report to Congress for the Year 1977—Board of Governors Federal Reserve System." Commerce Clearing House Credit Guide (January 10, 1978).

119. "Two Consumer Groups Sue for Fed's Interest Data." American Banker (September 18, 1973), p. 3.

120. "U.S. Agency Plans Rules for S & L's to Prevent Discriminatory 'Pre-Screening' of Customers." Wall Street Journal (February 24, 1978), p. 32.

121. U.S. Congress House Committee on Banking Subcommittee on Consumer Affairs. "Do Financial Regulatory Agencies Listen to Consumers?" (December 1976).

122. U.S. Government Manual. Washington, D.C.: Government Printing Office, 1977.

123. "Wave of Consumerism Viewed As Challenge, Not Threat." _American Banker_ (March 20, 1973), pp. 6, 23.

124. Welfing, Weldon. _Mutual Savings Banks_. Ohio: Press of Case Western Reserve University, 1968.

125. Wheeler, Mark C. "Banking Must Catch Approaching Wave of Consumerism; Trade Organizations Have Vital Role in Creating Proper Image." _American Banker_ (March 23, 1976), p. 7.

126. White, Horace. _Money & Banking_. Ginn & Company, 1935.

127. Wilcox, James A. _A History of the Philadelphia Savings Fund Society, 1816-1916_. New York: Lippincott, 1916.

128. Wolf, Alvin. _Lobbies and Lobbyists_. Boston: Allyn & Bacon, 1976.

4

CONSUMERISM AND THE CLOTHING INDUSTRY

Gloria J. Fenner

INTRODUCTION

In the clothing industry, textile fibers (wool, fur, cotton, and synthetics) are made into finished men's, women's, and children's wear. Over the years, a number of problems have been associated with clothing products, concerning such issues as: labeling of fiber content, the control of fashion by designers, quality, preservation of wild animals, flammability, and care labeling. Since the early 1900s, consumers and government have tried to resolve these issues in favor of the buying public.

This chapter details the history of consumerism in the clothing industry, examines existing consumer groups, delineates the role of government in the clothing industry, and considers the responses of the industry and individual companies to consumerism.

THE HISTORY OF CONSUMERISM IN THE CLOTHING INDUSTRY

The First Era: Early 1900s

The earliest consumer issue involved informative labeling, but interest came from within the industry. In 1902, woolgrowers' associations representing several states favored passage of a bill removing used wool from the market because of excessive competition from companies using shoddy (a name for a type of reused wool) wool and other firms labeling products filled with cotton as all wool [49, pp. 70-71].

In 1916, the control of fashion by Paris designers was a topic of discussion as U.S. firms began to create their own designs and do quite well. To compete, Paris opened offices in New York in 1917 in order to maintain control over fashion styles [73, p. 428]. Petite ladies, modeling elegant clothing, inspired women of different builds to purchase garments that were not as attractive on themselves. Some U.S. citizens, unable to see many Paris fashions, relied upon written advertisements [7].

Those concerned with endangered animals were critical of women's vanity. Minnie Madden Fiske wrote a 1921 article concerning the cruelty and waste in trapping animals that were made into garments not essential to health or comfort. Trappers stated that three-fourths of the animals found in traps were worthless for pelts. The fur trade reasoned that if animals were not trapped, they would have killed one another [33]. By 1924, an increased production of fake furs took place, limiting the number of animal pelts. However, the marketing of these products caused the Federal Trade Commission (FTC) to become concerned. The commission banned the advertising of the products as "fake fur," "imposter otter," "imitation fur," "pretend leopard," or other similar names [109]. This ruling was not incorporated into law for many years.

The Second Era: Emerging Issues

Until 1929, fashion designers were not confronted with complaints about their control over styles from any consumer groups. Women wore impractical and uncomfortable styles when designers introduced them. But in 1929, the Young Women's Christian Association (YWCA) heavily criticized long skirts, trains, and corsets: "Down with the corset and up with the hemline should have been the slogan of every woman who did not want to be bullied into doing something as undesirable as it was unwelcome" [51, p. 40]. Despite this pressure on designers to halt the introduction of longer styles, women accepted them by 1930 [11].

Woolgrowers continued to insist on protective legislation during the 1930s. In 1939, the Wool Products Labeling Act was enacted. The act eliminated deceptive practices involving products labeled as pure wool and introduced content labeling. Since woolgrowers advocated and benefited from this law, its consumer benefits were by-products, not prime concerns.

Wool labeling improved the quality of wool products, but there were problems with other textiles. In the 1940s, many defects in synthetic fabrics were discovered: shifting of yarns in laundering, slippage of seams, weakening when wet, excessive shrinkage in washing, nonfast colors, inability to wash at a temperature of 160 degrees, and inability to use a strong family soap solution in laundering [78, p. 225].

Consumers also had quality expectations that were not satisfied because of deficiencies in fabrics. They wanted improvements in: eye value or good appearance, which included beauty, attractive finish, and a good feel to the hand; ease of laundering; color fastness; and tensile strength, meaning good wearing quality. These factors all related to wearability and satisfactory service [78, p. 224].

Flammability was an important issue that did not result in consumer outcries until tragedies struck [69]. The push for flame retardant clothing, apparel resistant to burning, was mainly governmental [110]. On January 27, 1945, the California State Legislature passed a bill governing the manufacture or sale of flammable or "explosive" fabrics. The bill was practically unenforceable because its definition of flammability was limited to cotton cloth in the natural state. However, further research and legislation were inspired. By 1947, four bills were introduced in Congress, three in the House and one in the Senate [62, p. 114].

During this period, extensive research was undertaken by the American Association of Textile Chemists and Colorists. Its goal was to segregate dangerous fabrics from harmless ones by employing a machine that evaluated the rate of burning. The best method established the rate of burning by measuring the speed at which a flame could travel over the surface of a fabric suspended on a specimen rack at a 45-degree angle. Other techniques were developed by the National Bureau of Standards and the Fire Marshal of California [44, p. 141]. By 1948, the vertical Bunsen flame test was probably the best-known test used in identifying nonburning fabrics and assessing the relative efficiency of flameproof properties [62, p. 114].

Among the fabrics used in manufacturing apparel, the most flammable were those of cellulosic origin, such as cotton and rayon. Fibers of animal origin were not as flammable [89, p. 133]. At this time, an inexpensive, permanent flame-proofing treatment that could be applied to fabrics had not been developed. Therefore, information about flammability was needed.

In the late 1940s, the Federal Trade Commission became involved in the controversy concerning deceptive fur practices. Labels identifying the animals from which pelts were taken and the locations in which they were discovered were found to be false. As Congressman Robert Hale of Maine stated:

> The language of the fur trade—you'll hear it when you shop for furs—is so largely aimed at concealment that not even salespeople can keep track of the humble origins of some of the glamorized words; so a mere Congressman might be forgiven, if I certainly never knew until yesterday that Hudson seal was muscrat [91, p. 39].

Racoon-dyed opossum was actually all opossum. Northern seal was really rabbit. Both Australian chinchilla and Russian marten came from the United States, where before becoming coats they were known as opossum. Bombay lamb did not come from Bombay, nor did Persian lamb come from Persia [91, p. 190].

Naming furs was only one aspect of deception in the fur trade. Quality claims were also fraudulent. Cheap furs were passed off as high quality and old furs as new. Pieces of furs, like paws, tails, bellies, and waste, were used to construct coats [49, p. 72]. The need for protective legislation was cited by James H. Francis of the National Board of Fur Farming Organizations: "Unfair practices are becoming so common in our industry that legislation is needed to require what should be a basic principle, that of simply telling the truth" [91, p. 38].

The Fur Products Labeling Act was passed in 1952. It was not enacted through the efforts of consumers, but because of the endeavors of the industry to achieve protection [49, p. 73]. The Flammable Fabrics Act was passed in 1953 as the result of injuries with brushed materials. Standard CS191-53, effective July 1954, was developed to prevent future introduction of hazardous materials and to remove highly flammable products from the market [110, p. 1].

Principal support for proper textile labeling came from within the industry, since problems had been encountered as cheap synthetics were represented as natural fibers. The Textile Fiber Identification Act (1958) was aimed at halting this deceptive practice [49].

In 1960, the American Standards Association created Standard L-22, which applied to finished woven knitted menswear, womenswear, and home furnishings. Some provisions of L-22 dealt with:

minimum performance, such as breaking strength, resistance to yarn slippage, and colorfastness in laundering;

performance requirements for special finishes, such as wrinkle and crease resistance, moth resistance, mildew, and rot resistance;

permanent labels, detachable labels, and certification of fabrics or products;

side effects, such as odor and brittleness; and

minimum performance for wash-and-wear and minimum-care products [66, p. 8].

Standard L-22 was voluntary and never became mandatory.

Conservationists continued their fight for the protection of wild animals. The International Union for the Conservation of Nature and Natural Resources called for the cessation of the killing of spotted cats in a 1964 resolution, but this resolution had no noticeable effect. Later, conservationists proposed a complete ban on the importation of rare furs into the United States and Europe. This proposal also failed [39, p. 52].

The Current Era of Consumerism

In 1966, Esther Peterson, a presidential advisor, became involved with the quality and performance of apparel on the federal level. Consumers had complained of contradictory labels appearing on garments and damage caused by washing or ironing through methods too severe for certain fabrics. Peterson established the Industry Advisory Committee, composed of people representing fiber, fabric, and apparel manufacturers, retailers, dry cleaners, and launderers, to rectify the situation. The committee's first goal was to develop a glossary of terms that would fit on labels and be easily understood [40, p. 48].

The Voluntary Industry Guide for Improved Permanent Care Labeling of Consumer Textile Products" was introduced in 1967 [98]. However, consumers remained dissatisfied since the high costs of the guidelines precluded manufacturers from following them, tags were not permanently affixed to garments, and there were many falsities on tags. Betty Furness commented, "Many women had discovered that the phrase 'never need ironing,' could use a parenthetical warning: 'If you don't mind a little wrinkled' " [40, p. 48].

While consumers complained among themselves, they rarely joined together or complained to manufacturers. A 1969 mail survey showed that only 25 clothing and linen complaints and 14 home-furnishing complaints were registered over a two-and-one-half-week period [92, p. 164].

In between the consumer and manufacturer, the retailer has acted as the mediator in solving problems. Until the last decade, dissatisfied consumers had faced difficulties with manufacturers in returning goods. Retailers proposed a policy for manufacturers in 1969 that required manufacturers to buy and use an automatic washer, an automatic dryer, adequate examining tables, and a dry cleaning machine or the services of a dry cleaner [99, p. 74]. The equipment would be utilized to test the appearance, retention, colorfastness, and durability of garments, and make sure there were no open seams or missing buttons. By employment of this system of quality control, product defects would drop drastically and retailers would reduce the problems they encountered.

Despite the retailers' proposal, quality remained an issue in the 1970s. For example, the quality of ladies' ready-to-wear has been affected by a lack of inspection at every stage in production, the dwindling supply of skilled labor, a lack of pride on all sides of the industry, and built-in obsolescence of styles [72]. Cost-cutting, to hold prices down, has led to reduced seam allowances and garments with few or no pockets. Retail chains developed their own control systems to check on garment quality, since manufacturers showed little concern about product defects.

The early 1970s fashion trend was toward short dresses and skirts. Eve Merriam wrote, "Women have been so bewitched and brainwashed that they seem incapable of resisting the most arrant nonsense. Anything wacky can be sold in the name of fashion" [84, p. 113]. Merriam's comments referred to the power of designers over women. But the 1970s also witnessed men being engulfed by fashion trends, such as wide lapels and ties. Today, fashion affects everyone.

Conservationists continued their struggle to save animals in the 1970s. Timme & Sons, a manufacturer of fake furs, capitalized on the issue of animal conservation with its campaign, "Fur coats should not be made of fur" [100, p. 7]. The campaign was opposed by furriers, since it was aimed at reducing the sales of real fur coats. In 1971, Paris designers supported fake furs, since they could closely simulate real furs.

During 1972, the Federal Trade Commission initiated action to inform consumers of the care necessary to retain purchased qualities in items after usage [50]. After care labeling rules were implemented, complaints about the laundering performance of garments abated.

In the mid-1970s, consumers became concerned about the safety of clothing products. The Department of Commerce was pressured to prohibit the sale of children's sleepwear, sizes 0-6X, which failed to meet flammability standards. The chemical Tris was developed to retard flammability in sleepwear and clothing for children. However, in 1977, tests by the National Cancer Institute on rats and mice who were fed Tris showed increased incidences of kidney, lung, stomach, and liver tumors [101].

On April 8, 1977, the Consumer Product Safety Commission (CPSC) called for a ban on all children's sleepwear containing Tris, since children could ingest unsafe residues on the garments. The commission had no evidence of danger to humans at this time, but felt the tests on rats and mice were sufficient. One firm, Spring Mills of South Carolina, filed suit against the commission on the ground that its ruling would force the company to buy back $2 million of garments treated with Tris. In May 1977, a federal judge nullified the commission's order until full hearings were held. The final court ruling occurred in July 1978. The commission was allowed to file injunctions forbidding sales of Tris-treated products to consumers, but could not void previous transactions [9, 104, 110].

During 1976 and 1977, consumer surveys were conducted regarding quality. In 1976, about one-half the respondents said they had not returned one garment in five years because of poor quality; one-quarter said they had returned one garment. The 1977 survey indicated that about 70 percent of the respondents had made no returns for poor quality. Despite these results, the majority of consumers, approximately 70 percent, were dissatisfied with quality and felt garments were more poorly made than in the past [80, p. 62].

The control over fashion by designers has changed as new competition has entered the market. Designers from Australia, Israel, the United States, and other countries have competed successfully with Paris and provided consumers with greater choices [102]. Diversification has brought benefits.

ACTIVE CONSUMER GROUPS

Throughout the twentieth century, consumer and consumer-related groups have stressed the need for consumer protection. The influence of these groups has grown from a weak beginning. The American Farm Bureau Federation, an association then representing 500,000 women, began its support for textile labeling in 1919. The American Home Economics Association, then totaling 11,000 members, started its support for general fabric identification legislation around the same time [32, p. 262]. Neither group has pursued clothing issues since these early times.

The Young Women's Christian Association expressed its opposition to the flapper kilt and then longer skirts in 1929. Its fight to stop these styles was not successful [8, p. 39]. Since this controversy, the YWCA has remained silent in regard to the clothing industry.

In 1939, the New York City Federation of Women's Clubs, part of the General Federation of Women's Clubs, backed textile legislation. The club represented the view of more than 200,000 New York women [32, p. 937]. The club has not been engaged in other clothing issues.

During the 1970s, consumer interest in the clothing industry increased dramatically. Consumers' Research tested children's pajamas by Sears that claimed to be flame retardant, and upheld the claim. It also found that Nomex nylon (used in underwear), dynel, and other fibers were inherently flame retardant, depending upon cost, absorbency, and comfort [34]. Consumers Union tested flammable sleepwear, prior to the introduction of Tris, and found all the samples of 72 models of children's sleepwear sizes 0-6X failed the flame test, except for Sears [10].

Two fire prevention organizations expressed concern with flammable garments. The National Fire Protection Association developed and published information in order to minimize the effects of fires and explosions, and conducted safety education programs. Association files contain many records of severe injuries and deaths attributable to clothing fires. It has made substantial efforts to inform the public of the hazards associated with flammable clothing [32, p. 691].

Action for the Prevention of Burn Injuries to Children was formed in 1972 by the parents of burn victims. Its objective is to educate the public about burn prevention and the possible consequences of fire, with emphasis on safer clothing and other products. Due to this group, Massachusetts has passed more burn legislation than any other state [32, p. 724]. Despite the efforts of these and other groups, a complete elimination of flammable garments has not occurred.

The Environmental Defense Fund, with a membership of 40,000, petitioned the Consumer Product Safety Commission to ban the sales of Tris because of the National Cancer Institute's test results. Tris was subsequently banned, and another product, Fyrol FR-2, was substituted. The fund now wants manufacturers to put warning labels on garments, fearing that Fyrol FR-2 may be carcinogenic [96, p. 28]. Other chemicals, like those in permanent press garments, are under analysis to determine their side effects [32, p. 368].

Individual consumerists have worked for consumer protection in clothing. Ralph Nader has stressed the need for improved flammability standards and a goal of nonflammable garments [83]. Betty Furness, due to her own experiences, has found it necessary to push for better launderability of garments, since regular washing can ruin some garments. She wants the FTC to form appropriate rules.

GOVERNMENT

The clothing industry is regulated by three federal government agencies: National Bureau of Standards, Federal Trade Commission, and the Consumer Product Safety Commission. These agencies are responsible for the enforcement of a variety of laws and rules affecting the clothing industry. For purposes of continuity, the agencies are discussed in the order of their origination.

National Bureau of Standards

The National Bureau of Standards was founded in 1901. It consists of four institutes (Basic Standards, Material Research, Applied Technology, and Computer Science and Technology) and the Office for Information Programs. The bureau is under the control of the Department of Commerce, and strives to ensure a sound measurement system, scientific and technological services for industry and government, a technical basis for equity in trade, and technical services to promote public safety [94, p. 2].

In 1947, the bureau conducted a study to determine the cause of clothing ignition. Accidental burns occurred most frequently with rayon and cotton fabrics that have long, fine naps. Light rayon net, sometimes used in veils, dresses, and trimmings, burned rapidly [89, p. 133]. After the passage of a new flammability standard in 1967, fabrics were tested again by the bureau. Fabrics that passed the standard continued to take lives. The Commerce Department promulgated better standards and tests for products, and recommended that all garments have flame-resistant qualities [18, p. 40].

A 1975 study was conducted to determine the relationship between the various factors causing apparel fires in order to reduce human and economic loss. Human factors, such as age, sex, and defensive ability, were involved as well as product flammability. Voluntary and/or mandatory flammable standards were found to be necessary to offer a minimum level of consumer protection [71].

The Federal Trade Commission is responsible for enforcing Bureau of Standards regulations.

Federal Trade Commission

The FTC was formed in 1914 and given powers to aid consumers in 1938 with the passage of the Wheeler-Lea Amendment. Several federal laws affecting the clothing industry are under the jurisdiction of the FTC: Wool Products Labeling Act, Fur Products Labeling Act, Textile Fiber Identification Act, Flammable Fabrics Act, and the Permanent Care Labeling Rule.

Wool Products Labeling Act

The Wool Products Labeling Act was passed in 1939 in order to

protect manufacturers, producers, distributors and
consumers from the unrevealed presence of substitutes
and mixtures spun, woven, knitted, felted, or otherwise

manufactured wool products, and for other purposes
[88, pp. 22, 67].

The act dealt with defining terms, such as wool, reused wool,
and reprocessed wool. Generic names and percentages of fibers had
to be included on tags, exclusive of permissive ornamentation. Violators could be fined up to $5,000 and/or imprisoned for up to one
year. The Federal Trade Commission was responsible for investigating and prosecuting firms that did not comply [88].

In 1960, the Hunter Mills Corporation was found in violation
of the portion of the act that dealt with giving the percentage of wool
in garments. The company used nylon, rayon, acetate, and other
fabrics in garments marked 100-percent reused or reprocessed wool.
On December 6, 1960, Hunter Mills was ordered to cease misbranding [27].

More recently, H. Myerson & Sons and Windsor Fabrics were
accused of representing wool products as all silk and not stamping,
tagging, or labeling wool products in accordance with the act. On
February 25, 1971, both companies were ordered to cease-and-
desist misbranding products [29].

While consumers were given information as to the fabrics
contained in a garment, they were not adequately informed as to the
characteristics of these fabrics. Consumers had to learn about fiber
properties on their own [74, p. 5].

Fur Products Labeling Act

The Fur Products Labeling Act was legislated in 1952. It
required retailers to attach tags on every fur and fur-trimmed garment. The tags had to include: the true name of the animal from
which the skin was taken; the country of origin of the skins if imported;
a statement of alteration if the fur was dyed, bleached, or otherwise
changed; a breakdown of less valuable furs if contained in the garment;
and the identification number of the store [4, p. 49]. The act also
covered the labeling of fur products containing material other than
fur and misrepresentation of prices when advertising furs [86].
The Federal Trade Commission was empowered to issue cease-and-
desist orders to stop misrepresentation.

In 1961, the Hoving Corporation was accused of misbranding,
false and deceptive invoicing, and false and deceptive advertising of
fur products. White mink muffs and sets of muffs, hats, and ascot
chokers were made from the waste fur of minks (tails, bellies, and
so on), and the retailer, Bonwit Teller, did not inform customers
of this. Hoving was found guilty of misbranding and deception. A
cease-and-desist order was granted, and no fine imposed [26].

During the same year, the Federal Trade Commission found 22 items in the stock of Morton's Incorporated to be incorrectly labeled. Morton's failed to disclose the name of the animal producing the fur, misrepresented sales prices in advertising, and did not maintain adequate records. The United States Court of Appeals determined that Morton's used false and deceptive advertising, and issued a cease-and-desist order for this. The recordkeeping did not violate provisions of the act [28].

No other Federal Trade Commission actions have resulted from the Fur Products Labeling Act.

Textile Fiber Identification Act

The Textile Fiber Identification Act was passed in 1958. As part of the act, 17 manmade fibers were identified and defined. Its provisions involved: stating the percentages of different fibers found in the garment on the tag; generically labeling only fibers amounting to 5 percent or more of the garment; stating that unknown fibers were contained in the garment; and listing the manufacturer, marketer, and country of import [87].

Under this act, the FTC has prosecuted two companies for violations. Transair Incorporated was accused of improper stamping, tagging, and labeling of garments, poor maintenance of records, and false, misleading, and deceptive statements and representation in 1961. The company was ordered to cease and desist these practices [30]. In 1971, H. Myerson & Sons was ordered to cease and desist false and deceptive advertising of textile products and the use of generic names of fiber trademarks without making full fiber content disclosures [29]. Neither company was fined.

Flammable Fabrics Act

During 1945, several small boys were fatally burned when the cowboy chaps they were wearing, made of highly flammable rayon, burst into flames. Six years later, sweaters imported from the Far East caused several burns and deaths after the piled rayon fabric of which they were composed ignited. Public and congressional concern over these and other incidents resulted in the Flammable Fabrics Act of 1953 [65, p. 38].

The act called for legal limits on the flammability of outerwear, underwear, many hats, long gloves, and hosiery [63, p. 55]. The Flammable Fabrics Act was amended in 1967 to make it more effective and fund further research [69, p. 19]. The amendment brought new efforts in the search for less flammable fabrics. Synthetic flameproof fabrics for women's nightwear, lounging robes, and other household uses were developed. The new fabrics, dynel by Union Carbide and verel by Eastman Chemical Products, burned only where the flame touched them and did not support fire [65, p. 40].

The Secretary of Commerce called a 1968 meeting of his advisory committee on flammability, but formal procedures for a new children's sleepwear standard were not begun until 1971 and enacted until 1972. As of July 29, 1973, children's sleepwear had to meet the standard or not be sold [50, p. 69]. Children's sleepwear, sizes 7-14, manufactured after May 1, 1975, had to employ permanent labels to warn consumers and provide proper care instructions [83].

In 1972, the Federal Trade Commission issued cease-and-desist orders to M. Grossman & Son and Betmar Hat, after it found them manufacturing flammable berets. The Court of Appeals overruled the commission, finding that the berets did not cover the neck, face, or shoulders and therefore did not violate the act [25]. The FTC has not prosecuted other cases under this legislation.

Permanent Care Labeling Rule

The Permanent Care Labeling Rule was enacted in early 1972 in order to inform consumers of the best procedures for laundering garments. The rule stated that: garments had to come with care labeling information; clothing fabrics for home use had to include care information; labels had to use words and phrases; information had to be legible for the life of the garment; different labels were needed for different care instructions; no promotional language was allowed; and items that did not have to be dry cleaned had to be labeled as such [50, p. 64]. Exemptions also were specified for certain garments and clothing.

The Permanent Care Labeling Rule helps to keep garments in good wearing condition and reduces returns to manufacturers.

Consumer Product Safety Commission

The Consumer Product Safety Commission was created in 1972. During the same year, the Flammable Fabrics Act was placed under its control. Since the CPSC was responsible for the collection and dissemination of information regarding hazardous products as well as the creation and enforcement of safety standards, it worked with the Bureau of Standards to develop flammability standards. The CPSC could prohibit the sale of garments not meeting specific standards.

In the clothing area, the commission's major concern involved the flame-retardant chemical Tris and its relation to cancer. The commission banned Tris in 1977, went through several court cases, and finally spread the cost of the ban among chemical manufacturers, textile mills, apparel manufacturers, and retailers [90, 101].

INDUSTRY RESPONSES TO CONSUMERISM

Industry responses to consumerism are examined via a review of the relevant literature and through responses of trade associations to a primary study.

Industry Responses as Reported in the Literature

Industry responses to consumerism have been most evident during periods when legislation has been under consideration. After passage of legislation or cessation of consumer efforts, industry responses have diminished. Six issues have received the greatest industry reactions: wool labeling, fur trade, flammability, textile labeling, quality control, and care labeling.

Wool Labeling

Prior to enactment of the Wool Products Labeling Act in 1939, Congress held 20 years of hearings. Two early bills, French-Capper and Lodge-Rogers Honest Merchandise, were introduced in 1921; neither was enacted [79, p. 90].

French-Capper called for compulsory labeling of all woven fabrics in which wool was utilized. Manufacturers and distributors of woolen and worsted fabrics opposed this law, contending consumers would not benefit and costs would rise. These industry representatives also felt unduly pressured, since many items were excluded from the law. The bill was advocated by woolgrowers. The Lodge-Rogers Honest Merchandise Bill was endorsed because consumers would receive protection without additional costs or standards. Consumers would be protected from fraud and misrepresentation of all commodities, and given redress against offending sellers [79, p. 19].

By the time the Wool Products Labeling Act was under final discussion, more than 90 percent of the manufacturers of woolen garments opposed it. Representatives of the United Infant's and Children's Wear Association and the National Association of Men's Clothing Manufacturers claimed it would be impossible to identify fiber content due to the section-work system [42]. Other objections centered on the cost of administering label requirements, the support woolgrowers and woolen manufacturers would receive, the stigma placed on reprocessed wool, and fiber content not supplying consumers with information pertaining to wearing properties [49, p. 71].

Fur Trade

In 1948, protective legislation of the fur trade was desired by many groups in order to halt fraudulent practices of industry members. The National Board of Fur Farming Organizations sponsored a bill in Congress aimed at stopping misrepresentations by fur manufacturers in the labeling of products [91, p. 38].

Industry groups that gained from unrestricted competition opposed any legislation. They claimed mandatory labeling would be expensive and burdensome, excessive, misrepresentative, and insufficient [49]. In 1951, legislation that partially protected and informed consumers was passed.

E. F. Timme and Sons, the leading advocate of fake fur purchases, published advertisements in the June 1970 editions of Women's Wear Daily and the Daily News Record calling for the preservation of wild animals. These advertisements were criticized strongly by the Council of American Fur Organizations, which claimed the advertisements exaggerated the situation since some animals on Timme's list were abundant [17]. In 1973, Timme produced two television commercials lauding women for not taking part in the extinction of wild animals. Real fur representatives, trade associations, unions, and garment manufacturers filed suit in United States District Court to obtain an injunction against the showing of the commercials. Timme was upheld by the Supreme Court in 1974 [97].

Flammability

A relatively simple test was developed for fabric flammability. The method was adopted as an industry standard and incorporated in the Flammable Fabrics Act of 1953. The act also eliminated easy-to-ignite brushed fabrics and prohibited the introduction of hazardous materials. Initially, the act met with few negative industry reactions. This was due in large part to the laxity of the law [69, p. 19].

When a new flammability standard for children's sleepwear was promulgated by the Federal Trade Commission in 1971, the American Apparel Manufacturers Association contested the deadline for making sleepwear flame retardant. Industry representatives said more time was needed to accomplish the standard's provisions and voiced concern about higher prices. Later the association reconsidered, supported the new standard, and even advanced the effective date of the standard [10].

The most effective chemical developed for flameproofing children's sleepwear was Tris-BP. When the Consumer Product

Safety Commission banned the sale of products containing Tris in 1977, industry reaction was completely negative. The American Apparel Manufacturers Association said:

> With friends like the Commission, the consumer needs no enemies. Ultimately, the ban on Tris will be self defeating. Women will not find children's sleepwear in the store [5].

Since the June 1977 findings had been called preliminary, the industry felt the ban was imposed too hastily, without consideration of the effect on the sleepwear industry and its employees [5].

Textile Labeling

The Textile Fiber Identification Act of 1958 received its principal support from within the industry. The act was intended to protect producers of expensive fabrics from deceptive practices by producers of low-cost fabrics, as well as protect consumers. Advocates of the law included cotton, wool, fur, and farm interests who perceived synthetics as threats to business [49, p. 73].

The act was opposed by the Textile Fabrics Association, which asserted that consumers were interested in the wearing qualities of garments and not with textile labeling. The association felt consumers lacked knowledge about the properties of generic names of manmade fibers, and considered the cost of employing separate labels to be high [60].

Quality Control

In 1971, the Textile Quality Control Association described its major objective as the promotion and exchange of information that would assist operating mill workers in their efforts at manufacturing better quality textiles at lower costs [36, p. 32]. Later, retailers made a major attempt to develop quality control systems. Chains instituted procedures, such as checking total garment construction and care labeling instructions. These procedures forced manufacturers to set up similar systems [81]. Small retailers and manufacturers were unable to employ sophisticated quality control procedures because of high costs.

Care Labeling

An Industry Advisory Committee was established in 1966 by Esther Peterson, a presidential advisor. The committee helped create the "Voluntary Industry Guide for Improved Permanent Care Labeling." However, voluntary compliance was not forthcoming, and the Federal Trade Commission enacted a Trade Regulation Rule making it mandatory for every textile product to carry a permanent label. Industry reaction to this was negative, as members wanted to employ "exception" labeling [107, p. 49]. Every textile item now carries a mandatory label.

Trade Association Responses to Primary Study

Ten clothing trade associations were contacted and asked to respond to a mail questionnaire. Three associations answered the survey: American Apparel Manufacturers Association (AAMA), Men's Fashion Association (MFA), and the National Outerwear and Sportswear Association (NOSA). One association, United Infants' and Children's Wear Association, replied by stating it had no policy toward consumerism. Six associations did not respond at all, despite a follow-up letter: Associated Fur Manufacturers, Clothing Manufacturers Association, Greater Blouse, Shirt and Undergarment Association, Greater Clothing Manufacturers Association, International Ladies Garment Workers Union, and National Dress Manufacturers Association.

All three associations feel their products are of top quality. Two think consumerism has caused no noticeable effects because of consumer-oriented practices; one believes consumerism has had a detrimental effect. One association has a committee to deal with consumer problems. All the associations send representatives to testify before government committees, usually when asked. Two provide speakers for consumer groups, if requested. The associations differ on their long-run views toward consumerism from no impact to stricter regulation.

Table 4.1 contains abbreviated responses for the participating trade associations. Every association did not answer each question. Open-ended responses were interpreted by the author.

COMPANY RESPONSES TO CONSUMERISM

Company responses to consumer issues have been limited since many firms express their opinions through trade associations rather than individually. The following reports on the reactions of the few companies cited in the literature or responding to a primary study.

TABLE 4.1

Clothing Trade Association Responses to Study

Question 1	Generally speaking, how does your association feel about the consumer movement?
AAMA	Individual consumers who have had unsatisfactory experiences or seek information are helped. There is no involvement with the consumer movement.
MFA	Members favor giving consumers good quality, value, and performance. Garment manufacturers are responsive to consumer needs and wants.
NOSA	The consumer movement is not threatening, because high quality products are produced.
Question 2	How has the consumer movement affected the companies that belong to your association?
AAMA	Companies lean over backward to give consumers satisfaction and answer complaints. These policies have existed for many years and are not a result of consumer pressure.
MFA	Regulations regarding chemical fixatives have generated concern and detrimental effects. There should be greater research and consultation by government before establishing legislation.
NOSA	There has been no noticeable effect.
Question 3	Has the association created a position, panel, or department to deal with the effects of the consumer movement?
AAMA	The Consumer Affairs Committee, comprised of apparel suppliers and manufacturers, informs the industry of general consumer problems and is involved with consumer education.
MFA	Due to a small budget, no department has been created. Research and legal staffs are necessary to deal effectively with the consumer movement.
NOSA	No.

(continued)

Question 4	Does the association provide representatives to appear before government committees examining consumer issues?
AAMA	Technical expertise is provided; a representative, the association's legal counsel, and technical staff personnel appear.
MFA	Other associations are more active in this area, but representatives are sent when requested.
NOSA	Representatives are provided upon request.
Question 5	Does the association provide speakers to appear before national and/or local consumer organizations?
AAMA	No speakers are provided.
MFA	Speakers are provided upon request.
NOSA	Speakers are provided upon request.
Question 6	What do you believe to be the long-term impact of consumerism on the industry you represent?
AAMA	There will be little impact beyond that which has occurred already. The role of the apparel manufacturer is to produce quality products at the lowest possible prices, generate stockholder profits, and unskilled and semiskilled jobs.
MFA	It is impossible to judge the long-term impact because no one can predict the future direction of the consumer movement.
NOSA	There will be continued attention to quality details, expansion of testing facilities, and very strict adherence to labeling laws.

Source: Compiled by the author.

Company Responses as Reported in the Literature

Fashion, wool labeling, flammability, fur trade, quality, and care labeling are issues to which some individual companies have addressed themselves.

Fashion

For more than 50 years, designers have worked to develop popular fashions. Paul Poiret, the top courtier of the 1920s, understood women's desires for uniqueness and displaying affluence. The Poiret style of unlined, uncorseted dresses of oriental contour were quite popular. In 1937, Schiaparelli used padding in suit shoulders. The 1940s brought shirtwaist dresses and masculine coat styles for women. During the 1950s, casual and relaxed styles were offered. Sports clothes and loose fitting apparel were desirable [84]. In the 1960s and 1970s, new designers have entered the market and have offered a great diversity of styles to satisfy all types of women and men.

Wool Labeling

In 1939, a spokesman for Bamberger, a Newark retailer, said the demand by the public for information data was understandable; yet, the company opposed wool labeling on the ground that it would not help consumers judge the value or usefulness of products [14]. Only manufacturers of high quality garments supported the labeling act; many retailers and manufacturers opposed it. No companies have commented in this area since the Wool Products Labeling Act was implemented.

Flammability

Since the original flammability standard of 1953 was not strictly enforced, company responses were unnecessary. By 1973, the situation changed as a new standard for children's sleepwear was introduced. Some companies, including J. C. Penney, Montgomery Ward, and Sears Roebuck, voluntarily offered children's clothing and adult sleepwear that would satisfy the flame-retardant standard. In 1976, Penney developed a free over-the-counter brochure informing consumers about flame-retardant products. Sears also published a brochure. Advertising, labeling, and use displays were other techniques used by retailers to inform consumers [83].

When Tris was banned, company comments were critical. For example, a spokesman for Hollywood Needlecraft of Los Angeles said, "Small manufacturers like us don't have the profit margins to withstand the loss that may come from the ban" [1, p. 46]. A spokesman for Cassie Cotillion of New York stated, "If Tris is banned, it could put a lot of companies out of business" [1, p. 46]. The abruptness and costs of the ban were heavily attacked.

Fur Trade

In 1961, furriers criticized both fake fur manufacturer Russell Taylor for making inexpensive, lightweight, and nonallergenic furs, and conservationists for overstating the problem of animal extinction. During the 1970s, Timme, another fake fur manufacturer, was accused of deceptive practices by real fur manufacturers. The purchase of real furs has continued by consumers [100].

Quality

The Monsanto Company, which is not a garment manufacturer but a producer of fibers, began a "Wear Dated" program in 1962. This program offered a one-year guarantee for apparel containing its fibers; refund or replacement would be given. Monsanto employed a quality control procedure that involved top quality fibers, extensive testing of fabrics and garments, and laundering of garments according to care labels [53].

In 1975, Sears, Penney, and Montgomery Ward established quality control systems. Sears set minimum standards for weight, thread count, and colorfastness of fabrics and apparel. Penney used a computerized surveillance program. Montgomery Ward laundered apparel according to care labels. None of these companies was satisfied with the quality control techniques of manufacturers [47].

Care Labeling

Sears and Montgomery Ward became involved with care labeling in 1970, before mandatory rules were enacted. Sears realized that objections would be encountered to its placing labels in sheer garments, but without laundering information, consumers would be unable to properly care for these garments. Montgomery Ward developed 28 combinations of instructions for care labels [40, p. 118].

Some companies opposed care labeling. In 1970, one knitwear manufacturer said:

An industry which is dominated by fashion and is highly seasonal is faced with the fact that they make many fabrics without being completely sure how they will actually be called upon to perform, AND THEY ARE PUSHED IN THIS DIRECTION BY THE CONSUMER [40, p. 49].

Permanent care labeling was made mandatory in 1973 and continues today.

Company Responses to Primary Study

Ten clothing manufacturers were contacted and asked to participate in a study on consumerism. Only two companies responded: Levi Strauss and Munsingwear. Eight companies chose not to respond, even after a follow-up letter: Aileen, Blue Bell, Bobbie Brooks, Hart, Shaffner and Marx, Jonathan Logan, Manhattan Industries, V. F. Corporation, and Warnaco.

Capsule responses by Levi Strauss and Munsingwear to individual questions appear in Table 4.2. The answers have been abbreviated by the author. Since only two companies participated in the survey, overall conclusions cannot be made.

THE OVERALL EFFECTS OF CONSUMERISM

Following are a discussion of the overall impact of consumerism in the clothing industry and an evaluation of the performance of consumers, government, the industry, and individual firms.

Impact of Consumerism

Consumerism has generated a great deal of action by government and company groups. Government has implemented many pieces of legislation, and a number of associations and companies have fought against them.

Fiber content acts (wool, fur, and textile) sought to provide more information about garment composition. Opponents of these acts commented that they would confuse and not help consumers. After passage, violations, which were few in number, were prosecuted by the Federal Trade Commission. However, only cease-and-desist orders were given; there were no fines or prison sentences.

Critics frequently complained about the arbitrary setting of fashion trends by designers, but consumers continued to buy new clothing that was displayed. Recently, competition has lessened the designers' control over fashion.

Conservationists and manufacturers of false furs had some success in restraining the slaughter of wild animals. Nonetheless, many consumers still purchase real furs.

TABLE 4.2

Clothing Company Responses to Study

Question 1	The Consumer: What type of policy do you have for handling complaints? Do you have an in-house consumer advocate? Do you have an educational program?
Levi Strauss	Complaints are processed by quality assurance departments on an individual basis. If a defect is due to improper care, the garment is returned with an explanation. There is no in-house consumer advocate, but, the Chief Counsel and Director of the company is a director and active member of the National Consumer League. There is no participation in any structured educational program.
Munsingwear	Consumer inquiries receive typed responses within five days. Merchandise is replaced when necessary. General Managers and Merchandise Managers answer complaints. There is no in-house consumer advocate; all employees are informal consumer advocates. Educational materials are distributed to high schools and colleges. Meetings are held to educate retail sales clerks.
Question 2	The Product: What type of product-related information is made available to the public? What procedure do you follow to ensure product and service quality? Are you modifying or changing your products in response to consumerism?
Levi Strauss	Product information is limited to care labels and hang tags. Products are constantly changed and modified in response to consumers. A Product Integrity Department sets standards throughout the company. Each division has a Quality Assurance Department and makes careful inspections.

(continued)

Table 4.2 (continued)

Munsingwear	There is no direct product-related information for consumers. Illustrated catalogs are sent to retailers; information enclosures are provided to consumers. Products are not modified in response to consumerism, but in response to fashion trends and consumer desires. Merchandise is frequently inspected and tested for defects.
Question 3	Outside Influences: What type of consumer regulations affect your operations? How do you respond to outside consumer pressure? How do you evaluate the effects of consumerism on your company?
Levi Strauss	Regulations deal with fiber content labeling, care instructions, flame retardance, truth-in-advertising, etc. There is no response to outside consumer pressures, but to anticipated consumer needs. The effects of consumerism cannot be determined since the company's concern predates the movement.
Munsingwear	Regulations have not had an adverse effect. Content and care labeling have increased costs. Consumer pressure is handled via a complaint procedure and by correcting problems. It is difficult to measure the impact of consumerism, since the company is consumer-oriented.

Source: Compiled by the author.

A number of manufacturers opposed flammability standards on the basis of higher costs, but demands by the National Fire Protection Association and Action for the Prevention of Burn Injuries to Children resulted in strict standards. A flame-retardant chemical, Tris, was developed for children's sleepwear. Unfortunately, testing showed possible links to cancer, and treated garments were not allowed to be sold. Various court cases were brought by industry members to slow down the ban on Tris and spread the costs more equitably. It has been quite difficult to find a replacement for Tris that is not carcinogenic.

Some retailers and manufacturers created thorough quality control programs, while many others did not. Voluntary efforts with care labeling proved to be ineffective. Compulsory Federal Trade Commission rules were necessary.

Evaluation of Consumerism

It is possible to understand the objections to wool, fur, and textile acts. While the Federal Trade Commission has attempted to protect consumers, it has been involved with content labeling without education. In addition, these acts have caused garment prices to rise. On the other hand, information is essential for consumers to make intelligent decisions.

For several decades, consumers bought fashions originating in Paris, and then from other fashion capitals, without regard for utility and personal taste. Recently, shoppers have shown less interest in fashion centers and purchased according to their own desires and not those of designers.

Consumers have shown little interest in the conservation of wild animals. Efforts by conservationists and fake fur manufacturers have not convinced shoppers to avoid the purchase of real furs. Status and vanity have persisted.

The introduction of improved flammability standards was necessary, but the rush to Tris, which was an effective flame retardant, occurred without proper testing for side effects. In this instance, the industry did its best to meet government standards and was then castigated for doing so.

Every year about 5,000 people die and 250,000 are injured as a result of burns involving flammable fabrics [69]. Since 1973, only a children's sleepwear standard, for sizes 7-14, has been adopted. While no retardants should be introduced without proper testing, standards in areas outside children's wear need considerable tightening.

Several companies have done excellent jobs in establishing quality control procedures. Too many have not upgraded their procedures because of high costs or lack of concern. Retailers have become scapegoats for manufacturers, as consumers complain to them.

Care labeling instructions have benefited consumers and the clothing industry. Consumers are able to maintain garments longer and in better condition. Manufacturers and retailers have less returns due to improper customer care.

Consumer group pressure has been small in comparison to the variety of issues that concern them. Consumers have not done a good job of organizing or following through to improve practices in the clothing industry. Safety has been pursued only after serious injuries or deaths.

It has been covernment intervention that caused labeling, nonflammability, care labeling, and other laws to be enacted and standards set. However, government actions can be faulted in two ways. First, penalties have been too lenient and standards too lax. Second, the government has not done enough to recognize responsible companies and encourage self-regulation.

On the whole, the clothing industry has not done well in policing itself. Some members have incited government actions. On safety issues, there should have been more cooperation with the government. Overall, trade associations have not taken leadership positions in responding to consumer issues.

At the company level, firms frequently have ignored consumerism. Companies have battled each other, not in the interests of consumers but in their own interests, over rules and regulations. A few progressive companies have responded well to consumer problems.

FUTURE OUTLOOK

The future of consumerism in the clothing industry will evolve as it has in the past—slowly.

Labeling laws will expand as information about chemicals and other materials found in fabrics is required on labels. Care labeling will include leather clothing, and washing instructions will contain temperature descriptions, drying methods, and bleaching and ironing advice.

Fashions will constantly change, as in the past, but consumers will not buy fashions they do not like. Desires for status and uniqueness in clothing will continue.

The conservationist cause will struggle, since support will grow very gradually. Conservationists will stress statistics about endangered animal species and fake fur purchases. Consumers will still buy real furs at high prices.

Flammability will be a topic of greater concern as accident data are released. Safe flame retardation will be a major goal. Parents will exhibit care in purchasing children's clothing.

Quality control procedures will remain virtually unchanged, due to the costs of administering programs by retailers and manufacturers. Relatively untested imports will have many quality defects, such as open seams and missing buttons. Because of this, consumer complaints and returns will increase.

Additional consumer groups do not appear forthcoming. Only in the area of safety will new groups arise. The government will become more involved with animal conservation. It will sustain its concern about flammability. The Consumer Product Safety Commission will become involved with classifying apparel items and testing for flammability.

The clothing industry and its companies will oppose consumer legislation on the basis of higher costs. Voluntary self-regulation seems difficult and doubtful. Cooperation with government will increase.

RECOMMENDATIONS

Recommendations are made for consumer groups, government, the industry, and individual companies.

Consumer Groups

Consumers must work through formalized groups in order to present their views effectively. Presently, there are established groups that have not been active in the clothing area for several years, if at all. Women's organizations, educational organizations, and health associations must take more interest.

Consumer education must be improved. Information about flammability, fiber content, and so on are presently inadequate. Manufacturers' registration numbers, which have been used in lieu of company names, need to be explained so that comparison shopping will be possible and encouraged.

Government

The government should encourage self-regulation before enacting legislation. Adequate time must be provided for industry compliance with new laws. Penalties must be enforced more stringently; cease-and-desist orders are insufficient for illegal business practices. The government should make animal conservation an important issue, require chemical additives on labels, indicate potential hazards on labels by using symbols, set quality control standards, and test the quality of imports.

The Industry and Companies

The industry and its companies must be responsive to consumer needs, cooperate with government, and work toward a system of self-regulation. They should realize that the successful resolution of consumer issues, including content labeling, quality, flammability, and care labeling, helps the industry and its companies as well as consumers.

Fashion changes should be more gradual and less drastic. Uniform sizing is needed for consumers to judge correctly their sizes in garments made by different manufacturers and to reduce the shabby condition of some garments caused by excessive trying-on to determine the correct size. Improved care labeling would aid consumers and the clothing industry. Voluntary guidelines, if not implemented and followed, will be superseded by government regulations.

BIBLIOGRAPHY

1. "A Flame Retardant Ban Dishevels an Industry." Business Week (April 18, 1977), pp. 45-46.

2. "Agony and Finery." New York Times (October 4, 1975), p. 26.

3. "Are Women Interested in Paris Fashions?" Reader's Digest 79 (July 1961), pp. 87-91.

4. Bachrach, Max. "Now There's a New Law Against Furs." Good Housekeeping 135 (August 1952), pp. 49ff.

5. Bleiberg, Robert M. "Pajama Game? The Ban on Tris Is Very Serious Business." Barrons 57 (June 6, 1977), p. 7.

6. Bush, Paul. "Tris Case Holds Lessons for Marketing Managers." Marketing News 11 (April 7, 1967), p. 4.

7. "Can the American Manufacturer Force Styles?" Printers Ink (October 12, 1922), pp. 10-11.

8. Carter, Caleb. "Fake Furs Unlimited." Canadian Magazine 88 (November 1937), pp. 14ff.

9. Charlton, Linda. "The Facts About Tris Don't Leave Much Choice." New York Times (July 3, 1977), p. D3.

10. "Children's Flammable Sleepwear—A Progress Report." Consumers Union (February 1972), p. 106.

11. Clark, F. S. "Who Sets Fashions—And How?" Review of Reviews 31 (January 1930), pp. 53-58.

12. "Clothiers Could Reap $55 Million As Senate OKs Aid in Tris Ban." Miami Herald (January 21, 1978), p. 1.

13. "Consumer Agency Issues New Warning on Tris." New York Times (August 20, 1977), p. 8.

14. "Consumers Learn, But Not Sure What." New York Times (March 9, 1939), p. 37.

15. Coughlin, W. E. "Meeting Consumer Needs in Textiles." American Dyestuff Reporter 34 (June 18, 1945), pp. 253-54ff.

16. Dall, W. B. "Enter a New Era of Informative Labeling." Textile World 91 (February 1941), pp. 80-81.

17. "Despite Plaints, Timme Ads Will Still Say, 'Fur Coats Shouldn't Be Made of Fur'." Advertising Age 41 (June 15, 1970), p. 97.

18. Dishon, C. "Fireproofing Our Children." Today's Health 49 (January 1971), pp. 38-41ff.

19. Earnshaw, Karen. "Up from Down Under." New York Post (February 27, 1978), p. 34.

20. Edgerton, E. M. "Consumer Protection in Informative Labeling." American Dyestuff Reporter 133 (November 20, 1944), pp. 496-99.

21. Engel, James; Wales, Hugh; and Warshaw, Martin. Promotional Strategy. Homewood, Ill.: Richard D. Irwin, 1975.

22. "Explosive Sweaters." Newsweek 39 (January 21, 1952), p. 29.

23. Fabricio, Roberto. "After a Fashion, Garment Makers Expect You to Buy More Clothes." Miami Herald (January 22, 1978), p. 7.

24. "Fake Furs Win Warm Friends." Chemical Week 108 (January 20, 1971), pp. 32-33.

25. Federal Reporter. FTC v. M. Grossman & Sons Inc. & Betmar Hats Inc., 458, no. 71-1197 (April 25, 1972), 1,277-81.

26. ____. Hoving Corp. vs. FTC, 290, no. 343, Docket 2664, 19.1 (1965).

27. ____. Hunter Mills Corp. vs. FTC, F 20 284 (1961), 70-71.

28. ____. Morton's Inc. vs. FTC, 286, no. 5675 (1961), 155.

29. Federal Trade Commission Decisions. H. Myerson & Sons vs. FTC, Docket no. 8808 (February 25, 1971), 464-84.

30. ____. Transair Inc. vs. FTC (April 5, 1962), 694-705.

31. Feigenbaum, A. V. "Quality Control." Western Apparel Industry (April 1971), pp. 46-50.

32. Fisk, Margaret. Encyclopedia of Associations. Gale Research Co., USA, 1977.

33. Fiske, Minnie Madden. "What a Deformed Thief This Fashion Is: Cruelty of Trapping." Ladies Home Journal (Summer 1921), pp. 20-21.

34. "Flame Retardant Textiles for Consumers." Consumer Bulletin 53 (September 1976), pp. 4ff.

35. Fortess, Fred. "Fashion Plus Performance, A New Dimension for the Industrial Engineer." The Bobbin (March 1968), pp. 38-47.

36. ____. "Quality Control in Apparel Manufacturing." Textile Bulletin (June 1971), pp. 32-36.

37. "Four Ask Wool Labels." New York Times (March 11, 1939), p. 30.

38. "FTC Aide Endorses Plan to Toughen Textile Caretags." Wall Street Journal (August 25, 1977), p. 8.

39. "Fun Furs." New Yorker 43 (May 20, 1967), pp. 32-33.

40. Furness, Betty. "The Cost of Living." McCalls 98 (October 1970), pp. 48-49ff.

41. "Furs by Any Other Name." New York Times (December 9, 1951).

42. "Garment Men Oppose Wool Labeling Bill." New York Times (March 3, 1939), p. 39.

43. Goldthwait, F. "Consumers Are Demanding More Durability in Textiles." Textile World 75 (March 9, 1929), pp. 1,669-70.

44. Hager, Herman. "Flammability of Wearing Apparel." American Dyestuff Reporter 36 (March 24, 1947), pp. 141ff.

45. "Handling Flammability Problems." Stores (May 1973), pp. 14ff.

46. Herrmann, Henry F. "The Informative Labeling of Textiles—A 25-Year Review of Pros and Cons." American Dyestuff Reporter 35 (December 12, 1946), pp. 616-17ff.

47. Hertz, Eric. "Big 3 Chains Rap Fabrics, Apparel." Women's Wear Daily (June 2, 1975).

48. Howard, K. "How Paris Sets the Styles." Ladies Home Journal 37 (November 1920), pp. 17ff.

49. Howard, Marshall. "Textile and Fur Labeling Legislation: Names, Competition, and the Consumer." California Management Review 14 (Winter 1971), pp. 69-80.

50. "How the New Clothes Labels Can Help You." Redbook 136 (September 1972), pp. 62ff.

51. Hurst, F. "Must Women Go Back to Tripping Over Their Trains?" Literary Digest 103 (November 16, 1929), pp. 39-51.

52. "Informative Textile Labeling." American Dyestuff Reporter 29 (December 9, 1945), pp. 656-62.

53. "Is Quality Fashionable—Testing Apparel Performance Can Turn Fashion Inside Out." New York Times, advertising supplement (April 21, 1974), p. 7.

54. Ivins, Molly. "The Constant in Fashion Is the Constant Change." New York Times (August 15, 1976), p. D6.

55. Johnston, L. G. "Consumer Complaints from New Fabrics and Finishes." American Dyestuff Reporter 38 (January 24, 1949), pp. 65-66.

56. "Judge Strikes Down Safety Ban on Tris." New York Times (June 24, 1977), p. 9.

57. Kearney, Paul William. "Are You Dressed to Kill?" Woman's Home Companion 80 (May 1953), pp. 36-37.

58. Kent, Patricia. "Quality Lag Vexing to Us, Firms Claim." Women's Wear Daily (February 20, 1970).

59. Klemesrud, Judy. "What I Hate About Clothes." New York Times Magazine (August 25, 1974).

60. Klurfeld, Arthur M. "Textile Labels Opposed, Letter to Editor." New York Times (May 21, 1958), p. 52.

61. Koshetz, Herbert. "Comeback for Hair of the Camel." New York Times (April 20, 1975), p. C15.

62. Little, R. W. "Trends in the Evolution of Fire Resistant Textiles." American Dyestuff Reporter 37 (February 23, 1948), pp. 114-18.

63. London, M. "How the Flammable Fabrics Act Affects You." Textile World 104 (September 1954), pp. 55-58.

64. Lyle, Dorothy. Performance of Textiles. New York: John Wiley and Sons, 1977.

65. Manchester, Harland. "What You Should Know About Flammable Fabrics." Reader's Digest 98 (May 1967), pp. 37-38ff.

66. "Minimum Fabric Performance Specified in New ASA Standard." Textile World (April 1960), pp. 8-9.

67. Morris, Bernadine. "Fashion: Not Enough Choice." Stores (July 1970), pp. 8-10.

68. ____. "The Haute Couture: Expensive, Influential and Enduring." New York Times (July 30, 1977), p. 20.

69. Nader, Ralph. "The Burned Children." New Republic 165 (July 3, 1971), pp. 19-21.

70. "Naming Textiles Is Not Enough—Consumers Want to Know About Performance." Consumer Bulletin 42 (June 1959).

71. NBS Technical Note 867, U.S. Department of Commerce National Bureau of Standards. "Relationships of Garment Characteristics, and Other Variables to Fire Injury Severity." The Cotton Foundation (June 1975), pp. 1-36.

72. Nemy, Enid. "Declining Quality in Clothes: The Makers and Sellers Tell Why." New York Times (December 10, 1974).

73. Nesbitt, J. "Paris Again Fashioning the Fashion World." Illustrated World 27 (May 1917), pp. 428-38.

74. "New Wool Labels, What They Can Mean to Consumers." Consumers Research Bulletin 10 (January 1941), pp. 4-6.

75. 1977/1978, U.S. Government Manual. Published by the Office of the Federal Register, National Archives and Records Services, and General Services Administration, 1-882.

76. "Now You Can Tell When to Wash and When to Dry-Clean Your Clothes." Consumer Bulletin 55 (September 1972), pp. 2ff.

77. Peach, Robert. "Customer Returns: Problems or Symptom." Journal of the AATCC 123 (November 5, 1969), pp. 23-26.

78. Pferfle, L. C. "What the Consumer Seeks from the Textile Manufacturer." American Dyestuff Reporter 32 (May 10, 1943), pp. 224-25.

79. "Protest Compulsory Labeling of Textiles." Textile World (March 8, 1924), pp. 19ff.

80. "Quality Control: But Sam, You Made the Pants Too Long." Clothes (April 15, 1976), pp. 61-65.

81. "Quality Control: More Than Just a Ripple." Clothes (September 1, 1975), pp. 29-31.

82. Quant, Mary. "The Young Will Not Be Dictated To." Vogue 148 (August 1, 1966), pp. 86ff.

83. "Ralph Nader Reports." Ladies Home Journal (March 1976), p. 58.

84. Ratcliff, J. D. "Paris Fashions Come to Main Street." Reader's Digest 79 (July 1961), pp. 87-91.

85. Robinson, Dwight E. "The Meaning of Fashion." In Inside The Fashion Business by Jeannette E. Jarnow. New York: John Wiley & Sons, 1965.

86. "Rules and Regulations Under the Fur Products Labeling Act," as amended May 15, 1961, Federal Trade Commission.

87. "Rules and Regulations Under the Textile Fiber Products Identification Act," effective March 3, 1960, Federal Trade Commission.

88. "Rules and Regulations Under the Wool Products Labeling Act of 1939," effective July 15, 1941, Federal Trade Commission.

89. Sandholzer, W. M. "Accidents from Highly Flammable Clothing." Journal of Home Economics 39 (March 1947), pp. 133-34.

90. Slom, Stanley. "Fifteen Chemicals Used with Fabrics Spur Health Queries." Wall Street Journal (May 27, 1977), p. 9.

91. Sontheimer, M. "Is It Really A Fur Coat?" Good Housekeeping 127 (November 1948), pp. 38-39ff.

92. Steiniger, Lynn, and Dardis, Rachel. "Consumers Textile Complaints." Journal of the AATCC 3 (July 1971), pp. 161-65.

93. "Subcommittee Flogs Velesiocol Over Tris." Chemical and Engineering News (May 23, 1977), p. 17.

94. Taylor, Russell. "Action People." Marketing Communications 299 (February 1971), pp. 13-14.

95. "10 Most Frequent Quality Slipups Retailers Hate." Menswear (May 28, 1976), pp. 48-49.

96. "The Chemicals Around Us." Newsweek (August 21, 1978), pp. 25-28.

97. "The Real vs. the Fake." Broadcasting 87 (December 2, 1974), pp. 33-34.

98. "This Is No Way to Wash the Clothes." Consumer Bulletin 37 (February 1972), p. 106.

99. Thompson, Robert. "A Retailer's View of Quality Problems in the Clothing Industry." The Bobbin (September 1968), pp. 74-84.

100. "Timme Ads for Fake Furs Point Finger At Lollabrigida Tiger Skins, Heckel Seal Coat." Advertising Age 41 (March 2, 1970), p. 8.

101. "Tris Ban Demanded by EDF." Chemical Marketing Reporter 211 (February 14, 1977), pp. 3ff.

102. "Trying to Bolster Sales with 'The Big Is in Look'." Business Week (August 17, 1978), p. 36.

103. Udell, Gerald, and Fischer, Philip. "The FTC Improvement Act." Journal of Marketing 41 (April 1977), pp. 81-86.

104. U.S. Consumer Product Safety Commission. News Release. Washington, D.C.: July 17, 1978.

105. "U.S. to Ease Restraints on Sleepwear Fabrics." New York Times (September 18, 1977), p. 26.

106. Van Horne, Harriet. "The Shape of Things to Come: Sloppiness and Slease." New York Post (March 6, 1978), p. 27.

107. "What Fur Labels Must Tell You." Changing Times 27 (July 1973), p. 47.

108. "What You Need to Know About Flammable Fabrics." Consumer Bulletin 50 (March 1967), pp. 16-17.

109. "Why You Can't Call Fake Fur a Fake." Consumer Bulletin (February 1924), pp. 24-25.

110. "Why the Concern About Flammability?" Flame Resistant Apparel 1977 Report of the Technical Advisory Committee, AAMA.

111. "Will Consumers Benefit from the New Textile Labeling Act?" Consumer Bulletin 43 (March 1960), p. 9.

5

CONSUMERISM AND HOUSEHOLD PRODUCTS

Donald E. Bonin

INTRODUCTION

The household products industry encompasses a variety of products. The scope of this analysis will be limited to those items normally found under the kitchen sink or in the medicine cabinet. Included are cleaners, soaps, oven cleaners, shaving creams, hair dyes, shampoos, insecticides, cosmetics, dentifrices, and furniture polishes.

Although the unit prices of most products are in the two-dollar range, total sales in 1977 were $6.5 billion for cleansers, soaps, and detergents. Cosmetic care products and toiletries accounted for $7.33 billion [107]. In 1977, Procter & Gamble, Colgate-Palmolive, Warner-Lambert, and Bristol-Myers each had revenues of well over $2 billion [106].

In this chapter, consumerism and household products are examined in historical terms, and the responses of consumer groups, government, the industry, and individual companies are studied.

THE HISTORY OF CONSUMERISM IN
THE HOUSEHOLD PRODUCTS INDUSTRY

Early Issues

Between 1783 and 1865, three state laws and one federal law concerning flour, importation of adulterated drugs, and purity of food were passed [122]. In 1899, a National Consumers League was founded to encourage consumers to buy household products produced under fair working conditions [19]. A pure food and drug act was passed in 1906, as meatpackers commonly left rodent hair in canned meat [101]. During this period, there were few household products as they are known today [122].

In 1913, Engineering Record pointed out the hazards of white lead and benzene in paint [57]. At the same time, a household headache remedy, bichloride tablets, was determined to have caused deaths and injuries. Yet, nothing was done about the product for years [83].

During the early 1920s, consumer activity was limited. Buying cooperatives were designed to help consumers, but proved ineffective [19]. Starting in the late 1920s, consumer issues came into focus. F. J. Schlink and Stuart Chase wrote Your Money's Worth, and discussed "slick salesmanship" and high prices involving mouthwash, toothpowders, floor cleansers, and nonhousehold products [94]. The government tested some items, but did not give consumers access to the findings [122].

Emerging Issues

Consumers' Bulletin, begun by Schlink, reported on items like toothpowders, the ingredients that went into them, their costs, and how consumers could make their own [19]. At about the same time, the dangers of poisons in headache remedies with secret ingredients were disclosed [95]. The hazards of carbon tetrachloride, used in household cleaning products and spot removers, were discovered by scientists [92]. Silver polishes were found to contain potassium cyanide, which could emit harmful fumes [59].

During the mid-1930s, the Joint Committee for Sound and Democratic Consumer Legislation was founded. It was staffed by executives from companies like Bristol-Myers and Colgate-Palmolive. The intent of the committee was to stop or amend consumer legislation [92].

In 1939, Good Housekeeping magazine ran into trouble because its seals of approval and guarantees to the public were found to be exaggerated and false for many common household products advertised in the magazine. Cosmetic, medical, and dental experts felt the products did not live up to claims. Many well-known products were involved: Jergens Lotion, Woodbury Soap and Face Cream, Guardsman Finish Furniture Polish, and Murine eye drops. Good Housekeeping blamed communists for its problems, feeling they had infiltrated the consumer movement [120].

In 1940, Ponds and Jergens put vitamins in their face creams. Both claimed the vitamins would be absorbed through the skin, making one more beautiful. In reality, it was better for consumers to ingest vitamins than rub them into the skin [120].

Listerine claimed that it killed germs that caused colds, prevented colds, and stopped dandruff and halitosis. The basic ingredient was eucalyptus-flavored alcohol; a bottle of wine had the same therapeutic effect [66]. At this time, some popular headache remedies, such as Bromo Seltzer, were made of chemicals that caused consumers to become mentally deranged [5].

Colgate-Palmolive advertised that its toothpaste killed bad breath germs and had special ingredients to combat halitosis. Ipana said it strengthened gums, but it really irritated them. Despite complaints of irritated gums by U.S. sailors, Ipana continued to advertise its medicinal value [20].

Senator Estes Kefauver held congressional hearings on monopoly power and price administration in 1957. The prices of household products were high; there were fake shortages of product ingredients for items like floor wax [19]. During the same year, two University of Pennsylvania dermatologists discovered tumorlike cell masses (granulomas) could be caused by allergies to a deodorant ingredient called zirconium [22].

In 1958, Listerine claimed it was an Asian flu remedy, since there was no scientific evidence to prove it did not cure the illness. Advertising messages were adapted to evolving maladies [42]. Colgate-Palmolive advertised in 1960 that is dentifrice gave protection from dental disease. The product contained "Gardol," which promised to solve the problem of tooth decay. Many consumer groups and government agencies called upon Colgate to prove its assertions, which it was unable to do successfully [8].

Soap, floor wax, deodorant, bleach, and other household products were sold underweight in 1961. Package weights were expressed as fractions, like 11 7/8 ounces, to make price comparisons difficult [61]. Senator Phillip Hart proposed federal labeling and packaging legislation to end this practice. California consumer officials stated that cosmetic jars were deceptive because they appeared to contain more of the cosmetic than they actually did. Plastic and glass bottles/jars had extra-thick or false bottoms [14]. Despite these incidents, federal fair labeling and packaging legislation was not enacted until 1966.

Modern Era

During 1963 and 1964, Rise shaving cream advertised on television by shaving the cream off sandpaper. Consumers and the Federal Trade Commission (FTC) felt this commercial was deceptive in its ease of shaving, but Rise continued the campaign for two years until the courts ruled it could not [97].

In 1964, Regimen, a diet supplement, was advertised as having therapeutic values. It incorrectly implied that the user would look and feel younger by using the product. Geritol was another item that came under criticism from the federal government for making claims about keeping users young and healthy [64].

Packages were found to be dangerous, especially to children. For example, insect spray cans could easily dispense poisonous insecticides into a child's face; metal cans would leak due to corrosion; easy-open aspirin bottles made ingestion easy; chemical drain openers and bleach could be easily spilled; spray deodorants and room deodorizers were highly flammable; and pressure aerosol cans were subject to explosion. Lawsuits against manufacturers resulted in increasingly higher jury judgments [91].

Beginning in 1968, toiletry and soap manufacturers had to adhere to new fair packaging and labeling regulations. These regulations specified that a soap box had to contain the name of the manufacturer and its address, the packer, and the ZIP code [115]. At the same time, consumerists called for more explicit listing of ingredients in order to help people with allergies and to know what to do in case of swallowing [35].

In the early 1970s, unit pricing and price per ounce were legislated for supermarkets by several states and cities. This allowed comparison shopping and reduced confusion regarding terms such as king, family, and super [43, 122]. Detergents were criticized by health, environmental, and consumer groups for containing ecologically unsafe phosphates. Many communities, including Suffolk, New York, banned the sale of phosphate detergents [108].

During the mid- and late-1970s, consumer issues ranged from deceptive marketing of cold remedies to carcinogens in hair dyes.

The marketing of over-the-counter cold medicines and syrups, whose effectiveness was doubtful, came under attack in 1976. Cures for psoriasis, colds, pimples, hemorrhoids, and bad breath were among the items sold extensively. One well-known cold medicine, Vicks Nyquil, was 50 proof, 25 percent alcohol by content. An examination of the warning label on the bottle revealed that the user was to consult a physician if he or she had high blood pressure, heart disease, diabetes, or a thyroid disease [29]. Many doctors stated that the simple advice of taking aspirin, drinking liquids, and getting bed rest would suffice instead of a cold medicine, which could do more harm than good [10].

Insecticides such as the Shell "No Pest Strip" also caused concern in 1976. The strip killed bugs via a slow time-released vapor action. The vapor was odorless and tasteless. This made it possible for people to be exposed for long periods of time. No one knew the long-term hazards of exposure [12].

In 1977, benzene, a petrochemical derivative used in rubber cement, paint remover, furniture polish, floor wax, spot remover, and lubricants, was found to be very flammable. In addition, when vapors were inhaled, they could lead to blood cancer (leukemia) [81]. The issue was resolved finally on March 27, 1978, when the Consumer Product Safety Commission (CPSC) banned benzene [2].

Some common household products, such as patching/spackling compounds and cement/glue powders, were found to contain asbestos. Asbestos was known to cause lung cancer, and had been banned in talcum powder [39]. In April 1977, asbestos was banned from spackling compounds, but stock on store shelves could be sold until June 1978 [112].

The safety of hair dyes was questioned in 1977 and 1978. Some of the dyes were absorbed through the skin when applied to the hair and scalp, and were suspected of causing cancer. The dyes were exempt from the Food and Drug Administration laws of 1938. It was difficult for the government to have warning labels placed on products because of lengthy court cases. As of this writing, hair dyes remain on store shelves [40].

ACTIVE CONSUMER GROUPS

While there are no consumer groups whose primary focus is household products, many general groups have been involved when particular situations or problems have interested them. Consumers' Research, founded in 1928, rates household products in its monthly magazine and yearly manual called Consumers' Research. Of the 33 major product categories evaluated by Consumers' Research, four involve household products: cosmetics and beauty aids, cleaning and polishing supplies, soaps and detergents, and shaving equipment and supplies. Products are rated "Recommended," "Intermediate," and "Not Recommended." Household products are tested in the organization's New Jersey facilities, where in-home conditions are simulated. Products are evaluated on the basis of safety, effectiveness, quality, and performance [84].

A number of times, research and testing have found faults in household products. For example, the February 1978 issue of Consumers' Research pointed out that some nonphosphate detergents contained sodium carbonate and soda ash, which could cause problems for the user. Instead of the chemical completely washing out of clothing, it became a stiff, greasy, and rough residue. It also made clothes yellowish and dull, and could reduce the fire-retardant ability of some finishes. The magazine provided suggestions on how to solve these problems [89]. Other household products that recently have been tested include laundry detergents, floor waxes, and removers.

Consumers Union, founded in 1936, is the publisher of Consumer Reports. Household products are tested for quality, cost, safety, and effectiveness. Consumer Reports has been especially active in evaluating furniture wax, soap, detergent, shaving cream, paint, dishwashing liquid, and silver polish. In addition to its magazine ratings, Consumers Union has a staff of lawyers, based in Washington, D.C., which files class action suits on issues such as flammability of home products (including spray containers and mattresses) and pushes for legislation to have manufacturers disclose the ingredients on cosmetic products [122].

The February 1978 issue of Consumer Reports tested silver care products and found one to be extremely dangerous. Gorham Silvermaker Silver Polish was judged to be highly flammable, and this was not marked clearly on the label. Consumer Reports felt users should have been warned and the manufacturer required to adhere to federal hazard legislation affecting this product [100].
In its March 1978 issue, Consumer Reports showed a pictorial comparison of two cans of Sure deodorant. Both cans were identical in price and package, with the exception of their weights: one can held 14 ounces, the other 12, a 14-percent price increase [78]. Other household products tested and rated by Consumers Union in the last two years include: laundry bleach, drain cleaner, spot remover, hand lotion, dishwashing liquid, freezer wrap, insect repellent, and toilet soap. In addition, the proper way to identify solid weight in many household products was covered in an article.

The Consumer Federation of America, started in 1967, is the largest national consumer advocacy organization in the United States with 220 member organizations. It is interested in product pricing, quality, servicing, and guarantees, and lobbies to present consumer views and pass consumer legislation. The federation has had minimal impact on household products, although it does comment to the government on regulations regarding household products and over-the-counter drug products [75].

Truth in Advertising, founded in 1973 and located in Mantairie, Lousiana, has chapters throughout the United States. It supports consumers when household product advertisements are found to be false or deceptive [75].

The Interagency Committee on Product Information, a federal government organization of representatives from 22 agencies, wants to develop a program for:

disseminating general product information that the
government acquires in buying consumer products

and for sharing the skill and knowledge of government purchases with the public in a fair and useful manner [75].

If a consumer wants to know which home products the government has bought, he or she can find out from this committee. Up to this point, final consumers have rarely asked for this information, but institutional buyers have.

The American Council on Consumer Interests, founded in 1953 and now with over 3,000 members, stimulates the exchange of ideas among consumer groups and disseminates information about consumer problems. It distributes a newsletter that is a source of information for new publications and material on household products [75].

The Federation of Homemakers, established in 1959 and now comprised of 6,000 members, is a consumer education organization of individuals who are "seeking to inform homemakers of the potential harm families incur from ingesting chemically treated foods" and to "acquaint consumers with the work, responsibilities, and problems of the Food and Drug Administration" [75]. The group distributes information on pending and recently passed federal food, drug, and cosmetic laws.

The Federation of Homemakers also has given statements and urged members to write legislators regarding color additives, lipstick ingredients, the use of pesticides on farms and around the house, and other dangerous products or substances. The group pushed for the Hazardous Substances Act of 1963, which partly dealt with flammability and caustic dangers. Until the formation of the Consumer Product Safety Commission, the federation acted as a self-appointed watchdog for product safety [75, 90].

Student Legal Action Organizations are comprised of public-interest law students who identify unfair business practices and pursue the issues in court. Some groups that have been active and/or successful are: Breathers for the Reduction of Atmospheric Hazards to the Environment (BREATHE); For Improved Labeling to Terminate Hazards (FILTH); Law Students Association for Buyers Education in Labeling (LABEL); Move to End Deception in Advertising (MEDIA); Students Opposed to Advertised Pollutants (SOAP); and Students Resisting Aerosol Fluorocarbon Emissions (STRAFE) [75]. The organizations began at George Washington University's National Law Center.

GOVERNMENT

Several government agencies are responsible for enforcing federal legislation and dealing with companies that utilize illegal

practices to harm consumers of household products. The major
agencies are: Department of Commerce (DOC); Federal Trade
Commission; Food and Drug Administration (FDA); Health, Education, and Welfare (HEW); Environmental Protection Agency (EPA);
and the Consumer Product Safety Commission. These agencies are
discussed chronologically, based on their date of establishment.

Department of Commerce

The Department of Commerce, founded in 1901 as part of the
Treasury Department, is now a cabinet-level office that includes
the National Bureau of Standards. The department has encouraged
companies to minimize the variety of package sizes they offer on a
voluntary basis. For example, one cough medicine manufacturer
could make up to ten different package sizes. In 1972, DOC established guidelines for the cough medicine industry to follow. It suggested that three or four package sizes would be more suitable to
the consumer and cheaper for the manufacturer [11]. This illustrated
the agency's promotion of uniformity in weights and measures.

The Department of Commerce prints pamphlets on many household products (not by brand name) such as paints, cleaners, and
glues. For instance, a consumer who wanted to find information
on adhesives could write for "Adhesives for Everyday Use" [56].

Federal Trade Commission

The Federal Trade Commission, established in 1914 and
amended in 1938, is empowered to prohibit unfair or deceptive
business practices and contains the Bureau of Consumer Protection.
The commission seeks to prevent deceptive labeling and packaging,
misconceptions, and false claims concerning any food, drug,
cosmetic, or other household product [53].

The FTC constantly has been involved with Listerine because
of assertions made by the manufacturer. During the 1940s, the
FTC tried to stop Listerine from advertising that it could prevent
dandruff, prevent and cure colds, and stop halitosis. The case went
to court, but was not resolved [66]. In 1957, the FTC stopped
Listerine from claiming it could cure the Asian Flu but could not
stop claims about cold prevention [42]. In 1972, the FTC began a
case against Listerine that ended up in the Supreme Court and was
not resolved until April 1978. The Supreme Court ruled that $10
million of advertisements had to contain the phrase, "will not help
prevent colds or sore throats or lessen their severity" [47].

The FTC and Carter's Products, makers of Carter's Little Liver Pills, battled for 16 years. The commission felt the word "liver" should be deleted from the product's name since it had nothing to do with the liver, and that Carter's advertising was false and misleading. In 1959, the California United States Court of Appeals upheld the FTC. The case cost the federal government $1 million [124].

In 1960, the FTC forced Colgate to cease advertising that its dentifrice offered full protection, and it released information as to how truthful toothpaste claims were [46, 58]. Also during 1960, the FTC was able to have the advertising of Anacin, Excedrin, and Bayer changed to reflect the fact that they did not relieve tension [58].

The FTC investigated false deodorant advertising in 1973. Companies claimed deodorants would keep users cool and calm and prevent perspiration. The assertions were found not to be true, and the FTC pressured the companies to alter their advertisements [45]. In addition, the FTC won a 13-year conflict with the makers of Geritol in 1973. The company was told it could not say Geritol cured "tired blood" and was fined $812,000 for misleading advertising [49, 110].

Food and Drug Administration

The Food and Drug Administration, founded in 1931, seeks honest and informative labeling of products as well as safety and proper warnings for hazardous products. The FDA is involved primarily with food, drugs, and cosmetics, and also sets standards for quality, identity, and contents of products.

The FDA did a study in 1960 and found 39 percent of the tested packages to be shortweighted. This problem included soap, laundry detergent, and dishwashing compounds. The packaging industry was quite worried about the situation [31, 111]. In 1962, the FDA further investigated shortweighting and looked at "economic class" violations, where the buyer was cheated out of money by deception. There were 105 seizure cases due to short weight and 28 due to inconspicuous net content and ingredient statements. At the request of President John Kennedy, the FDA began a strict enforcement program of new labeling requirements for hazardous or deceptive household articles [31].

During 1972, soap and detergent manufacturers were told they would have to state the phosphate contents in their products. The manufacturers were reluctant to do so, but consented to FDA wishes [113]. The FDA realized asbestos was a carcinogen in 1973 and began investigating which products contained asbestos. Many cosmetic and toiletry products, such as talcum and face powders, were found to use asbestos as a base or filler. The FDA stepped in to control the asbestos fiber levels used in these household products [39].

In 1973, there were reports that feminine hygiene sprays caused infections and irritations. Gynecologists said soap and water were just as effective and safer. The FDA proposed warning label guidelines so users would be aware of the risks of the sprays [38]. Late in 1975, it was suspected that chloroform, which was used in many cough medicines and mouthwashes, caused cancer [32]. The FDA investigated and initially concluded there was no safety hazard; six months after this, chloroform was banned in all cosmetics and cough medicines because tests revealed it to be a carcinogen. Chloroform was contained in over 2,000 products [27, 33].

The FDA became involved with bubble bath products during early 1977 when some users reported urogenital infections. The FDA proposed regulations warning users of the infections that could be caused [37]. Later in the same year, many cosmetic products applied to the face and eyes were discovered to bring about serious infections. It was possible for some users to go blind if not treated properly. For example, a mascara application wand would pick up micro-organisms when placed on the eyelid. The wand was then returned to the bottle, where the micro-organisms proliferated. An infection would be applied to the eye area as the wand was reused. The FDA wanted manufacturers to add preservatives that would prevent the growth of micro-organisms [41]. On March 15, 1977, the FDA banned the use of bizmuth citrate, a common chemical in cosmetic hair dyes that caused scalp irritation and was suspected of being carcinogenic [28].

Health, Education, and Welfare

The Department of Health, Education, and Welfare, created in 1953, is a cabinet-level department and contains an Office of Consumer Affairs. In 1972, HEW conducted hearings on the Consumer Product Safety Act. The purpose was to set consumer product safety standards. For household products, these concerned flammability and hazardous substances in cleaning products [53].

Environmental Protection Agency

The Environmental Protection Agency was established as an independent agency in 1970. It monitors everything from radiation in the environment to the regulation of chemicals used in the environment. For example, Raid insect spray was monitored to be sure the toxicity level of the pesticide would not be a threat to food or air [53]. In 1972, benzene emissions were added to the EPA's hazardous air pollutants list. As mentioned earlier, benzene was suspected of leading to cancer [26].

During the last few years, the EPA has removed fluorocarbons from household spray-can products. In 1975, there were 300 household aerosol products on store shelves, including insect sprays, cooking pot coatings, oven cleaners, hair sprays, and deodorants. Although the products were convenient, scientists and health officials worried about their usage since incorrect storage could lead to an explosion [122]. In addition, some people experienced eye irritation or respiratory discomfort [102]. Some deaths occurred as teenagers inhaled sprays, such as Pam, to get high. There were also accidental misfirings or misdirected spray angles that resulted in sprays in users' faces [122].

Vinyl chloride, a fluorocarbon propellant, was banned because it was suspected of causing cancer. Other fluorocarbons were banned since they were considered harmful to the earth's ozone layer and could increase the chances of skin cancer. By January 1978, there were no products on store shelves that contained fluorocarbons [30].

Consumer Product Safety Commission

The Consumer Product Safety Commission, created in 1972, protects the public from consumer products that might lead to injury. It evaluates product safety and develops guidelines. In 1974, the CPSC banned a dangerous disposable cigarette lighter that had an 18-inch flame, and set standards for butane lighters. The standards allowed flames to go no higher than six inches [122]. Despite these regulations, on February 14, 1978, a television station in New York broadcast that there were four burnings a day from lighters, and the flames were much higher than eight inches. While the standards existed, enforcement seemed to be a problem [6].

Many issues are still pending before the CPSC. For instance, the acceptability of asbestos in glues and toxic chemicals in paints has not been resolved. Consumers still own products with benzene, since it was not banned in all consumer products until mid-1978 [1]. Homemakers have not been clearly warned about the presence of asbestos in 3,000 products.

Since 1973, the CPSC has issued just three standards. The cigarette lighter was the only household product affected [65]. S. John Byington, chairman of the CPSC, came under harsh criticism and resigned under pressure on February 20, 1978. As of early 1978, the commission had a backlog of 180 cases, many of which involved household products [112].

Major Consumer Legislation

There are nine major federal laws to which the household product must conform: Food, Drug, and Cosmetic Act; Insecticide, Fungicide, and Rodenticide Act; Air Pollution and Prevention and Control Act; Hazardous Substances Labeling Act; Fair Packaging and Labeling Act; Poison Prevention Packaging Act; Consumer Product Safety Act; Consumer Product Warranty Act (Magnuson-Moss); and Toxic Substances Control Act. Many of these laws have been amended because technological advances and new research have shown particular products to be unsafe, faulty, or ineffective. These laws are summarized in chronological order in Table 5.1.

INDUSTRY RESPONSES TO CONSUMERISM

The industry's responses to consumerism have been obtained from secondary and primary research. An examination of these responses follows.

Industry Responses as Reported in the Literature

The household products industry has many trade associations that usually are staffed by executives of the companies they represent. The associations normally keep a low profile and avoid publicity. An examination of trade association responses to consumerism over the last several years shows the roles these groups have assumed.
In 1962, the Toilet Goods Association opposed FTC amendments regarding the labeling of cosmetics. A spokesman said:

> Quite frankly, I do not believe the commission has any
> authority over packaging of cosmetics since there is
> a law that gives the authority to the FDA [123].

During the same year, New York City considered banning the sale of aerosols that contained flammable propellants. The Chemical Specialties Manufacturers Association formed a special committee to lobby and work against the ban. Their efforts were successful [123].

TABLE 5.1

Federal Legislation Affecting Household Products

Legislation	Year Enacted	Key Provisions
Food, Drug, and Cosmetic Act	1906	Regulates the safety of ingredients of many household products, mandates that claims must be proven
Insecticide, Fungicide, and Rodenticide Act	1947	Prevents high levels of poisons that may be toxic to humans and the environment, requires these products to be labeled clearly
Air Pollution and Prevention and Control Act	1955	Protects and enhances air quality, covering household products that emit dangerous substances into the air
Hazardous Substances Act	1960	Regulates hazardous products that may cause harm, injury, or illness as a result of handling or using
Fair Packaging and Labeling Act	1966	Provides basic information, including product identity, place of manufacture, quantity, conspicuous printing, and uniform lettering; requires small products to use inserts for information, rather than labels
Poison Prevention Packaging Act	1970	Prevents children from opening or ingesting products that are dangerous by requiring childproof caps

(continued)

Table 5.1 (continued)

Legislation	Year Enacted	Key Provisions
Consumer Product Safety Act	1972	Protects the public against unreasonable risks of injury associated with consumer products, fosters research and prevention, and provides for recalls of unsafe products
Consumer Product Warranty Act (Magnuson-Moss)	1975	Defines warranties and what may be said in them, distinguishes between full and limited warranties
Toxic Substances Control Act	1976	Requires the government to publish data collected by manufacturers on chemical substances and mixtures and their effect on health and the environment; regulates harmful substances and mixtures, without unnecessary economic barriers to innovation; protects employees from being fired for exposing dangers

Source: Compiled by the author.

Chemical Week, a trade publication, had a 1963 article about deceptive jars with false bottoms. The Toilet Goods Association contended that the jars were not deceptive; in some cases, the jars contained more, not less, product [63]. In 1964, Advertising Age, an industry publication, considered the Rise Shaving Cream case and questioned how far companies could go before deeming advertising deceptive. There also was concern over how far the FTC would go in issues such as this [97].

During 1965, Modern Packaging, an industry publication, voiced its displeasure with the proposed Truth-in-Packaging Bill. In an attempt to stop the bill, Modern Packaging and its supporters sponsored a 50-state survey of weights and measures chiefs, and attempted to work out their own standards for label and quantity statements. The publication hoped this would stop consumer complaints and eliminate the push for the Truth-in-Packaging Bill [121].

In 1966, a Chemical Specialties Manufacturers Association meeting featured two speakers from Union Carbide who talked about improving hair sprays. New ideas were presented for reformulating hair spray chemicals in a manner that users' hair would hold up better in rain and humidity, thus minimizing consumer complaints [67].

The FDA, FTC, and DOC were in the process of amending the new Fair Packaging and Labeling Act in 1967, when the Grocery Manufacturers of America expressed the hope that its members would have the opportunity to regulate the industry [54]. In 1968, an FDA commissioner presented a speech to the Joint Conference on Cosmetic Sciences. He informed the group that members would have to do better jobs of policing themselves and develop improved systems of checks and balances. The commissioner specifically cited microbiological contamination, which caused spoilage and created harmful organisms in cosmetic products [52].

In 1969, Modern Packaging noted concern over the proposed Poison Prevention Packaging Act, which would cover economic poisons involving what the government defined as household chemical products. The packaging industry felt this would be costly to business and the consumer. It also thought the industry was being informally indicted and that the responsibility of poison prevention fell to the final consumer [76].

The Toilet Goods Association expressed dissatisfaction in 1970 about government activity in cosmetic regulation. The government wanted to require firms to prove cosmetics were safe to use. This policy would have forced manufacturers to use expensive laboratory/animal testing on all cosmetic products. The association felt it was already doing a good job in this area and needed no further legislation [69].

Before implementation of the Poison Prevention Packaging Act, a committee was formed under government supervision to determine the best manner for carrying out the act. The packaging industry was represented on this committee [55].

The Cosmetic, Toiletry, and Fragrance Association anticipated legislation in 1972 requiring toiletry manufacturers to list ingredients on their products. It developed its own proposals for self-regulation, which the FDA thought were defensive [105]. At the same time, the Soap and Detergent Association lost a federal court case over Chicago's right to legislate a ban on no-phosphate detergents. The association said the issue interfered with the consumer's right to buy and hindered interstate commerce [103].

Also in 1972, the packaging industry was told it would have to make childproof caps and closures for household chemical products. The industry was reluctant to incorporate the changes, since they would raise packaging costs [34]. However, six years later, the Glass Packaging Institute stated:

> The protective closures that save youngsters' lives by
> keeping them from swallowing hazardous substances
> such as drugs, lye, and furniture polish (substances
> the young can't distinguish from good food) are called
> resistant caps (or CRC's). Developed by the closure
> industry in cooperation with government, CRC's are
> now required by law on all oral prescription drugs and
> on an ever-growing number of household products [51].

According to the Consumer Product Safety Commission, there was a 63-percent drop in aspirin deaths of children under five from 1972 to 1975 [51].

Late in 1972, the drug industry and the FDA clashed over the assertions made by antacid manufacturers. The industry opposed proposed legislation and regulation requiring companies to prove how well their products would reduce acidity levels in stomachs. A spokesman for the Proprietary Association said the regulation was unnecessary, since consumers' past experiences would be used to judge how effective products were [105].

Beginning in 1974, the Cosmetic, Toiletry, and Fragrance Association petitioned the FDA to amend cosmetic labeling regulations involving aerosol propellants and warning labels on hygiene sprays [18]. The head of the association, who was also a Bristol-Myers vice-president, helped negotiate regulations for ingredients and aerosol labeling of hygiene sprays [15]. Three years later, the association lost its bid to exempt fluorocarbon label warnings on small aerosol fragrance bottles [17]. The Toiletry Merchandisers Association, after a long struggle, decided to abide by FDA proposals to phase out most aerosol items having fluorocarbons by 1978 [114]. Manufacturers resisted because of heavy capital investments in this form of packaging.

During the mid-1970s, the Manufacturing Chemists Association tried to prove aerosols posed no threat to the environment. The association also commented that its results would not be believed by the government if they showed no threat. It therefore called upon the government to prove or disprove the impact of aerosols [21].

In 1975, the Soap and Detergent Association was investigated for anticompetitive tactics. An industry spokesman called the allegations untrue and said the FTC investigation would show how intense competition was within the industry.

The drug industry wanted the FTC to withdraw strict labeling and ingredients laws on over-the-counter medicines in 1976 [77]. The National Association of Broadcasters and the Proprietary Association felt warning labels on items such as aspirin and antacids would reduce the effectiveness of their advertising. The FTC defended its action by criticizing new industry maladies like "file cabinet headaches" [16]. In April 1976, the Cosmetic, Toiletry, and Fragrance Association denied that hair dyes could be linked to cancer. It felt the products were safe, and had been proven so over a period of years [16]. The Toiletry and Cosmetic Association started to develop an ingredient safety review program in 1976. This program of self-regulation filed information, evaluated ingredients, and assisted small producers with limited laboratory resources [13].

The January 1977 issue of Modern Packaging contained an article on the government's packaging legislation activity. The publication said no type of packaging was safe from consumer and government pressure and that there already was too much legislation [72]. The May 1977 issue of Paperboard Packaging reported on the Environmental Protection Agency and its interest in containers used in household products. The Paperboard Packaging Council and the American Paper Institute monitored an EPA project on glass and plastic packaging; they thought paper was superior, since it was biodegradable and the others were not [80].

Later in 1977, the Cosmetics, Toiletry, and Fragrance Association recommended to members and other manufacturers how they could print ozone damage warnings on small labels away from principal labels. At the same time, the Chemical Specialties Manufacturers Association tried to raise $150,000 from members to launch a public relations campaign supporting fluorocarbons [1].

Trade Association Responses to Primary Study

Fourteen trade associations in the household products industry were asked to participate in a survey on consumerism. Four associations answered the questionnaire: Glass Packaging Institute (GPI), National Soft Drink Association (NSDA), Paperboard Packaging Council (PPC), and the Soap and Detergent Association (SDA). One association, Aluminum Foil Container Manufacturers Association, sent a short letter and literature, but the material did not relate to consumerism. Nine associations did not respond, despite two requests: American Brush Manufacturers Association, American Pet Products Manufacturers Association, Can Manufacturers Institute, Composite Can and Tube Institute, National Association of Glue Manufacturers, National Broom and Mop Council, Pesticide Formulators Association, Plastic Containers Manufacturers Institute, and the Toiletry Merchandisers Association.

The four associations' attitudes toward the consumer movement are basically positive. However, the tone of the responses reflects a degree of skepticism, such as the Glass Packaging Institute referring to "the so-called consumer movement."

The associations believe operations are affected by consumerism, particularly through increased costs. Two have a position or panel for dealing with the consumer movement. Three of the associations send representatives to appear before the government. The associations usually are not responsive to speaker requests by consumer groups, although on occasion a representative is sent. Predictions about the long-term impact of consumerism vary from declining in importance to generating new regulations.

Table 5.2 contains the condensed answers of the four participating associations. Each association did not answer each question. Open-ended responses were interpreted by the author.

COMPANY RESPONSES TO CONSUMERISM

The responses of household products companies to consumerism have been collected from secondary and primary data. An examination of these responses follows.

Company Responses as Reported in the Literature

Household products companies have acted in a manner similar to their industry representatives: they have maintained low profiles

TABLE 5.2

Household Products Trade Association Responses to Study

Question 1	Generally speaking, how does your association feel about the consumer movement?
GPI	There is concern about the "so-called consumer movement."
NSDA	Consumer interests and concerns are welcome.
PPC	The consumer movement is supported. There is worry about some "fringe elements" in the movement who feel packaging is wasteful.
SDA	Consumers who express their views are highly beneficial to society in general. There are reservations about groups who use consumerism to promote their own interests.
Question 2	How has the consumer movement affected the companies that belong to your association, in regard to household products?
GPI	Consumer/environmental legislation regarding mandatory deposits on beverage containers in Oregon has resulted in the loss of 450 jobs in the glass bottle and can industry.
NSDA	Companies are required to spend more money and energy on items such as returnable bottles, leading to higher costs for consumers.
PPC	An example of the effect is a company that was prohibited from putting a dishwashing detergent in a milk-carton-type package due to possible confusion by minors.
SDA	Companies interview consumers to determine their needs and communicate with them about resultant changes.
Question 3	Has the association created a position, panel, or department to deal with the effects of the consumer movement?
GPI	None is indicated.
NSDA	No, the organization is small.
PPC	There is no formal position, but there is a Public Affairs Department to deal with consumer issues.
SDA	There is no formal position, but there is a Consumer Information Department.

(continued)

Table 5.2 (continued)

Question 4	Does the association provide representatives to appear before government committees examining consumer issues?
GPI	No provision for representatives is indicated in the association's response.
NSDA	Officers testify before Congress, FDA, FTC, EPA, and other government bodies. They cooperate and help develop standards to protect the public.
PPC	The association may petition or appear before government groups, when the matter is of particular interest to the paperboard packaging industry.
SDA	Representatives appear before federal, state, and local governments regarding soap and detergent issues.
Question 5	Does the association provide speakers to appear before national and/or local consumer organizations?
GPI	This cannot be determined from the association's response.
NSDA	As a rule, none is provided, but speakers do attend meetings of consumer organizations like the Consumers Federation of America.
PPC	Speakers are provided to appear before local and national consumer organizations.
SDA	Due to the organization's small size, there is no regular program. Occasionally staff members present talks when invited.
Question 6	What do you perceive to be the long-term impact of consumerism on the industry you represent?
GPI	In some states, such as Washington, the industry is levied a tax to support a "Litter Control Act." This increases the industry's awareness of issues, but will eventually lead to higher costs for consumers.
NSDA	There will be a long-range effect. For the effect to be positive, consumers, industry, and government must work together.
PPC	There is uncertainty about the long-term effect, since it is unclear which way consumerism will go. There will probably be demand for additional printed information on packages and contents due to consumer interest.
SDA	When consumer groups represent legitimate interests of people, consumerism will help the dialogue between manufacturers and consumers.

Source: Compiled by the author.

144

and avoided publicity. A review of a cross-section of company responses over the last 30 years shows the orientation they have taken.

During the 1940s, slack-full packages, larger than what appeared to be in them, were a problem. FDA regulations governed how much a product could be slack-filled, and most companies responded to government pressure to eliminate the problem. For example, Bristol-Myers and Lambert Pharmaceutical made it possible to reduce toothpaste carton volume by up to 54 percent. As a result, paper was saved, a better package was made, and the government appreciated the cooperation [62].

In 1946, toothpaste companies, including Colgate-Palmolive, reluctantly changed their advertising to eliminate claims of stopping halitosis. Ipana, Pepsodent, and Iodent also were involved. Colgate-Palmolive had to defend its advertising again in 1960, this time regarding Colgate Rapid Shave and Colgate toothpaste with Gardol. Also in 1960, Purex decided to develop a more honest advertising campaign [20, 86].

Ever since it introduced Crest toothpaste, Procter & Gamble advertised that test results proved the product was better than any other toothpaste. But in 1962, the company stopped this type of advertising since the results could not be proven [85]. Merck Pharmaceutical, maker of Sucrets throat lozenges, signed a 1964 consent order agreeing to stop advertising that its product killed staph germs [68].

In 1967, Colgate-Palmolive recalled some Ajax laundry detergent after consumers experienced a "little problem with one small batch." The company estimated refund costs of $250,000 to $750,000 [104]. During mid-1973, Colgate, Lever Brothers, and Procter & Gamble tried to prevent Chicago from banning phosphate detergents; the companies lost. At the same time, the three companies decided it was cheaper to abandon Dade County, Florida, than defend themselves in court [14]. Within a week, Colgate changed its policy and decided to sell nonphosphate detergents in Dade County [82].

During 1973, Miles Laboratories, maker of Alka-Seltzer, was criticized by the FTC for false and misleading advertising that resulted in consumers buying a medicine for the wrong illness. Labels were changed to portray more accurately the uses of the product [104]. Also in this year, Gillette recalled two new deodorants that caused irritations on test subjects. To avoid consumer complaints and litigation, the company thought it best to withdraw the products from the market [50].

Prior to the uproar over fluorocarbons, S. C. Johnson & Company used the ingredient in its furniture wax line. In response to consumer pressure and pending legislation, the company dropped the propellants in 1975 [96]. In 1976, a Senate committee wanted to see more informative labeling on antacid products such as Gelusil, Pepto-Bismol, and Alka-Seltzer. Miles Laboratory said no extra information was needed. The committee felt Alka-Seltzer was an antacid with aspirin, which could upset a user's stomach. In response, Miles introduced a new form of Alka-Seltzer without aspirin [44].

In 1977, it seemed that Bristol-Myers had two attitudes toward consumerism. The company refrained from using fluorocarbons and was quite vocal in its anti-aerosol campaign [1]. In contrast, its booklet on product information, edited by Bess Myerson, stated there was "no evidence that hair dyes pose a threat to health" [3]. Hair dyes represented 12 to 15 percent of the company's gross revenue.

Company Responses to Primary Study

A mail survey was sent to ten household products companies, five of whom answered the questions: Dow Chemical, DuPont, Procter & Gamble (PG), Texize, and WD-40. Five other companies did not respond, despite two requests: Devcon Corporation, Drackett, Johnson Wax, Luminall Paints, and 3M.

The five participating companies indicate they have formal policies for processing complaints and make efforts to resolve them. Three of the companies have consumer complaint departments. Two have in-house consumer advocates. There are some educational programs, with emphasis on brochures and product information. All the companies have established procedures to ensure high quality products and services. Four of the companies do not indicate whether consumer regulations have had an impact on their operations and provide little information about their reactions to consumer pressures. Three of the companies feel consumerism has a positive effect on their operations. Overall, the companies are becoming more consumer-conscious and responsive to government and consumer pressure.

Table 5.3 shows the individual answers of the responding companies. These answers have been summarized and classified by the author.

THE OVERALL EFFECTS OF CONSUMERISM

In this section, the impact of consumerism in the household products industry is detailed, and the effectiveness of the consumer movement is evaluated.

TABLE 5.3

Household Products Company Responses to Study

Question 1	The Consumer: What type of policy do you have for handling complaints? Do you have a consumer complaint department? Is there a consumer advocate in-house? Do you have an educational program or participate in educational programs for consumers?
Dow	There is a program called "Product Stewardship," which regards quality in manufacturing, care of the environment, and concern for the ultimate disposal of products. Complaints are individually handled by each department. There is a consumer communications group within the Health and Consumer Products Department, covering products like Saran Wrap and Dow Bathroom Cleaner. The company does not have an in-house consumer advocate or formal educational programs.
DuPont	Every complaint and question is handled on an individual basis. Problems are investigated, and remedies and adjustments sought. The preservation of customer goodwill is important. There is no consumer complaint department, but a consumer affairs coordinator oversees complaints. Several persons serve as consumer advocates, including a technical manager and a legal advisor. Consumer brochures are developed and published.
PG	The policy is to resolve complaints quickly, and respond to every consumer and inquiry. A consumer section is responsible for interfacing with consumers and utilizes a toll-free telephone number. There is no in-house consumer advocate. The response is unclear as to whether or not educational programs are sponsored.
Texize	Each individual consumer contact, including complaints, is analyzed and a response provided. A consumer relations department, under the vice-president of sales, handles complaints. The Director of Consumer Relations is an in-house advocate who actively represents consumers in planning and marketing. A teaching kit with a sound filmstrip, handouts, and other

---

(continued)

Table 5.3 (continued)

	aids is available for educational and consumer groups. Other devices are planned.
WD–40	The company has only 21 employees and attempts to resolve every problem individually. There is no complaint department; complaints are processed by the technical director and the company president. The firm has no in–house advocate, and its response does not indicate if it provides educational materials or programs.
Question 2	The Product: What type of product–related information is made available to the public? Are you modifying or changing your products in response to consumerism? What procedures do you follow to ensure product and service quality?
Dow	The company is willing to provide information about products. It is aware of the consumer and considers changing a product to satisfy customers. A quality assurance program verifies that all products meet company, government, and industry specifications.
DuPont	The Product Information Service routes questions to the person best able to answer them. Consumers are important, but changes are usually caused by technical developments and market research, not outside influences. There is a quality assurance program, and consumer satisfaction is occasionally monitored.
PG	The Customer Services Department provides product information when asked. Products are changed in response to consumers. An example is the reformulation of soap ingredients to satisfy different water conditions. An extensive quality assurance program includes market research, chemical analysis, and simulated household conditions.
Texize	The Customer Relations Department handles requests for product information. Product changes or modifications are made when consumer responses indicate they are necessary. A Quality Assurance Department uses computerized checks and random sampling to verify proper quality.

(continued)

WD-40	Information is available through advertising brochures. The company's response to consumer requests for modifications is not indicated, nor is its quality assurance procedure.
Question 3	What type of consumer regulations affect your operations? How do you respond to outside consumer pressures? How do you evaluate the effect of consumerism on your company?
Dow	Dow's response does not indicate what regulations have an effect. It applies the tenets of "Product Stewardship," meaning concern for the consumer. The company does not say how it evaluates consumerism.
DuPont	Consumer regulations have minimal impact; labeling and maintenance have improved. The company does not reveal how it responds to outside consumer pressures. Consumerism has helped improve some products, but also has caused higher prices.
PG	The company does not indicate what regulations affect the company, how it responds to outside consumer pressure, or how it evaluates the effect of consumerism.
Texize	All regulations pertaining to advertising, labeling, promotion, etc.—that relate to the industry—have an impact on company operations. The Consumer Relations Department is responsible for adherence. Consumer pressure has increased awareness of and participation in consumer education. Consumerism has increased the company's efforts to deal with the consumer.
WD-40	The company's response does not indicate how regulations have affected it or how the firm responds to consumerism. The company is conscious of consumer liability claims.

Source: Compiled by the author.

Impact of Consumerism

Consumerism in the household products industry has resulted in the creation of trade associations to protect and represent companies. The associations view consumerism as a mixed blessing. It hinders consumers' freedom of choice, causes people to lose jobs, increases costs, and leads to excessive government control. Some associations have advocated self-regulation in order to limit government intervention.

Associations are particularly distressed about the contradictory laws in different states. For example, Oregon requires soft drinks to be sold only in glass-deposit bottles. Some states ban pull-tab cans. Other states allow all types of packaging [74].

Industry associations have increased their research into consumer desires and recommended changes in products to meet these desires. Technical, legal, and market research are now used to measure the long-term effects of household products in terms of health, environment, and safety. Senator Moss of Utah has stated that ten years ago the industry would have reacted negatively to any proposed consumer legislation; today it is more accommodating and works toward reasonable solutions [70]. Others are not so positive. Frank McLaughlin of the Office of Consumer Affairs finds the industry is still antagonistic toward consumerism, with a "modest trend" toward the movement [70].

The impact of consumerism on household products companies has varied, depending on the company. DuPont feels it has not been hampered by too many consumer regulations, but its products have improved and prices have risen. Texize, the maker of Fantastik spray cleaner, thinks consumerism has had a profound effect on its operations, requiring adherence to a number of regulations and the creation of a consumer relations department.

Procter & Gamble, Colgate-Palmolive, and Lever Brothers have all been involved with one or more consumer issues over the last 40 years, as they have been charged with deceptive packages, hazardous ingredients, misleading advertising, and short-weighting. Because of these practices, new laws and agencies have developed. As a result, small companies, like WD-40, question how a company can be held liable for injury when a minor goes through a neighbor's garbage and accidentally swallows a hazardous substance.

An executive director for Consumers Union sees companies making superficial changes due to consumerism. According to this spokesperson, in-house consumer advocates have no tools or power. This view is supported by Consumer Federation of America. Many companies, including Johnson Wax, disagree and feel they are making real efforts to please consumers [70].

Currently, consumerism in the household products industry is in a period of nongrowth and on shaky financial ground. As in the recent past, products are recalled and hazardous products appropriately labeled.

Evaluation of Consumerism

Consumerism has had a significant impact on the household products industry, although there is no consumer group whose main interest is household products. According to a former director of the National Association of Manufacturers, consumerism may have a "limited life" because it has a hard-to-define constituency and disorganized membership [70]. This may account for many companies' defensive rather than progressive strategies.

Consumer legislation has led to safer and more informative products. Large companies, however, exert substantial power and are rarely penalized by fine or imprisonment of executives for violations of laws. Legislation normally is oriented to "long-run efficacy" [19]. Companies realize the punishment by government is not overburdening.

Consumerism in the household products industry has had costs as well as benefits. Most product modifications result in higher prices to consumers, a factor harshly criticized by business. Costly legislation, such as the Consumer Product Safety Act, has not proven effective as the CPSC has initiated very few actions or policies affecting household products. This agency must develop and enforce substantially more regulations if it is to justify its expenditures. The CPSC also could help remove the confusing and contradictory state laws on product safety by specifying clear federal standards.

In terms of regulation and self-regulation, there seems to be a balance. There are now nine laws that govern the household products industry; most were enacted because companies did not need consumer and legislator warnings. Today, the industry is more aware of consumerism and employs trade associations to police itself and monitor consumer issues in order to minimize legislation. There is no significant legislation concerning household products that is pending at this time, with the exception of an FDA law regarding hair dyes.

FUTURE OUTLOOK

Consumerism will not grow, and active consumer groups will stay approximately the same size in the future. Issues will be the same as in the past: safety, information, fair weighting, and honesty. Because of the relative satisfaction with household products, their widespread availability, and low prices, the consumer movement will concentrate in other areas.

There will be little increase in government legislation. Existing agencies will be given more authority to enforce the nine laws already enacted, particularly those involving safety and hazardous substances.

The industry will have to adhere to tighter safety standards. A number of companies will "cease attempting to annihilate one another, and begin the process of rational informed debate" [74]. This will result in more self-regulation. Companies will realize that although consumerism may be bothersome and costly, ignoring it will result in lost sales and increased government involvement. Industry and company representatives will continue to speak out on issues they feel place the industry in a bad light, and fight against consumer legislation.

RECOMMENDATIONS

Recommendations are offered for consumer groups, government, the industry, and individual household products companies.

Consumer Groups

Since there are no consumer groups directly involved with household products, organizations such as Consumers' Research should become more involved and apply pressure for informative labeling, uniform sizes and weights, and safer ingredients. Washington-based consumer groups should participate more actively in hearings and lobby for legislation. They should concentrate on better implementation of existing laws and regulations, and push for faster governmental decision making, particularly those involving hazardous products. Consumer groups also could press for a law requiring products to be proven safe prior to their introduction, which is the reverse of the current policy.

Government

Existing laws and agencies are strong enough to do an effective job of protecting consumers and their rights, but some agencies are not aggressive enough in pursuing violations or preventing and stopping potential health hazards. Agencies should develop programs, enforce laws, and act quicker. There should be more cooperation among government, industry, and consumers.

The Industry

Recent legislation and the consumer movement have raised the industry's consciousness; nonetheless, it is still leery of consumerism. This could be resolved by having trade associations cooperate and communicate more with consumer groups. The industry should remember that consumerism was born out of neglect and became more responsive to consumer desires. If an issue arises, the trade associations involved should try to resolve it through self-regulation. There should be less fighting with government agencies, since it lowers the industry's image and credibility.

Companies

Many companies are making conscientious efforts to improve their public images, but there needs to be more research on consumer desires and powerful in-house consumer advocates. Companies must stop fighting against practices that protect consumer safety and rights. Good communications and responsiveness to consumer problems will increase companies' success and lessen government intervention.

BIBLIOGRAPHY

1. "Aerosols under Siege." Drug and Cosmetic Industry 120 (June 1977), pp. 28-33, 38-40.

2. "Benzene Banned by CPSC." CBS Evening News, Channel 2, New York, N.Y. (April 27, 1978).

3. "Bess Myerson Chided on Booklet Saying Hair Coloring Harmless." New York Times (November 4, 1977), p. 30.

4. "Big Three Choose Chicago for Phosphate Showdown." Chemical Week (June 7, 1972), p. 16.

5. "Bromide Backfire; Five Makers of Headache Remedies Cited by F.T.C." Business Week (October 31, 1942), p. 22.

6. "Butane Lighters." Channel 2 News, New York, N.Y. (February 14, 1978).

7. Campbell, Persia. Consumer Representation in the New Deal. New York: Columbia University Press, 1940, pp. 107-09.

8. "Colgate Defends Gardol Ads, Hits F.T.C. Bad Faith." Advertising Age 31 (February 1, 1960), pp. 1-2.

9. "Colgate Told Not to Imply Full Protection; Past Cooperation Isn't Proof Gardol Ads Won't Offend Again." Advertising Age 31 (August 8, 1970), pp. 1-2.

10. "Comments to F.D.A. Protesting the Continued Marketing of Unproven Cough and Cold Drugs." Washington, D.C., Health Research Group, #429 (December 8, 1976).

11. "Commerce Department Guides Will Cut Number of Liquid Cough Products." American Druggist (January 24, 1972), p. 28.

12. "Congressional Testimony on EPA and the Testing of Pesticides (Using DDVP and the No-Pest Strip As a Case Study)." Washington, D.C., Health Research Group, #376 (April 9, 1976).

13. "Cosmetic and Toiletry Industry Develops Industry Safety Review Program." Commerce America (November 11, 1976), p. S1.

14. "Cosmetic Jars Are Deceptive, Says California Official." Advertising Age 34 (January 28, 1963), p. 2.

15. "Cosmetic, Toiletry and Fragrance Association Assesses Exemption for New Label Regulations." Drug and Cosmetic Industry 116 (April 1975), pp. 42-43.

16. "Cosmetic, Toiletry and Fragrance Association Denies Cancer Link in Hair Dyes." Chemical Market Reporter (April 5, 1976), p. 1.

17. "Cosmetic, Toiletry and Fragrance Association Loses Aerosol Appeal." Drug and Cosmetic Industry (March 1976), p. 71.

18. "Cosmetic, Toiletry and Fragrance Association Petitions the F.D.A. to Amend Cosmetic Labeling Regulations." Chemical Market Reporter (January 14, 1974), p. 21.

19. Creighton, Lucy Black. *Pretenders to the Throne*. Toronto/ London: Lexington Books, D. C. Heath & Co., 1976.

20. Cunningham, R. M. "Toothpaste Ads vs. the Truth." *New Republic* LL (March 4, 1946), pp. 313-15.

21. Davis, Donald A. "Ozone Ordeal Goes On." *Drug and Cosmetic Industry* 116 (February 1975), pp. 74ff.

22. "Deodorant Allergy Causes Tumor Growth." *Science Newsletter* 72 (November 30, 1957), p. 344.

23. "Detergent Industry Investigated by F.T.C. for Anti-Competition." *Wall Street Journal* (June 13, 1975), p. 2.

24. Dow Chemical Company Literature and Response (February 1978).

25. DuPont Chemical Company Literature and Response (February 1978).

26. "EPA Includes Benzene Emissions on 'Hazardous Air Pollutants' List, Permanent Standards to Come." *Wall Street Journal* (June 1, 1972), pp. 2ff.

27. "F.D.A. Bans Chloroform for Cosmetics and Cough Medicines." *Journal of Commerce* (June 30, 1976), p. 5.

28. "F.D.A. Bans Use of Bismuth Citrate in Cosmetic Hair Dyes." *Chemical Market Reporter* (November 21, 1977), p. 4.

29. "F.D.A. Criticizes Drug Blending in Cold Preparations." *Advertising Age* (February 9, 1976), p. 1.

30. "F.D.A. and E.P.A. Propose Time Table to Phase Out Fluorocarbons by April 15, 1978." *Wall Street Journal* (May 12, 1977), p. 1.

31. "F.D.A. Is Casting Vigilant Eye at Groceries and a Glare Fall on Soaps, Washing Compounds." *Oil, Paint and Drug Reporter* 18 (March 26, 1962), p. 54.

32. "F.D.A. May Ban Chloroform Use in Cough Medicines, Mouthwashes and Related Products." *New York Times* (December 31, 1975), p. 4.

33. "F.D.A. Says Chloroform Drugs Will Stay on Market, No Evidence of Any Safety Hazard." Chemical Market Reporter (January 5, 1976), p. 3.

34. "F.D.A. Order for Child-Proof Closures on Household Chemicals to Raise Packaging Costs." Chemical Week (October 25, 1972), p. 21.

35. "F.D.A. Outlines Rules for Listing Package Contents." Advertising Age 38 (March 20, 1967), pp. 1ff.

36. "F.D.A.'s Panel Urges Tougher Restrictions on Analgesic Ads." Advertising Age (September 25, 1976), pp. 1, 8.

37. "F.D.A. Proposes Warning Labels for Bubble Bath Products." Household & Personal Products Industry (March 1977), p. 8.

38. "F.D.A. Proposes Warning Labels for Feminine Sprays." Wall Street Journal (June 21, 1973), p. 8.

39. "F.D.A. to Control Asbestos Fibers in Cosmetics and Toiletries." Chemical Week (March 7, 1973), p. 13.

40. "F.D.A. Urges Warning Labels for Hair Dye." New York Times (January 5, 1978), p. B10.

41. "F.D.A. Wants Mascara and Other Eye Cosmetics to Aid Preservatives." Wall Street Journal (October 11, 1977), p. 23.

42. "Flu and Fingernails." Consumer Reports 23 (May 1958), pp. 236-37.

43. Friedman, Monroe. "Consumers Use of Informational Aids in Supermarkets." Journal of Consumer Affairs (Summer 1972), pp. 72-89.

44. "F.T.C. May Extend Label Warning for Antacid Ads." Wall Street Journal (April 6, 1976), p. 6.

45. "F.T.C. Orders Antiperspirant Ad Maker to Document Claims." Wall Street Journal (May 25, 1973), p. 1.

46. "F.T.C. Releases Toothpaste Ad Data." Advertising Age (July 24, 1972), p. 1.

47. "F.T.C. Upheld on Listerine's Ads as Supreme Court Bars a Review." New York Times (April 4, 1978), p. 3.

48. "F.T.C. Widens Sphere; Assumes Jurisdiction Over Misleading Labeling." Business Week (May 11, 1940), p. 44.

49. "Geritol's Bitter Pill; F.T.C. Complaints Against Advertising." Time 101 (February 5, 1973), p. 62.

50. "Gillette to Recall Two New Antiperspirants." Wall Street Journal (October 2, 1973), p. 13.

51. Glass Packaging Institute Response and Literature. Pamphlet on Closure Tops, Washington, D.C.

52. "Goddard to Cosmetic Makers: More Self-Regulation Needed." Drug and Cosmetic Industry 102 (May 1968), p. 66.

53. Government Manual, 1977-78. Office of the Federal Register, National Archives and Records Service. Under G.S.A., pp. 249-540.

54. "Government Guidelines, Federal, State, and Local Actions." Modern Packaging 50 (May 1977), pp. 195ff.

55. "Government Guidelines, Federal, State, and Local Actions." Modern Packaging 44 (July 1971), p. 80.

56. Guide to Federal Consumer Services. Washington, D.C.: Office of Consumer Affairs, Executive Office of the President, p. 18.

57. "Hazards of Painting." Engineering Record 68 (November 8, 1913), p. 509.

58. "Headache Remedy; F.T.C. Complaints Against Analgesic Advertising." Time 99 (May 1, 1972), p. 48.

59. Henderson, Yandell. "Household Health Hazards." Scientific Monthly 33 (July 1933), pp. 63-64.

60. "House Kills Revised Consumer Agency Bill." Advertising Age (November 7, 1977), p. 12.

61. "How Can Deceptive Packaging Be Controlled or Eliminated?" (Symposium). Modern Packaging 35 (October 1961), pp. 67-68.

62. Jannsen, W. F. "The Slack-Fill Problem." Modern Packaging 22 (April 1949), pp. 144-47ff.

63. "Jars Get into a Jam." Chemical Week 92 (March 9, 1963), pp. 47-49.

64. "Kastor-Hilton Is Fined $50,000 for Regimen Ad Role." Advertising Age 36 (January 28, 1965), pp. 1ff.

65. Kurtz, Howie. "This Commission May Be Hazardous to Your Health." Newsday (February 20, 1978), p. 31.

66. "Listerine Test, F.T.C. Action Against Lambert Pharmacal Company." Business Week (April 18, 1942), p. 50.

67. MacFarland, J. H., and Scott, R. J. "Formulating Hairsprays to Satisfy the Consumer." Drug and Cosmetic Industry 98 (February 1966), p. 41.

68. "Merck Replies to F.T.C. Sucrets Complaint; Defends Ad Warning." Advertising Age 35 (October 12, 1964), p. 84.

69. "Microbial Contamination—F.D.A., Industry Views Are Still Far Apart." Drug and Cosmetic Industry 107 (November 1970), pp. 38ff.

70. Miller, William H. "Consumerism on the Wane?" Industry Week (June 28, 1976), pp. 35-38.

71. Moody's Industrial News Reports 49 (April 4, 1978), pp. 2,650-938.

72. Mullins, P. E. "There Are No Safe Packages." Modern Packaging 50 (January 16, 1977), p. 16.

73. Nadel, Mark V. The Politics of Consumer Protection. New York: Bobbs-Merrill, 1971, pp. 35-41.

74. National Soft Drink Association Response and Literature. Quote from Letter (January 1978).

75. National Trade and Professional Associations of the United States and Canada and Labor Unions. Washington, D.C.: Columbia Books, 1977.

76. "Next U.S. Goal: Childsafe Containers." Modern Packaging 42 (July 1969), p. 36.

77. "Over-the-Counter Drug Producers Want F.T.C. to Withdraw Advertising Rule." Chemical Marketing Reporter (March 1, 1976), p. 7.

78. "Package Magic." Consumer Reports (May 1978), p. 132.

79. Paperboard Packaging Council Response and Literature (February 1978).

80. "Paperboard Rated Unfavorably in EPA Study Comparing Materials for Milk Containers." Modern Packaging 62 (May 1972), pp. 48ff.

81. Petition to CPSC to Ban All Products Containing Benzene, Including Some Paint Removers and Rubber Cement Because Benzene Causes Leukemia. Washington, D.C.: Health Research Group (May 5, 1977).

82. "Phosphate Washout." Chemical Week (June 6, 1972), p. 16.

83. "Poison Headache Remedy—Bichloride Tablets." New York Times (May 30, 1913), p. 6.

84. Policy Literature from Consumers' Research.

85. "Procter & Gamble Accepts Consent Order from F.T.C. On Ad Claim for Crest." Advertising Age 33 (March 5, 1962), pp. 3ff.

86. "Pure Purex Ads; Soap Company Adopts an Honesty Policy." Broadcasting 58 (May 9, 1960), p. 32.

87. "Recommendation to F.D.A. on Alka-Seltzer Ad Would Hurt." Wall Street Journal (November 11, 1972), p. 8.

88. "Regimen Maker, Kastor-Hilton Indicted in New York." Advertising Age 31 (June 20, 1960), pp. 3ff.

89. "Residue on Clothes." Consumers' Research (February 1978), p. 3.

90. Response from Federation of Homemakers, from letter dated February 17, 1978.

91. Rohan, T. M. "Warning Sounded, Make It Safe; Jury Claims Against Manufacturing by Those Using Their Products Continue to Rise." Iron Age 199 (February 23, 1967), p. 43.

92. Rorty, J. "Consumers vs. the N.R.A." Nation (March 14, 1954), pp. 295-97.

93. ____. "Consumers vs. the N.R.A." Nation 138 (March 21, 1934), pp. 322-24.

94. Schlink, F. J., and Chase, Stuart. Your Money's Worth: A Study of the Waste of the Consumer Dollar. New York: Macmillan, 1927.

95. Schlink, F. J., and Kollet, Arthur. "Poison for Profit." Nation 135 (December 21, 1932), pp. 608-10.

96. "S. C. Johnson & Son To Drop Fluorocarbons Propellant from Consumer Products." Wall Street Journal (June 19, 1975), p. 29.

97. Seligman, D. "Presents the Great Sandpaper Shave, A Real Life Story of Truth in Advertising." Fortune 70 (December 1964), pp. 130-33ff.

98. "Shades of Tugwell, New York City Board of Health Proposes Stringent Drug, Cosmetic, and Advertising Control." Business Week (October 19, 1935), p. 22.

99. "Should the Cosmetic Label Tell It Like It Really Is?" Chemical Week (January 12, 1972), p. 37.

100. "Silver Care Products." Consumer Reports (February 1978), p. 104.

101. Sinclair, Upton. The Jungle. New York: Doubleday, 1906.

102. "Skin Irritation, Inhalation Toxicity Studies of Aerosols Using Methylene Chloride." Drug and Cosmetic Industry 120 (January 1977), pp. 238-40.

103. "Soap and Detergent Association Attacks Legality of Chicago's Phosphate Ban." Chemical Week (June 7, 1972), p. 16.

104. "Some Ajax Is Withdrawn As Users Complain." Advertising Age 38 (August 7, 1967), p. 1.

105. Spivak, Jonathon. "F.D.A. and Drug Industry Headed for Clash over Effectiveness of Antacid Products." Wall Street Journal (November 27, 1972), p. 8.

106. Standard & Poor's Industry Survey (March 2, 1978), p. H22.

107. Standard & Poor's Industry Survey 145 (November 24, 1977), p. H5.

108. Steinfield, J. L. "Behind the Great Phosphate Flap." Reader's Digest 103 (November 1973), pp. 170-74.

109. Texize Chemical Company Response and Literature (February 1978).

110. "That Reckless Feeling, F.T.C. Crackdown on Geritol Advertising." Newsweek 81 (February 5, 1973), p. 78.

111. "30% of Packages Shortweighted, F.D.A. Study Finds." Advertising Age 31 (July 11, 1960), p. 106.

112. Thomas, J. "Performance of Consumer Agency Disappoints Its Early Supporters." New York Times (January 30, 1978), p. A1.

113. "To Accept F.D.A. Order on Labeling Household Products; Procter & Gamble." Advertising Age (May 10, 1972), p. 1.

114. "Toiletries Manufacturers Ready to Abide by F.D.A. Proposals to Phase Out Most Aerosol Items." Daily News (October 18, 1976), p. 5.

115. "Toiletries, Soap; Ground Rules Set on Package Law." Oil, Paint and Drug Reporter 193 (March 25, 1968), pp. 4ff.

116. U.S. Code Annotated. New York: West Publishing. These texts contain all consumer laws applicable to the household products industry.

117. Veblen, Thorstein. The Theory of the Leisure Class. New York: Macmillan, 1915.

118. "Vitamins Rebuffed; F.D.A. and F.T.C. Opposed to Claims for Vitamin Content of Face Creams." Business Week (September 20, 1941), p. 30.

119. WD-40 Company Literature and Response (December 1977).

120. "What Is False Advertising? F.T.C. Case Against Good Housekeeping." Business Week (December 23, 1939), pp. 24-26.

121. "Who Needs the Hart Bill?" Modern Packaging 38 (January 1965), pp. 83ff.

122. Wolf, Alvin. American Consumers: Is Their Anger Justified? Englewood Cliffs, N.J.: Prentice-Hall, 1977.

123. "Won't Ban the Bombs (N.Y.C. Rules on Flammable Aerosol Propellants)." Chemical Week 97 (July 14, 1962), p. 42.

124. "Word: Carter's Little Liver Pills." Time 73 (June 29, 1959), p. 46.

6

CONSUMERISM AND LEAD, ASBESTOS, AND FLUOROCARBONS

Paul R. Saueracker

INTRODUCTION

Lead, asbestos, and fluorocarbons have been used in consumer products for many years. While the occupational health problems associated with lead and asbestos have been known for quite a while, the possible harmful effects of fluorocarbons have been known for about six or seven years. In recent years, the use of these minerals and chemicals in consumer products has been intensely analyzed. Research has influenced many manufacturers to reduce or replace lead, asbestos, and fluorocarbons in a number of consumer products. Three specific industries form the basis of this investigation: paint and coatings (lead), building products (asbestos), and cosmetics and toiletries (asbestos, fluorocarbons).

Paints and coatings containing lead, which may be used on interior or exterior surfaces that are accessible to children or their toys and furniture, are potentially hazardous. The ingestion of paint chips by children can cause anemia, abdominal colic, brain damage, and death [51]. The total paint and coatings industry produced 965 million gallons of paints and coatings with a value of almost $5 billion in 1976 [68]. Four companies accounted for 32 percent of all production: Sherwin-Williams, DuPont, PPG, and SCM [49].

Asbestos fibers are used in vinyl-asbestos flooring products, and can represent up to 30 percent of the total weight of the product. As the products wear or are removed when replaced, asbestos fibers may be released into the environment and ingested by consumers. This may lead to asbestosis, asbestotic pneumoconiosis, and meso-thelial tumors, primary malignant tumors of the pleura and peri-toneum [4]. Total 1976 sales in the resilient floor-covering market were $1.7 billion. Vinyl-asbestos floor coverings accounted for about 40 percent of these sales [44]. The major manufacturers are Armstrong Cork, GAF, Flintkote, and Congoleum.

Another building use of asbestos fibers is in patching and spackling compounds, where the asbestos provides reinforcement and improved trowelability during application. These fibers may be released into the air when products are mixed or sanded. Inhalation exposes the consumer to the risks of asbestosis and mesothelioma [31]. Specific information about the size of the market is not available. The major producers of patching and spackling compounds are National Gypsum and U.S. Gypsum.

Asbestos fibers and fluorocarbons have been used in cosmetics and toiletries. Asbestos fibers in talc, found in bath and face powders, pose a potential health hazard, since studies indicate the ingestion of fibers may lead to asbestosis and mesothelial tumors [4]. Fluorocarbons, employed as propellants in aerosols, may lead to a reduction in the earth's ozone layer. This would allow greater amounts of ultraviolet radiation to reach the earth's surface and neighten the incidence of skin cancer [2]. Cosmetic and toiletry sales were approximately $7.3 billion in 1976, with 43 percent in toilet preparations and cosmetics [43]. The major cosmetic and toiletry manufacturers are Avon, Gillette, Revlon, and Johnson & Johnson.

In this chapter consumerism and lead, asbestos, and fluorocarbons are described historically and from the perspectives of consumer groups, government, the industry, and individual companies.

THE HISTORY OF CONSUMERISM AND LEAD, ASBESTOS, AND FLUOROCARBONS

Studies that lead in paint could cause nonoccupational health problems were not conducted until the late 1940s and early 1950s [47, 48]. It was not confirmed that asbestos could lead to nonoccupational health problems until the 1960s [69, 70]. The possible harmful effects of fluorocarbons did not become known until the 1970s [2].

Lead in Paint and Coatings

The hazardous nature of lead poisoning has been known since the second century B.C. [51]. Exposure to low levels of inorganic lead results in insomnia, fatigue, and constipation. Continued exposure causes anemia, colic, and neuritis. Additional exposure leads to loss of appetite, weakness, headaches, and occasionally double vision. Advanced lead poisoning in children can lead to brain damage and death [74].

Lead-based paint has been the major source of lead poisoning in children. Beginning in the late 1940s, clinical studies showed a relationship between lead poisoning in children and residence in older housing coated with lead-based paint. Young children peeled and ate loose flakes. Prior to World War II, lead in paint was common [51]. In 1955, the American Standards Association developed a standard specifying that paints for toys, furniture, and interiors of dwellings should not contain "harmful quantities" of lead. The standard, known as ANSI Standard Z66.1, limited lead content to less than 1 percent in the final dried solids of fresh paint. The level was based upon clinical tests and the sophistication of equipment then available for measuring paint samples. It took many years before a few states and municipalities passed ordinances requiring conformity with ANSI Standard Z66.1 [51].

Laws on the lead content in paint were enacted in three states: Illinois and Kansas in 1958 and Connecticut in 1967. Similar laws were passed in municipalities: Baltimore in 1963, Philadelphia in 1966, and St. Louis and Cleveland in 1970 [51]. In 1971, provisions of the federal Lead-Based Paint Poisoning Prevention Act took precedence and reduced the need for state and local legislation.

In 1963, Consumer Bulletin issued its first report about the hazards of lead in paint: "Lead: Killer of Young Children." The article stated that pigments in interior paints were common causes of mental deficiency and death in children until the early 1950s [52].

The Lead-Based Paint Poisoning Prevention Act, passed by Congress in 1971, defined lead-based paint as one containing more than 1 percent lead. The law also sought to identify areas of sub-standard housing and remove the hazards of lead-based paint. The act was amended in 1973 and reduced the amount of lead in paint to 0.06 percent, the level developed by the American Academy of Pediatrics. The Consumer Product Safety Commission (CPSC) raised the level to 0.5 percent in late 1974 [64]. The act was amended again in 1976. As a result, CPSC ruled in 1977 that paints could contain no more than 0.06 percent lead, with certain specific exemptions [14].

Three general consumer articles were published in national magazines to help consumers learn about the hazards of lead pig-ments. The first article on lead poisoning appeared in the New Republic in 1969, and reported that approximately 225,000 children might have been suffering from lead poisoning induced by eating paint chips containing lead [29]. In 1972, Reader's Digest provided additional information, estimating that 400,000 children ate paint chips and 100 to 200 of these died each year. Thousands suffered brain damage [73]. A general review of lead in paint was provided in the New Republic in 1975. The article confirmed Reader's Digest's estimate of 400,000 children suffering from lead poisoning, and reported on the Lead-Based Paint Poisoning Prevention Act and its amendments [64].

Even with strict regulations and consumer awareness, lead poisoning has continued to affect young children. A 1977 New York Times article reported 502 cases of lead poisoning in New Jersey during 1975 and 635 for the first eleven months of 1976 [22]. Testing also continues, as organizations examine children for signs of lead poisoning [54].

Asbestos in Building Products and in
Cosmetics and Toiletries

The occupational health hazards of asbestos were first detected in England and France in the early 1900s, when workers were found to be suffering from pulmonary fibrosis. Postmortems indicated the workers had severely scarred lungs containing numerous asbestos fibers [69]. Dr. W. E. Cooke, an English physician, first used the term asbestosis in 1927 to describe individuals with severely scarred lungs due to asbestos fibers [17]. In 1935, the relationship between asbestos and cancer was identified in the case of a South Carolina textile worker. The relationship was firmly established in 1947, as British factory workers with asbestosis had a high incidence of lung cancer [4].

Guidelines for acceptable dust concentrations in the asbestos industry originated in 1938. The first actual standard was set in 1946 by the American Conference of Governmental Hygienists, which allowed a total of 5 million particles of dust per cubic foot to be inhaled by factory workers [11].

Mesothelial tumors, primary malignant tumors of the lining of the lung and abdominal cavities, have been very rare. However, in 1960 the relationship between these tumors and asbestos was established when 33 cases of pleural mesothelioma were uncovered in South Africa in an asbestos mining area [69].

The initial studies indicating that nonoccupational exposure to asbestos fibers could result in health problems were conducted in 1960. Many South African patients found with mesothelioma malignancies did not have occupational exposure to asbestos, but lived with asbestos workers or near asbestos mines. In Finland, individuals with asbestos-related health problems were found to live in an area with an asbestos mine [70]. A 1963 study in South Africa indicated that products used by people could lead to asbestos-related diseases, the first sign asbestos had "become a modern urban hazard" [69, p. 6]. These findings were confirmed in 1966 by Dr. I. J. Selikoff, a professor at Mount Sinai, who reported the presence of asbestos bodies in about half of the lung autopsies he performed in New York City [70].

Despite these findings, the major emphasis of research and technical conferences in the mid-1960s involved the occupational health hazards of asbestos fibers. The American Conference of Government Industrial Hygienists, a private group that set safety standards for industrial exposure to various products, did not set a limit specifically for asbestos until 1969. The limit was 12 fibers, each more than five microns in length, per cubic centimeter of inhaled air [66].

Two Ralph Nader-sponsored groups investigated the occupational hazards and, to a lesser extent, the nonoccupational hazards of asbestos in the early 1970s. The Study Group on Air Pollution reported that asbestos was becoming a common airborne city pollutant caused by the wearing away of brake linings, the spraying of asbestos to fireproof steel girders, and the release of fibers when buildings were razed [23]. The Study Group on Disease and Injury on the Job examined asbestos health hazards in the modern industrial environment, and concluded that there were few lungs "not exposed to microscopic asbestos fibers" from pipe insulation, floor tiles, plastics, sealants, patching compounds, and automotive brake linings [66, p. 21].

Popular magazines published articles about asbestos and the hazards of exposure to it. In 1968, the New Yorker wrote on the health problems related to asbestos fibers and reviewed the history of occupational studies linking the inhalation of asbestos fibers with asbestosis and mesothelioma [13]. A 1972 article in the New Republic summarized governmental efforts to limit employee exposure to asbestos fibers in the air. It cited Johns-Mansville's New Jersey plant, the largest asbestos factory in the world, where 60 plant workers exposed to airborne asbestos fibers had died of mesothelioma in the preceding eight years [85]. The history of industrial exposure to asbestos fibers in Pittsburgh Corning's Texas asbestos pipe-covering plant was detailed in a 1973 article in the New Yorker, including the company's attempt to remove all signs of the existence of this facility when it was closed. The plant was completely dismantled under armed guard and buried on the company's property [10].

During the early 1970s, consumers learned they were being exposed to asbestos fibers occasionally associated with the talc used in bath powder and foot powder products. In 1971, as much as 25 percent asbestos was found in two samples of talcum powder [5]. The Food and Drug Administration initiated tests employing electron microscopy and X-ray diffraction techniques. By 1973, the tests showed 10 percent of 200 talcum products then on the market contained 2 to 4 percent asbestos impurities, as manufacturers apparently had changed the grade of talc in their products [45].

In 1976, the first report by a national consumer group appeared when Changing Times published an article about the nonoccupational hazards of asbestos. The article discussed the many products that were produced with asbestos and used in vehicles, buildings, and homes. Some asbestos fibers became loose, entered the air, and eventually lodged in lungs where they could possibly cause asbestosis and mesothelioma [3]. A December 1976 New York Times story stated that talc containing asbestos fibers was still being sold and used in consumer products, such as spackle and patching compounds, without proper health labeling. This practice allowed consumers to be exposed to asbestos fibers above the level set by law [63]. The Consumer Product Safety Commission banned asbestos in spackling and patching compounds in late 1977. Included in the ban were asbestos in artificial fireplace logs and artificial fireplaces, which released asbestos fibers when gas fires were lit in these units [79].

The New York Times reported in late 1977 that rocks containing asbestos fibers were being used to surface roads and parking lots. When vehicles drove over these surfaces, asbestos fibers could be released into the atmosphere and inhaled by the public [75].

Fluorocarbons in Cosmetics and Toiletries

Fluorocarbons have been used as aerosol propellants for antiperspirants, deodorants, and hair sprays. Their use began in the early 1950s and increased rapidly after the development of a suitable valve [2, 9, 39]. The first detection of fluorocarbons in the earth's atmosphere was documented over western Ireland in 1970. Initially, this was thought to be harmless, since the gases were known to be chemically inert. The inertness made fluorocarbons ideal propellants, as they did not react with the ingredients they propelled [9, p. 47].

In early 1974, Rowland and Molina of the University of California at Irvine published a report proposing that fluorocarbons were a major contributor of chlorine atoms to the upper atmosphere. The chlorine atoms reacted with the ozone, resulting in a net destruction of the ozone layer [2, 9, 58]. If the ozone layer was reduced because of fluorocarbon emissions, excessive amounts of ultraviolet radiation would reach the earth's surface and lead to greater occurrences of malignant skin cancer. It has been estimated that a 10-percent decrease in the ozone layer would result in a 20-percent increase in ultraviolet radiation, causing an additional 60,000 to 200,000 diagnosed cases of skin cancer in the United States [2, p. 12].

In 1974, 1975, and 1976, the Natural Resources Defense Council petitioned CPSC to ban consumer products containing fluorocarbons as propellants. Similar petitions were filed with the Food and Drug Administration (FDA) and the Environmental Protection Agency (EPA) in 1976. The petitions were granted in 1976 and 1977 [21].

Two national magazines published articles on fluorocarbons in 1975. The Nation wrote "Hair Spray in the Ozone: The Politics of Freon," which discussed the problems DuPont faced as it built a major fluorocarbon facility in Texas at a time when several large consumer products manufacturers already had announced their intentions to reduce the use of fluorocarbons as aerosol propellants [58]. The New Yorker printed an article reviewing the history of fluorocarbon propellants, initial reports indicating their potential adverse effect on the ozone layer, and the reactions by government and industry to these findings. The government had asked the National Academy of Sciences to conduct a study of the fluorocarbon problem. Industry responded by saying the theory was hypothetical, but would sponsor a three-year study to test it [9].

During 1976, the National Academy of Sciences established a panel to review the evidence that fluorocarbons could deplete the ozone layer. The panel then estimated that approximately 7 percent ozone depletion was probable [20, p. 3]. However, DuPont and others continued to "insist that the ozone-depletion theory is still unproved, and that further new chemistry may be discovered that undermines the theory" [76, p. 38]. DuPont believed a ban should occur only after controlled tests showed actual damage to the ozone.

The Consumer Product Safety Commission, Food and Drug Administration, and Environmental Protection Agency supported the consumerists' view that waiting further could lead to severe damage to the ozone and increases in skin cancer. In March 1978, the agencies released a three-point plan to rule out nonessential uses of fluorocarbon propellants in aerosol products. After October 15, 1978, fluorocarbon propellants could not be manufactured or ordered. After December 15, 1978, products containing fluorocarbon propellants could not be manufactured. After April 15, 1979, processors could not initially introduce a product containing a fluorocarbon propellant into interstate commerce [30].

The chemical industry has tried to gather additional information regarding the effects of fluorocarbons. The Manufacturing Chemists Association established a global network of air-monitoring stations funded by fluorocarbon producers. In early 1978, over $5 million was committed for this project. One goal of the study was to determine if natural sinks, which removed fluorocarbons before they reached the ozone layer, existed in the atmosphere [55].

The next phase in the fluorocarbon controversy involves the possible imposition of controls on the use of fluorocarbons for refrigeration and air conditioning, and as blowing agents in urethane foam [76]. As of this writing, regulatory hearings had been scheduled [76].

ACTIVE CONSUMER GROUPS

Two consumer groups have had a major impact on federal legislation and the actions of regulatory agencies responsible for the potential hazards of lead, asbestos, and fluorocarbons: the Center for the Study of Responsive Law and Natural Resources Defense Council, Inc. (NRDC).

Center for the Study of Responsive Law

The Center for the Study of Responsive Law was founded in 1968 by Ralph Nader. Its primary aim has been to bring current major issues, including air and water pollution and occupational health and safety, to public and official discussions. Three of the Center's study groups have had an impact on hazardous minerals and chemicals: Study Group on Air Pollution, Study Group on Disease and Injury on the Job, and the Health Research Group.

During the summer of 1969, the Study Group on Air Pollution (composed of graduate students in law, medicine, science, and engineering under the supervision of an attorney) examined the operations of the National Air Pollution Control Administration (NAPCA). The findings were published in a book entitled Vanishing Air. The occupational and nonoccupational hazards associated with lead and asbestos were documented in a clear and technical fashion [23]. This study group has since disbanded, and its activities are now included within the Health Research Group.

The Study Group on Disease and Injury on the Job consisted of medical, law, and engineering students and young lawyers who analyzed occupational hazards in the work environment during 1971 and 1972. In particular, it investigated the battle for the Occupational Safety and Health Act of 1970 and its impact on the 1971 work environment. Findings were published in a book entitled Bitter Wages. Information about the occupational hazards associated with lead and asbestos and the length of time for regulatory agencies to act and prepare guidelines were detailed. United Kingdom legislation was found frequently to predate the laws passed in the United States [66]. This study group was also disbanded and incorporated into the Health Research Group.

The Health Research Group monitors industry and regulatory agency actions regarding air pollution and disease and injury on the job. On December 13, 1976, the group sent a report to the Occupational Safety and Health Administration (OSHA) stating that the Vanderbilt Company of Connecticut was producing industrial talc containing asbestos without properly protecting workers or placing the mandated health warning label on packages of talc sold to customers. Final consumers were exposed to asbestos fibers in products such as spackle and patching compounds, which were produced from the talc. In early 1977, the Department of Labor ruled that the Vanderbilt Company could no longer produce the talc without informing workers and customers that it contained asbestos [50].

Natural Resources Defense Council, Inc.

The Natural Resources Defense Council, Inc. was organized in 1970; by 1977, it had 35,000 members. The Council "is dedicated to protecting America's endangered natural resources and to protecting and improving the quality of the human environment" [21]. Some of the areas with which NRDC has been involved are toxic substances, air and water pollution, and the international environment. It has organized teams to monitor the performance of several key federal agencies as they carry out their environmental responsibilities.

The primary tactic of the council has been to file petitions with appropriate agencies. For example, NRDC was the first group to file petitions to ban consumer products with fluorocarbons as propellants. Petitions were filed in 1974, 1975, and 1976. Eventually petitions were filed with the Consumer Product Safety Comsion, the Food and Drug Administration, and the Environmental Protection Agency. In late 1976, all three agencies announced their intentions to regulate fluorocarbons in aerosol sprays [21, pp. 33-34].

In July 1976, the council petitioned CPSC to ban wall-patching compounds with asbestos, since asbestos fibers were released into the air when the compounds were sanded or mixed. Inhalation by the consumer would increase the risk of cancer. On July 29, 1977, CPSC proposed that patching compounds containing asbestos be banned [21, p. 35].

The council also has filed comments with various government agencies. For example:

In 1975, NRDC filed comments on the proposed standard for workplace exposure to asbestos promulgated by the Occupational Safety and Health Administration.

The comments criticized OSHA for establishing a standard based on health effects other than cancer. Since asbestos is a known human carcinogen, only a standard which prohibits exposure to asbestos fibers adequately protects human health [21, p. 35].

GOVERNMENT

Four government agencies are primarily responsible for regulating the use of lead, asbestos, and fluorocarbons: Food and Drug Administration, Occupational Safety and Health Administration, Environmental Protection Agency, and Consumer Product Safety Commission.

Food and Drug Administration

The Food and Drug Administration, formed in 1931, protects the country against impure and unsafe foods, drugs and cosmetics, and other potential hazards [83, p. 263]. For fiscal 1979, the FDA had a budget of $294.3 million and about 7,350 employees [80, p. 377].

The FDA monitors cosmetic products to be sure they do not contain any poisonous or deleterious substances and are not contaminated in any manner that could be harmful to the health of the consumer. The manufacturer has the prime responsibility for assuring product safety. In fulfilling its role, the FDA conducts research on the health implications of cosmetic ingredients, maintains a test program of cosmetics on the market to ensure compliance, and keeps a cosmetics registry for the voluntary registration of cosmetic formulations, manufacturing facilities, and adverse consumer reaction reports to cosmetics [25, p. 93].

Research on the safety of cosmetic ingredients is performed by the FDA's Bureau of Foods [83]. The FDA followed up reports of harmful health effects caused by the presence of asbestos in talcum products with an intensive research program to develop an analytical method for the accurate determination of low levels of asbestos contamination in talc, less than 1 percent [27, p. 113]. The FDA cooperated closely with other federal agencies in studying the problems associated with fluorocarbons [26, p. 103].

Although the FDA is the major agency involved with the safety of cosmetic products, cosmetic programs received only $2.8 million out of a total budget of $250 million in fiscal 1977 [25, p. 157]. As of 1974, about 20 chemists were responsible for evaluating the safety of approximately 15,000 to 20,000 cosmetic formulations [87, p. 2].

Occupational Safety and Health Administration

The Occupational Safety and Health Administration was established by the Occupational Safety and Health Act in 1970. OSHA

> develops and promulgates occupational safety and health
> standards; develops and issues regulations; conducts
> investigations and inspections to determine the status
> of compliance with safety and health standards and regu-
> lations; and issues citations and proposes penalties for
> noncompliance with safety and health standards and
> regulations [83, p. 376].

For fiscal 1979, OSHA was given a budget of $162.7 million and had about 2,660 employees, 80 percent of whom were involved with inspecting work facilities [80, pp. 626-27].

From its investigations, OSHA has proposed standards for various substances in order to maintain the health and safety of workers. For example, in 1971 and 1972, OSHA established a standard for workplace exposure to asbestos. The standard set a limit of five fibers per cubic centimeter of air, a significant reduction from the previous limit of 12 [37]. The limit dropped to two fibers on July 1, 1976, and has remained at this level [36]. An attempt to reduce the level to 0.5 fibers per cubic centimeter of air has not been successful [35].

OSHA regulations and research have provided the basis for consumer-oriented proposals and legislation by Congress and consumer groups.

Environmental Protection Agency

The Environmental Protection Agency was established as an independent agency on December 2, 1970. One objective of the EPA is "to serve as the public's advocate for a livable environment" [83, p. 490]. The EPA's fiscal 1979 budget was $84 million, covering about 2,300 employees [80, p. 377].

In October 1976, the EPA and the FDA "announced their intentions to regulate the use of fluorocarbons in aerosol sprays" [21, p. 34]. This occurred after the Natural Resources Defense Council and several other consumer groups filed petitions because they felt the EPA was not acting quickly enough to regulate the use of environmentally harmful fluorocarbons.

On November 10, 1977, the EPA announced it would undertake a study to develop an asbestos standard for the production and use of crushed stone containing asbestos. In particular, the EPA would identify serpentine rock quarries and evaluate samples of rocks from these quarries. If the production and use of this rock were found to release asbestos fibers into the air, the EPA would propose appropriate regulations [32].

Consumer Product Safety Commission

The Consumer Product Safety Commission was formed in 1972 and charged with protecting the public against unreasonable risks of injury associated with consumer products. The CPSC establishes guidelines for hazardous minerals and chemicals in consumer products, and has the ultimate authority to ban products [83, p. 480]. To carry out its provisions, the CPSC had 960 employees and a budget of $41.5 million in fiscal 1979 [80, p. 854].

The commission tries to balance safety and costs, and seeks participation by consumer and industry representatives when making decisions. Individuals and organizations have the right to petition the CPSC to take regulatory action on any product within its jurisdiction [81, p. 4]. The CPSC has responded to several petitions by the Natural Resources Defense Council with rulings on fluorocarbon use [33].

The CPSC is empowered to regulate the amount of lead in lead-based paint under amendments to the Lead-Based Paint Poisoning Prevention Act of 1971. Regulatory actions have been taken by the commission since 1974 to meet its obligations under the act.

On May 11, 1977, the CPSC, EPA, and FDA proposed a three-step program to phase out propellants by April 15, 1979. The program was finalized on March 15, 1978 [30]. In 1977, in response to petitions filed by the Natural Resources Defense Fund and Consumers Union, the CPSC banned wall-patching compounds containing asbestos. Asbestos could not be included in consumer patching compounds produced or introduced into commerce after January 16, 1978; all stocks had to be removed from sale by June 12, 1978. Commercial patching compounds that were allowed to contain asbestos could not be used in residences, schools, hospitals, public buildings, or any other areas where consumers normally were present [21, 31].

Vinyl-asbestos floor coverings are not regulated by the CPSC at this time, since the asbestos fibers are locked in by vinyl resin and do not become airborne.

Major Consumer Legislation

Many federal laws are enforced by the preceding agencies. The most important are: Food, Drug, and Cosmetic Act, Hazardous

Substances Act, Occupational Safety and Health Act, Clean Air Act, Lead-Based Paint Poisoning Prevention Act, and the Consumer Product Safety Act. These laws are summarized chronologically in Table 6.1.

There have been no major court cases involving lead, asbestos, and fluorocarbons, since petitions filed with the relevant agencies by consumer and environmental groups have resulted in regulations and enforcement.

INDUSTRY RESPONSES TO CONSUMERISM

The data obtained from the literature reveal that industries using lead, asbestos, and fluorocarbons have not wanted legislation and regulatory agencies. Throughout the early 1970s, the industries attempted to weaken proposals for regulating these substances. Following are a review of industry responses reported in the literature and the results of a survey with leading trade associations.

Industry Responses as Reported in the Literature

The general attitude of industries utilizing lead, asbestos, and fluorocarbons is illustrated by a comment made by a representative of the American National Standards Institute at a November 1977 meeting of the National Paint & Coatings Association (NPCA). The representative doubted "that anyone anticipated the consumer movement would last as long as it has," and believed "businessmen didn't think the consumer movement would make headway, much less emerge with the widespread support it has today" [16, p. 32].

Lead in Paint and Coatings

The National Paint & Coatings Association attempted to moderate the impact of the Consumer Product Safety Commission by proposing lead standards to meet the requirements of the Lead-Based Paint Poisoning Prevention Act. In January 1973, the NPCA announced that a 1 percent lead level in paint was safe, but the industry planned to use a 0.5 percent lead level to provide consumers with an "additional margin of safety." The NPCA said no scientific evidence supported lower lead contents [61, p. 28].

The NPCA gave the Midwest Research Institute of Kansas City a grant to conduct an animal feeding study of lead compounds in modern paint from December 1972 to July 1973. Animals fed samples of old white lead paint acquired lead poisoning. Those fed samples of modern paint, with up to 2 percent insoluble lead pigments, "pro-

TABLE 6.1

Federal Legislation Affecting Lead, Asbestos,
and Fluorocarbons

Legislation	Year Enacted	Key Provisions
Food, Drug, and Cosmetic Act	1938	Deems cosmetics adulterated if they bear or contain any poisonous or deleterious substances that may injure users when they follow directions
Hazardous Substances Act	1960	Requires the proper labeling of products containing substances or mixtures of substances that are toxic and could cause injury or illness, complements voluntary standard ANSI Z66.1
Occupational Safety and Health Act	1970	Investigates work environments, generates data used for consumer-oriented problems like asbestos
Clean Air Act	1970	Enhances the quality of air resources, regulates the amount of fluorocarbons released into the atmosphere
Lead–Based Paint Poisoning Prevention Act	1971	Provides direct protection to consumers by limiting the amount of lead in paints and coatings to 0.06 percent for consumer paint made after June 22, 1977
Consumer Product Safety Act	1972	Establishes CPSC, sets and enforces product safety standards, allows consumer petitions, provides for product recalls

Source: Compiled by the author.

duced no detectable changes" [57, p. 39]. The insoluble lead in
modern paint chips was not absorbed from the gastrointestinal tract
at low lead levels.

In 1973, the Lead-Based Paint Poisoning Prevention Act was
amended, and the CPSC was required to determine if the lead level
should be reduced to 0.06 percent. On September 26, 1974, the
National Paint & Coatings Association filed a petition requesting the
lead level to remain at 0.5 percent. After a public meeting, the
CPSC issued a final regulation leaving the lead level at 0.5 percent
[64].

During 1976, the CPSC again evaluated the safe lead level in
paint. The NPCA filed a petition proposing the standard for household paint prohibit the deliberate inclusion of lead as an ingredient,
but allow up to 0.2 percent lead as an inadvertent contaminant, since
some pigments might be naturally contaminated with lead [62]. On
February 16, 1977, the CPSC reduced the lead level in paint to 0.06
percent as required by law, as it could not determine what level
between 0.06 and 0.5 percent was safe [34]. In March 1977, the
NPCA filed a petition requesting exemptions from the 0.06 percent
rule for nine special purpose coatings that could not be ingested by
children [60]. Congress approved several of the exemptions in
August 1977.

In February 1978, the president of the NPCA indicated a continuing distrust of regulatory agencies, which were "able to regulate
a substance under the authority of whichever of the four agencies
has the strictest guidelines for that particular substance" [67, p. 20].

Asbestos in Building Products and in Cosmetics and Toiletries

Although the health hazards associated with asbestos were well-
documented during the 1960s, the Asbestos Information Association
prepared and ran a 1971 series of advertisements stating: "Without
asbestos, life for all of us would be a lot more hazardous." As
E. B. Weiss concluded, with the available public information about
asbestos, it would have been better if the industry had remained
silent [86, p. 19].

A progressive stand was taken by the Cosmetic, Toiletry, and
Fragrance Association (CTFA), which prepared a data sheet on
cosmetic talc in 1976 mandating that cosmetic talc could not contain
asbestos fibers. The association said an examination of over 2,000
samples of modern cosmetic talc did not reveal any asbestos fibers.
The cosmetic talc producers reacted quickly when the asbestos
hazard was discovered [18].

The patching and spackling compound industry was divided in presentations before the Consumer Product Safety Commission. Some manufacturers supported the ban on asbestos; others did not. The CPSC eventually did ban respirable free-form asbestos in consumer patching products [31]. The vinyl-asbestos industry has not responded publicly to the asbestos problem, since its fibers are locked in by vinyl resin and are not considered a threat to the consumer.

Fluorocarbons in Cosmetics and Toiletries

The harmful effects of fluorocarbons on the earth's ozone layer have been known for several years. During this time, many industry groups, including the Chemical Specialties Manufacturers Association (CSMA), representing aerosol manufacturers, and the Council on Atmospheric Sciences (COAS), an industry group formed to respond to fluorocarbon questions, fought the ban on fluorocarbon use. After their efforts failed, they tried to show the industry had met the challenge.

In March 1975, COAS held a news conference outlining the aerosol industry's research program to deal with the ozone issue and the objectives of COAS. The objectives were to comment on industry research and work with government, to coordinate with government research, to recommend a government-leading agency, and to support government atmospheric research. COAS was supported by 19 worldwide fluorocarbon manufacturers and administered by the Manufacturing Chemists Association [41, p. 5].

On September 30, 1975, COAS stated that fluorocarbon harm to the environment was only a theory that needed two to three years to prove or disprove, and that the industry was spending $5 million for research projects at 19 universities in the United States, Canada, and Britain [19, p. 38]. A September 1976 statement by the National Academy of Sciences said fluorocarbons appeared to affect the environment adversely, but more study was needed before the government should ban this ingredient. COAS said the report vindicated its position regarding additional research, which the industry planned to conduct [59]. Shortly thereafter, the FDA stated it would seek to ban all nonessential uses of fluorocarbons as aerosol propellants. CSMA said it could not accept the proposed phase-out of nonessential use, nor could it accept the proposed warning label [6].

On May 11, 1977, the FDA, EPA, and CPSC announced plans to end formally the nonessential use of fluorocarbons as aerosol propellants. The executive director of the Chemical Specialties Manufacturers Association, who was also a member of the Council on Atmospheric Sciences, replied that: the ozone depletion theory had not been proven conclusively; the National Academy of Sciences had recommended a two-year delay for additional studies; and fluorocarbon use was down 40 percent since 1973. Both CSMA and COAS opposed the new ruling during the 30-day comment period [1]. On May 16, 1977, the CSMA Aerosol Division authorized $150,000 to undertake a major public relations and advertising campaign to prevent a consumer revolt against all aerosols, and hoped to raise a total of $250,000 for the campaign [1, p. 31].

Eventually, individual companies began to use nonfluorocarbon propellants in their products in order to meet government proposals and consumer requests. In August 1977, CSMA's executive director commented that "a concerted effort to reduce fluorocarbon usages is being made to alleviate consumer concerns about the environment" [84, p. 16].

Trade Association Responses to Primary Study

Eight trade associations involved with lead, asbestos, and fluorocarbons were sent a mail questionnaire on consumerism. After two requests, three associations agreed to participate in the study: Aerosol Education Bureau (AEB), Chemical Specialties Manufacturers Association (CSMA), and the Cosmetic, Toiletry, and Fragrance Association (CTEA). Three associations did not respond at all: Asbestos Textile Institute, Lead Industries Association, and the National Paint & Coatings Association. Two associations replied by referring the questionnaire to another association: Lead-Zinc Producers Committee and Society of Cosmetic Chemists.

Two of the cooperating associations believe they are responsive to consumerism. All three associations describe self-regulation efforts and the effectiveness in reacting to consumer issues. Two associations employ departments to handle consumerism. Two send representatives to government hearings and would send speakers to consumer groups when invited. All three associations predict continued responsiveness to consumers and their needs.

Table 6.2 contains the condensed responses of the associations. Answers were classified and phrased by the author.

COMPANY RESPONSES TO CONSUMERISM

Company responses to consumerism were obtained by investigating the published literature and sending out a mail questionnaire to specific companies. They are described in this section.

TABLE 6.2

Lead, Asbestos, and Fluorocarbon Trade Association
Responses to Study

Question 1	Generally speaking, how does your society feel about the consumer movement?
AEB	Any answer would be an opinion and the association only deals with facts.
CSMA	The association is actively involved with consumer affairs. Four hundred manufacturers are aided in producing and marketing safety and effective products. Consumers are educated. Technical standards are set.
CFTA	The industry is very competitive and must be responsive to consumer needs.
Question 2	How has the consumer movement affected the companies that belong to your association, in regard to the use of lead, talc (asbestos), and fluorocarbons?
AEB	The industry continues to convert to alternative propellants in place of fluorocarbons. Only about 20 percent of aerosols now contain fluorocarbons.
CSMA	Consumerism has had little effect, because nonaerosol products and alternate forms of propellants were developed. Seventy-five percent of fluorocarbons were removed voluntarily by 1977, almost 87 percent by 1978.
CTFA	The talc specification requires that no asbestos be present. The industry is converting to nonfluorocarbon propellants.
Question 3	Has the association created a position, panel, or department to deal with the effects of the consumer movement?
AEB	The association itself responds to consumer requests for information.
CSMA	Consumer affairs is handled through a Communications Department. A wide variety of information is disseminated. The association belongs to the National Planning Council for Poison Prevention Packaging Week and the American National Standards Institute

(continued)

Consumer Panel. Your Child and Household Safety has been published.

CTFA The Public Information Department answers consumer inquiries and aids consumers.

Question 4 Does the association provide representatives to appear before government committees examining consumer issues?

AEB Representatives are not provided.

CSMA Representatives appear before congressional committees and other hearings. Safety data, scientific findings on health effects, usage information, and other types of data are presented.

CTFA The association has testified at congressional hearings as well as at FDA hearings.

Question 5 Does the association provide speakers to appear before national and/or local consumer organizations?

AEB Speakers generally are not provided.

CSMA Speakers would be provided if invited.

CTFA Every effort to comply is made when speakers are requested.

Question 6 What do you perceive to be the long-term impact of consumerism on the industry you represent?

AEB Any alert industry will be responsive to consumers' needs and attempt to provide them with the best possible products.

CSMA The industry is and will be involved with consumerism on a wide range of issues. Responsiveness and interaction will continue through surveys, consumer affairs offices, advisory committees, focus groups, and government-consumer-industry programs.

CTFA The industry will continue to be sensitive to consumer wants and needs.

Source: Compiled by the author.

Company Responses as Reported in the Literature

While trade associations speaking for their industries have argued consistently against the enactment of regulations restricting the use of lead, asbestos, and fluorocarbons, many individual companies have reacted positively to proposed regulations and prepared new or modified products.

Lead in Paint and Coatings

Major producers of consumer paints consistently have made products that have met or exceeded federal regulations. For example, a 1974-75 Consumer Product Safety Commission study showed that 95 percent of the samples of latex paint it tested had less than 0.06 percent lead, although the standard at this time was 0.5 percent. Of the solvent-thinned paint tested, 68 percent had less than 0.6 percent lead; only 7.6 percent of these paints contained more than 0.5 percent lead [15].

In March 1970, DuPont voluntarily discontinued manufacturing paints containing lead, with the exception of one lead primer paint containing 0.5 percent lead. Prior to this, DuPont paints had up to 6.5 percent lead, but were adequately labeled [24]. The company's commitment to lead-free consumer paint products was reaffirmed in a letter from DuPont to the CPSC on March 22, 1977, which supported the 0.06 percent lead level: "We have long had an interest in the removal of any lead-based paint hazard to children. This letter underscores our ongoing advocacy of that objective" [15, p. XIII].

The Glidden-Durkee Division of SCM has supported efforts to remove lead from paint. In a 1977 letter to the CPSC, the company agreed with the 0.6 percent lead level in consumer products, stating: "Glidden has been pursuing an active program to remove all lead compounds from consumer goods since 1971. That goal was achieved in 1973" [15, p. XIII].

PPG Industries also has reacted to potential lead regulation. By 1972, 90 percent of its consumer paints had a lead content level ranging from zero to 0.06 percent, far below the federal lead standard at that time [65]. In a letter to the CPSC on March 22, 1977, the company wrote that it recommended the 0.06 percent level and was:

> pleased to see that the Commission has resolved all evidence concerning the safe level of lead on the side of safety by recommending the lowest level which is achievable under present technology [15, p. XIII].

During March 1977, Sherwin-Williams sent a letter to the CPSC, saying that the company "has and continues to strongly support efforts to reduce the possibility of ingestion of materials harmful to children." Also:

> Sherwin-Williams has over the last four years removed lead driers and pigments from consumer type paint for architectural use. We are conforming to the practice of not adding lead-containing compounds to these paints and restricting the known level of lead contamination from our raw materials so that the finished product will contain less than 0.06% lead in the non-volatile paint [15, p. XIII].

Asbestos in Building Products and in Cosmetics and Toiletries

Companies using asbestos or talc that contained asbestos in their products have faced particular problems. In the cosmetics area, any hint that products were hazardous quickly affected sales. Consequently, cosmetics manufacturers had to react quickly to protect their market positions.

In 1971, initial reports on talc powders indicated all samples contained asbestos, with some having asbestos concentrations of 5 to 25 percent. Johnson & Johnson immediately announced that its tests, and tests conducted for it by independent laboratories, showed no asbestos in any Johnson & Johnson talc [5, p. 16]. By 1973, a New York University researcher found that of 200 samples of talcum powder tested, 80 percent had no asbestos, 10 percent had 1 to 2 percent asbestos, and only a few had 10 to 20 percent asbestos [28, p. 16]. Asbestos in cosmetic talc products was eliminated by 1976, as determined by a study of the Cosmetic, Toiletry, and Fragrance Association [18].

Vinyl-asbestos floor-tile manufacturers have not been affected by consumerism, as asbestos is still used in their products. In a telephone interview, the executive director of the Resilient Floor Coverings Institute said the tile manufacturers belonging to his organization did not anticipate any problems with the use of asbestos in their products. To his knowledge, there were no changes in formulation to reduce asbestos content [56].

Fluorocarbons in Cosmetics and Toiletries

Cosmetic and toiletry manufacturers have been influenced by the fluorocarbon controversy. However, individual manufacturers had anticipated the consumer movement against fluorocarbons and developed alternative packages and propellant systems for their hair sprays, deodorants, and antiperspirants.

In 1973, Bristol-Myers commissioned a series of studies to determine which type of deodorant product (pump spray, stick, lotion, or cream) consumers would prefer if aerosols were no longer available. By a sizable margin, the pump spray was preferred over other nonaerosol alternatives. Ban Basic deodorant pump spray was introduced in eight western states in 1975 and nationally in 1976 [7, pp. 23-29]. In 1976, Bristol-Myers announced all of its leading brands were being made in nonaerosol form [6]. By 1977, research developed a nonfluorocarbon aerosol, and Ultra Ban II was sold as "the first environmentally safe aerosol marketed nationally" [8, p. 7].

Gillette's 1974 Annual Report mentioned that questions had been raised about fluorocarbon propellants and their possible negative effects on the ozone layer. Gillette continued "to explore product alternatives that could be used if research shows that fluorocarbons used in aerosols are a harmful factor" [78, p. 20]. A 1975 advertising campaign announced the company's development program for alternatives to fluorocarbons [58]. In 1976, Right Guard deodorant stick was introduced nationally. Gillette predicted stick deodorant sales would rise from 5 percent of total deodorant sales in 1975 to 10 percent in 1976 [42, p. 1].

During 1975, Alberto-Culver announced that carbon dioxide would replace fluorocarbon propellants in hair spray [40]. At about the same time, S. C. Johnson & Sons unveiled a plan to have hydrocarbons replace fluorocarbons as aerosol propellants [40]. Clairol also said it would eliminate fluorocarbon propellants in 1975 [58]. In December 1976, Avon revealed that it was switching all of its aerosol fragrances, both existing and new products, out of aerosols and into pump sprays [46].

Company Responses to Primary Study

Mail questionnaires on consumerism were sent to 13 companies involved with lead, asbestos, and fluorocarbons. Six companies completed the survey: Avon, DuPont, Gillette, PPG, Revlon, and SCM. Five others sent materials, but did not respond to the survey or said they could not participate: Armstrong Cork, DeSoto, GAF, Pfizer, and Sherwin-Williams. Two companies did not reply at all, despite two mailings: Flintkote and Johnson & Johnson.

Four of the responding firms have some process for handling consumer complaints. Three companies have decentralized complaint systems and one a centralized system. All educate consumers through product booklets. All the companies use trained sales personnel or product bulletins to provide product-related information to the public. Five companies modify products to satisfy consumer needs. Five companies utilize extensive quality control procedures to ensure product quality. Four feel that governmental regulations have had a great impact on operations, but do not believe they are subjected to outside consumer pressure.

Table 6.3 shows the responses of the companies to each question. Answers have been condensed and categorized by the author. Many questions were not answered by the respondents.

THE OVERALL EFFECTS OF CONSUMERISM

The impact of consumerism on lead, asbestos, and fluorocarbons and an evaluation of consumerism in this area are detailed below.

Impact of Consumerism

Consumerism has had a major impact on most of the industries and companies included in this analysis. The actions of consumer groups and government agencies have resulted in the elimination of many hazardous minerals and chemicals from consumer products. Most large paint companies have reduced the level of lead in consumer paints to far less than 0.06 percent. Children are no longer exposed to lead poisoning from newly painted residential surfaces.

The use of asbestos has been banned from spackling and patching compounds, so that consumers are protected from inhaling asbestos fibers while mixing or sanding these products. Cosmetic producers now utilize asbestos-free talc in their talcum products, eliminating the danger of consumers inhaling asbestos fibers. The vinyl-asbestos floor-tile industry has been unaffected by consumerism. Asbestos fibers in these products are locked into the floor tile by a vinyl resin and cannot be inhaled by the consumer. Accordingly, consumer groups and government agencies have not taken actions to have asbestos removed from floor-tile products.

Fluorocarbon aerosol propellants have been taken out of deodorants, antiperspirants, and hair sprays. Companies now use environmentally safe aerosol propellants or pump sprays to dispense these consumer products.

Evaluation of Consumerism

Although consumers are protected from hazardous minerals and chemicals, the costs associated with this protection must be

TABLE 6.3

Lead, Asbestos, and Fluorocarbon Company Responses to Study

Question 1	The Consumer: What type of policy do you have for handling complaints? Do you have a consumer complaint department? Is there a consumer advocate in-house? Do you have an educational program or participate in educational programs for consumers?
Avon	Consumers are supplied with product-use booklets. No answers are indicated for other parts of this question.
DuPont	Complaints are directed to the specific group marketing the product. A formal education program exists for consumers, including the preparation and distribution of literature.
Gillette	The Consumer Service Department handles consumer communications. The company's interests are best served when consumers are satisfied. There is no formal consumer education program, but product-use booklets are provided to consumers.
PPG	Complaints usually are handled by field salespeople or regional sales managers. There is no in-house advocate for consumers. Consumer education is through product bulletins.
Revlon	Consumers are given product-use booklets. No answers are indicated for other parts of this question.
SCM	Most complaints are handled at the store level with a corporate follow-up system. The company does not have an in-house consumer advocate. Consumers are educated through how-to booklets.
Question 2	The Product: What type of product-related information is made available to the public? Are you modifying or changing your products in response to consumerism? What procedure do you follow to ensure product quality?
Avon	Product-use booklets are available. No answers are indicated for other parts of this question.
DuPont	Product-related information is provided. Products are modified because of comments and suggestions made by consumers, not consumerism. Product quality is ensured through strict control procedures.
Gillette	Product-use bulletins are disseminated. There are no reactions to consumerism; rather, the company tries to satisfy consumer needs. Product quality is maintained by extensive quality control and safety procedures.

(continued)

PPG	Sales personnel are trained to aid consumers in selecting the proper product. How-to bulletins also are provided. Products are modified to meet consumer needs and government regulations, not because of consumerism. All products must pass quality control checks.
Revlon	Product-use booklets are provided. The company is always responsive to consumer needs and preferences. Product quality is assured by very stringent quality control procedures.
SCM	All product labels provide information on proper product use. Products are modified to meet consumer needs. Product quality is ensured through control procedures.
Question 3	Outside Influences: What type of consumer regulations affect your operations? How do you respond to outside consumer pressures? How do you evaluate the effect of consumerism on your company?
Avon	No answer is indicated for this question.
DuPont	The major effect of outside influences is the reformulation of products to meet federal regulations. The company is not subjected to outside consumer pressure. It strives to maintain the good reputation of products that carry the company name.
Gillette	State and federal regulatory agencies affect company operations. There is no outside consumer pressure. Consumerism has led to avoiding even the appearance of wrongdoing.
PPG	Regulations issued by federal agencies influence operations. Substantial efforts are made to comply with these regulations. Consumerism tends to increase product costs and delay new product introductions.
Revlon	No answer is indicated for this question.
SCM	Regulations regarding product formulation have had the most impact. Consumer legislation proceedings are followed to be aware of outside consumer pressures. The performance of products in the marketplace is the best criterion to evaluate the effect of outside influences on the company.

Source: Compiled by the author.

evaluated. For example, during 1971 discussions about lead levels in paints, it was estimated that replacing lead-based pigments with lead-free ones would cost $2-to-$5 per pound, up from $0.20 per pound. These costs would be passed on to consumers [53, p. 42].

The Consumer Product Safety Commission estimated labor costs for the construction of new homes and the renovation of existing homes would increase by $50 to $125 million during the first year asbestos was banned in spackling and patching compounds. Per-unit costs would rise by $10 to $60. All costs would be passed on to consumers [31].

Several estimates indicate the ban on fluorocarbons will have a total cost of about $1 billion. Almost $600 million will be absorbed by aerosol marketers and captive fillers through lost sales and the costs of developing alternative systems [77, p. 30]. Eventually, most of these costs will be passed along to consumers.

Despite the costs enumerated above, the benefits of consumerism in these industries outweigh them. In 1975, the surgeon general estimated 400,000 children had high blood lead levels due to eating paint chips [64, p. 12]. Today, children are not exposed to this hazard in newly painted residential surfaces.

In 1971, reports indicated that all tested talcum-powder products contained asbestos fibers, exposing consumers to increased risks of cancer [45]. Now consumers are not subjected to this hazard.

It was estimated in 1975 that continued use of fluorocarbon aerosol propellants could result in an additional 60,000 to 200,000 diagnosed cases of skin cancer per year in the United States alone [2, p. 12]. The ban on fluorocarbons has removed this danger. Thus, in all cases, the costs of reducing or eliminating hazardous minerals and chemicals have resulted in the eradication of potential health hazards for millions of consumers.

It is concluded that government regulations are necessary, or else hazardous products would still be on the market. As a former director of New York City's Bureau of Lead Poisoning remarked when several paint companies violated their own voluntary standard on the level of lead in paint and did not properly label the hazard:

> The disappointing aspect is that the voluntary standard
> had appeared to be accepted by the industry. But it
> was violated by a number of paint companies, including
> some of the biggest ones. This invites government
> regulation where there need not be any, if they do their
> own policing [53, p. 41].

In 1977, the Ideal Toy Company recalled 60,000 Snoopy toy banks because they contained more lead than federal law allowed [72, p. 16]. Would a company recall products without federal regulations?

FUTURE OUTLOOK

Consumerism will continue and result in the production of items that are safe to the consumer and the environment. Existing consumer groups will monitor industry actions and petition government agencies to establish guidelines to protect consumers and the environment from hazardous substances. The groups will become more effective as their technical expertise increases.

The government will propose regulations causing manufacturers to control further the hazardous substances found in their products. Regulations will be passed more quickly as agencies better coordinate their actions. Dominant agencies will be designated for issues based on the agencies' expertise with specific hazardous substances and powers from enabling legislation.

Industry associations still will oppose regulations proposed by agencies and consumer groups, calling them excessively cautious and expensive. The associations will recognize consumerism as a force and distribute consumer-oriented literature and films to aid consumers in using products.

Companies will find innovative ways to meet proposed government regulations in order to maintain their positions in the marketplace. Companies will provide extensive consumer-oriented literature on product use, establish formal education and complaint departments to deal with consumer inquiries, and develop quality control procedures to test the effects of products in the environment, not the laboratory.

RECOMMENDATIONS

Recommendations are suggested for consumer groups, government, the industries, and individual companies.

Consumer Groups

Consumer groups should continue to press for regulations that ensure safe products for the consumer and the environment. The groups should improve their technical capabilities and thereby convey better information to government and industry. They should judge accurately the technological problems and costs associated with their proposals, set realistic timetables for eliminating hazardous substances, and estimate the costs to be passed on to consumers.

Government

Government agencies need to be responsive to consumer groups and industry representatives when developing regulations. They should acquire more in-house expertise instead of relying upon outside consultants. Industry problems and costs should be assessed before issuing regulations and balanced against consumer demands. The time needed to prepare regulations must be shortened, as it now takes years from the detection of a hazardous substance to the promulgation of final rules. Interagency cooperation is essential.

The Industries

The industries must cease playing a negative role and take an active part in proposing legislation to protect consumers. If a possible health hazard exists, industry must make it known to the proper government agency. Industry also should propose workable timetables for correcting hazards, based on technical capabilities, and estimate the costs to business and the consumer. Associations should sponsor advertisements and press releases that alert the consumer to potential problems, and offer industry-recommended safety procedures. This information will supplement and balance that provided by consumer groups.

Companies

Companies must take more active interest in their trade associations' responses to consumerism and see that all firms make safe products. All companies are harmed when one or more violate the letter or spirit of the law. Companies must continue their efforts to meet consumer desires and government regulations. Trade associations should not advocate fewer standards than the companies they represent. Individual firms also must add in-house consumer advocates and formal complaint departments, strengthen consumer education programs, and better train sales personnel to advise consumers about the proper techniques for handling and using products.

BIBLIOGRAPHY

1. "Aerosols Under Siege." Drug and Cosmetic Industry 120 (June 1977), pp. 28-29ff.

2. Amed, K. A. "Unshielding the Sun . . . Human Effects." Environment 17 (April/May 1975), pp. 6-14.

3. "Asbestos." Changing Times 30 (November 1976), pp. 37-38.

4. Asbestos. National Research Council, Committee on Biologic Effects of Atmospheric Pollutants. Washington: National Academy of Science, 1971.

5. "Asbestos in the Boudoir." Chemical Week 109 (July 14, 1971), p. 16.

6. "Bid to Ban Fluorocarbons Sparks Anger, Surprise." Advertising Age 47 (October 25, 1976), pp. 8ff.

7. Bristol-Myers Annual Report, 1976. New York, N.Y.

8. Bristol-Myers Annual Report, 1977. New York, N.Y.

9. Brodeur, P. "Annals of Chemistry: Aerosol Sprays." New Yorker 51 (April 7, 1975), pp. 47-50ff.

10. ____. "Asbestos Dangers at Pittsburgh Corning Corporation Factory, Tyler, Texas." New Yorker 49 (October 29, 1973), pp. 44-48ff.

11. ____. Expendable Americans. New York: Viking Press, 1973.

12. ____. "The Magic Mineral." New Yorker 44 (October 12, 1968), p. 117.

13. ____. "Relationship Between Pneumoconosis, Asbestosis and Mesothelioma." New Yorker 44 (October 12, 1968), pp. 117-18ff.

14. "CPSC Lead-in-Paint Regulations Okayed—Industry 'Wins' Some Exemptions." American Paint & Coatings Journal 62 (September 12, 1977), pp. 9-10.

15. Consumer Product Safety Commission. Final Environmental Impact Statement on Lead Content in Paint, vols. I and II. Washington: Consumer Product Safety Commission, May 1977.

16. "Consumerism Is Here to Stay and Paint Industry Must Live with It, Conventioners Told." American Paint & Coatings Journal 62 (November 14, 1977), pp. 30ff.

17. Cooke, W. E. "Pulmonary Asbestosis." British Medical Journal 2 (1927), pp. 1,024-25.

18. Cosmetic, Toiletry and Fragrance Association, Inc. Cosmetic Talc. Washington: Cosmetic, Toiletry and Fragrance Association, Inc., 1976.

19. Davis, Donald A. "Aerosols and the Ozone—Industry Efforts Don't Shake Environmentalists." Drug & Cosmetic Industry 117 (November 1975), pp. 37-39ff.

20. Dickinson, J. W., Jr. "Aerosols, Ozone." CFTA Cosmetic Journal 9 (July/September 1977), pp. 2-5.

21. Docket. New York: Natural Resources Defense Council, Inc., 1977.

22. "Elizabeth Lead-Poisoning Clinic May Become a Model." New York Times (February 16, 1977), p. B7.

23. Esposito, J. C. Vanishing Air. New York: Grossman, 1970.

24. "Eye Lead Paint Bills." Chemical Week 107 (September 2, 1970), p. 24.

25. FDA Annual Report, 1976. Washington, D.C.: Department of Health, Education and Welfare.

26. FDA Annual Report, 1975. Washington, D.C.: Department of Health, Education and Welfare.

27. FDA Annual Report, 1974. Washington, D.C.: Department of Health, Education and Welfare.

28. "FDA Plans to Impose Limits on Asbestos in Certain Cosmetics." Wall Street Journal (February 26, 1973), p. 16.

29. Featherstone, J. "The Silent Epidemic." New Republic 161 (November 8, 1969), pp. 13-14.

30. Federal Register, 43FR 11301 (March 17, 1978).

31. ____. 42FR 63354 (December 15, 1977).

32. ____. 42FR 58543 (November 10, 1977).

33. ____. 42FR 42780 (August 24, 1977).

34. ____. 42FR 9404 (February 16, 1977).

35. ____. 40FR 47652 (October 9, 1975).

36. ____. 37FR 11318 (June 7, 1972).

37. ____. 36FR 23207 (December 7, 1971).

38. Flintkote Corp. Annual Report, 1975. White Plains, N.Y.

39. "Fluorinated Hydrocarbons—Salient Statistics." Chemical Economics Handbook, Section 658.20300 (September 1975), Menlo Park, Calif. SRI International.

40. "Fluorocarbon Ads, Proposals Under Attack." Advertising Age 46 (July 14, 1975), p. 8.

41. "Fluorocarbon Group Outlines Industry's Research Program to Deal with the Ozone Issue." Chemical Marketing Reporter 207 (March 3, 1975), pp. 5ff.

42. "Gillette Sets National Launch of Right Guard Stock." Advertising Age 27 (July 5, 1976), p. 1.

43. "Health Care, Drugs and Cosmetics, Basic Analysis." Standard & Poor's Industry Survey, section 2 (March 2, 1978).

44. "Home Furnishings, Basic Analysis." Standard & Poor's Industry Survey, section 2 (March 9, 1978).

45. "How Pure Is Talcum?" Chemical Week 112 (March 7, 1973), p. 13.

46. "How to Sell Him, Her." Chemical Week 119 (December 8, 1976), p. 20.

47. Ingalls, T. H.; Tiboni, E. A.; and Werrin, M. "Lead Poisoning In Philadelphia, 1955–1960." Archives of Environmental Health 3 (November 1961), pp. 575–79.

48. Jacobziner, H. "Lead Poisoning in Childhood: Epidemiology, Manifestations and Prevention." Clinical Pediatrics 5 (May 1966), pp. 277–86.

49. Kline Guide to the Paint Industry, 4th ed. Fairfield, N.J.: Charles H. Kline & Co., 1975.

50. "Labor Agency Cancels Its Safety Exemption on Industrial Talcs." Wall Street Journal (February 3, 1977), p. 34.

51. Lead: Airborne Lead in Perspective. National Research Council, Committee on Biologic Effects of Atmospheric Pollutants. Washington: National Academy of Science, 1972.

52. "Lead: Killer of Young Children." Consumer Bulletin 46 (October 1963), pp. 36-40.

53. "Lead Paint Is an Inside Problem." Chemical Week 109 (December 15, 1971), pp. 41-42.

54. "Lead Poisoning Tests Scheduled." New York Times (February 3, 1977), p. 21.

55. "MCA Seeks to Find Fluorocarbon Life." Journal of Commerce (February 14, 1978), p. 6.

56. Mauer, Robert. Executive Director, Resilient Floor Coverings Institute, Washington. Telephone interview (July 5, 1978).

57. Midwest Research Institute. Lead Paint Ingestion Study. Scientific Circular no. 800. Kansas City, Mo.: Midwest Research Institute, 1974.

58. Mitchell, Sean. "Hair Spray in the Ozone: The Politics of Freon." Nation 220 (June 28, 1975), pp. 775-78.

59. "NAS Report Calls for Additional Study Before Any U.S. Fluorocarbon Crackdown." Chemical Marketing Reporter 210 (September 20, 1976), pp. 3ff.

60. "NPCA Asks for Lead Exemption for Nine Coatings." Coatings 29 (April 11, 1977), p. 31.

61. "NPCA Is Launching New Study to Determine Safe Lead Limits." Chemical Marketing Reporter 203 (January 8, 1973), p. 28.

62. "NPCA Proposes Lead Regulation for Home Paints." Chemical Marketing Reporter 210 (September 20, 1976), pp. 4ff.

63. "Nader's Group Says Safety Agency Allows Illegal Labeling on Product." New York Times (December 15, 1976), p. B15.

64. Needleman, Herbert L. "How Much Lead Is Too Much? Little Flakes of Poison." New Republic 173 (January 25, 1975), pp. 12-15.

65. PPG Industries Annual Report, 1972. Pittsburgh, Pa.

66. Page, J. A., and O'Brien, M. W. Bitter Wages. New York: Grossman, 1973.

67. Roland, Robert A. "Are U.S. and Business Headed for Compatibility?" American Paint & Coatings Journal 62 (February 6, 1978), pp. 16-17ff.

68. Sales Survey, 1976. Washington: National Paint & Coatings Association, 1977.

69. Selikoff, I. J. "Asbestos." Environment 11 (March 1969), pp. 3-7.

70. ____ and Hammond, E. C. "Community Effects of Non-Occupational Environmental Asbestos Exposure." American Journal of Public Health 58 (September 1968), pp. 1,658-64.

71. Sive, M. R., ed. Environmental Legislation, A Sourcebook. New York: Praeger, 1976.

72. "Snoopy Bank Recalled Due to Lead in Paint." Wall Street Journal (September 14, 1977), p. 16.

73. Spencer, S. "America's Tragic Silent Epidemic." Reader's Digest 100 (April 1972), pp. 59-60ff.

74. Stellman, J. M., and Daum, S. M. Work Is Dangerous to Your Health. New York: Pantheon, 1973.

75. "Study of Rock Quarries for a Cancer Clue Is Set." New York Times (November 20, 1977), p. 48.

76. Tannenbaum, J. A. "Fluorocarbon Battle Expected to Heat Up As the Regulators Move Beyond Aerosols." Wall Street Journal (January 19, 1978), p. 38.

77. "The Aerosol Ban Has Lost Its Sting." Business Week (May 30, 1977), pp. 30-31.

78. The Gillette Co. Annual Report, 1974. Boston, Mass.

79. "Three Cuts in Asbestos." Chemical Week 120 (May 4, 1977), p. 17.

80. U.S. Bureau of the Budget. The Budget of the U.S. Government, Fiscal Year 1979—Appendix. Washington, D.C.: U.S. Government Printing Office.

81. U.S. Consumer Product Safety Commission. Annual Report, July 1, 1974-June 30, 1975. Washington, D.C.: 1975.

82. U.S. Department of Labor. Sixty-Fourth Annual Report, Fiscal Year 1977. Washington, D.C.: U.S. Government Printing Office, Superintendent of Documents.

83. U.S. Government Manual, 1977/78. Washington, D.C.: Office of the Federal Register, National Archives and Records Service, General Services Administration.

84. "Union Carbide Plans to Halt Fluorocarbon Production in Fall." Chemical Marketing Reporter 212 (August 8, 1977), pp. 3ff.

85. Vare, R. "Inhaling Cancer: Asbestos Under Fire." New Republic 167 (July 7, 1972), pp. 13-15.

86. Weiss, E. B. "Here's How Not to Act If Your Industry Comes Under Scientific Attack." Advertising Age 42 (December 27, 1971), p. 19.

87. Winter, R. A Consumer's Dictionary of Cosmetic Ingredients. New York: Crown, 1974.

7

CONSUMERISM AND THE MAIL-ORDER INDUSTRY

Susan A. Levey

INTRODUCTION

Mail-order retailing encompasses shipping, billing, or otherwise contacting consumers via the mail. This form of retailing has existed since New World settlers received goods from their countries of origin. Today, consumers order a variety of products, from plants to furniture, through the mail.

The development of consumerism in the mail-order industry has gone through three distinct phases. At the turn of the century, various groups tried to foster better consumer habits and set standards for the industry. Initial consumer laws were proposed. The 1930s saw increased awareness on the part of individual consumers, as the depression made them more critical of business and business practices. From the 1960s to the present, there has been a great deal of legislation designed to curb abuses in the mail-order industry.

The history of consumerism, consumer groups, government activities, and the responses of the industry and individual companies to consumerism in the mail-order industry are detailed in this chapter.

THE HISTORY OF CONSUMERISM
IN THE MAIL-ORDER INDUSTRY

Early Era

Mail order began to flourish in the 1830s, mostly in the New England area [44, p. 17]. By the late 1800s, the bulk of the U.S. population lived on farms and in rural communities. People looked to mail order for merchandise they could not obtain elsewhere. Retail store expansion did not take place on a broad enough scale to

improve small-town and rural shopping. Communication and transportation facilities were poor. Stores had inadequate stock and slow
turnover. Limited merchandise assortments were sold. High prices
were caused by the need for long-term consumer credit [132, p. 383].

The first regulations aided in the industry's development and
involved the distribution of catalogs and merchandise to the rural
public. In 1879, mail-order publications were classified as "aids
in the dissemination of knowledge," permitting promotional pieces
to be mailed at the rate of 1¢ per pound. In 1891, John Wanamaker,
the postmaster general and "merchant king," proposed the rural free
delivery (RFD) system to eliminate the physical isolation of farmers,
which was adopted in 1896. The Parcel Post Act of 1912 reduced
the postage rate on packages over four ounces in weight. Restrictions
limiting the sizes of packages were liberalized from 1912 to 1914
[132, p. 384].

Mail-order firms took advantage of the new regulations. The
first well-known firm, started by Aaron Montgomery Ward in 1872,
attempted to lower the high costs of retail store selling. Sears,
Roebuck and Company stressed the same objective. Both firms
sought to reach rural customers with limited retailing facilities [44,
p. 2]. Mail-order catalogs helped to educate consumers and retailers
about merchandising, and led to increased demand for goods and
services [87].

Sears and Ward dominated mail-order retailing at the turn of
the century. They communicated with consumers by offering new
and different methods of promotion, such as credit, special interest
catalogs, and premium incentives. The major issues at this time
were misleading advertisements, social pressure, credit selling,
and unordered merchandise.

Misleading Advertisements

Sears heavily advertised in magazines catering to mail-order
firms and attempted to have consumers order its catalog. "Come-
on" items were described in exaggerated language, which Sears
justified with the comment that prices were lower than any competitor.
The catalog was referred to as the "great wishbook" or "consumer's
guide" in order to upgrade the image of mail order [26, p. 6].

Social Pressure

In the early 1900s, small-town merchants feared the growing
popularity of mail-order purchases and joined together for action
against those who would buy through the mail. Several techniques
were used to discourage mail-order customers, including organized
pressure groups, legislative lobbies, catalog burnings, and the social

ostracism of mail-order patrons [132, p. 386]. The target of these activities was the unfair competition of mail-order houses that exaggerated claims about the products they sold.

The Federal Trade Commission (FTC) issued a formal complaint in 1918 against 117 lumber dealers and the editor of the Mississippi Valley Lumberman, charging a conspiracy to injure mail-order houses. The lumber dealers and the newspaperman first attempted to prejudice customers against the mail-order lumber business by interfering with salesmen who appeared at housing sites. The lumber dealers then filed suit accusing various mail-order houses of making false statements in advertising. The advertisements had alluded to a "lumber trust" and characterized lumber dealers as thieves and robbers. The mail-order firms were told to halt such practices [155].

Another attempt by retailers to influence consumers not to buy mail-order merchandise was made in 1935. A number of hardware manufacturers formed the American Institute of Fair Competition and pledged to sell merchandise only through independent hardware retailers, excluding chain stores and mail-order houses. They felt this policy would increase the volume sold by independents and enable them to counter the low prices of competitors. The American Institute of Fair Competition, called a "campaign of prejudice" by one wholesaler, did not succeed [91].

Credit Selling

Sears extended credit to customers in 1913, Ward in 1923. Various credit plans were tested: no money down, no charge for credit, and credit for preferred customers only [26, p. 8]. Abuses occurred because of the built-in obsolescence of products, substandard merchandise, and debt promotion [125]. Laws designed to curb credit abuses were not enacted until the 1970s.

Unordered Merchandise

Customers were able to receive merchandise on approval and could choose to keep what they wanted. However, as the use of mailing lists and automated equipment increased, consumers began to complain that they received unordered merchandise. By 1927, consumer complaints grew to the point that the Post Office stopped allowing COD and insurance privileges for vendors of clothing and other merchandise who sent unsolicited shipments to consumers. No regulation existed to prevent unordered merchandise from being sent, on approval, to consumers whose names appeared on mailing lists. Customers who acknowledged receipt of items were liable for payments or had to return the items to the vendor [107]. The Post Office aided companies by providing proof of delivery.

In 1927, the Post Office banned the wholesale tracing of un-ordered goods by mail-order firms. Mass requests for proof of delivery were disallowed; only individuals or reputable businesses could trace occasional stray shipments. At this time, Congress sought to declare the sending of unordered merchandise illegal. Poor public representation at hearings prevented the proposed bill from reaching the floor of Congress [107].

Although not fully protected by law, consumers had rights that were explained by consumer groups, chambers of commerce, and other organizations. Stamps had to be provided for the return postage on unordered merchandise; a fraud was committed if this was not done. The recipient was under no obligation to return or maintain unordered merchandise, although it could not be worn or used. A consumer also could charge storage rates, which he or she could set. After a certain period of time, the goods could be sold to cover storage charges. In addition, consumers were advised to inform companies they knew about the legalities surrounding unordered merchandise, which would stop all collection procedures and future deliveries of unordered products [97].

Second Era

Consumer awareness and sophistication increased during the late 1920s and 1930s, causing mail-order firms to use special letters to identify customer grievances and elicit comments [90]. In 1932, Berth Robert-Gross, Incorporated, which sold semifinished dresses, developed a customer service policy of answering all inquiries within two days of receipt. Every Berth Robert-Gross product had an abso-lute guarantee, which was described in an understated manner in advertisements. Catalogs carried a complete description of every dress sold [82].

Mailing lists were criticized for not reflecting proper customer information. One recipient objected because he was addressed as "Miss" instead of "Mr." on a mailing piece [34]. Mail-order sales were found to be related to whether or not the consumer was given a bargain, good merchandise, distinctive merchandise, or conven-ience [42]. Lotteries, contests, free merchandise, deceptive adver-tising, credit purchasing, and mail-order real estate were popular topics of discussion or investigation.

Lotteries

"Endless chain" sales or lotteries appeared in the late 1920s. The first case involved the Tribond Sales Corporation, which had issued contract forms containing individual coupons labeled A, B, and C to consumers who paid $4 toward the final price of $10 for a lot of hosiery. Customers were given one year to sell the coupons to three other purchasers at $2 each or remit the remaining price personally. In 1927, the Court of Appeals found this practice to be illegal, since the success of coupon holders was dependent on their ability to sell extra coupons. An element of chance existed as to whether the additional coupons could be sold [23].

By 1933, over 100 chain schemes still originated out of New York City. The schemes dealt with fountain pens, wallets, razor blades, golf balls, and other merchandise. Usually, consumers were promised commissions after their fourth sale. If the chain did not break, the commission would be quite large. The problem with the schemes was eventual saturation and the inability of people to make four sales [45]. The Better Business Bureau attempted to regulate lotteries. In Statute 3005, the Post Office prohibited lotteries and set guidelines for postmasters to follow if schemes were uncovered.

Contests

The Post Office sought to ban cartoon-solution-type contests under the antilottery law, which outlawed all gift enterprises or schemes in which the award of prizes was dependent on chance. P. Lorillard held an Old Gold cigarette contest in 1937 that was marred by the emergence of at least ten "authorities" selling correct, but not guaranteed, answers to the contest. Although Lorillard ran advertisements warning against hucksters, authorities found that the damage was already done [3].

Free Merchandise

After World War II, mail-order firms promoted heavily to obtain shares of growing spending power. Some new promotional methods resulted in legislation to protect consumers [120]. One of the first postwar problems with mail-order sales involved the use of the word "free" in advertising. In 1948, the Federal Trade Commission issued complaints against the Literary Guild, Classics Club, Detective Book Club, Book-of-the-Month Club, and the Cadillac Publishing Company because they did not comply with free offers. The word free was supposed to indicate a gift or gratuity. If a customer had to purchase another product or perform some service, then the item received was not free. In addition, the seller could not recover the cost of the free item from the immediate transaction nor substitute an inferior product for the advertised free product [47].

Deceptive Advertising

The Federal Trade Commission ruled that using the term "selected families" was illegal when it implied consumers were contacted because of their distinctive characteristics. In 1949, the FTC ordered Americana Encyclopedia to stop saying its "publication is available only to selected individuals under special conditions," since this was not true [73, p. 136].

Credit Purchasing

During 1955, Spiegel introduced its Budget Power plan, similar to department store credit, in response to consumer demand for additional types of credit-purchasing plans. At this time, Spiegel divested itself of retail stores and became exclusively a mail-order operation. Some companies modified monthly billing statements to show the exact amounts owed, instead of fixed carrying charges. Sears began a 30-day free credit plan in April 1959 [78].

Mail-Order Real Estate

Consumers were victims of phony real estate promotions in the 1950s. They were sent letters offering the privilege of buying property in advance of others, when the land was being sold at its regular price in a general offering. At this time, New York State developed tight controls over any advertiser selling within the state, even if it was located within another state. The promoter had to fill out a questionnaire with information on ownership, topography, water tables, and improvements. An inspector from the state's Division of Licenses visited the development, at the developer's expense, to verify all advertised claims. Ohio and Michigan enacted similar requirements [11].

Modern Era

The modern era of consumerism in the mail-order industry began in the 1960s as the industry rapidly expanded and consumers sought to assert their rights. By 1961, sales were several billion dollars per year, and five million people were employed. As Printer's Ink commented, "direct mail is emerging from the medicine man stage" [35]. In the modern era, fair trade, lotteries, contests, and privacy have been important issues, and new uses have been found for mail order.

Fair Trade

Fair trade laws allowed manufacturers to establish uniform retail prices for their merchandise if they so desired. Several mail-order firms violated state fair trade laws by discounting the prices of merchandise. These firms then had difficulty placing advertisements as states honored the laws. However, the Court of Appeals upheld the right of Masters Mail Order Company to sell its goods at discount prices in fair trade states because its location was in Washington, D.C., which had no resale price maintenance law [103].

In 1975, District Sound and Audio Warehouse of Washington, D.C., challenged manufacturer United States Pioneer for the right to advertise lower prices in fair trade states. This challenge was one factor behind the eventual elimination of fair trade [17, 144].

Lotteries

Chain-referral selling resurfaced in the 1960s. In June 1967, the Postal Inspection Service conducted 234 investigations that resulted in 34 convictions. The lottery had consumers believing they would pay little or nothing for merchandise, or make money, if they referred the names of acquaintances to various businesses. In its prosecutions, the Postal Inspection Service had to prove intent to defraud [99].

Contests

Procter & Gamble sponsored ten contests in 1968, and in seven of them awarded no prizes. Ford Motor Company said it would award more than $2 million of cars and merchandise from 1967 to 1976, but actually gave out $34,534 of prizes. House subcommittee investigations found that soap companies awarded 1.9 percent, automobile companies 1.5 percent, and mail-order firms 2.6 percent of the prizes offered [98]. The low prize payoffs were due to the way winning ticket numbers were chosen. Winning numbers were drawn from the total contest mailing. If a winning number was not mailed back to the company, the prize was not awarded to anyone.

Contest abuses have included: the number of advertised prizes outnumbering the actual prizes distributed, advertisements of contests after prizes were awarded, and certain sections of the country favored to increase sales.

Privacy

The Privacy Protection Study Commission set forth three recommendations for the regulation of mailing lists in July 1977, after testimony from various users of direct-mail advertisements. First, a person or company engaged in interstate commerce would not be required by law to remove a consumer's name and address from a mailing list. This could be accomplished on a voluntary basis through the cooperation of mailers. Second, organizations that made their members' names and addresses available for mailing list rental had to inform the members of this practice and give them the opportunity to indicate if they wished to have this information made available. The organizations had to respond to members' requests for inclusion or deletion. Third, each state was to review the direct-mail uses of state records for solicitation purposes and devise procedures to prevent the release of the names of those individuals who did not want to receive miscellaneous solicitations [121].

New Uses of Mail Order

Over the last several years, new uses have been found for mail order, including: fund raising, attracting students to college courses, advanced instructions for salespeople, automobile promotions, and cents-off coupons. Consumers have learned that mail order can provide new and unique products in a convenient fashion [76].

Many new laws were enacted in the 1960s and 1970s to protect consumers from deceptive or misleading mail-order practices. The laws concern merchandise delivery, warranties, negative option selling, and other operations. These laws are enumerated in the government section of this chapter.

ACTIVE CONSUMER GROUPS

While a number of general and specific consumer organizations had an impact on U.S. business in the early part of the twentieth century, consumer groups only recently have begun to have a significant impact on the mail-order industry. The majority of consumer groups continue to ignore the mail-order industry as a specific concern. Three consumer organizations have been the most important in this area: Consumers Union, Truth in Advertising, and the Center for the Study of Responsive Law. Other groups may be active in the mail-order industry, but a thorough search did not reveal any.

Consumers Union

Consumers Union, founded in 1936 and currently staffed by 350 people, evaluates a wide range of consumer products and business practices. Data on products sold by mail and guidance on how to purchase through the mail have been disseminated. The organization represents consumers at government hearings and provides grants to universities and consumer groups. The group's publication, Consumer Reports, recently has had articles on mail-order practices.

In 1974, Consumers Union sued BankAmericard and American Express in a U.S. District Court in Washington, D.C., because the credit card companies had told merchants they were required to bill credit card customers and cash customers at the same prices. Consumers Union considered this unfair, since merchants kept 100 percent of the selling price if the item was paid for in cash and 95 percent of the selling price if the item was charged. The organization accused the companies of violation of antitrust laws [139]. As a result of the suit, American Express and BankAmericard agreed to allow merchants to offer discounts for cash payments and remove the ban on discounts from merchant contracts. In return, Consumers Union dropped the antitrust suit [128].

A 1976 Consumer Reports article discussed the problems of getting and disposing of junk mail. It explained how consumers could have their names removed from mailing lists and how list compilers generated their lists. For example, R. H. Polk had a list of 55 million owners of automobiles and trucks, which it purchased from state motor vehicle bureaus [95].

Book clubs were studied by Consumer Reports in 1977. They were rated on the basis of: overall satisfaction, price, titles offered, delivery time, shipment of books requested, correct filling of orders, billing and crediting, complaint handling, and the quality of paper, printing, and binding. The Book-of-the-Month Club and Literary Guild received average ratings [10].

In 1979, Consumer Reports published an article on buying health aids by mail. It was highly critical of the claims made by bust developers, wrinkle removers, diet pills, protein supplements, reducing devices, baldness remedies, and aphrodisiacs [31].

Truth in Advertising

Truth in Advertising, established in 1973, has 37 regional and local chapters. All are concerned with the elimination of deceptive, unfair, and misleading advertising. Several committees carry out the objectives of the organization, including one specifically geared toward mail order [61]. No information was uncovered regarding the actual actions of Truth in Advertising's mail-order committee.

Center for the Study of Responsive Law

The Center for the Study of Responsive Law was organized in 1968 by Ralph Nader. In 1975, the center conducted a study that found that consumers experienced problems with one out of every four purchases. Only one-third of the problems were reported to anyone, with only 1 percent commenting to a consumer agency, government agency, or court. The five areas of greatest consumer difficulties, in descending order, were: car repairs, appliance repairs, mail-order items, housing repairs, and toys. The study recommended improved court procedures for small claims, improved business complaint procedures, and more awareness on the part of government agencies [18].

GOVERNMENT

Two government agencies have most of the responsibility for regulating the deceptive or misleading practices of the mail-order industry: Federal Trade Commission and the Post Office.

Federal Trade Commission

The Federal Trade Commission, established in 1914 and amended in 1938, deals with the "unfair or deceptive acts or practices" of the mail-order industry. Actions have been taken in various areas: misleading advertising, deceptive advertising of guarantees, deceptive pricing, advertising allowances, negative option plans, free and similar representations, and shipment of merchandise.

Misleading Advertising

The FTC took its first steps against deceptive advertising in 1918. At that time, Sears was ordered to cease and desist from making "false and misleading" claims in advertisements, wherein it stated coffees and teas were purchased from Japan when they were actually bought from importers in the United States. The FTC also cited Sears for not dealing fairly with customers, since they were led to believe Sears' plumbing goods were easy to install; they were not. In addition, Sears did not inform consumers it might have been illegal not to employ a licensed plumber [7].

In 1948, the FTC charged Doubleday, Book-of-the-Month Club, Walter J. Black, and Cadillac Publishers with deceptive advertising [51]. Book-of-the-Month Club was accused again in 1953 [22,

p. 229]. Each company had advertised for new members by stating in large print across the top of a page of advertising that a free book would be given. A coupon was shown in much smaller print in the advertisement. This coupon, when signed and sent to the company, constituted a contract to purchase at least four books per year. The FTC said the clubs had made misleading use of the word free, since an additional purchase was required, and issued a cease-and-desist order.

Recently, the FTC has sought to stop various mail-order companies from engaging in deceptive practices. In 1975, Shaklee Corporation of California agreed to a consent order and ceased setting prices and imposing restrictions on the resale of its food supplement, cosmetic, and other household products [129]. During the same year, the FTC charged Jay Norris, Federated Nationwide Wholesalers Service, Garydean Corporation, P-N Publishing, Pan-Am Car Distributing Corporation, Joel Jacobs, Mortimer Williams, and Kenneth Mann with making deceptive claims about their products. As of this writing, the FTC is seeking to bar these companies from making unsubstantiated claims about their products, which include roach powder, television antennas, socks, and taxicabs. The FTC wants the companies to include an address and telephone number for consumer complaints in all advertisements [104].

In 1977, Amrep Corporation, two subsidiaries named Rio Rancho Estates and ATC Realty, and four executives were convicted of mail fraud and violation of the Interstate Land Sales Act. The defendants had been charged with defrauding investors in the sale of $200 million of lots near Albuquerque, New Mexico [2]. Also during 1977, the Jewelry Club of America was accused of committing a fraud by failing to deliver merchandise ordered by customers in 22 states and Canada. The company was accused further of failing to advise customers of their right to request and receive refunds [102]. Two other companies, Make-Up Club of America and RPHI, pleaded guilty in 1977 to federal charges that they fraudulently sold jewelry and cosmetics through the mail, and placed misleading advertisements in magazines [144].

Deceptive Advertising of Guarantees

In 1942, Raladam Company was ordered to cease and desist selling a fat-reducing remedy, because alleged misleading and deceptive statements were made to further sales. The statements dealt with weight loss and injured competition [22, p. 213]. The Clinton Watch Company was ordered to cease and desist from advertising a lifetime guarantee without clear disclosure of the service charges for repairs in 1961 [22, p. 214].

Advertisements for guarantees and warranties must include: product or parts covered, exclusions, durations, guarantor performance and responsibility, and what is meant by lifetime [53].

Deceptive Pricing

During 1937, the Standard Education Society was ordered to cease and desist from advertising that a set of books was given away to consumers and only a looseleaf extension service had to be purchased. It was found that the price charged for the looseleaf service was the regular standard price for both [22, p. 228]. A thorough search of the literature and government documents was unable to locate more recent actions on deceptive pricing.

The FTC's guidelines for pricing require: real sale prices, showing the regular and sale prices, the elimination of misleading bargain offers, and truthfulness [54].

Advertising Allowances

Spiegel was ordered to cease and desist from using certain types of advertisements in 1969. It was determined that an advertisement amounted to an unfair method of competition if the meaning and impression of it in the mind of the reader arose not only from what was said within the advertisement but from what was implied as well [22, p. 211].

The guideline for advertising allowances, based on the Robinson-Patman Act, deals with competitive inequalities in interstate commerce when services or facilities are provided to customers in connection with the distribution of a product for resale. Services covered by the guidelines are: advertising, handbills, catalogs, demonstrations, display materials, special packaging, accepting returns for credit, and prizes or merchandise for promotional contests. The services must not be misleading and should provide equitable treatment for all customers [55].

Negative Option Plans

The FTC created guidelines for negative option selling plans on June 7, 1974. Under negative option plans, members of mail-order clubs were advised in advance of selections available for shipment. If merchandise was not wanted, members had to inform the clubs, or it would be shipped automatically. The FTC guideline required consumers to be informed of: how to act when a selection was not wanted, minimum purchase obligations, cancellation rights upon fulfillment of contract obligations, the identity of the selection ten days prior to shipment, guaranteed postage for the return of an

unannounced selection, the frequency of announcements, and the right
to receive alternate products if introductory or bonus items could
not be shipped within four weeks [48, 49, 116, 150, 151].

The FTC sought to ban negative option selling in 1975, but
members of the mail-order industry persuaded it to abandon this
action [119].

Free Merchandise

In 1957, the American Medical Association informed the FTC
of a deceptive free trial offer by the Vitasafe Corporation, a mail-
order vitamin house. Investigation by the FTC concluded that a
requirement to send 25¢ did not constitute free. In addition, Vitasafe
sent vitamins to consumers after they requested that their names be
removed from mailing lists. Vitasafe agreed to stop these practices
[106].

The guideline for use of the term free in advertising stipulates
that a customer pay nothing for one article and the regular price for
the other products. All conditions pertaining to the free item must
be disclosed within an advertisement [52].

Shipment of Merchandise

During 1975, the FTC established a rule that required a mail-
order seller to refund the purchase price of prepaid merchandise if
it could not be shipped within 30 days. The refund would be sent
automatically, without a customer having to demand it. Exceptions
to the rule were permitted when customers were informed of longer
delivery times prior to their remittance and/or the company obtained
written consents from buyers to fill orders after 30 days [22]. The
customer could cancel during the waiting period and receive a refund.
Refunds for charge card customers were to be credited within one
billing cycle. Refunds of cash could not be limited to company
vouchers and had to be issued within seven days of a customer's
request [113].

In 1977, the Jewelry Club of America was accused by the FTC
of failing to advise customers of their right to request and receive
refunds if ordered merchandise was not shipped within the advertised
period [102].

Post Office

Since 1872, under provisions of the Postal Fraud Statute, the
Post Office has denied the use of the mail to those who would defraud
the public. Criminal regulations provide for up to five-years impris-

onment and a $1,000 fine for each mailing offense promoting a fraudulent scheme. Civil laws provide for the suspension of business-mailing privileges, after a hearing before a postal department officer finds fraudulent practices [99, pp. 80-81]. In 1962, Congress revised the postal laws without altering their substance [119]. Some of the consumer issues affected by the Post Office are: lotteries, unlawful matter, pandering advertisements, detention of mail, and unordered merchandise.

Lotteries

The Post Office is able to act against people engaged in a lottery. It can direct the local postmaster to return the mail to the sender, marked as a violation, or it can forbid the payment of any money order or postal note to a person engaged in a lottery scheme, and return the money to the sender [119, p. 69].

Unlawful Matter

The Post Office is allowed to return mail to the sender and/or forbid postal order or postal note payments, if satisfactory evidence is obtained that a firm is obtaining money or items of value in exchange for "obscene, lascivious, indecent, filthy, or vile" material [119, p. 73].

In 1977, the Supreme Court upheld the rule that individuals were subject to a federal ban on sending obscene matter through the mails, even though the state of origin had permissive standards. Jerry Lee Smith was convicted for mailing issues of Intrigue magazine, pamphlets, and allegedly obscene films [86].

Prohibition of Pandering Advertisements

People or companies offering for sale matter considered to be sexually provocative by an addressee are prohibited from mailings of such materials. Also, the sender cannot rent for mailing lists the names of those not wishing to receive mailings. Violators may be prosecuted by the attorney general [119, p. 76].

In 1976, Al Goldstein and Jim Buckley, publishers of Smut and Screw, "the world's dirtiest papers," were convicted of mailing obscene materials. Larry Flynt, publisher of Hustler, went on trial in January 1977 in Cincinnati, Ohio, charged with pandering obscenity and engaging in organized crime [117].

Detention of Mail

Mail privileges may be curtailed for parties accused of mail fraud, if proceedings are being prepared. In 1973, International

Term Papers had its mail privileges revoked, while the attorney general proved a fraud existed involving a scheme to deceive a third party through the misrepresentation of materials [119, p. 75]. In 1976, the Post Office issued a mail-stop order against Cecily Vane, a company selling a method of bust enlarging. The Post Office takes action against five to six businesses each year [85].

Mailing of Unordered Merchandise

Mailing unordered merchandise is considered an unfair method of competition and an unfair trade practice, except for clearly marked free samples or merchandise mailed by charitable organizations soliciting contributions. Merchandise sent in violation is considered free to the recipient, who may dispose of it in any manner without obligation to the sender. The merchant cannot send any bill or dunning communication [119, p. 79].

Other Federal Protection

The Consumer Credit Protection Act of 1968 requires the disclosure of credit terms and annual rates of finance charges in dollars as well as percentages [116, p. 82]. Provisions cover enforcement, finance charges, guidelines for credit transactions, extortionate credit policies, and restrictions of garnishment [112, p. 82].

The Fair Credit Reporting Act of 1970 enables consumers to review their credit dossiers. Reporting mechanisms must be certified as fair and impartial. The consumers are allowed to correct or delete erroneous or obsolete information [112, p. 73]. In August 1977, New York enacted a law requiring credit bureaus, employers, insurance companies, and others to notify consumers that they were being investigated and allow them to inspect their credit files [13].

The Fair Credit Billing Act of 1974 requires creditors to disclose all the information pertaining to borrowers' accounts in a clear manner on all billing statements. Credit card billings cannot be issued for merchandise that has not been delivered [56, p. 51,594; 122]. The act also makes provisions for correction of billing errors. Disputed amounts may not be reported to credit bureaus while an investigation is underway. In 1977, the FTC ruled that four retail companies operated by Genesco had handled credit balances of charge account customers in an unfair and deceptive manner, and awarded $800,000 in customer refunds [75].

The Equal Credit Opportunity Act of 1974 prohibits discrimination in the issuance of credit. It covers all credit transactions and requires that applicants be informed as to the reasons for denial of credit. Fines may be given out for each violation [79, 127].

State Consumer Protection

Individual states have established laws to protect consumers who purchase through the mail. For example, state attorney generals are able to employ temporary injunctions to restrain companies from deceptive business practices while trials are underway. Such action was taken against the Record Club of America in 1975 because it continued to accept orders it might not have been able to fill after it had filed a bankruptcy petition. New York State's attorney general obtained an injunction when some customers were advised merchandise was unavailable and were offered a credit or refund [74, p. 101; 96].

In 1977, Unique Ideas was enjoined from engaging in unlawful acts relating to false information contained in its mailings, which described a work-at-home system for selling mink novelty items. Two-and-a-half million letters were sent after a New York injunction was obtained. The company was found in contempt of court [74, p. 102].

The Virginia attorney general investigated the actions of Malpractice Research, which in 1977 offered a mail-order "review of potential malpractice cases" by anonymous physicians [20]. The results of the investigation could not be determined.

INDUSTRY RESPONSES TO CONSUMERISM

The reactions of the mail-order industry to consumerism were obtained from a comprehensive search of published literature as well as a questionnaire to leading trade associations. These reactions are described below.

Industry Responses as Reported in the Literature

For decades, the mail-order industry has sought to establish and maintain a favorable image with the public. As far back as 1922, a noted mail-order consultant said business "has been conducted on honorable and high-grade lines. The customer is always right" [125]. The industry's view of itself has remained unchanged since this statement was made.

General Activities of the Industry

One function of mail-order trade associations is to transmit information to members and consumers. For example, in 1975 the Direct Mail/Marketing Association (DMMA) reported to the news media that many mail-order companies would offer their customers a variety of options concerning their placement on mail listings [94]. Public service announcements were placed in magazines. Responses to these announcements revealed that many more consumers wanted to be added to mailing lists than desired to be deleted [111].

During February 1977, the Mail Advertising Association International aided member firms that had to curtail production due to lack of fuel and extremely poor weather conditions. Association officials conducted a membership survey to ascertain who needed help in making deadlines and who could provide assistance to others. Later in 1977, DMMA was advised by an industry representative that its role was to offer help for firms entering the industry, improve teaching programs, encourage blacks and women to become active, and increase sharing of ideas among industry members [64].

A second function of trade associations is to act as a representative of the industry before government agencies or consumer groups. The Mail Order Association of America and the Parcel Post Association provided their members' opinions during 1972 FTC hearings on refunds for cancelled orders. The associations suggested businesses show intentions to comply with the FTC rule on refunds, rather than maintain extensive records of each customer transaction [56, p. 51,592].

In 1973, the FTC tried to ban negative option selling. The industry suggested self-regulation as an alternative measure and presented arguments to the FTC stressing the importance of this marketing technique. The industry agreed to describe the terms of negative selling plans within advertising materials and allow subscribers a minimum of ten days to refuse any selection [115].

The Mail Order Association of America and the Direct Mail/Marketing Association commented in 1975 on the FTC's 30-day rule, which required customer requests for refunds to be acted upon within seven working days after the receipt of the request. The industry argued that ten days would be fairer [56, p. 51,592].

On February 20, 1976, the Associated Third Class Mail Users appeared before the Court of Appeals to request that first-class rates be 13 cents and not the 25 cents proposed by the Post Office [66]. The Mail Advertising Service Association tried to attain reduced rates for third-class mail in 1976. These rates would apply to mail presorted by carrier routes or walk sequences [68].

In August 1976, industry responses to a proposed House bill, which would have prohibited the use of mailing lists with the names of persons under the age of 18, caused the sponsor to drop the bill. An FTC inquiry and industry pressure on the specific company involved with this practice resulted in the company ending its policy [70].

Industry testimony in February 1977 helped the New Jersey attorney general convict executives of the Elgin Ten Division of G. Martin Frank, Ltd., of fraudulent schemes. Consumers had been sold franchises, supposedly enabling them to sell bulk quantities of pens to large businesses [65]. The American Association of Nurserymen helped Pennsylvania obtain an April 1977 conviction and penalties against American Consumer for deceptive advertising practices. The company had advertised nursery products under various company names and generated numerous consumer complaints. It was fined $45,000 in civil penalties and investigative costs [62].

Direct Mail/Marketing Association

The foremost trade association in the mail-order industry is the Direct Mail/Marketing Association, which was established in 1917 for the purpose of securing cooperative action for the advancement of direct advertising. The association represents more than 1,600 companies, with offices in New York and Washington, D.C. DMMA is the only trade association to cover the whole industry [40]. In 1958, the Business Mail Foundation was formed, and is now affiliated with DMMA. It spends $2 million annually [39].

DMMA has set guidelines to be followed by responsible companies, regarding: clear and understandable statements, matching performances with promises and products with claims, refunding money promptly, keeping mailings on a high standard of decency, and adhering to high principles of business in all dealings with the public [40].

DMMA has seven special interest services to provide members. The Public Affairs Council represents members in court and before legislatures, and works to improve relations with consumers. It also publishes Public Affairs Report, which comments on the latest trends in consumer activity, legislation, and court action. The Information Council runs a worldwide hotline that gives immediate answers to members' questions. The Loan Library contains direct-mail campaigns, including information on their creation and performance. The Direct Mail/Marketing Manual has basic information on how to run a campaign and rules for success. Education involves special conferences, seminars, workshops, meetings, and institutes. Forum Councils are available for the discussion and resolution of member problems. These councils exist for business and catalog mailers, marketing specialists, insurance specialists, fund raisers, list brokers, and telephone marketers. Fellowship programs allow businesspeople to meet and exchange information [40].

The DMMA has a Mail Order Action Line for consumers. Of the complaints received, 85 percent relate to nonmember firms. The Action Line tries to resolve problems when consumers are not satisfied with company responses. In particular, it provides consumers with information about the processing of mail orders [37, 39]. DMMA also offers a Mail Preference Service, which allows consumers to choose whether or not to have their names appear on mailing lists. From 1971, when the service was started, until the end of 1977, 191,424 households enrolled in the service. Of these, 65 percent asked to be added to lists and 35 percent selected the name-removal option [39].

In July 1976, DMMA issued a 22-point guideline for advertising. It listed FTC and Post Office regulations, and the Better Business Bureau Code of Advertising. The DMMA's Ethics Committee, which generated the guidelines, investigates complaints and takes action when warranted [36]. DMMA also works with other associations, such as: Marketing Club of New York, Chicago Association of Direct Marketing, Direct Marketing Club of California, and the Philadelphia Direct Marketing Merchants Association [29].

Better Business Bureau

There are 146 Better Business Bureaus (BBB) throughout the United States, with a central office in Washington, D.C. Of 384,000 complaints received by bureaus during the first six months of 1977, the most (17.75 percent) pertained to mail order. Approximately 84.5 percent of the mail order complaints were settled with BBB intervention. In processing complaints, the BBB contacts firms and attempts to have them resolve the problems. The bureau follows up if a problem is not resolved [69].

Delay in delivery is the most common complaint regarding mail-order sales. Other major criticisms include failures to: deliver prepaid merchandise, provide refunds for unordered goods, act on complaints, and answer letters of complaint [113].

In 1974, the New York BBB investigated work-at-home schemes that required sending money in advance and offers of business opportunities promising instant wealth. During 1977, the Newark BBB said over 60 mail-order frauds operated in New Jersey, including work-at-home schemes, weight-reducing aids, aphrodisiacs, and miracle-cure devices [130].

The National Advertising Division of the Council of Better Business Bureaus investigated ten national campaigns in 1977. Six promoted justifiable facts. The other campaigns did not meet BBB standards [41]. In April 1978, the Long Island BBB restated its position that Jay Norris Corporation did not meet its standards. Although the FTC had earlier issued an order prohibiting the firm from unfair, misleading, and deceptive practices, over 200 complaints were received at the beginning of 1978 [6].

The BBB recently has added arbitration to its complaint resolution process. Under the system, both consumers and company representatives can agree to meet with unpaid, but trained, volunteers to try to solve their disagreements. Thus far, decisions have been distributed evenly between consumers and firms. The technique is still experimental and limited to certain locations [15].

Annually, BBB and DMMA meet with representatives of the Consumer Protection Office of the Post Office, the fraud branch of the Postal Inspection Service, and the consumer advocate of the Post Office [29].

Trade Association Responses to Primary Study

Ten trade associations representing the mail-order industry were asked to participate in a study on consumerism. None of the associations replied to the questions in the survey. Two supplied materials: Direct Mail/Marketing Association of New York (DMMA-NY) and Mail Order Association of America (MOAA). One association, Mail Advertising Service Association International, said its members are technicians who service advertisers, but do not deal directly with consumers. Seven associations did not reply at all, after two requests: Association of Second-Class Mail Publishers, Associated Third-Class Mail Users, Chicago Association of Direct Marketing, Direct Mail/Marketing Association of Washington, D.C., Direct Selling Association, National Star Route Carriers Association, and Parcel Post Association.

The lack of participation precludes any summary observations about trade association beliefs and policies. Table 7.1 attempts to place the materials provided by the two responding associations into the format of answers to the survey.

COMPANY RESPONSES TO CONSUMERISM

Company responses to consumerism have been reported in the literature and a primary mail survey. They are examined below.

TABLE 7.1

Mail–Order Trade Association Responses to Study

Question 1	How does your association feel about the consumer movement?
DMMA-NY	The materials sent do not indicate an answer to this question.
MOAA	The materials sent do not indicate an answer to this question.

Question 2	How has the consumer movement affected the members who belong to your association in regard to mail-order sales?
DMMA-NY	The materials sent do not indicate an answer to this question.
MOAA	The materials sent do not indicate an answer to this question

Question 3	Has the association created a position, panel, or department to deal with the effects of the consumer movement?
DMMA-NY	The Mail Preference Service has been designed to meet the desire of some consumers to reduce their mail advertising on a nonselective basis, and to counter the public image that mail advertisers are insensitive to consumer attitudes.
MOAA	The materials sent do not indicate an answer to this question.

Question 4	Does the association provide representatives to appear before government committees examining consumer issues?
DMMA-NY	Information on the Mail Preference Service has reached the public through congressional communications.
MOAA	The association is concerned with matters relating to the Postal Service and federal regulatory agencies.

(continued)

Table 7.1 (continued)

Question 5	Does the association provide speakers to appear before national and/or local consumer organizations?
DMMA-NY	Information on the Mail Preference Service regularly appears in newspaper action-line columns and is included in consumer-oriented broadcasts throughout the country.
MOAA	The materials sent do not indicate an answer to this question.
Question 6	What do you perceive to be the long-run impact of consumerism on your industry?
DMMA-NY	The materials sent do not indicate an answer to this question.
MOAA	The materials sent do not indicate an answer to this question.

Source: Compiled by the author.

Company Responses as Reported in the Literature

Company reactions to consumerism may be viewed from two perspectives: companies seeking to understand why consumers purchase through the mail, and company responses to consumerism and the reforms it has brought.

Understanding and Satisfying the Consumer

Early Montgomery Ward catalogs, first issued in 1872, stressed "guaranteed net prices quoted in plain figures." This contrasted with the widely followed practice of charging high prices. Montgomery Ward also offered convenience and quality to customers [90]. In 1924, the chairman of Sears wrote an article for System magazine, stating that Sears had to supply what was ordered to please customers. The retailer's policy of send-no-money advertisements, begun in 1884, allowed customers to see merchandise in advance of payments and minimize risks [127].

The Book-of-the-Month Club was started in 1926 in an attempt to reach a new market [80]. A division of the club was added in 1971 to sell limited editions of high quality graphics and sculpture [84]. By 1974, the club introduced its Quality Paperback Service, which had monthly selections of paperback books at $3.95 and up [21].

Maxwell Sroge, owner of a mail-order company and a well-respected analyst, estimated high sales in 1972 for kitchen appliances, tools under $30, watches under $30, luggage sets under $30, tableware sets under $30, tools over $30, vacuum cleaners, radios under $30, watches over $40, and cookware sets under $40 [100]. For 1974, the president of DMMA estimated 700 million separate transactions, $50 billion in sales, and 10 percent of all consumer purchases were through the mail [30].

In a 1974 marketing study, Fred D. Reynolds analyzed why consumers bought from mail-order catalogs. He found that these shoppers sought time and place convenience, bought items not always available through local stores, and accepted a higher degree of risk than store shoppers [124].

In 1977, Peter Nieman established Aristera Organization, a mail-order business catering solely to left-handers [16]. Other firms with specialized audiences were: Rodale Press, natural foods and organic gardening; L. L. Bean, outdoors; and Eddie Bauer, camping and hiking [71]. Sunset House initiated an approach of selling a variety of new and unusual products [152].

Recently, Literary Guild instituted a rating system, similar to the one used for movies, to warn customers that certain selections might offend certain readers [108].

Reactions to Consumerism

Important consumerism issues have been initiated or resolved by company actions or reactions, including the 30-day rule, misleading advertising, costs of credit, unfair practices, privacy, and sweepstakes.

30-Day Rule. From March 27 to March 29, 1972, the FTC held public hearings, and from September 8, 1971, to April 28, 1972, it received written statements from firms regarding the 30-day rule for unordered merchandise and services. Many individual companies participated.

The president of Sunset House supported the 30-day rule, saying:

> There are those who will promote an item by mail—
> without any inventory and will accumulate customer
> orders when received—and then, and only then, initiate
> action to procure merchandise [56, p. 51,586].

Popular Services, Columbia House, and Sears said 30 days were not sufficient to allow sellers to determine whether or not they could ship merchandise promptly. They felt the rule allowed only seven to ten days, since sellers had to prepare and mail delay notices, and receive them back, all within 30 days [56, p. 51,589]. Because of these and other comments, the FTC allowed consumers to consent to delays of up to 30 days instead of 15 [56, p. 51,590].

Based on testimony from Jay Norris and Frederick's of Hollywood, the FTC decided not to invoke an absolute recordkeeping requirement as long as documentary proof of systems and procedures was available. Frederick's stated that recordkeeping "would seriously discriminate against small companies that are not geared up to automated processing and recordkeeping" [56, p. 51,588].

Frederick's, Popular Services, Downe Communications, and Sears testified that seven working days for refunds to be processed and sent to buyers was an unworkable requirement [56, pp. 51,592-93]. Columbia House asked for a more flexible definition of refund of credit sales [56, p. 51,592].

Prentice-Hall reported that an average of 122 orders per week were received and categorized as illegible or incomplete, and therefore, unfillable. The FTC ruled orders had to contain all necessary information before the 30-day rule could be applied [56, p. 51,592]. Book-of-the-Month Club and other negative option sellers expressed concern for the rule's effect on their programs. To handle this, the FTC developed a special negative-option rule [56, p. 51,593]. Time,

Incorporated and other magazine publishers expressed the view that their response rates from subscription efforts would decrease if they had to disclose the period of time before the first issues would be mailed. The FTC did not change the rule for magazines [56, p. 51,595].

Seed and nursery firms contended their items could not be shipped within 30 days, but at the proper time for planting. The FTC agreed, and excluded the sale of seeds and plants from the rule [56, p. 51,595]. Mail-order photofinishers also were exempted, after they convinced the commission that delays were due to theft or loss, not "mere" shipping delays [56, p. 51,596].

Misleading Advertising. Grolier, a direct-mail and door-to-door marketer of encyclopedias and educational books, negotiated with the FTC to settle a 1971 complaint. The FTC wanted salespeople to identify the company and the fact that they were salespeople prior to entering the home, since complaints had been received that Grolier personnel misrepresented their identities. At this time, Grolier began a customer-relations campaign [81].

On an NBC news report in 1976, Betty Furness informed viewers that certain publications, such as Popular Mechanics, would refuse to print mail-order advertisements that offered "hopeless opportunities" [66].

In February 1977, Fingerhut Corporation agreed to settle a suit brought by the San Francisco district attorney's office, which had charged the firm with "false and misleading advertising and other violations of state and federal consumer protection laws" [60]. Fingerhut was accused of advertising that a $79.95 recorder could be purchased for $29.95, without disclosing the tie-in purchase of 15 cassette tapes. The total price was $176.52. The company paid $100,000 in civil penalties to avoid further litigation.

Cost of Credit. During March 1977, the FTC said Gulf Oil had violated the Truth-in-Lending Act by not clearly and conspicuously disclosing the cost of credit for installment buying. Gulf agreed to cease this practice without admitting any guilt [83]. Also in 1977, the FTC ordered Diners Club, Carte Blanche, ARCO, Federated Department Stores, and City Stores Company to refund more than $3 million to customers who overpaid bills [147].

Unfair Practices. In 1975, the FTC ordered Spiegel to stop suing allegedly delinquent credit customers outside the counties where they lived or signed credit purchase contracts. Spiegel argued it had stopped the practice in 1971 [134].

Privacy. A representative of American Express testified before the Privacy Protection Study Commission in 1975 that recipients of unsolicited mail advertisements did not need legislation to have their names deleted from mailing lists. Voluntary compliance with individual requests was all the protection needed. The commission upheld this contention [13].

Sweepstakes. At a January 1977 luncheon, a speaker from Sunset House called sweepstakes a valuable promotion tool. The speaker added that sweepstakes had to be credible to consumers, since they did not respond to gimmicks [67]. In February 1977, an advertising executive said the negative sweepstakes publicity of the 1960s had been eliminated by assurances "all prizes will be awarded." At this time, Reader's Digest announced the odds of winning a prize in its contest were one out of 269 [137].

Company Responses to Primary Study

Ten companies with sizable mail-order sales were asked to participate in a mail survey. Two companies answered the questions: Book-of-the-Month Club (BMC) and Publisher's Clearing House (PCH). Two firms said replies would be forthcoming, but they were never received: Columbia House and Time-Life Books. Despite two mail requests and telephone contacts, six companies did not respond at all: Alden's, Ambassador International, American Express, Collector's Guild, Grolier, and Sunset House.

Table 7.2 shows the summarized responses of Book-of-the-Month Club and Publisher's Clearing House. Not every question was answered by the two companies. Overall generalizations are not possible because of the lack of responses.

OVERALL EFFECTS OF CONSUMERISM

Following are an examination of the impact of consumerism and an evaluation of consumerism in the mail-order industry.

Impact of Consumerism

Although consumerism has existed since the inception of the mail-order industry, the modification of company and industry practices because of consumer input has not occurred until the modern era. Early consumerism aided the growth of the industry, as govern-

TABLE 7.2

Mail-Order Company Responses to Study

Question 1	The Consumer: What type of policy do you have for handling complaints? Do you have a consumer complaint department? Is there a consumer advocate in-house? Do you have an educational program or participate in educational programs for consumers?
BMC	The complaint department processes all complaints with personal letters or phone calls. There is no in-house consumer advocate. There is no educational program.
PCH	The company policy is "The Customer is always right—and, even when she's wrong, we treat her as though she were right." A Magazine Action Line was established in 1973 to resolve subscription problems. The Customer Service Department employs 100 people to answer customer letters or toll-free phone calls. The Director of Consumer Affairs is an in-house advocate who reports to the Vice-President of Operations. Two educational booklets describe company services.
Question 2	The Product and Service: What type of product-related information is made available to the public? Are you modifying or changing your products or services in response to consumerism? What procedure do you follow to ensure product and service quality?
BMC	No product-related information is made available. Products and services are the best available.
PCH	Two booklets on PCH are distributed. There is no need to change or modify products or services. The lowest available prices for magazine subscriptions are offered with a guarantee of complete satisfaction. "Free Trial on Approval" invitations help assure complete satisfaction before payment. A program of test orders helps to monitor dates of subscription starts, publisher resolution of complaints, and timely responses. An internal Consumer Council also evaluates billing problems and cancellations, and tries to develop new and improved procedures.

(continued)

Table 7.2 (continued)

Question 3	Outside Influences: What type of consumer regulations affect your operations? How do you respond to outside consumer pressure? How do you evaluate the effect of consumerism on your company?
BMC	The company accepts any product for return and reimburses customers for postage. There are no "consumerism" product problems.
PCH	The FTC's 30-day rule has an impact. The company takes responsibility, by offering positive or negative options to those subscribers whose first issue of a magazine is not available as soon as possible. There are few outside pressures, as a result of the policy of customer satisfaction and cooperation with the Better Business Bureau and Postal Service. PCH encourages responsive consumerism. The Magazine Action Line and Consumers Council seek to eliminate consumer problems. The company belongs to the Direct Mail/Marketing Association and the Society of Consumer Affairs Professionals in Business. The Director of Consumer Affairs participates in interviews, projects, and workshops to stress the consumer-oriented attitude of PCH.

Source: Compiled by the author.

ment regulations created a favorable atmosphere for expansion. Retail businesses brought suit against mail-order companies, charging unfair competition, but consumer demand for the variety of merchandise and convenience that mail order provides grew rapidly.

In recent years, consumers and government have reacted to improper uses of credit, unsolicited merchandise, poor customer service functions, lotteries, contests, misuse of the word free, late delivery, deceptive advertising, and invasion of privacy. Consumer Reports has published several articles on mail-order schemes and gimmicks and rated company performance.

The Federal Trade Commission and the Post Office have the major responsibility for regulating the mail-order industry. Both have used their powers to eliminate unfair or deceptive business practices. Several states also have acted to discontinue fraudulent mail-order policies.

Trade associations have developed procedures for dealing with consumer issues and have testified before Congress. Regulations have been revised, due to association presentations. Individual companies have had similar effects on proposed legislation. Many now call their customer service departments "consumer affairs" departments. Internal policies have been changed to conform with FTC rulings and cease-and-desist orders. Costs have been passed along to consumers.

In October 1977, Congress defeated an amendment to the FTC Act that would have made companies that violated cease-and-desist orders liable to class action suits [88]. Trade associations and individual companies do not have the ability to eliminate dishonest mail-order firms, but they do publicize the practices of these firms.

Evaluation of Consumerism

Since consumer problems have recurred over the years, the success of guidelines prohibiting unfair or deceptive practices is questionable. Consumer issues cannot be resolved with the current resources of the FTC and the Post Office.

Trade associations and companies, while having consumer-oriented policies, have done a poor job of informing consumers of their existence. For example, the burden of telling consumers about how mailing lists work, what data businesses retain from them, and removing names from mail listings should be borne by companies, not consumers. The costs of this would be offset by the positive publicity generated.

Many unsuspecting people are still bilked by less-than-honest mail-order schemes. They require further legislative protection.

The FTC and Post Office may allow too much industry input when developing guidelines. Consumer groups frequently have too little input, sometimes because of underrepresentation in this industry.

Trade associations and companies have generated some self-regulation, but not enough. The DMMA has done the best job in this area, although it gave a weak response to the mail questionnaire it was sent. The major thrust of self-regulation has been the attempt of trade associations and companies to offer modifications of proposed government guidelines, and then support their passage. The industry must work harder to eliminate dishonest firms.

As a 1976 Consumer Reports article on mailing lists and privacy concluded, consumerism issues in the mail-order industry are not easy:

> it's unclear how a mandatory system would work and who would administer it. How, for example, do you accommodate a person who wants to be taken off some lists but not others? Should mass compilers like Donnelley and Polk bear the cost of sending name-removal forms to 60 million households? If a person wants to be taken off all lists, is that for one year, five years, or a lifetime? The questions are difficult indeed [95, p. 542].

FUTURE OUTLOOK

No consumer group will evolve to concentrate on the mail-order industry. Therefore, the influence of the general groups, which focus on issues from time to time, will remain limited. Overall reform will not be advocated because of this issue-oriented approach. Interaction among consumer groups, industry associations, and government will not expand rapidly.

The lack of a federal consumer agency will result in little, if any, forward movement in mail-order consumerism. Problems will continue to be resolved in a case-by-case manner. Local and state agencies will become more involved in reducing fraudulent mail-order practices. The outcome of this will be a confusing maze of consumer regulations that will affect consumers and the industry.

Trade associations will continue to have limited regulatory influence on members. Their prime functions will remain the staunch advocation of industry positions and information for members and consumers. They will appear before more state, local, and consumer organizations.

Large, ongoing mail order companies generally will comply with consumer and government requests on a voluntary basis. They will develop departments and policies to handle consumer-oriented issues. The companies will better educate both employees and consumers. Some dishonest companies will continue to fluorish; in some cases they will be prosecuted and reopen under new names.

RECOMMENDATIONS

Recommendations follow for consumer groups, government, the industry, and individual companies.

Consumer Groups

The consumer groups concerned with mail-order abuses should develop a channel of communication among consumers, industry, and government agencies. This would best be accomplished by the establishment of a national consumer group specifically involved with the mail-order industry. This group could be a clearinghouse for state and local organizations. Lobbying also would be increased and be more effective.

Government

In the absence of a federal consumer agency, the Federal Trade Commission and the Post Office must receive greater resources and authority to police the mail-order industry. The public needs to be better informed about unfair business practices. The agencies should be given the power to initiate class action suits on behalf of consumers. Communication with the industry should be improved, while at the same time balancing business inputs with consumer needs. More stringent self-regulation should be encouraged.

The Industry

Trade associations must become more active policymakers, and influence their companies to adopt codes of ethics and follow consumer-oriented policies. Better self-regulation will reduce the need for government action. Improved and frequent communications with consumers, explaining the mechanisms of mail-order schemes and how to avoid them, are essential.

Companies

Individual companies must be honest and informative. They should seek voluntarily to correct poor practices, and quickly respond to consumer complaints. Programs should be set up to assure the quality of advertising, screen operations, and pinpoint potential problems before they get out of hand. A consumer orientation should be pursued enthusiastically. Complaint departments and in-house consumer advocates should be developed. Favorable publicity from the enactment of these policies will enhance company reputations and sales.

BIBLIOGRAPHY

1. "Ads and Consumers." Newsweek 14 (July 3, 1939), p. 38.

2. "AMREP, 4 Executives and 2 Units Convicted on Land Sale Charges." Wall Street Journal (January 25, 1977), p. 6.

3. "Ban Old Gold Type of Contests?" Business Week (May 22, 1937), pp. 25-26.

4. Beem, Eugene R. "The Beginnings of the Consumer Movement." In William Thomas Kelley, ed., New Consumerism: Selected Readings. Columbus, Ohio: Grid, 1973.

5. ___. "The Consumer Movement, 1930 to World War Two." In William Thomas Kelley, ed., New Consumerism: Selected Readings. Columbus, Ohio: Grid, 1973.

6. Better Business Bureau of New York. "A Report to Business." 3 (April 1978).

7. "Big Mail Order House Collides with Federal Trade Commission." Domestic Engineering 85 (December 7, 1918), p. 371.

8. Blood, Jack. "Montgomery Ward Spells Out New Direct Mail Approach." Merchandising Weekly 104 (October 16, 1972), p. 6.

9. Board of Governors of the Federal Reserve System. What You Ought to Know About Federal Regulation "Z" Truth in Lending. Washington, D.C.: July 1969.

10. "Buying Hardcover Books." Consumer Reports 43 (September 1977), pp. 505-09.

11. "Buying Lots by Mail? Beware!" Changing Times 11 (December 1957), pp. 17-19.

12. "Book-of-the-Month Tests Paperbacks." New York Times (January 8, 1974), p. 27.

13. Burns, John F. "Mail-Order Officials Defend Practices at Hearing Here." New York Times (November 13, 1975), p. 36.

14. "Carey Signs a Bill Aimed at Holding Down Auto Insurance Premiums." New York Times (August 17, 1977), p. 4.

15. Carper, Jean. "You Can Get Your Money Back." Reader's Digest 108 (May 1976), pp. 106-09.

16. Cavanaugh, John. "Getting Things Left." New York Times (May 22, 1977), p. 12.

17. Cerra, Frances. "Four Hi-Fi Makers Accept Prohibition on Fixing of Prices." New York Times (August 19, 1975), p. 1.

18. ____. "Study Finds Shoppers Have Problems with 25% of Purchases." New York Times (June 16, 1976), p. 50.

19. "The Changing Mail Orders." Financial World 124 (August 11, 1965), p. 20.

20. Charlton, Linda. "Company Offering Mail-Order Review of Potential Malpractice Scrutinized." New York Times (March 9, 1976), p. 16.

21. Cohn, David L. The Good Old Days. New York: Simon and Schuster, 1940.

22. "Commerce and Trade." United States Code Annotated, Title 15. St. Paul, Minnesota: West Publishing, 1973.

23. "Coupon Selling Scheme Declared Illegal." Printer's Ink 139 (May 12, 1927), pp. 19-20.

24. Creighton, Lucy Black. Pretenders to the Throne. Lexington, Mass.: D. C. Heath, 1976.

25. "Crimes and Criminal Procedure." United States Code Annotated, Title 18. St. Paul, Minnesota: West Publishing, 1973.

26. Crown, Paul. How to Build Your Mailing Lists. Dobbs Ferry, N.Y.: Oceana Publications, 1973.

27. "DMMA Ad Hoc Subcommittee's Guide for Self-Regulation of Sweepstakes Promotions." Printed by the DMMA, Washington, D.C.

28. "Deceptive Mail-vertising." U.S. Office of Consumer Affairs Consumer News 6 (August 2, 1976), p. 1.

29. Delay, Robert F. President's Report. DMMA Newsletter, December 1977.

30. ____. "Retail Direct Marketing Is Only Tip of Direct Marketing Iceberg." Advertising Age 45 (September 30, 1974), p. 65.

31. "Delusions of Vigor: Better Health by Mail." Consumer Reports 44 (January 1979), pp. 50-54.

32. Dembner, S. Arthur. "A Weeding-out in Mail Selling." Printer's Ink 278 (January 5, 1962), p. 48.

33. Devlin, Stanley. "Comparative Analysis of the Two Great Mail Order Companies." Magazine of Wall Street and Business Analysis 86 (June 1950), pp. 263-65ff.

34. Dickinson, Roy. "Irate Subscriber Registers Protest." Printer's Ink 137 (November 1926), pp. 93-95.

35. "Direct Mail: Finding New Growth, New Stature." Printer's Ink 274 (January 27, 1961), pp. 28-34.

36. Direct Mail/Marketing Association, Inc. "Guidelines for Ethical Business Practice of the Direct Mail/Marketing Association, Inc." (July 1976).

37. ____. "Mail Order Action Line." Undated fact sheet.

38. ____. "Mail Preference Service." Undated pamphlet.

39. ____. "Public Affairs Report." (December 1977.)

40. ____. "Why Membership Is Important to You?" Undated pamphlet.

41. Dougherty, Philip. "Advertising." New York Times (October 17, 1977), p. 17.

42. Drake, Maxwell. "Why Is a Mail-Order Buyer?" Printer's Ink 149 (December 5, 1929), pp. 102ff.

43. Eastman, R. O. "Small Leak in Consumer Good-Will Can Make a Big, Bad Puddle." Printer's Ink 233 (October 6, 1950), p. 31.

44. Emmet, Boris, and Jeuck, John E. Catalogs and Counters. Chicago: University of Chicago Press, 1950.

45. "Endless Chains." Business Week (February 1, 1933), p. 11.

46. "FTC Considers Alternate Rule." Publisher's Weekly 201 (April 10, 1972), p. 30.

47. "FTC Cracks Down on Free Goods Offers." Business Week (July 17, 1948), pp. 68-69.

48. "FTC Rule on Delayed Delivery of Mail Order Merchandise to Be Effective February 2, 1976." Memo from John Jay Daly to DMMA Members (October 25, 1975).

49. "FTC Tells Mail Firms to Stop in 30 Days or Else." Merchandising Weekly 107 (October 27, 1975), pp. 3ff.

50. Faber, Doris. Enough! The Revolt of the American Consumer. New York: Farrar, Straus & Giroux, 1972.

51. "Federal Trade Commission Charges Book Firms with Deceptive Use of the Term 'Free'." Publisher's Weekly 154 (July 17, 1948), pp. 203-05.

52. Federal Trade Commission. "Guide Concerning the Use of the Word 'Free' and Similar Representations." (November 16, 1971.)

53. ____. "Guides Against Deceptive Advertising of Guarantees." (April 26, 1960.)

54. ____. "Guides Against Deceptive Pricing." (January 8, 1964.)

55. ____. "Guides for Advertising Allowances and Other Merchandising Payments and Services." (August 4, 1972.)

56. ____. "Mail Order Merchandise." In Federal Register 40 (November 5, 1975), pp. 51,582-97.

57. ____, and the U.S. Postal Service. "Shopping by Mail? You're Protected!" Undated pamphlet.

58. ____. "Trade Regulation Rule Concerning the Use of Negative Option Plans by Sellers in Commerce." Effective June 7, 1964.

59. ____. "Unordered Merchandise—Consumer Bulletin No. 2." 1972.

60. "Fingerhut to Settle Suit Filed by San Francisco Over Ads, Other Issues." Wall Street Journal (February 23, 1977), p. 3.

61. Fisk, Margaret, ed. Encyclopedia of Associations. Detroit: Gale Research, 1977.

62. Friday Report. Garden City, N.Y.: Hoke Communications (April 8, 1977).

63. ____. (April 15, 1977.)

64. ____. (February 11, 1977.)

65. ____. (February 4, 1977.)

66. ____. (February 6, 1976.)

67. ____. (January 14, 1977.)

68. ____. (June 18, 1976.)

69. ____. (November 11, 1977.)

70. ____. (September 10, 1976.)

71. ____. (September 30, 1977.)

72. ____. (September 3, 1976.)

73. Geller, Eric. "Selling Encyclopedias." In David Sanford, ed., Hot War on the Consumer. New York: Pitman Publishing, 1969.

74. "General Business Law 1977-1978." In McKinney's Consolidated Laws of New York Annotated, Book 19. St. Paul, Minnesota: West Publishing, 1977.

75. "Genesco Is Ruled Liable by FTC Judge on Credit." New York Times (January 12, 1977), p. 5.

76. Gillett, Peter L. "In-Home Shoppers—An Overview." Journal of Marketing 40 (October 1976), pp. 81-88.

77. Gold, Gerald. "Consumer Beware," New York Times (May 16, 1974), p. 47.

78. "Good Year for Mail Order Firms." Financial World 112 (August 19, 1959), pp. 5-6.

79. Greenhouse, Belinda. "Wilson Attacks Banks' Sex Bias." New York Times (February 8, 1974), p. 34.

80. Gridley, Don. "Building Repeat Sales for a Mail-Order Business." Printer's Ink 138 (February 24, 1927), pp. 211-12ff.

81. "Grolier Hopes to Settle FTC Tiff by Negotiation." Advertising Age 42 (July 19, 1971), p. 2.

82. Gross, Nathan (as told to Don Gridley). "This Business Grew by Getting Close to the Consumer." Printer's Ink 158 (January 7, 1932), pp. 17-20.

83. "Gulf Oil Agrees to State That Mail Order Prices Include Credit Costs." Wall Street Journal (March 25, 1977), p. 38.

84. Hartley, William D. "I'll Send Away Now So That Someday My Prints Will Come." Wall Street Journal (December 21, 1976), p. 11.

85. Henry, Diane. "U.S. Blocks Leaflet on Bust Enlarging." New York Times (July 21, 1976), p. 20.

86. "High Court Upholds Obscenity Conviction." New York Times (May 24, 1977), p. 23.

87. Higley, Merle. "What the Consumer Wants and Will Pay For." Printer's Ink 227 (April 15, 1949), pp. 38-40

88. "House Kills Plan on Suits by Defrauded Consumers." New York Times (October 14, 1977), p. 5.

89. "How the Mail-Order House Handles the Fake 'Lost' Order." Printer's Ink 150 (March 13, 1939), pp. 41-42ff.

90. "How and Why the First Mail Order House Started." Printer's Ink 146 (January 3, 1929), pp. 129-30.

91. Howe, Andrew M. "Close Communion Selling." Printer's Ink 171 (May 16, 1935), pp. 37ff.

92. Hurja, A. O. "How a Mail Order House Brought Back Lost Customers." Printer's Ink 138 (March 24, 1927), pp. 49-50.

93. "Is Mail Order Buying Spreading From the Country to the City?" Printer's Ink 118 (May 4, 1922), pp. 146ff.

94. "Junking Junk Mail." New York Times (July 27, 1975), p. 13.

95. "Junk Mail: Getting It—And Getting Rid of It." Consumer Reports 41 (September 1976), pp. 540-42.

96. "Lefkowitz Warns on Record Company." New York Times (February 17, 1975), p. 25.

97. "The Legality of Selling Unordered Goods by Mail." Printer's Ink 139 (May 26, 1927), pp. 111-12.

98. Lewis, James, ed. The Consumer's Fight-Back Book. New York: Award Books, 1972.

99. Magnuson, Warren G., and Carper, Jean. The Dark Side of the Marketplace. Englewood Cliffs, N.J.: Prentice-Hall, 1968.

100. "Mail Offers Big Business, Sroge Says." Advertising Age 44 (January 29, 1973), p. 32.

101. "Mail Order Discount House Finds Trouble in Placing Triumphal Acts." Business Week (June 22, 1951), p. 15.

102. "Mail Order House Cited." New York Times (October 22, 1977), p. 51.

103. "Mail Order House Eliminates Customer Complaints." American Business 29 (January 1959), p. 44.

104. "Mail Order Operation Based in New York Is Accused by FTC." Wall Street Journal (October 9, 1975), p. 2.

105. "Mail Order Selling Now Reaches Almost Every Class." Printer's Ink 140 (September 15, 1927), pp. 195-96ff.

106. "Mail Order Vitamin Firm Accused by AMA." Printer's Ink 268 (August 7, 1959), p. 14.

107. "Mail Tracer Service Barred to Unordered Goods Vendors." Printer's Ink 140 (September 22, 1927), p. 44.

108. Mitgang, Herbert. "More Readers Using Clubs As Bookstores in Mailboxes." New York Times (October 23, 1977), p. 61.

109. "Mixed Results for the Mail Orders." Financial World 110 (September 10, 1958).

110. "More About Who Buys Goods by Mail." Printer's Ink 128 (July 24, 1924), pp. 69-70ff.

111. "More People Want Junk." New York Times (November 14, 1975), p. 61.

112. Murray, Barbara B. "Major Federal Consumer Protection Laws, 1960-1970." In Barbara B. Murray, ed., Consumerism: The Eternal Triangle. Pacific Palisades, Calif.: Goodyear Publishing, 1973.

113. "New Ground Rules Cover Mail Order Purchases." Consumer Reports 41 (February 1976), pp. 64-65.

114. "New Merchandising Methods of a Big Mail Order House." Printer's Ink 112 (September 23, 1920), pp. 137ff.

115. "New Rules for Negative Option Reflect Current Sell Methods." Advertising Age 44 (February 19, 1973), p. 3.

116. "Notice of Rulemaking Proceedings for the Establishment of a Trade Regulation Rule Relating to the Use of Negative Option Plans by Sellers in Commerce." Issued by the Federal Trade Commission (May 13, 1970).

117. "Obscenity Trial in Ohio Resumes with Defense Seeing Threat to Others." New York Times (January 31, 1977), p. 37.

118. Pettingill, H. E. "Customers Decided on This Manufacturer's Retail Outlets." Printer's Ink 132 (July 16, 1925), pp. 17-19.

119. "The Postal Service." In United States Code Annotated, Title 39. St. Paul, Minnesota: West Publishing, 1962.

120. Prior, Faith. "Today's Consumer Movement." In Loys L. Mather, ed., Economics of Consumer Protection. Danville, Illinois: Interstate Printers and Publishers, 1971.

121. Privacy Protection Study Commission. "Personal Privacy in an Information Society." July 1977.

122. Public Law 93-475. "Title III—Fair Credit Billing." (October 28, 1974.)

123. Public Law 93-495. "Title V—Equal Credit Opportunity." (October 28, 1974.)

124. Reynolds, Fred D. "An Analysis of Catalog Buying Behavior." Journal of Marketing 38 (July 1974), pp. 47-54.

125. Rosenbaum, S. G. "More People Than Ever Buying by Mail." Printer's Ink 118 (March 9, 1922), pp. 10ff.

126. Rosenfels, I. S. "Where Is Retail Mail Order Business the Thickest?" Printer's Ink 114 (February 3, 1921), pp. 53-54.

127. Rosenwald, Julius. "Why You Can't Do Too Much for Customers." System 46 (December 1924), pp. 709-12.

128. Rugaber, Walter. "American Express Lifts Its Ban to Stores' Discounts for Cash." New York Times (April 18, 1974), p. 1.

129. "Shaklee Corp. Consents to Order by the FTC." Wall Street Journal (October 28, 1975), p. 2.

130. Sheppard, Jr., Nathaniel. "Newark Termed Mail-Fraud Base." New York Times (May 6, 1974), p. 1.

131. Shimek, John Lyle. Billions of False Impressions: An Anthology of Deception. Chicago, Ill.: Concepts of Postal Economics, 1970.

132. Smalley, Orange A. "Market Entry and Economic Adaption."
In Hilma P. Holston, ed., Business History Review. Harvard
Graduate School of Business Administration. Massachusetts:
Harvard Press, 1962, pp. 372-401.

133. Smith, Roger H. "The Publishing and Selling of Mail Order
Books." Publisher's Weekly 205 (June 10, 1974), pp. 24-27.

134. "Spiegel Inc. Ordered to File Suits in Court Closer to the
Accused." Wall Street Journal (September 2, 1975), p. 7.

135. Springer, John L. Consumer Swindlers and How to Avoid Them.
Chicago: Henry Regnery, 1970.

136. Sterne, Michael. "Poor Are Victimized As Money Orders
Fail." New York Times (January 26, 1977), p. 7.

137. Stone, Bob. "Black Clouds Blow Over As Sweepstakes Are
Reformed." Advertising Age 48 (February 14, 1977), pp. 44-
54.

138. Subcommittee on Consumer Affairs. Give Yourself Credit.
Washington, D.C.: U.S. Government Printing Office, 1977.

139. "Suit for Consumers Says Credit Cards Hurt Cash Buyers."
New York Times (February 21, 1974), p. 21.

140. "Summary of the Magnuson-Moss Warranty Act and Federal
Trade Commission Rules." Prepared by the Merchandising
Division of the National Retail Merchants Association. Undated.

141. "That Pestiferous Guarantee." Printer's Ink 151 (May 20,
1930), pp. 146ff.

142. "Trial and Error Mark a Promotion." Printer's Ink 274
(January 27, 1961), p. 54.

143. "Two Credit Card and Store Concerns Ordered to Refund
Overpayments." New York Times (February 17, 1977), p. 56.

144. "Two N.J. Cos. Plead Guilty to Mail Fraud." New York Times
(February 17, 1977), p. 83.

145. "Unfail Trade." Newsweek 11 (March 28, 1928), p. 35.

146. "U.S. Pioneer Faces Tough Fight in Fair Trade M.O. Cases." Merchandising Week 107 (January 13, 1975), pp. 3ff.

147. "Unsolicited Merchandise Again Before Congress." Printer's Ink 158 (February 11, 1932), pp. 112ff.

148. Updegraff, Robert R. "Visualizing the Development Possibilities of Mail Order Markets." Printer's Ink 6 (March 1923), pp. 50ff.

149. Wadsworth, Ralph K. "How Many Times Will a Customer Buy by Mail?" Printer's Ink 121 (October 26, 1922), pp. 121-22.

150. Wagner, Susan. "FTC Documents Rule on Negative Option Selling." Publisher's Weekly 203 (February 26, 1973), pp. 105-06.

151. ____. "FTC Proposes Rule on 'Negative Option' Selling." Publisher's Weekly 201 (February 14, 1977), pp. 40-41.

152. "When the Needless Is Essential." Business Week (December 12, 1972), pp. 50-52.

153. "When Not to Go into the Retail Mail Order Business." Printer's Ink 115 (June 2, 1921), pp. 25-26.

154. "Who Buys from the Mail Order Catalogue?" Printer's Ink 111 (April 15, 1920), pp. 90ff.

155. "Will File Complaint Against Mail Order Houses." American Lumberman (January 12, 1918), pp. 36-37.

156. Winkler, M. "Humanizing the Mail Order—Our Way to 1400% Greater Volume." Magazine of Business 45 (April 1924), pp. 478-80.

8

CONSUMERISM AND THE PETROLEUM INDUSTRY

Alan D. Gaines

INTRODUCTION

Companies in the petroleum industry are involved with petroleum, natural gas, coal, petrochemicals, and nuclear energy. There is a discernible trend toward an "energy industry" [20]. For example, Continental Oil owns a coal firm, a petrochemical company, produces components for nuclear power plants, and has interests in natural gas [30]. Exxon has a chemical division. Occidental Petroleum owns the country's third largest coal producer.

Virtually all large petroleum firms are similar in their organization and operating structures. They are engaged in every aspect of the business: production, exploration, pipeline transportation, refining, and service stations. The average company has considerable control over supply, although this is declining because of OPEC, and prices.

In this chapter, the historical and current effects of consumerism in the petroleum industry are examined. The activities of consumer groups, government, the industry, and individual companies are presented and analyzed.

THE HISTORY OF CONSUMERISM IN THE PETROLEUM INDUSTRY

The petroleum industry has gone through three eras of consumerism, with the last being the most important. Individual consumer groups have not been much of a factor until recently. The government has been and continues to be the major watchdog of the industry. The eras of consumerism are delineated by the level of government regulation and intervention.

First Era

The first era lasted from the mid-1860s until the late 1800s. During this time, the government sought to ensure competition and was not really concerned about consumer protection, which was a by-product of some government activities.

Before 1850, thousands of very small firms existed. Revenues and profits also were small. During the late 1850s, firms started to grow and consolidate into larger, more efficient ones. Then holding companies emerged and several layers of bureaucratic structure developed. Cutthroat competition, corruption, and price-fixing were common [45].

At this time, prices were set by trade associations [44]. Fuel was sold to some areas at higher prices than in others. Locations that had shortages, often contrived, were charged high prices. In some instances, oil was handled by five or six middlemen, each of whom earned a commission. "Gentlemen's agreements" among firms were frequent, although illegal [45, p. 50]. Pools were formed where most or all of the firms fixed prices and shared markets.

During the late 1860s, pools came under fire from various groups, and another corporate structure was sought: the trust. Under this device, company stock was held by trustees in joint, rather than individual, accounts, so that stockholders gave up individual interests in their own companies and received a proportionate share in the total property and income of the entire trust. The powers of trustees were similar to those now held by directors of corporations [45, p. 185].

The government began to feel that the oil industry was not operating in the public interest in the 1870s. Since the trust mechanism allowed the supply of crude oil to be controlled, it represented a monopoly to the government. Several attempts were made to have industry self-regulation, but the companies did not react to government pressure. In 1879, Standard Oil was asked by government officials to hold down its profit margins and distribute petroleum products at fair prices throughout the country. This action failed [45, p. 304].

In 1882, Ohio instituted antitrust proceedings to dissolve the Standard Oil Trust. The Ohio Supreme Court stated that consumers as well as competition had rights:

> Much has been said in favor of the objects of the Standard Oil Trust and what it has accomplished. It may be true that it has improved the quality and cheapened the costs of petroleum and its products to the customer.

But, such is not one of the usual or general results of a monopoly, for that is what it is. Experience shows that it is not wise to trust human cupidity where it has been the opportunity to aggrandize itself at the expense of the public and the consumer [51, p. 14].

The Standard Oil Trust was ordered dissolved by the Ohio Supreme Court in 1892 on the grounds that illegal agreements had been made between Standard Oil and the railroads, and that Standard Oil dumped products overseas, controlled the supplies and prices of crude oil, and did not know the meaning of "social responsibility" [56, p. 19]. Several smaller firms were created. The Federal Interstate Commerce Act of 1887 and the Sherman Antitrust Act of 1890 were by-products of this case.

Second Era

The second main era lasted from the breakup of Standard Oil until the 1950s. This era saw the advent of the modern form of corporate structure. There were no longer trusts or pools. Individual firms were large, powerful overseas, and decentralized. Regulations limited price-fixing, corruption, and rates of return. Federal legislation was extensive: the Clayton Act in 1914, Federal Trade Commission Act in 1914, and the Securities and Exchange Act of the 1930s. Flagrant violations of law were countered with immediate government action. Yet, until 1951, consumerism was relatively dormant.

In 1951, a group of stockholders filed a class action suit against New York Oil, charging the company with manipulating stock prices and shareholder asset value [98]. It was alleged that reported earnings were held down, causing low valuation of stock. Company directors then would buy the stock and sell it at higher prices after true earnings were released. The New York Supreme Court ruled for the stockholders in 1953. The management of New York Oil was disbanded, and four members were fined heavily [58]. This was the first major case won by shareholders of any oil concern since passage of the Security and Exchange Acts. Standard Oil of New Jersey, now Exxon, acquired New York Oil in 1957.

The stockholders of Wyler Oil and Gas sued the firm in order to oust the board of directors, who were accused in 1952 of unfair trading of stock and production control. The state of Kansas charged the company with price-fixing. In 1954, Wyler was forced to reorganize; after failure to do so, it went bankrupt [29, 48].

During 1957, the stockholders of Judd Oil and Gas were able to discharge the entire board of directors because of stock manipulation [97]. Also in 1957, officials of Oilex, a small natural gas and transmission firm, were indicted and convicted of falsifying reported earnings to stockholders and debtors. The company went into Chapter Eleven in 1960, and its assets were distributed to stockholders and debtors [93, 69].

Modern Era

The modern era has been characterized by the growth of giant, multinational energy corporations that developed through a series of consolidations and mergers in the 1960s and the internal growth of the industry. The current oil industry in the United States is dominated by the "seven sisters": Exxon, SoCal, Gulf, Mobil, Texaco, British Petroleum, and Royal Dutch Petroleum. The first four companies are members of Aramco and control crude oil from Saudi Arabia, Kuwait, and the Arab Emirates. They are known as the "four sisters."

Many court cases have arisen since the early 1960s. Some have been similar to the stock manipulation, price-fixing, hoarding, and cartel suits brought in earlier years. Others have dealt with false or deceptive advertising and other consumer issues. Following, in chronological order, are the most important cases.

In 1961, Gulf was charged with false advertising for its no-nox gasoline. Customers claimed Gulf deceptively said the gasoline would increase mileage [32]. Texaco was sued on the same ground in 1962 [65]. The State Court of California upheld both companies, since it found that there was a chemical difference between these gasolines and others on the market. This difference could increase mileage for the average driver [16].

Amerada Petroleum, Wainoco Oil, Texas International Oil, and El Paso Natural Gas were accused by Texas Eastern Transmission Company of the illegal formation of a cartel to control gas and oil supplies and prices in a four-state area in 1966. Amerada pleaded innocent and was exonerated. The other firms pleaded no contest and were fined [49, 5].

Shell, Mobil, and Indiana Standard were charged with deceptive advertising of additives in motor oils and gasolines in 1969 by the Federal Trade Commission (FTC). The California Supreme Court forced the companies to stress that their additives worked for the average driver, not all drivers [31].

During 1971, Texaco was alleged to overcharge service station dealers for gasoline. A court order required the company to remit the difference between a fair price and what the dealer had been paying [4]. Exxon was charged with mishandling petroleum in 1972. The use of many middlemen raised prices for consumers, while the middlemen made profits. Exxon was fined $10,000 by the New York Department of Consumer Affairs [26]. In 1973, Davis Oil, the largest independent crude oil refiner, sued Exxon, Mobil, Phillips Petroleum, and Coastal States Gas on the basis of discriminatory pricing practices and attempts to monopolize the industry. The case was won by Davis in 1975, after reaching the Texas Supreme Court. It was the first time an independent had ever won a substantial judgment against any of the larger internationals [86, 33].

Exxon, Mobil, Gulf, SoCal, and Arco were charged with hoarding gasoline in order to take advantage of rising daily prices during the 1973 Arab oil embargo. Many states, including New York, New Jersey, and Connecticut, filed suit. The companies pleaded no contest, and were fined heavily by the respective state attorneys general [13]. Also in 1973, Gulf, Exxon, Shell, Mobil, Texaco, SoCal, Indiana Standard, Hess, Sohio, and Arco were accused of price-fixing and employing a loose cartel to control the supply of crude oil. All the firms pleaded no contest and were fined [68].

The Gulf bribery case occurred in 1974. The company admitted making illegal payments to foreign officials and was fined. In 1975, Gulf stockholders sued the firm for falsifying reported earnings, which led to a decline in the price of common stock. The California Supreme Court found Gulf guilty and fined it [62, 40]. Six other oil companies reported the use of illegal payments overseas; some were fined [62].

The Justice Department filed a 1975 suit against the oil companies on the basis of restraint of trade. It called for divestiture of nonoil businesses [44]. The case is yet to be settled.

Independent gasoline marketers sued Gulf, Texaco, and Sun Oil in 1975 for allegedly attempting to eliminate independent service stations, raising leases by unfair amounts, and setting high prices. The marketers won their case in 1976. Leases and other costs were reduced in many instances, and retroactive payments were received by independent station operators [57, 86].

In 1976, Shell, Amerada Hess, Sun Oil, Superior Oil, Mesa Petroleum, and Coastal States Gas reported illegal payments had been made overseas. All were fined, although not as much as previous companies [9]. The Atomic Energy Commission (AEC) charged Exxon, Conoco, and United Nuclear with forming a "nuclear cartel" to push for more lenient legislation in the construction of atomic breeder reactors in 1976. The firms pleaded no contest and were not fined [66].

Recently, it has become evident that most gasolines of a similar type, such as lead free, regular, and premium, are priced within pennies of each other at the service station. Since company rates of return vary greatly, the similarity in prices has been questioned. Oil companies usually follow the actions of Exxon, which has been the price leader [17].

Despite the fact that pump prices have increased dramatically, gasoline has been something of a loss leader:

> The big oil companies didn't give a damn about gasoline
> marketing: it was just a necessary evil. The purpose
> of the service station was to keep pumping gasoline,
> whether at a profit or not, so that companies could
> make their large profits at the wellhead [47, p. 5].

The oil companies say wellhead costs are similar. This is where prices are determined.

The value of the new synthetic oils has been disputed. The leader in this area is Mobil, with Mobil One oil. The companies claim the average automobile can ride up to three times longer between oil changes by using the new products. In most instances, they are up to five times more expensive [92].

During the last year, as the oil crisis worsened with the events in Iran and the price hikes by OPEC, U.S. oil companies have come under intense criticism regarding prices, possible hoarding, allocation of supplies, profits, and the scarcity of alternative fuels. This criticism and potential government actions will not let up in the near future.

ACTIVE CONSUMER GROUPS

There has been little consumerism activity in the petroleum industry. As W. P. Tavoulareas, president of Mobil, has said:

> The lack of the organized consumer is eminently evident
> in our industry. It seems that the public has left it to
> the industry as a whole to do much of their own self-
> regulation. As for the overall health of this gesture,
> this remains to be seen [91, p. 2].

Three consumer groups have had the most impact on the petroleum industry: Petroleum Watchdog, Consumers Union, and the Sierra Club.

Petroleum Watchdog

Since the oil embargo of 1973-74, Ralph Nader has monitored the industry through his Petroleum Watchdog division. A staff of 20 to 50 people work in this division and constantly survey activities within the petroleum industry. Inconsistencies are investigated, and when necessary, lawsuits are filed.

In 1976, on behalf of independent gasoline retailers, Petroleum Watchdog sued the four sisters, plus Shell and Texaco, for the purpose of ensuring a competitive atmosphere in which independents could operate. Restraint of trade and unfair transportation and pricing tactics were charged. Petroleum Watchdog maintained that larger firms held back supplies of crude oil and gasoline in order to raise prices, making it difficult for independents to compete with them. A lower court in California ruled in favor of the oil companies in 1976 [37, 64]. Petroleum Watchdog and Power Test, the largest independent marketer of gasoline, appealed the ruling. Some provisions of the initial lawsuit have been adopted by four states: California, Oklahoma, Arizona, and Texas. These states now require a fair pricing system for independents [43].

Consumers Union

Consumers Union, publisher of Consumer Reports, has shown some involvement with the petroleum industry. Throughout the late 1960s and the 1970s, Consumer Reports reviewed different gasolines and motor oils, including additives.

In 1969, Consumers Union initiated a suit charging the petroleum industry with deceptive and misleading advertising. Despite oil company assertions, Consumers Union tests showed additives to be similar in chemical configuration and operational results. The California Supreme Court ruled in January 1970 that there were enough differences in the additives for the companies to differentiate them in a fair and proper manner. The court also decreed that the firms had to place disclaimers in their advertisements that stated conditions varied according to driving and servicing [78, 79]. The court appeared to accept the contention of a former director of the American Petroleum Institute:

> Gasoline additives all have the basic configuration
> continuity, but do differ in a way that each particular
> additive performs a regulated and different function
> within each specific gasoline. In other words, the

same additive would not react the same within a different
gasoline. Each gasoline, therefore, gets the most
individual benefit from its own particular additive,
thus for the benefit of the consumer [80].

At the height of the Arab oil embargo in 1973, Consumers
Union sued the oil industry for hoarding gasoline. Consumers Union
said gasoline was being sold to areas that were willing to pay price
increases. The New York State attorney general charged all the
major east coast dealers, such as Exxon, Texaco, Gulf, and Mobil,
with withholding gasoline. Stiff fines were levied on the firms, which
pleaded no contest [1, 101].

Sierra Club

An environmental group, with considerable lobbying power,
is the Sierra Club of California. In January 1977, the Sierra Club
sued Exxon Nuclear, Conoco International, United Nuclear, and
Gulf Oil for allegedly employing a nuclear cartel to influence key
Senate members to ease the safety and construction restrictions for
breeder reactors. The club was not opposed to individual lobbying,
but felt the combined efforts of the firms were excessive [28]. The
firms stopped their joint lobbying.

Other Consumer Groups

Many small pressure groups formed just before or since the
1973-74 Arab oil embargo, including: Energy Free America in 1972,
Watchful Eye on Energy in 1974, Energy Independent America in
1974, Consumer Energy Committee in 1974, Energy Educational
Services in 1975, and Energy Conscious America in 1976. The most
influential of these groups has been Energy Independent America,
which has employed letter-writing campaigns, concentrated protests,
and educational programs.

Occasionally, citizens have joined together on a particular
oil-related issue. For example, Concerned Citizens of Long Island
was upset about offshore drilling rights on the Long Island Sound.
The group initiated a suit calling for a ban on this drilling because
of fear of an oil spill and damage to the area's fishing industry [7].
As of this writing, the case was still pending.

GOVERNMENT

The petroleum industry is under strict regulation at the federal and state levels. There are five primary federal agencies that are responsible for regulating the industry: Justice Department, Interstate Commerce Commission (ICC), Federal Trade Commission, Environmental Protection Agency (EPA), and Department of Energy (DOE). Their activities are discussed in detail below.

Other government agencies also have some responsibility for the petroleum industry, but mainly on a secondary level: Agency for Energy Policy and Planning, Atomic Energy Commission, Federal Pipeline Authority, Federal Planning Commission, Federal Power Commission, Interstate Pipeline Commission, Interstate Transport Authority, Senate Energy Commission, Department of Commerce, and Department of the Interior.

Justice Department

The Justice Department was established formally as an executive department reporting to the attorney general in 1870. The department operates against the formation of monopolies or monopolistic practices, and acts on illegal restraints of trade. Antitrust proceedings and litigation are tools of the department.

Both the Federal Trade Commission and the Justice Department have similar divestiture suits pending against the major international oil companies. The Justice suit is far less radical [94]. The suit was initiated in July 1977 and calls for the horizontal divestiture of nonoil assets by U.S. petroleum companies. Networks involving petroleum would remain unchanged [14].

Interstate Commerce Commission

The Interstate Commerce Commission was formed in 1887 as a result of the Standard Oil case. Originally oriented toward railroad operations, the ICC now is involved with all types of interstate business. The commission regulates the interstate transit of petroleum and natural gas, and issues guidelines regarding quantities shipped, methods of transportation, and safety. Limited regulation of interstate pipelines is undertaken by the ICC; the majority of pipeline legislation is under the jurisdiction of the Federal Pipeline Authority [17].

From time to time, the ICC has sued and subsequently fined oil companies and pipeline firms for rule violations. No significant consumer benefits resulted from these cases. Generally, when the commission won a decision, a small fine was imposed and the case closed [17, p. 19].

Federal Trade Commission

The Federal Trade Commission, created in 1914 and involved with unfair competition and restraint of trade, seeks to ensure that crude oil is not mishandled or illegally hoarded, and that false or misleading advertising claims are not made.

In 1971, the FTC brought a suit against STP for "false and misleading effectiveness claims and representations for STP oil and gas treatments, and STP filters" [2, p. 3]. The FTC said that every car "does not have to use STP products in order to reduce friction and increase engine efficiency"; and "Any representation of benefit for STP's additives must be based upon competent and reliable testing sources in order to substantiate scientific data" [2, p. 3].

Under the threat of court action, then STP chairman Andy Granatelli and president Craig Nelson appeared at various FTC hearings. As a result of the hearings, STP agreed that future advertising claims would be substantiated scientifically. In further action, the company was fined heavily and published the following corrective advertisement in the February 13, 1978, Business Week, as well as other publications:

> FTC NOTICE: As a result of an investigation by the Federal Trade Commission into certain allegedly inaccurate past advertisements for STP's oil additive, STP Corporation has agreed to a $700,000 settlement. . . .

The FTC began a case in 1975 calling for the complete reorganization of major domestic oil companies via vertical divestiture. This would force integrated producers to divide their operations by function, permitting each firm to control only one aspect of the business: production, pipeline transportation, refining, exploration, or marketing [94]. The case has not been settled yet.

Environmental Protection Agency

The Environmental Protection Agency, formed in 1967, regulates pollution levels for the disposal of organic, chemical, and nuclear wastes. In both 1975 and 1976, EPA delayed construction of the Alaska pipeline, costing the petroleum industry billions of dollars in lost revenues during the delay. The EPA was concerned about faulty welds at crucial points in the pipeline [74]. During 1976, EPA sued the Exxon Pipeline Company for dumping violations that caused unnecessary pollution and health hazards. The company pleaded no contest and was fined [35].

The EPA also has been involved with the building and development of atomic breeder reactors. Almost all the major petroleum companies are active in this area. For various reasons, usually health or safety, EPA has delayed the building of reactors in heavily populated areas. In September 1977, it enumerated various precautionary measures to be taken during and after the construction of breeder reactors [39].

The EPA lobbied for clearer and more effective legislation of gasoline octane ratings in 1977. Before EPA's interest, octane was measured under two conditions to determine ratings. Companies used ratings obtained by research octane, which measured gasoline under mild conditions and gave high ratings, such as 94, for regular gasoline. Motor octane measured gasoline under harsh conditions and gave low ratings, such as 86, for regular gasoline. These ratings were not used by companies. Through EPA pressure, the Cost of Living Council determined that octane ratings should be simple averages of research octane and motor octane. These average ratings now appear on U.S. gas pumps [21].

Department of Energy

The Department of Energy, formerly the Federal Energy Administration, was made a cabinet-level department in 1977. DOE is responsible primarily for examining energy bills, setting natural gas prices, setting efficiency standards for oil-related products and by-products, and developing and approving a national solar energy schedule. The major objectives are the reduction of foreign oil imports and the vulnerability to external pressures, and the attainment of renewable and inexhaustible sources of energy for sustained economic growth [84].

DOE has an Office of Consumer Affairs to enable consumers to participate in national policy and program determinations. Conservation literature is available for consumers from the department.

DOE does not regulate the petroleum industry by using threats of litigation or fine. These actions are undertaken by other regulatory bodies at the request of DOE. The department does expect individual companies to incorporate national policies into their own corporate planning and act responsibly.

The National Petroleum Council, created in 1946 (well before DOE), is a federal advisory committee that reports to the departments of Energy and the Interior. The council advises, informs, and makes recommendations to these departments on matters pertaining to the petroleum industry. It has issued over 200 reports since 1946, many of which have led to new legislation or policies [65]. For example, "Offshore Drilling and Petroleum Resources Under the Ocean Floor" resulted in regulations for new offshore and onshore oil and natural gas production [67].

The council feels consumerism is not yet a powerful bloc, but will be: "The future impact will be of a more positive nature, forcing firms into safer environmental practices" [65, p. 22].

Congressional Subcommittees

At different times, congressional subcommittees have been formed to hold hearings regarding practices within the petroleum industry. For example, in 1975 and again in 1977, Senate hearings subpoenaed Exxon, Sohio, Gulf, and Texaco to investigate illegal overseas payments [99]. Since the hearings, and without government threats, many companies have explained publicly their overseas payments [6].

INDUSTRY RESPONSES TO CONSUMERISM

The responses of the petroleum industry to consumerism are found in the literature and in a mail survey with leading trade associations.

Industry Responses as Reported in the Literature

Trade associations have conducted their own independent research studies and testified before governmental hearings in order to "keep a close and harmonious relationship with government forces affecting the industry and our customers" [44, p. 13]. A president of the American Petroleum Institute (API), the largest and most active trade association in the industry, has said:

> We reserve the right to disagree with various legislation which we find will not act in the best interests of the consumer. We will continue to work with the government, as we have done in the past, for the

legislation we feel will reform the industry, and aid
in the national interest of the public and the nation
[44, p. 17].

Throughout the late 1940s and 1950s, the industry, particularly
the American Petroleum Institute, worked with state supreme courts
to correct what it perceived as abuses against the public. For example, API worked with New York Oil stockholders to correct abuses
resulting in "fraudulent practices which would be detrimental to the
public, and the credibility of the industry overall" [8, p. 23].

In 1968, API and the National Petroleum Refiners Association
assisted the Federal Trade Commission in its case against Mobil,
Shell, and Indiana Standard. The FTC accused the companies of
deceptive advertising. The two associations prepared reports on
different gasolines and additives to spell out more clearly chemical
differences, if any [17]. The API cautioned about the advertising
of these products:

Positive effort should be undertaken in order that the
consumer is properly represented where advertising
of petroleum based products is concerned, making sure
there is truth and fact present in all claims [88, p. 32].

The API, the National Petroleum Refiners Association, and
the Pennsylvania Crude Oil Association backed STP in 1971. This
time the API said:

The fact is, STP has used independent scientific testing
procedures which prove the claims made to be true.
These claims should have the right to be advertised,
and we at the Institute will continue with our legal
efforts to support STP [88, p. 32].

Regarding current issues, the industry continues to oppose
regulation of natural gas pricing and any form of restructuring
(divestiture). Although trade associations have differed with government viewpoints, all legislation has been followed after enactment.

The American Petroleum Institute remains as the most dominant organization. It has 146 paid lobbyists in Washington, D.C.
The National Petroleum Refiners Association is second with 40
lobbyists [100, p. 1,879]. Executive lobbying by associations is
extensive, and the lobbyists are considered the most influential,
persuasive, and wealthy in Washington [10].

Some members of Congress have been severely critical of the
persuasion methods used by the associations [10, p. 3]. A former
director of the American Trial Lawyers Association has stated:

Many oil lobbies, directed by either company or trade association officials, are schooled on the "art of government," focusing major efforts at key points and persons whereby decisions are made and policy determined and converted into action. They utilize methods they deem appropriate for their circumstances within the limits of their resources, policies, and ethics. For most groups, their resources and policies are known by now. However, their ethical outlook and methods regarding this area leave much to be desired by some, including myself [11, p. 13].

Tools of oil lobbyists have included bribery, sexual favors, gifts, and political favors [11, p. 14]. In some instances, lobbyists have been fined or jailed [63].

Trade Association Responses to Primary Study

A mail questionnaire on consumerism in the petroleum industry was sent to eight major trade associations. Two responded: American Petroleum Institute (API) and Oil Spill Control Association of America (OSCAA). Six associations did not reply, after two requests: Independent Refiners Association of America, Mid-Continent Oil and Gas Association, National Energy Producers Council, National Petroleum Refiners Association, Pennsylvania Grade Crude Oil Association, and the Society of Independent Gasoline Marketers of America.

The American Petroleum Institute submitted a detailed and comprehensive reply. It included samples of consumer information. The API classifies consumerists as adaptionists (education-based), protectionists (government as protector), or, reformers (activists). It supports adaptionists; it is opposed to divestiture.

The Oil Spill Control Association of America sent a briefer response. Individual questions were not answered; a general statement was written. The association has broad objectives, centering on improved communication and professionalism.

Because of the number of nonresponses, a general summary cannot be developed. Table 8.1 contains condensed and categorized answers from the two participating associations. Answers were categorized by the author.

TABLE 8.1

Petroleum Trade Association Responses to Study

Question 1	Generally speaking, how does your association feel about the consumer movement?
API	Activities of this type are no longer a passing fad. Although private consumers are weak in general, the movement as a whole will continue to assert itself as a persuasive and powerful influence on business and governmental decisions.
OSCAA	There is no response indicated for this question.
Question 2	How has the consumer movement affected the companies that belong to your organization?
API	The movement has affected the firms to varying degrees. While it is not directly responsible for declining public confidence in the oil industry, it has caused some confidence to be lost regarding the expertise of the industry, leadership, the wisdom of self-regulation, and the overall veracity of the industry.
OSCAA	Standards have been developed to prevent unnecessary pollution caused by spills and the needless destruction of marine life. Member firms have become more ecologically and safety-minded over the last decade.
Question 3	Has the association created a panel, position, or department to deal with the effects of the consumer movement?
API	In 1977, a Committee on Consumer Affairs was created to monitor, evaluate, and report on developments in the consumer movement. The External Liaison Department allows industry members to meet directly with public interest groups. The Public Relations Department publishes educational material for the consumer's benefit.
OSCAA	The Public Liaison Department enables members to communicate with consumers.

(continued)

Table 8.1 (continued)

Question 4   Does the association provide representatives to appear before governmental committees examining consumer issues?

API   The institute has appeared before Senate Select Committees as well as other hearings examining consumer issues. The effects of particular issues on consumers are related.

OSCAA   The association has never been asked to appear, but would do so if requested.

Question 5   Does the association provide speakers to appear before national and/or local consumer organizations?

API   The Public Affairs Department coordinates this activity by scheduling company speakers on almost every energy issue. The institute has 34 state petroleum councils, each of which has a speakers bureau and programs for consumers.

OSCAA   Speakers are provided to various public interest groups, concentrating on subjects of current interest to the oil and hazardous materials spill control industry.

Question 6   What do you perceive to be the long-term impact of consumerism on the industry that you represent?

API   The industry must regain consumer confidence in order to solve the energy problem. Socially desirable industry actions will become more commonplace. Antitrust legislation probably will continue and produce changes within the industry, although not of a sweeping nature.

OSCAA   There is no response indicated for this question.

Source: Compiled by the author.

254

COMPANY RESPONSES TO CONSUMERISM

The responses of individual petroleum companies to consumerism have been reported in the literature and obtained through a primary study with leading companies.

Company Responses as Reported in the Literature

Individual firms have reacted differently in the way they have responded to consumerism. Some companies have made statements about issues affecting the petroleum industry. These are leader firms. Others have preferred not to comment at all and remained in the background. A third grouping of firms has followed the positions taken by the leader firms. Very rarely have companies publicly differed from each other on energy-related issues.

The consistently outspoken firms include Exxon, Mobil, and Shell. The relatively silent firms include Amerada Hess, Arco, Gulf, Texaco, Indiana Standard, Sohio, Sun, and Superior. Followers include Conoco, Phillips Petroleum, and SoCal.

As early as the 1920s, Standard Oil of New Jersey, now Exxon, spoke out against the foreign dumping of petroleum in the United States. In the 1930s, the company explained its pricing procedures to the public. During the 1950s, the company appeared, unsubpoenaed, at a Senate hearing on stock manipulation, fraud, and tampering with reported earnings:

> We feel obligated to the public to explain the nature
> of our earnings. The industry, as well, should feel
> it necessary to do the same, in order to act in a
> respectable fashion which reflects the industry, its
> judgments, and its personnel [45, p. 79].

Two days later, Mobil appeared and explained the nature of its earnings and how they were determined.

In the midst of the oil and gasoline additive controversy in the late 1960s, Mobil and Shell made statements about their products before any suits were initiated. Soon thereafter, Exxon issued a similar release [83].

Both Shell and Mobil ran a series of advertisements in the New York Times, Wall Street Journal, and Oil and Gas Journal during the 1973-74 oil embargo. The advertisements detailed the industry's position and role with OPEC. Exxon utilized television spot advertising to explain which nations comprised OPEC, how they functioned, and how the industry was dependent on OPEC for crude oil [34, p. 14].

Critics have stated that the 1973-74 shortage of oil was in part contrived by the U.S. oil industry to boost sagging prices. Samuel Thorne, an oil consultant, said:

> excess hoarding and withholding of oil enabled prices to rise more than they should have. The use of boycotts in an industry such as this is unthinkable and inexcusable [87, p. 25].

The industry has consistently and strongly denied these allegations.

Recently, Exxon, Shell, and Mobil have used trade journal and newspaper advertisements to stress the need for a viable energy policy in the United States. Exxon and Conoco have met regularly with consumer and public interest groups to discuss atomic breeder reactors.

Company Responses to Primary Study

Fourteen large petroleum companies were sent a questionnaire on consumerism in the industry. Nine answered the questions: Arco, Conoco, Exxon, Indiana Standard (IS), Mobil, Phillips Petroleum, Shell (Royal Dutch Petroleum), SoCal, and Texaco. Two firms said it would be too costly to participate: Gulf and Sohio. Three others did not respond at all, after two letters: Amerada Hess, Sun Oil and Superior Oil.

The nine responses were fairly thorough. Virtually all the firms sent literature on a variety of consumer issues, their annual reports, and answers to the survey.

Three of the companies have centralized, specialized departments to handle complaints and other consumer matters. Five direct complaints to appropriate division managers, and do not use a centralized department. All the companies want to treat customers and dealers promptly and fairly, and have consumer complaint procedures. About half the firms have consumer advocates, usually in complaint or consumer relations departments. The others feel their employees are objective and work for the consumer's benefit, and so advocates are not necessary. All of the companies, except Texaco, have educational programs for consumers, some more extensive than others. Common topics are women drivers, gasoline conservation and economy, and emergency car repair.

All the companies publish some material on their products, including specifications, proper usage, and safety. Texaco supplies information only on request; the others distribute information at service stations. Each of the firms continuously modifies products and services and upgrades quality. This is due to industry desires to satisfy customers, not consumer pressure. All of the firms utilize some type of quality control department. Only two mention independent testing facilities, and one mentions follow-up marketing surveys.

Six companies feel federal and state regulations are a major concern. Several others do not reply to this question. Five of the companies say consumer pressure requires minimum industry compliance, but competition and the desire to please consumers are more important. The other companies avoid the question. Responses to the question on the effects of consumerism are quite mixed. Most firms do think the consumer movement will play an increasingly important role in the future.

The corporate reaction to consumerism is summed up in this statement by Shell:

> Together, corporations and consumers can increase understanding of consumer expectations and improve performance in the marketplace, as well as understanding problems from the perspective of the firm and the industry. Together, consumers and corporations can oppose any unnecessary legislation and/or regulations that are not in the consumer or the national interest. By joint consultation, business and consumer organizations can better anticipate impending shifts in public attitudes and the need to adjust to consumer programs [25, p. 10].

Table 8.2 contains question-by-question capsule responses from each participating petroleum company. Answers were categorized by the author.

THE OVERALL EFFECTS OF CONSUMERISM

The impact of consumerism in the petroleum industry and an evaluation of it are presented below.

Impact of Consumerism

Petroleum Watchdog has been the most powerful consumer group since its formation in 1973. Most of the other groups involved with the petroleum industry are much smaller in size and power. Today, the consumer has a greater voice on petroleum issues than

TABLE 8.2

Petroleum Company Responses to Study

Question 1	The Consumer: What type of policy do you have for handling complaints? Do you have a consumer complaint department? Is there a consumer advocate in-house? Do you have educational programs or participate in such programs for consumers?
Arco	Complaints are handled in a broad way, not clearly spelled out in the response to the question. A Customer Relations Department processes complaints and inquiries. There is no in-house advocate. Educational programs involve women drivers, automobile maintenance, gasoline economy, and the mechanical workings of a car. They are conducted by the Public Affairs Division.
Conoco	Complaints are directed to the appropriate division manager, who relays a reply within two to four weeks. The company tries to be objective and fair with customers. There is no specific complaint department. An in-house consumer advocate is located in the marketing division. Seminars on car care and repair, aid for women drivers, and emergency repairs are conducted by the Consumer and Distributor Affairs Group.
Exxon	Complaints are handled in a speedy and fair manner by the Consumer and Distributor Affairs Group. The company is concerned with its image as an industry leader. Investigators are sent out to research each complaint. The in-house consumer advocate heads the Consumer and Distributor Affairs Group. Programs are aimed at car care and repair for women drivers. A national speakers program is used.
IS	Six regional managers report to a manager of the Customer Relations Division and settle complaints within one week. An in-house consumer advocate is located in the Customer Relations Group. Seminars are held for women drivers. Materials on gasoline selection and car care are published.
Mobil	Regional customer complaint managers are assigned to each of the company's four regions. They coordinate activities and ensure fair and speedy responses, if possible at the service outlet level. The Customer

(continued)

	Relations Department includes a resale administrator, wholesale administrator, specialist programs, and staff coordination. There is no in-house advocate, but a vice-president heads Customer Relations. Most educational efforts are directed at women drivers.
Phillips	Complaints are routed to the proper group or division, and dealt with on an individual basis. Divisional managers are responsible for resolving complaints. While there is no in-house advocate, the Environmental and Consumer Protection Department is directed by a vice-president. The Public Affairs Department makes a variety of educational materials available to schools, community groups, and individuals, emphasizing a film series called "American Enterprise."
Shell	The company seeks to be prompt and fair, and is currently rewriting retail complaint procedures. A Customer Complaint Department formulates Shell's policies and replies to complaints and inquiries. The department has eight regional offices. There is an in-house consumer advocate who is on the same level as the vice-president of retail sales. Educational booklets on a wide range of subjects are heavily promoted and distributed.
SoCal	Complaints are sent to the Customer Service Division, which processes them. Inexpensive requests are resolved immediately; others are thoroughly investigated. Several in-house advocates are located in the Consumer and Public Affairs Department. Educational seminars and courses are conducted, and consumer and Better Business Bureau meetings are attended.
Texaco	Each complaint is investigated by the Field Marketing Organization. Monetary complaints are settled through arbitration. There is no in-house advocate, but the General Manager of Marketing is considered sensitive to consumerism. A booklet on car care is published.
Question 2	The Product: What type of product-related information is made available to the public? Are you modifying

(continued)

Table 8.2 (continued)

	or changing your products in response to consumerism? What procedure do you follow to ensure product and service quality?
Arco	Many brochures on specific products are distributed through retail service station outlets. An increase in self-service outlets is in response to consumer desires to save time and money. A research facility, a quality control department, and thorough training of independent dealers ensure quality products and services.
Conoco	Information about all company products is available at service stations. New products are announced and explained to dealers in publications designed especially for them. All products and services are modified and adapted to consumer demand. Extensive laboratory and field testing are conducted before any new product is marketed.
Exxon	Brochures on most of the popular product lines are available in service stations. Products and services are adapted to consumer demand, as determined through studies. Self-service outlets are growing. A quality control department, a research facility, an in-house laboratory, and an independent laboratory certify product quality. Products exceed government standards by 10 percent.
IS	Product information is available for most items, some required by law. Products are changed to satisfy customers, not because of consumer pressure. Quality control procedures are not described.
Mobil	Brochures on motor oil and gasoline are available at retail outlets. A quality control department and extensive laboratory research facilities are maintained.
Phillips	Brochures explain popular product lines; radio and television help increase consumer awareness. Since 1974, more specific and detailed testing of new products has been implemented. Phillips ranks first in the industry in the number of new patents for the last decade. Research facilities, a quality control department, and independent testing laboratories are used to ensure product quality.

(continued)

Shell	Product and safety information are provided for all products. Point-of-sale displays help consumers choose among different grades of motor oil and gasoline. Changes include self-service, super regular gasoline, a program for automobile care, and self-repair facilities. A complete quality control procedure, from refinery to service station, is employed.
SoCal	There is product information for gasoline, motor oil, transmission fluid, and additives. Products and services are changed to please consumers, not because of consumerism. Independent testing laboratories assist SoCal's own facilities for quality control.
Texaco	Information is published about most products. Some information is not readily available. Other information, such as gasoline volatility and additives, is not available at all. Products are changed to comply with government regulations and consumer desires, not consumerism pressure. Research laboratories, a quality control department, and outside testing laboratories verify product and service quality.
Question 3	Outside Influences: What type of consumer regulations affect your operations? How do you respond to outside consumer pressures? How do you evaluate the effect of consumerism on your company?
Arco	Federal, state, and local agencies control operations to a certain extent. The public, not consumerists, influences operations. There are restrictions on wholesale and retail pricing, volume, packaging, labeling, and credit cards. The company responds to consumer desires and competition. Consumerism expresses itself through legislation. Arco supports consumerism, but reserves the right to disagree on issues not in the public interest.
Conoco	Federal regulations have a major impact on operations. Conoco is sensitive to consumer pressures when it represents customer preference. The consumer movement is a strong motivation to update products and improve services to customers.

(continued)

Table 8.2 (continued)

Exxon	Outside pressure receives a response if the pressure is in the best interest of customers. The consumer movement is supported, but issues not in the interest of customers are refuted.
IS	A highly competitive marketplace dictates changes, not pressure from consumer groups. The company, through its wholly owned Amoco subsidiary, supports consumer desires and interests. However, not all consumer groups operate for the benefit of the average consumer. For example, divestiture would not be in the consumer's interest.
Mobil	A response to this question is not indicated in Mobil's reply.
Phillips	Various regulations and directives add greatly to the cost of operations. Consumerism is a positive force when the proper issues are involved.
Shell	Federal pricing regulations and possible future divestiture are important factors in operations. Shell supports consumer pressure for needed improvements in the marketplace, such as advertising and fraudulent practices; it opposes divestiture as not in the public interest. The movement gives the company an opportunity to respond to consumer expectations and desires, and gain a competitive edge. In the near future, all companies will be as responsive to consumerism as Shell is today.
SoCal	The list of regulations affecting operations is too long to describe. Consumer pressure, when it represents customer desires, is supported. Consumer pressure and customer satisfaction go together.
Texaco	The list of regulations is too long to enumerate. The Justice Department and the Environmental Protection Agency are important regulatory bodies. To the extent that consumer pressure can be identified and a legal response made, the company usually will do so. It is doubted that the consumer movement has had much impact on the petroleum industry.

Source: Compiled by the author.

ever before, although it is still limited and fragmented. Education programs and lawsuits regarding deceptive business practices have increased consumer awareness of petroleum issues. Legislation also has resulted from consumer group actions.

The president of Concerned Citizens of Long Island has made a statement that reflects the evolution of consumer groups in this area:

> The formation of this group was due in part to the continuing increase in consumer awareness regarding environmental rulings and procedures which will affect the average consumer in a specific area. We have groups like the Sierra Club, as well as Mr. Nader's excellent organization, to thank for affording us the possibility and courage to form and oppose rulings which we, the consumers, feel are not in our best interest, and which can be changed by standing up for what we feel is just [7, p. 18].

The prime responsibility for overseeing the petroleum industry has resided with the federal government. A number of court suits have resulted in fines being imposed on offending companies. Court rulings have affected pricing policy, distribution of crude oil throughout the country, storage of gasoline and petroleum by-products, advertising practices and claims, restraint of trade, illegal stock trading, and fraudulent reporting and restating of corporate earnings. Consumers now have direct liaisons with large federal agencies, such as the Federal Trade Commission, through divisions or departments.

Trade associations and companies have established procedures for dealing with consumer complaints. Most have created specific departments to carry out their policies. Public relations between firms and customers are becoming increasingly important. In-house consumer advocates are more common, and education programs have expanded. Products and services are constantly modified and improved.

Evaluation of Consumerism

Consumerism has had a substantial effect on the petroleum industry. However, this has been due mostly to government activity and not consumer groups. In the last dozen years, consumer groups have exerted a greater influence and are on the verge of becoming a powerful force. As Shell Oil concludes:

> The consumer movement has allowed the interaction
> of business and consumer of a positive nature. Feed-
> back is a great aid for both sides. Although these
> various groups are not yet too powerful or potent,
> they will continue to guide the industry in the formula-
> tion of planning and policy, with customer satisfaction
> as the primary directive [25, p. 6].

Despite these comments, many associations and firms have
exhibited mixed feelings and actions toward consumerism. They
claim to support consumer desires, yet oppose many consumer-
oriented proposals. Even now, the industry is accused of worsening
the gasoline and oil shortage in order to raise prices and profits.
    Some company statements still exhibit insensitivity to consumer-
ism. For example, Arco says:

> The industry and the company respond to customer
> preference, not consumer pressures. The products
> we sell are the best we have to offer. If any customer
> feels offended by Arco's products, services, prices,
> or image, he has the mobility to buy from any competi-
> tor he chooses [38, p. 2].

It is debatable whether or not consumers are able to choose where
to buy in the current gasoline and oil situation.
    Phillips Petroleum states:

> We feel that much of the negative flow directed to the
> oil industry by the consumer has been due to misunder-
> standing of the existing energy situation, and the hesi-
> tancy of many elected officials to learn about those
> problems and face up to them, regarding our real
> energy needs and their seeming inability to provide
> us with a workable energy policy [73, p. 10].

Phillips and other members of the industry likewise have failed to
inform consumers adequately and work to alleviate the energy problem.
    None of the concerned parties, consumer groups, government,
trade associations, or individual companies has coordinated its
activities and satisfactorily performed to solve short- and long-run
consumer energy problems. All must assume some responsibility
for the present state of affairs. A balance must be struck between
society and consumer needs and industry profits and shareholder
satisfaction.

FUTURE OUTLOOK

The near future will bring the formation of larger, broader-based consumer groups concentrating on the petroleum industry. Existing groups will expand their efforts in this area. All the groups will meet with corporate and government officials to improve communications. They will exert much more influence and carry out important lobbying functions. The groups will push for new government legislation and consumer protection.

Federal regulatory agencies will increase their involvement with the petroleum industry and place more restrictions on company operations. State and local agencies will widen their roles, particularly regarding distribution and ecology. Both consumer groups and government will continue to voice criticism of industry practices, while attempting to work closer with the industry. Important issues will be: availability of energy, product quality, prices, service, expertise of personnel, deceptive practices, prompt and fair responses to complaints, safety, and development of alternative energy sources. Consumer groups and government will be satisfied with proper self-regulation, but also will be skeptical of it.

Trade associations and companies will secure consumer feedback and opinions, placing organizational importance on market research, customer relations, in-house consumer advocates, and complaint-resolution systems. Seminars with consumer groups will become more frequent. Customer satisfaction audits, like the one established by Shell, will be used by more companies.

The views of Exxon will be widely accepted by the industry:

> Together, corporation and consumer organizations can increase understanding of consumer expectations and corporate costs, and improve overall performance in the marketplace. They can also oppose any unnecessary legislation that is not in the interest of the consumer and the nation. Via joint consultation, business and consumers can better anticipate impending shifts in public attitudes and the need to adjust to consumer-oriented programs [24, p. 8].

Corporate advertising, press releases, annual reports, and speeches will emphasize fair practices and openness with consumers. Emphasis on customer satisfaction at the retail level will increase.

The industry will try to resist intense government pressure regarding divestiture and natural gas pricing. Accusations of cartel formation, price-fixing, and hoarding will continue, but the industry will do a better job of interacting with consumer and government groups. Important court cases will be decided in the next few years. According to a former Department of Energy official:

> There's bound to be a major change in the structure of the oil industry within the next five to ten years. Forces have been unleashed here that cannot be stopped [95, p. 36].

The probable form of divestiture will be horizontal, with the companies forced to rid themselves of nonoil business, like coal, petrochemicals, and nuclear energy. Petroleum networks will remain as they are now.

As new energy sources are discovered, the petroleum industry may or may not be placed in a precarious position. Divestiture will hurt the industry severely, but without divestiture, the most progressive firms will continue to progress and grow. Cooperation with independent wholesalers and retailers will aid the industry in its fight against divestiture. In addition, effective self-regulation will be helpful for the industry.

RECOMMENDATIONS

Recommendations for consumer groups, government, the industry, and individual companies are offered below.

Consumer Groups

Larger, broader consumer groups must monitor the petroleum industry and be active in the development of new energy sources. The groups should meet regularly with corporate and government officials to discuss consumer issues. The groups must unite and form a more powerful lobbying bloc. The groups also must do a more effective job of educating consumers about energy use, energy conservation, and deceptive business practices.

Government

Restructuring or divestiture legislation should not be passed, since this is not in the national or consumer interest. Divestiture would do little to insulate the economy from the effects of petroleum shortages or embargos, because OPEC would not be influenced. Any legislation would involve sweeping changes in the distribution of assets, cash, debt, inventories, receivables, and management. This would take years to accomplish and occupy valuable government and corporate time that could be expended in creating a viable national energy plan. With the uncertainty of the industry, capital spending and new employment by the industry could fall off drastically.

In 1948, movie production and theater ownership were split through an antitrust decree. This relatively simple divestiture took seven years to complete [52]. By contrast, the complex petroleum industry could possibly take 25 years to assimilate divestiture smoothly.

The antitrust bills currently pending would primarily affect Gulf, Mobil, Exxon, SoCal, and Texaco. They would not affect foreign giants, like Shell and British Petroleum. This could subject domestic companies to unfair competitive pressures.

The top five petroleum companies control about 35 percent of domestic production; the largest, Exxon, controls only 8.5 percent. There are thousands of small and medium drillers. Twenty independents have built refineries since 1950. The penetration of non-branded marketers rose from 18 percent in 1965 to 34.5 percent in 1977 [87].

Some production opportunities require joint ventures, due to their size. Even Exxon could not have built the $8 billion Alaska pipeline by itself.

Despite these comments, the government must continue to monitor petroleum business practices to ensure the fairest prices possible, equitable distribution of scarce energy, honest advertising, and competition—but without divestiture. Of prime importance is that the government, with business and consumer input, develop a national energy program as quickly as possible and work to implement it.

The Industry and Individual Companies

The industry and individual companies must increase their efforts toward self-regulation. An industry-formulated energy plan is desired by the industry, although opposed by almost all consumer groups.

According to the Petroleum Economist:

In less than two generations Americans have switched from coal to petroleum and natural gas. One might expect that Washington would be interested in how and why this transpired, now that we appear headed in the opposite direction. There is no indication that this is so. Self-regulation has worked in the past, and with little or no help from Washington. Such action is a possibility in the future that should be considered [76, p. 27].

Based upon the scope and difficulties involved, the change-over from coal to petroleum was swift and smooth. The situation is different today since there is no cheap fuel on the horizon. Nonetheless, an aggressive plan for self-regulation and energy development would help consumers and reduce government interest in regulation.

Companies must strive to consider ecology, honesty and information in packaging and labeling, consumer issues, in-house consumer advocates, product and service modifications desired by consumers, fair pricing, equitable distribution of fuel, and a consumer-oriented attitude in management decision making and actions.

As Indiana Standard has noted:

The management of our company recognizes that the growth, profitability, and perhaps the very survival of our company and industry is increasingly dependent upon our ability to respond to changes regarding social and economic demands and desires, and our ability to maintain the respect and confidence of all who are stakeholders in our internal and external operations [89, p. 10].

Credibility about the industry on the part of consumers must be restored. Tracking studies by Yankelovich, Skelly, and White point out that the public, by the widest margin ever, has little confidence in the petroleum industry [102]. With consumer groups, government, the industry, and individual companies working together, consumer attitudes can be turned around and energy problems significantly reduced.

BIBLIOGRAPHY

1. Aaron, Carl. "Lefkowitz Fines Exxon, Texaco, Gulf and Mobil." New York Times (July 16, 1974), p. 10.

2. Alexander, George. "FTC Sues STP Corporation on Deceptive Advertising Claims." Wall Street Journal (September 4, 1971), p. 3.

3. ____. "STP Unit of Studebaker Worthington Accepts FTC Curb on Car Product Claims." Wall Street Journal (August 14, 1974), p. 2.

4. Alexander, Thomas. "Service Station Dealers Fight Back." Fortune 121 (February 1971), pp. 23-26.

5. "Alleged Cartel Charged by Texas Eastern Transmission." Wall Street Journal (March 5, 1966), p. 12.

6. Alworth, Hyman W. "Subcommittee Cites Three Internationals for Illegal Payments." Oil and Gas Journal 89 (May 1975), pp. 12-14.

7. Anders, Theodore. "Long Island Group Delays Offshore Drilling." Newsday (September 6, 1977), p. 18.

8. "A.P.I. Backs New York Oil Shareholders." Wall Street Journal (March 6, 1953), p. 23.

9. Atwater, Dr. William S. "Lobby Groups Modes of Operation." American Bar Association Journal 34 (Summer 1965), pp. 23-29.

10. ____. "Unethical Practices by the Oil Lobby in Washington?" American Bar Association Journal 29 (Summer 1965), pp. 34-38.

11. August, Franklin. "Industry Commentary." Oil and Gas Journal 24 (May 1976), pp. 12-15.

12. Awrens, Gerry. "Energy Plan or Self Sacrifice." Oil and Gas Journal 41 (January 1977), pp. 8-10.

13. Baldwin, C. George. "Commonwealth in Hoarding War?" Oil and Gas Journal 46 (May 1974), pp. 12-14.

14. Barry, Eunice. "Justice Department Sues Big Oil." Petroleum Economist 35 (June 1977), pp. 21-25.

15. Belsen, Robert. "Texaco Sued by Shareholders Group." Wall Street Journal (July 18, 1962), p. 9.

16. ____. "Industry Commentary." Oil and Gas Journal 34 (October 1976), pp. 13-15.

17. Benson, Samuel. "Regulatory Bodies and the Future of the Oil Industry." Petroleum Economist 4 (March 1977), pp. 17-19.

18. Birney, Robert H. Phillips Petroleum letter of response. (January 1978.)

19. Blauvelt, Howard W. "Conoco Chief Speaks Out Against Divestiture." Wall Street Journal (April 19, 1977), p. 16.

20. Boros, J. F. "The Seven Sisters, New Deal." Petroleum Economist 46 (July 1965), pp. 25-27.

21. Boyer, Steven. "The Feud Over Octane." Oil and Gas Journal 145 (May 1976), pp. 14-17.

22. Brent, Wayne. Gulf Oil letter of response. (January 1978.)

23. Bres, J. V. Exxon Incorporated letter of response. (January 1978.)

24. ____. "Exxon on Consumerism." Exxon Incorporated letter of response. (January 1978.)

25. Brothers, Marvin S. Shell Oil's Approach to Consumer Understanding. Bryer Press, December 1976.

26. "Business or Bribery." Wall Street Journal (June 5, 1974), p. 6.

27. Byrnes, William. "Editorial." Oil and Gas Journal 46 (May 1974), pp. 28-31.

28. Carlisle, Harvey. "Sierra Club Charges Cartel in Nuclear Energy." Wall Street Journal (November 13, 1976), p. 5.

29. Connors, H. C. "Wyler Oil to Go Under . . . Kansas Precedent?" Wall Street Journal (February 2, 1956), p. 19.

30. "Conoco Fights Back." Wall Street Journal (July 5, 1977), pp. 4, 19.

31. Cowan, Edward. "F.T.C. Charges False Advertising." Oil and Gas Journal 56 (May 1969), p. 32.

32. Crane, Stephen. "Gulf Oil Charged with Deceptive Advertising." Oil and Gas Journal 5 (May 1961), p. 6.

33. "Davis Oil Files Suit Against Four Firms." Oil and Gas Journal 18 (September 1973), p. 16.

34. Exxon Incorporated. Annual Report for 1977.

35. "Exxon Pipeline in Suit by E. P. A." Petroleum Economist 132 (January 1975), p. 4.

36. Farber, Jerold. Mobil Corporation letter of response. (December 1977.)

37. Feldman, S. "Petroleum Watchdog Still Watching." Oil and Gas Journal 34 (March 1976), pp. 11-14.

38. Glendening, P. F. Atlantic Richfield Company letter of response. (January 1978.)

39. "Guidelines Set by E. P. A. Regarding Breeder Reactors." Oil Daily 14 (May 1977), p. 6.

40. "Gulf Oil Admits Foreign Payments." Wall Street Journal (May 7, 1974), p. 12.

41. Halley, Gary. "Justice Department Files Suit Against Big Oil." Wall Street Journal (August 4, 1975), p. 5.

42. Hardaway, Dr. Francine R. Standard Oil Company of California letter of response. (January 1978.)

43. Hendrix, Connell. "The Petroleum Industry—Just How Fair Is Fair?" Petroleum Economist 34 (February 1961), pp. 4-6.

44. Hawkins, Wallace. "Trade Association Practices—Lawful or Unlawful?" Southwest Legal Foundation Report 45 (December 1950).

45. Hidy, Ralph W. Pioneering in Big Business. New York: Harper and Row, 1955.

46. Hirschfield, James P. "Exxon's Stake in the Future of the Consumer Movement." Petroleum Economist 149 (June 1976), pp. 22-24.

47. James, Arthur. "Pumping Up Profits." Oil Daily 11 (August 3, 1977), p. 25.

48. Jameson, H. F. "Dissident Shareholders Against Wyler Oil." New York Times (May 4, 1952), p. 23.

49. ____. "Texas Eastern Wins Litigation." New York Times (January 28, 1967), p. 25.

50. Jensen, William, Jr. "Corporate Socialism for Big Oil?" Oil and Gas Journal 121 (April 1976), pp. 11-15.

51. Kahn, Irving. "State of Ohio Supreme Court Action Stuns Industry." Reprinted from Proceedings of the Supreme Court of the State of Ohio, 1882, Oil and Gas Journal 12 (September 1959), pp. 34-36.

52. Kauper, Thomas. "Antitrust Experts Against Antitrust." Petroleum Economist 156 (March 1978), p. 11.

53. Leiter, Jeffrey. "Editorial—American Petroleum Institute and Divestiture." Oil Daily 11 (June 4, 1977), pp. 12-15.

54. ____. American Petroleum Institute letter of response. (January 1978.)

55. Levine, Harry S. "Self-Regulation or Self-Pity?" Oil and Gas Journal 134 (September 1976), pp. 8-11.

56. Little, Harvey Allen. "The Standard Oil Trust—A Bygone Era?" American Bar Association Journal 4 (April 1970), pp. 45-47.

57. Marshall, Franklin. "S.I.G.M.A. Files Suit." Oil and Gas Journal 11 (April 1975), pp. 30-32.

58. Mason, H. V. "Settlement for New York Oil Harsh." Wall Street Journal (October 5, 1953), p. 2.

59. ____. "Department of the Interior Ruling on Offshore Leases." Wall Street Journal (March 17, 1978), p. 8.

60. Meyers, Sharon. "A.P.I. Speaks Out for Industry." Oil Daily 9 (November 13, 1976), pp. 3-5.

61. Mobil Corporation. Annual Report for 1977.

62. Morgan, F. "Editorial Commentary." Oil and Gas Journal 23 (May 1975), p. 34.

63. Moss, John E. "How Unethical Is Unethical?" Fortune 12 (April 1974), pp. 34–38.

64. "Nader At a Loss." Wall Street Journal (December 5, 1976), p. 4.

65. National Petroleum Council. National Petroleum Council Background Information. National Petroleum Council Press, January 1978.

66. "Nuclear Cartel Charged Against Exxon, Others." Wall Street Journal (March 1, 1977), p. 2.

67. Offshore Drilling and Petroleum Resources Under the Ocean Floor, Summary, Final Reports. National Petroleum Council Press, 1976.

68. "Oil Cartel Alleged." Wall Street Journal (December 3, 1973), p. 7.

69. "Oilex in Chapter XI—Trustee Appointed." Wall Street Journal (September 5, 1960), p. 34.

70. "OPEC and Exxon Against the Industry." Petroleum Economist 119 (March 1976), p. 12.

71. Parkins, F. Continental Oil Corporation letter of response. (January 1978.)

72. Parkins, George. Texaco Incorporated letter of response. (December 1977.)

73. Phillips Petroleum Company. Annual Report for 1977.

74. "Pipeline in Delay . . . Again." Forbes 121 (April 1976), p. 17.

75. "Private Sector and Increasing Awareness." Oil Daily 7 (June 14, 1975), pp. 23–25.

76. "Pro Self-Regulation." Petroleum Economist 126 (February 1976), pp. 23–29.

77. Raye, George. "Gasoline Difference—Fact or Hoax?" New York Times (May 14, 1963), p. 18.

78. Raymond, Jason W. "Consumers Union Suit Against Big Oil." Oil and Gas Journal 11 (June 1969), pp. 15-19.

79. ____. "Consumers Union Suit in Settlement." Oil and Gas Journal 11 (March 1970), pp. 12-14.

80. Richards, Farley S. "Gasoline Additives—All Singing the Same Tune ?" Oil and Gas Journal 19 (September 1968), pp. 2-4.

81. Rogers, Kent. Shell Oil Company letter of response. (December 1977.)

82. Sandrickson, H. G. "Expertise or Advertise ?" Petroleum Economist 14 (June 1969), p. 45.

83. Sanford, O. P. "The Platformate Craze." Oil and Gas Journal 11 (June 1969), p. 14.

84. Schlesinger, James R. "Goals and Perspectives." United States Department of Energy Press. 1978.

85. Selvin, Roger David. "S.I.G.M.A. Settlement." Oil and Gas Journal 4 (April 1976), pp. 10-11.

86. ____. "Win Some, Lose Some . . . Davis Oil Versus the Industry." Oil and Gas Journal 4 (May 1976), pp. 14-16.

87. Shaye, Marc K. Oil Spill Control Association of America letter of response. (December 1977.)

88. Sivla, Randolph. "A.P.I. Speaks Out Against Deception." Oil Daily 10 (October 6, 1977), p. 32.

89. Swearingen, John. "Response '76—A Progress Report on Corporate Social Policy." Standard Oil Company of Indiana Press. 1976.

90. Tavoulareas, W. P. Mobil Oil Corporation letter of response. (December 1977.)

91. ____. "From Mobil to You." An advertisement. Oil and Gas Journal 45 (December 1976), p. 8.

92. "Test Data." Special Report Study. Consumer Digest 10 (1976), pp. 6-8, 15.

93. "Texas Firm Convicted." Wall Street Journal (June 4, 1958), p. 13.

94. "The Irresistible Giant—Oil." Forbes 119 (March 1976), pp. 10–12.

95. "The Irresistible Target—Big Oil." Forbes 116 (October 1976), pp. 34–37.

96. Thorne, Samuel. "1973—Could It Happen Again?" Oil and Gas Journal 43 (June 1976), pp. 24–26.

97. Thurber, T. T. "Judd Oil Board Ousted Via Class Action Suit." Wall Street Journal (September 5, 1957), p. 5.

98. Thurman, James. "New York Oil Sued." New York Times (May 14, 1951), p. 21.

99. United States Congress. Congressional Record 1,554 (May 23, 1975), p. 1,224.

100. ____. Congressional Record 1,658 (May 15, 1977), pp. 1,879–82.

101. Vice-President. "Suit Against Major International Oil Firms." Consumer Reports 23 (September 1973), p. 16.

102. Yankelovich, Skelly, and White. "Corporate Priorities Tracking Research Study." (Contained within the letter of response submitted by Mobil Oil.) Reprinted from "Study of Corporate Seminars," Petroleum Economist 117 (March 1975), pp. 18–23.

103. Zarb, Frank. "Break Up Big Oil?" Newsday (July 15, 1976), Nassau edition, pp. 7, 11.

9

CONSUMERISM AND THE PHARMACEUTICAL INDUSTRY

Joseph A. Bravate

INTRODUCTION

The pharmaceutical industry manufactures, promotes, distributes, and dispenses ethical and proprietary drugs and devices. The manufacturing of drugs has developed from simple, noncontrolled, nonstandardized methods of production to highly sophisticated, standardized, controlled, and often complicated processes. The industry has generated several procedures for ensuring reliability, quality, efficacy, and safety.

Product promotion is divided into two areas. First, mass media advertise products directly to consumers. This is the prime means for promoting proprietary drugs. Second, information is communicated to physicians by journal advertisements, direct mail, and sales personnel. Ethical drugs are promoted in this manner.

The pharmaceutical channel of distribution goes from manufacturer to retailer, manufacturer to hospital, or manufacturer to wholesaler to retailer. Ethical drugs must be prescribed by licensed physicians and dispensed by registered pharmacists. Proprietary drugs may be sold freely to consumers.

The pharmaceutical industry is deeply involved in research and development. New products must be rigorously tested for efficacy and safety before introduction on the market. The Food and Drug Administration (FDA) exerts tight control over pharmaceutical products.

The history of consumerism in the pharmaceutical industry, consumer groups, government, and the attitudes and actions of the industry and individual companies are examined in this chapter.

THE HISTORY OF CONSUMERISM
IN THE PHARMACEUTICAL INDUSTRY

Early Issues

During the latter part of the nineteenth century, chemical preservatives were placed in food to accommodate long-distance shipping. Many of the preservatives proved harmful. The market also was flooded with various elixirs and cures that were sold by traveling, self-styled "doctors." These products often consisted of bitters spiked with whiskey, rum, or gin; they were never labeled as such. Some of the items contained opium, cocaine, or other habit-forming drugs, while others were comprised entirely of sugar and water. Thousands of deaths and serious illnesses occurred from usage of these products [80].

Many firms did make wholesome and reliable medicines, but these were based on limited medical knowledge and the belief in caveat emptor, let the buyer beware. There was little consumer protection for health and safety. Labels did not identify ingredients, nor warn against overdoses [80].

State chemists grew increasingly aware of the dangers of harmful foods and drugs, and many urged Congress to enact federal food and drug laws. The first bill for the prevention of adulterated food and drugs was introduced in Congress in 1879. No action was taken at that time [42]. In 1883, Dr. Harvey W. Wiley became the chief chemist for the Department of Agriculture. He began a struggle to protect consumers, but was opposed by food and drug manufacturers who tried to discredit his positions and role [80].

Between 1879 and 1906, approximately 75 bills were put before Congress. In 1890, the only bill was passed. It prohibited the importation of adulterated food and drugs. During 1902, an aggressive drive for pure food and drug legislation was begun. The muckraker press publicized the dangers of adulterated and dyed foods and the hazards of unlabeled patent medicines containing opiates and large quantities of alcohol. This publicity aroused public opinion. Health organizations, such as the American Medical Association, also worked for the passage of legislation [2, 11].

Experiments with volunteers from the Bureau of Chemistry showed that many foods were adulterated and injurious to human consumption. Because of the experiments he conducted, Wiley found a powerful ally in President Theodore Roosevelt. Roosevelt put all his influence behind passage of a food and drug law after conditions asserted in The Jungle and The World's Work were substantiated [2].

In 1906, almost unanimously, Congress approved and Roosevelt signed the Food and Drug Act. Wiley was appointed to administer the act [120]. After Wiley started to enforce the law vigorously, his critics began a smear campaign to destroy his reputation and discredit the Bureau of Chemistry. Wiley was eventually cleared of all charges [80].

Although amendments to the 1906 law were subsequently made, the law proved to be inadequate in consumer protection. It was difficult to enforce, and some drug manufacturers continued to make exaggerated claims without risk of penalties. Dangerous drugs enjoyed unrestricted sales with insufficient content labeling. If a drug was not adulterated and its label not untruthful, it could be freely sold [24]. Technological advances also were not considered in the original law, and new methods of control were necessary [23].

Strengthening Consumer Protection

It became evident that the 1906 law required revision and strengthening to protect the public [43]. In the early 1930s, President Franklin Roosevelt appointed Rexford Tugwell assistant secretary of Agriculture, with official supervision of the Food and Drug Administration. Tugwell was responsible for dealing with abuses in the manufacturing and merchandising of food, drugs, and cosmetics [83].

The struggle for revised legislation began in 1933 with the introduction of the Tugwell Bill in Congress. Public support for the bill was not substantial. Critics said it would give the government too much control over products and interfere with consumer choice and the "right to self-medication" [13, 43, 58]. Newspapers were fearful of losing advertising revenue if they supported Tugwell [2].

The FDA dramatized the need for legislation by presenting an exhibit of useless and dangerous patent medicines, unsafe cosmetics, and adulterated foods. The exhibit was called "The Chamber of Horrors" by the press. A 1936 book, The American Chamber of Horrors, documented the FDA's case and made it available to wider audiences. Sixteen women's groups supported legislation [2]. In 1937, more than 100 people died from taking sulfanilamide [117]. Spurred by this tragedy, Congress passed the Food, Drug, and Cosmetic Act of 1938.

The new law dealt with the prevention of certain unsatisfactory drug practices, but it did not directly involve deceptive advertising or the lack of sufficient warnings in drug advertising. The Federal Trade Commission (FTC) was responsible for these matters [78]. The FDA sought to control drug advertising through its authority over labeling. During the 1940s, the FDA and FTC grappled over advertising issues [95].

In the 1940s consumer groups began to be heard. They demanded information in order to become more discerning buyers, and requested consumer education about the production and distribution of products [25]. An assistant attorney general initiated an investigation of pricing methods in the pharmaceutical industry in response to consumers. Possible antitrust violations and monopoly practices also were examined [94]. Litigation sought to establish firmly the FDA's jurisdiction over food, drugs, and cosmetics, from raw materials to consummation of retail sales [27].

To ensure the potency, sterilization, quality, safety, and efficacy of drugs, the Food, Drug, and Cosmetic Act was amended in 1945. The amendments covered new classes of drugs, such as penicillin and other antibiotics, by requiring certification that they met certain standards [117].

In the late 1940s, the Hoover Commission recommended that all laws relating to food, drugs, and cosmetics be rewritten, simplified, and compiled under a single title [113]. A commission task force said control of drug advertising should be transferred to the FDA, since the FDA and FTC had difficulties over jurisdiction. The FDA was equipped to deal with technical and scientific aspects of advertising [30].

Also during the late 1940s, prescription refills were opposed by the FDA unless physicians gave their express permission. Prior to this, pharmacists could refill all but narcotic or dangerous drug prescriptions upon the request of patients [48]. In the early 1950s, the government tried to legislate the dispensing of pharmaceutical products. At this time, government and manufacturers debated who had the final authority to determine which drugs required prescriptions; manufacturers previously had made most of the decisions [32]. The government sought to draw up a list of dangerous drugs and limit their sales to prescription only [35].

The Kefauver Committee investigated the pharmaceutical industry from the late 1950s to the early 1960s. It probed many practices, including pricing, the use of detail men, promotional literature, and the tendency toward monopolistic practices and high profit margins. The benefits of patents and the expenditures to convince physicians to prescribe brand names also were studied. Senator Estes Kefauver concluded that consumers paid unfair prices because of these factors [71].

Providing information about their new drugs, allegedly without mentioning potential side effects [3, 36], became a major function of manufacturers. Many doctors relied on this information [80]. By 1961, the government sought other methods to give doctors more objective information. Package inserts were viewed as one alternative, since they would deal with safety and efficacy in use [65].

In 1962, the Kefauver-Harris Drug Amendments were passed, after problems with thalidomide. The amendments were not supported by Congress when the Kefauver hearings investigated drug safety, and it made several recommendations. However, thalidomide use by pregnant mothers in Europe and Canada led to thousands of deformed babies, and resulted in the new legislation [117].

The FDA was analyzed by the Citizens Advisory Committee in 1962. The committee determined that the FDA needed to be reorganized and found some of its actions had not been in the best interest of the consumer. The FDA was advised to encourage voluntary industry compliance and a greater sense of responsibility [45].

Modern Era

During the 1960s, government and industry became more aware of consumer demands for information and safety [38, 74]. Several congressional committees investigated drug industry pricing practices in the late 1960s, especially as the government began to pay for drugs through medicare and medicaid [81].

In the early 1970s, the issue of generic versus brand names in prescription drugs, first examined by the Kefauver Committee, was of concern to the industry and government. Proponents of substitution laws claimed that allowing pharmacists to substitute generic equivalents for brand names would result in lower prescription costs for consumers [88]. Some opponents maintained substitution would have little effect on prices because the average prices of generics were rising faster than the average prices of brand names [89]. Others said the repeal of antisubstitution laws might lead to higher prices, since a number of pharmacists could choose to increase profit margins on generics rather than pass savings on to consumers [21].

Proponents of substitution stated that therapeutic equivalency should be assumed until proven otherwise [88]. Opponents claimed studies showed quality and bio-equivalency among all drug products were far from reality [87]. Doctors saw the repeal of antisubstitution laws as a threat to their complete authority over medical care. On the other hand, pharmacists desired a greater input into the drug-selection process [7].

Critics of the FDA were concerned over the delays in new product approvals in the 1970s; they said important medications were not reaching the public [67]. However, countering this was a strong concern for drug safety and efficacy. New drugs had to demonstrate safety, effectiveness, quality control, and proper informative labeling and instructions before introduction on the market [105].

As truth in advertising became a major issue, the FDA closely scrutinized advertisements by prescription drug manufacturers. In 1972, the industry was warned against making claims that were not backed by clinical evidence, particularly comparative advertisements [44]. Consumers started to demand that the FTC take action on over-the-counter drug advertisements that contained misleading efficacy claims, insignificant product differentials, and statements about treatments for interpersonal and human problems [121].

In 1973, some of the laws and regulations inhibiting prescription price advertising, and hence price competition, were tested [19]. Consumer studies showed that prescription prices varied greatly from one pharmacy to another. Consumers believed the posting of these prices would reduce these variations and serve consumer interests [121]. During the same year, consumers demanded understandable information on prescriptions. They sought clearer information as to product uses, directions, side effects, and the possible hazards of mixing medication with other drugs or foods [19].

The FTC tried to eliminate state laws and regulations that prohibited or restricted drug advertising in 1975. The FTC also sought to legalize price posting for prescription drugs [55]. At this time, the commission was not successful.

During the middle and late 1970s, antisubstitution laws were debated again. A number of states repealed the laws; others put off action or decided to retain the laws. Some states repealed the laws, but allowed physicians to write DAW (dispense as written) or DNS (do not substitute) [10].

Restrictive pharmacy ownership was a prominent topic in 1975. Proponents favored restricting pharmacy ownership to pharmacists. Opponents said this was not in the public interest. Chain drug retailers were concerned about the possibility of restrictive ownership laws, as were consumer groups representing retired persons and senior citizens. Consumers feared monopolies and higher prices [16].

As government expenditures for drug reimbursement grew through medicare and medicaid, the FTC and Health, Education, and Welfare (HEW) searched for ways to dispense quality drugs at costs fair to the industry and taxpayers. Two plans were considered: actual-acquisition-cost (AAC) and maximum-allowable-cost (MAC) [63]. The problem with AAC was the difficulty in determining actual costs for each pharmacist, since these costs were based on quoted prices, deals, discounts, and rebates. HEW recognized this problem and explored various means for estimating true costs [64].

The FTC proposed dropping the idea of a dispensing fee added to AAC and implementation of a reimbursement program based on AAC plus the difference between that figure and the pharmacist's usual-and-customary prices to the general public. This would set medicaid payments at each pharmacy's regular prices. To encourage competition, the FTC would support prescription price advertising, repeal of antisubstitution laws, and open ownership of pharmacies [53].

In 1976, the FDA proposed safety regulations to ensure sanitary conditions and standards for quality, purity, and potency in the production of pharmaceutical products [82]. The FDA also exerted responsibility for the safety of medical equipment [117]. The FDA requested improved industry information for new drugs to help speed up the assessment process [67].

The issue of prescription price advertising was resolved in 1976, when the Supreme Court ruled against the ban on this advertising [60]. During the year, several consumer and women's groups filed petitions urging that certain prescription drugs be accompanied by label warnings written for consumers [61]. The right for patients to be informed regarding drug therapy is an issue that is still being discussed.

In 1977, the Florida Mandatory Substitution Law was enacted, and was expected to have a significant impact on pending legislation in other states. The law required less expensive, generically equivalent drugs to be substituted for brand name drugs unless the consumer or physician requested otherwise. Many pharmacists and consumer groups felt the law allowed consumers to save money, while enabling pharmacists to use professional judgment in product selection [10]. The substitution issue remains unresolved in many states today.

ACTIVE CONSUMER GROUPS

The National Consumers' League was formed in 1898. The league and the General Federation of Women's Clubs voiced their views on pure food and drug laws and lobbied for their passage prior to enactment of the Food and Drug Act of 1906 [2]. Today, the National Consumers' League, with a membership of 25,000 and a staff of three, continues to apply organized consumer power to the marketplace regarding food marketing and health services [50].

During the struggle for food and drug legislation in the 1930s, various consumer groups sent representatives to congressional hearings to provide consumers' opinions of the Copeland Bill. The National Home Economics Association, American Pure Food League,

Consumers' Research, and the People's Lobby all stated the bill was not adequate and called for more substantial legislation, like the Tugwell Bill. The groups felt the Copeland Bill would not offer consumers enough protection [12, 150]. Consumers' Research is still influential today, as it tests a wide variety of consumer products and gives technical and related information to schools, colleges, adult education groups, and governmental agencies [50].

In 1962, the Citizens Advisory Committee, a nongovernmental panel, recommended changes in the organization, practices, and policies of the FDA. It emphasized the agency's role in consumer education [45].

The National Council of Churches, founded in 1950 and composed of 30 Protestant and Eastern Orthodox denominations, stated its intention of cracking down on over-the-counter drug advertising to the public and prescription drug advertising to doctors in 1973. The council felt drug advertising presented a pain-pill-pleasure model that encouraged the misuse and abuse of drugs. If a system for monitoring and reviewing advertisements was not implemented or proved unworkable, the council expected to work to ban all drug advertising to the public and physicians [17].

The Public Interest Research Group (PIRG), founded in 1970, became involved with prescription drug prices in 1973. The group studied pricing practices for prescription drugs in several pharmacies and found them to differ significantly. This illustrated to PIRG that price posting and advertising were necessary for prescription drugs. To put pressure on pharmacists, PIRG offered to support repeal of antisubstitution laws only if the pharmacists backed compulsory price posting [121].

The Consumer Federation of America, established in 1967 and now the largest national consumer advocacy organization, is involved with the pricing, quality, and costs of items, including drugs. The group serves as a clearinghouse for information and operates as a fact-finding body [50]. In 1973, the federation urged member groups to challenge in court the constitutionality and validity of laws and regulations that inhibited drug price competition. It asked the government to purchase only generic drugs and amend state laws to permit substitutions in prescriptions. The federation also urged affiliates to fight to allow pharmacies in supermarkets and general merchandise stores [19].

In 1976, the FDA established the Patient Prescription Drug Labeling Project. The FDA sought the opinions of consumer groups, medical associations, and pharmaceutical associations regarding product labeling information and inserts. While research was under way, several consumer organizations put a petition before the FDA urging that certain prescription drugs be accompanied by warning

labels for consumers. These groups were: Center for Law and
Social Policy on behalf of Consumers Union, Consumer Action for
Improved Food and Drugs, National Organization for Women,
Women's Equity Action League, and the Women's Legal Defense
Fund. The groups believed patients were not getting enough informa-
tion about the drugs they took and that many doctors were too rushed
to discuss medication with patients [61].

The consumer groups that initiated the 1976 petition are quite
active today, particularly Consumers Union and Consumer Action
for Improved Food and Drugs. Consumers Union, formed in 1936,
provides consumers with information on drug products, mostly for
over-the-counter drugs, and lobbies in Washington, D.C. Consumer
Action offers information on labeling and packaging of drugs, and
assists grassroots organizations [18, 50].

GOVERNMENT

Federal Agencies

The first federal agency to emerge as a protector of public
interests in the area of food and drugs was the Department of Agriculture, through its Division of Chemistry. As early as 1879, the
division began to investigate food and drug adulteration. It recommended a national food and drug law in 1880. No government action
resulted, so the problems of adulteration were examined again [117].
Through the division's efforts, legislation was enacted in 1906. A
crackdown on violators began shortly thereafter, under the direction
of Wiley [80].

Under the 1906 law, federal courts were responsible for
ascertaining the guilt of parties cited by the Bureau of Chemistry
and imposing penalties. Government officials were not allowed to
set penalties, or seize or destroy food and drug products [41]. The
Bureau of Chemistry did develop practices, policies, and technical
skills for food and drug protection. Legal procedures and inspection
techniques were established and applied in court actions. Judicial
decisions, which strengthened the law and revealed its weaknesses,
were won [80].

In 1927, a separate law enforcement agency was created, known
as the Food, Drug, and Insecticide Administration. This was changed
to the Food and Drug Administration in 1931 [117]. The FDA was
transferred from the Department of Agriculture to the Federal Security Agency, now Health, Education, and Welfare, in 1940 [80].
Amendments have since broadened the scope and control of the FDA.

With regard to the pharmaceutical industry, FDA activities now include regulation, inspection, standardization, certification, seizure, and recall. The FDA inspects plants where drugs are produced. It approves new drugs for safety and efficacy before they are allowed on the market. It approves every batch of insulin anu antibiotics before they can be used. Samples of drugs are constantly tested and analyzed. Prescription, nonprescription, and biological drugs are reviewed. The FDA also develops regulations for labeling drugs, makes sure that physicians are adequately informed about drugs, issues public warnings for dangerous products, and monitors recalls [119].

The Federal Trade Commission is the other federal agency most responsible for regulating pharmaceutical industry practices, since the advertising of food, drugs, and cosmetics falls under its jurisdiction. Congress placed false and deceptive advertising under the control of the FTC, and product labeling and inserts under the authority of the FDA. In 1977, the FTC investigated the possible anticompetitive effects of antisubstitution laws and offered two proposals for reducing prescription prices: repeal antisubstitution laws or limit trademark protection on brands to 20 years [57]. Recently, the FTC has won challenges against Anacin, Listerine, and other over-the-counter pharmaceutical products regarding overstated and misleading advertising.

Legislation and Court Cases

The Food and Drug Act of 1906 prohibited the interstate commerce of misbranded, adulterated, or poisonous or deleterious food and drugs. The act was intended to protect the public health and suppress fraud, and gave the government seizure power [42]. However, in the six years following passage, the major provisions of the law were deactivated by amendments [120].

In 1910, Hipolite v. the United States was the first case under the act to come before the Supreme Court. The case dealt with the validity of Section 10 of the law, which authorized the seizure of adulterated or misbranded food or drugs that were shipped between states and remained unloaded, unsold, and in original unbroken cartons. The Supreme Court upheld Section 10, allowing the government to continue with seizures [42]. In 1911, the McDermott v. Wisconsin case went to the Supreme Court. The Court sustained Sections 7 and 8 of the Food and Drug Act, regulating the branding of packages containing articles of consumption [42].

The Supreme Court determined in the 1911 United States v. Johnson case that the act did not prohibit false therapeutic claims.

It only banned false and misleading claims as to the identity of drugs. The Sherley Amendment was enacted in 1912 to overcome this ruling, by prohibiting fraudulent therapeutic claims on medicine labels [117]. The Sherley Amendment was upheld in the Eckman v. the United States case [42].

In 1931, the Supreme Court specifically held that the FTC could not prohibit false advertising unless competitors were injured. The ruling temporarily halted consumer pressure. As a result of the decision, the FTC was strengthened by the 1938 Wheeler-Lea Amendment, which declared unfair or deceptive practices to be illegal regardless of the impact on competition [2]. Wheeler-Lea brought the false advertising of food, drugs, medical and veterinary devices, and cosmetics under the jurisdiction of the FTC. Temporary restraining orders and criminal proceedings could be brought against violators [1].

The Federal Food, Drug, and Cosmetic Act of 1938 sought to protect consumers from health and economic injuries [43]. The law extended food and drug laws to cover cosmetics and devices, required safety clearance on new drugs before distribution, stipulated tolerances for unavoidable poisonous substances, authorized standards for containers of food, authorized factory inspections, allowed court injunctions to aid seizures and prosecution, and eliminated the Sherley Amendment requirement to prove intent to defraud in drug-misbranding cases [80, 117].

In the 1947 Sullivan v. the United States case, the Supreme Court confirmed the authority of the FDA to police the retail sale of drugs, which enabled the FDA to supervise the movement of drugs from manufacturer to ultimate consumer [48]. The Miller Amendment of 1948 also affirmed that the FDA was responsible for safeguarding goods in interstate commerce until they reached the final consumer. The FDA was allowed to seize misbranded or adulterated items after they completed their interstate journey [48, 117].

The Durham-Humphrey Amendment to the Food, Drug, and Cosmetic Act was passed in 1951. This law specifically required that drugs that could not be safely used without medical supervision had to be prescribed by a licensed doctor [117]. Pharmacists continued to be permitted to refill prescriptions and manufacturers were able to determine those products needing prescriptions and those sold over the counter [32]. Pharmacists could not label drugs requiring medical supervision as over-the-counter items [35].

The Supreme Court ruled in the United States v. Cardiff case of 1952 that the factory inspection provision of the Food, Drug, and Cosmetic Act was too vague to be enforced as criminal law. Congress passed the 1953 Factory Inspection Amendment to clarify the previous law. It required the FDA to give manufacturers written reports on inspections and analysis of factory samples [117].

In 1960, the FDA sought to control advertisements and circulars that were used to promote new drugs to the medical profession. This action was a response to charges by the Kefauver Committee that the FDA failed to guard consumers and the medical profession from substandard and overadvertised drugs. The FDA issued regulations in 1961, most importantly one requiring a package insert to be on or inside all prescription drug packages. The drug label would contain

> adequate information for its use, including indications, effects, dosages, routes, methods, and frequency and duration of administration, and any relevant hazards, contra-indications, side effects and precautions under which practitioners licensed by law to administer the drug can use the drug safely and for the purpose for which it is intended, including all purposes for which it is advertised or represented [47, pp. 85-86].

The Kefauver-Harris Amendments were passed in 1962 to foster a greater degree of drug safety and strengthen new drug clearance procedures. For the first time, drug makers were required to prove the effectiveness and safety of new products to the FDA before the products could be sold [117]. Drugs that were previously approved could be removed from the market, if information indicated they were hazardous to health or ineffective [80]. The amendments also clarified advertising regulations. The FDA was responsible for prescription drug advertising. The FTC had the authority to regulate over-the-counter drug advertising [118]. In the Upjohn v. Finch case in 1970, the Court of Appeals said the commercial success of a drug was not enough to substantiate its safety. This made enforcement of the 1962 amendment possible [117].

The Fair Packaging and Labeling Act was passed in 1966. It required consumer products moving in interstate commerce to be honestly and informatively labeled. Prescription drugs were excluded from this law, since Congress felt other regulations were adequate [116]. The act limited the FDA's authority on fair packaging and labeling to foods, drugs, and cosmetics. The FTC was responsible for other items. FDA enforcement was carried out by its Bureau of Foods, Bureau of Drugs, and Bureau of Medical Devices [118].

In 1970, the FDA determined that all packages of oral contraceptives had to contain information about their potential risks to enable women to make educated decisions as to whether or not to use these products. The rules were extended in 1973 to cover two other contraceptive drugs [115].

The Supreme Court upheld the authority of the FDA to be the final judge of drug safety and effectiveness in five 1973 drug effective-

ness cases. The FDA was allowed to deny hearings to companies
that could not show that significant factors were in dispute [115].
The court decision gave the FDA control over entire classes of
products by regulations rather than through time-consuming, case-
by-case litigation [117].

New labeling regulations appeared in the 1976 Federal Register.
Among the provisions was one that required information about effectiveness, contradictions, warnings, precautions, and adverse reactions to be furnished to each patient receiving oral contraceptives
[49].

In 1976, the case of Virginia State Board of Pharmacy v.
Virginia Citizens Consumer Council resolved the issue of prescription price advertising. The Supreme Court struck down the Virginia
prohibition against this category of advertising, and set a precedent
for decisions in other states [62, 112]. The Code of Federal Regulations established the exact content and format of prescription drug
price advertisements. Advertised prices would have to be in effect
for at least seven days. Special group discounts would have to be
specified. The advertisements for prescription drug prices had to
be physically separated from general merchandise advertisements
[107].

INDUSTRY RESPONSES TO CONSUMERISM

Following are pharmaceutical industry responses to consumerism, as reported in the literature and through a primary study.

Industry Responses as Reported in the Literature

The drug industry had mixed views toward the 1906 Food and
Drug Act. Some patent-medicine manufacturers pressured the
publications in which they advertised not to print stories about the
harmful ingredients in elixirs, ointments, pills, and potions.
Responsible food and drug manufacturers supported legislation [80,
p. 17]. After passage of the law, there was a general willingness
to cooperate with the government. The National Wholesale Druggists
Association (NWDA) informed members of regulations and how to
comply with them. NWDA was interested in high quality and standards. In 1927, it asked members to review their procedures for
quality maintenance of products and made recommendations to achieve
quality in biological products [99].

Through meetings, trade associations and government officials
were able to air their views to each other. At a session in 1929, the

government's use of multiple product seizures was explained and clarified. The industry was assured that the government was not trying to restrict drug sales, but was interested in stopping the sale of misrepresented drugs. Trade associations became aware of government rules, procedures, and positions, and a spirit of cooperation grew [72].

The NWDA supported discriminant use of multiple seizures, and encouraged members and other associations to maintain an atmosphere of cooperation with the Bureau of Chemistry. The American Drug Manufacturers Association and the American Pharmaceutical Manufacturers Association communicated with the government about industry standards [97, 98].

Industry response to the Tugwell Bill was generally and strongly unfavorable in 1933. The proprietary medicine industry was quite adamant in its opposition, and saw the law as an attempt to increase government control and the power of the Department of Agriculture [6]. The Proprietary Association felt the bill would prevent self-medication, establish tight manufacturing and distribution controls, secure reversals of court decisions, transfer authority from the FTC to the FDA, and increase the probability of multiple seizures [83]. The industry also believed voluntary inspections really would be mandatory, and feared an end to secret formulas since ingredients and their percentages would have to be stated on labels [15].

Even when the legislation was revised and reintroduced in 1934 as the Copeland Bill, industry response was very negative. The Proprietary Association still opposed the law [21]. Industry pressure caused the bill to be rewritten several times before its passage in 1938. By that time, many former opponents endorsed the law [22, 52].

The industry disapproved of many proposed FDA regulations to carry out the Food, Drug, and Cosmetic Act. For example, it believed proposed labeling rules would have made honest members guilty of misbranding and new drugs would be defined too broadly [95]. In the early 1940s, industry representatives took the position that manufacturers did not have to tell the government the exact amounts of ingredients in products in order to protect secret formulas [100]. Industry members also became involved in the jurisdictional dispute over advertising regulation between the FTC and FDA during this period [54].

In 1948, the American Drug Manufacturers Association opposed an FDA plan to announce periodically the approval of new drug applications and their manufacturers. The association felt the plan would interfere with company marketing plans and lead to a federal formulary [54].

After ten years with the Food, Drug, and Cosmetic Act, the pharmaceutical industry had a generally positive attitude. The American Pharmaceutical Manufacturers Association recognized the law as a strong and socially responsible one. The industry benefited through improved integrity, constructive development, the highest medical standards in history, and cooperation with government [51]. The Proprietary Association of America also found the act to have led to an improved industry and greater industry-government interaction [51]. At this time, two associations established a set of principles for drug plant sanitation, which was immediately endorsed by the head of the FDA [39].

In 1950, trade associations assisted in simplifying drug laws, as recommended by the Hoover Commission. The associations and the government cooperated and compromised in recodifying laws [113]. However, during the same year, the American Drug Manufacturers Association said the federal government was exerting too much control. This was considered a threat to scientific progress [5].

The industry was quite active in opposition to several government programs in 1951, including the Durham-Humphrey Bill. Manufacturers objected to a provision empowering the government to draw up a list of dangerous drugs and limit their sale to prescription only. This was viewed as a step toward socialized medicine and a limit to self-medication [32].

The American Pharmaceutical Association charged that the FDA exceeded its authority by questioning the rights of pharmacists to refill prescriptions without specific directions from doctors in the early 1950s. The association announced it would take legal action on the matter [93]. Despite this, pharmacists were not allowed to refill prescriptions without doctors' permission.

In 1953, the Proprietary Association and others said they would support a plant inspection bill if the scope of inspectors' authority was left to the courts to decide. The American Drug Manufacturers Association and the American Pharmaceutical Manufacturers Association both supported factory inspection [86].

When the Kefauver hearings began, industry officials were sure their prices could be justified on the basis of research and development costs [122]. By 1959, public relations efforts were employed to publicize the positive aspects of the industry, such as the benefits of drug research and increased life expectancy [91]. Industry spokesmen defended the promotion of branded drugs in the early 1960s by citing their quality and the incentive for additional research and development [28].

The Pharmaceutical Manufacturers Association criticized a 1961 FTC regulation on information inserts for the medical profession. The association contended that medicine costs would rise and information intended for doctors would reach patients [102]. The industry proposed a centralized information agency instead of inserts. The agency would maintain an up-to-date information file for physicians' reference [36]. The FDA rules were enacted, despite these objections and suggestions.

The Pharmaceutical Manufacturers Association took exception to the Kefauver Committee Report, and considered it an unjustified attack on the pharmaceutical industry. It saw restrictive provisions forcing many small companies out of business and the whole industry to reduce expensive research on life-saving drugs [70]. After amendments were passed because of the Kefauver report, the association agreed to cooperate with them and resolve disputed issues. The association also expressed a willingness to challenge unreasonable, unnecessary, and excessive interpretations of the law in the courts and before Congress [33].

In 1967, the association reported a settlement of the generic-name-every-time issue. Manufacturers would not have to include the generic name of a branded drug on its label or in advertising each time the brand name was mentioned [58]. In 1968, the National Association of Retail Druggists took a stand against the compulsory prescribing of generic name drugs. The association was interested in selling quality drugs, not in dispensing the lowest-priced drugs regardless of quality [91].

The Pharmaceutical Manufacturers Association took a strong stand against the repeal of antisubstitution laws in 1972. Physicians had a similar position and were not willing to give up some decision making to pharmacists. Pharmacists supported repeal, since they would then have greater decision-making powers. The Pharmaceutical Manufacturers Association did not feel lower prices would occur through substitution, and questioned whether generics were therapeutically equivalent [88].

The American Pharmaceutical Association favored substitution laws, saying the public would benefit if pharmacists played a role in the drug selection process [7]. In 1975, the association played an important part in gaining approval in Arkansas for pharmacists to be allowed to dispense brands other than the ones prescribed. It promoted substitution amendments in other states [9]. The association took a position on medicaid reimbursements to pharmacies, recommending professional fees be included in the payments [63].

The National Association of Chain Drug Stores voiced its disapproval of restrictive ownership legislation in 1975, stating that limits on pharmacy ownership would result in monopolies and lead to higher drug prices [84].

Retail trade associations defended price differentials among pharmacies, saying they were caused by variations in acquisition costs to pharmacists. They blamed manufacturers and wholesalers for the variations in these acquisition costs. The associations were against an FTC proposal to compel pharmacies to advertise prescription prices without any action against manufacturers and wholesalers [8]. In 1976, the two leading pharmacy organizations charged that the FTC had decided to end advertising restrictions without an investigation into the effects of this decision [56].

In 1976, an HEW plan for medicaid reimbursement was criticized by the National Association of Retail Druggists. The association said the payments for some drugs would be less than their costs [108]. As of this writing, the reimbursement issue has not been resolved; states have the discretion to utilize either of two plans.

The National Association of Chain Drug Stores reaffirmed its stand against substitution in 1977. It asserted its dedication to brand name pharmaceuticals and the responsibility of the physician to prescribe drugs [79]. The association continued to monitor state laws restricting pharmacy ownership, and was able to defeat 15 bills [111]. The association took a position on package inserts, saying that this information should be provided by physicians during office visits [79].

During 1977, the National Association of Retail Druggists opposed what it called the unprofessional practice of price posting and the burden placed on pharmacists by time-consuming patient and drug labeling information. The organization also said the repeal of antisubstitution laws would not be beneficial to pharmacists, because few states had acted to solve the pharmacists' liability problems under the new laws [111].

Trade Association Responses to Primary Study

A mail questionnaire on consumerism in the pharmaceutical industry was sent to ten trade associations. Four participated in the survey: Drug Wholesalers Association (DWA), National Association of Chain Drug Stores (NACDS), National Wholesale Druggists Association (NWDA), and Pharmaceutical Manufacturers Association (PMA). Six associations did not respond after two letters: National Association of Drug & Allied Sales Organizations, National Association of Pharmaceutical Manufacturers, National Association of Retail Druggists, National Drug Trade Conference, National Pharmaceutical Council, and Pharmaceutical Proprietary Association.

Overall, the responding associations view the consumer movement in positive terms and feel it has served to focus industry attention on consumer needs. The associations state that consumerism affects them differently, from no effect to restrictions through legislation. Only one association has a department to deal with consumerism. Two associations appear before government committees. One association says it provides speakers for consumer groups. Consumerism is perceived as having a growing influence on the industry. Hopes are expressed that consumers will act responsibly in their demands and allow the industry to satisfy them.

Table 9.1 contains the individual answers of the participating associations. Answers have been condensed and categorized by the author.

COMPANY RESPONSES TO CONSUMERISM

Company responses to consumerism in the pharmaceutical industry are revealed in the literature and through a primary study.

Company Responses as Reported in the Literature

In 1920, the director of advertising for Parke-Davis Company explained that pharmaceutical manufacturers had to advertise their branded products to doctors in order to generate enough sales to cover large research expenditures for new products and product improvements. These companies furnished expensive literature, advertised extensively in medical journals, mailed letters and pamphlets, and trained detail men. This process led to effective medicines and assisted physicians [75].

As early as 1925, companies struggled with the issue of restrictive pharmacy ownership. The Liggett Company complained about an act that required all members to be licensed pharmacists [73].

Representatives of Swan Meyers Company and Abbott Laboratories discussed the use of detail men in the 1920s. They felt that detailing was an effective and profitable form of sales promotion. Officials from Hynson, Wescott, and Dunning emphasized the importance of educating retail druggists [13].

A vice-president of Bristol-Myers criticized the Tugwell Bill in 1933, stating it would work a hardship on the drug and other industries [114]. Bristol-Myers and Colgate-Palmolive were among those opposing the Copeland Bill in 1934 [80]. After the 1938 Food, Drug, and Cosmetic Act was enacted, some manufacturers delayed the revision of their product labels. Many did not even read the law [104].

TABLE 9.1

Pharmaceutical Trade Association Responses to Study

Question 1	How does your association feel about the consumer movement?
DWA	An answer to this question is not indicated.
NACDS	There is constant involvement with the consumer movement, since members are health-care providers and retailers.
NWDA	There is sympathy with any sensible action taken to be sure consumers obtain the highest quality at the lowest reasonable cost.
PMA	The consumer movement has structured, formalized, and given a voice to the concerns of modern society, resulting partly from the complexity and depersonalization of the marketplace. Communication is important to keep business and consumers aware of each other's needs.
Question 2	How has the consumer movement affected the companies that belong to your association?
DWA	The wholesaler has not been affected to any extent. Only if the retailer is adversely affected will the wholesaler be affected.
NACDS	In some cases, unnecessary government regulations lead to higher prices for consumers.
NWDA	Pharmaceutical manufacturers traditionally have been consumer-oriented in both quality and price.
PMA	The greatest impact has been in the areas of federal and state legislation, which have influenced substitution of drugs, promotion, and advertising.
Question 3	Has the association created a position, panel, or department to deal with the effects of the consumer movement?
DWA	No position, panel, or department has been created.
NACDS	There is no formal position, panel, or department, but the organization has taken stands on drug information, prescription labeling, expiration dating, and packaging.
NWDA	No position, panel, or department has been created.
PMA	There are several positions, a panel, and a department. Efforts were begun before the consumer movement had any impact on the industry.

(continued)

Question 4	Does the association provide representatives to appear before government committees examining consumer issues ?
DWA	Spokespeople are not provided.
NACDS	Representatives testify before Congress or federal agencies to promote the organization's commitment to quality goods and services at the lowest possible prices.
NWDA	Spokespeople are not provided.
PMA	Representatives are sent to discuss issues directly related to the pharmaceutical industry.
Question 5	Does your association provide speakers to appear before consumer organizations ?
DWA	Speakers are not provided.
NACDS	An answer to this question is not indicated.
NWDA	Speakers are not provided.
PMA	A Speakers Bureau was established in 1968 to enable staff personnel and member firms to present talks in local communities throughout the country on issues of importance to consumers.
Question 6	What do you perceive to be the long-term impact of consumerism on the pharmaceutical industry?
DWA	The only possible impact would be on the supply-demand curve of the retailer. Anything enhancing competition is good; anything detracting from competition is bad.
NACDS	The consumer movement will continue to become a stronger voice in the federal decision-making process and how the industry conducts its business. It is hoped there will be continued efforts to maintain the balance between government protection and customer choice.
NWDA	It is hoped and believed that the long-term impact on the wholesale drug industry will be good.
PMA	Unless consumers understand that their ability to survive illnesses, not presently curable, depends on a continuation of the research capability of the industry, the vast majority of pharmaceutical companies will become merely commodity suppliers.

Source: Compiled by the author.

During the 1940s, several companies pointed out the steps they took to assure product sterility and quality. The installation of brass piping and the development of piping maintenance methods eliminated the problems of product discoloration and deterioration caused by insufficient sterility [101]. In 1941, Bristol-Myers reported its use of sterilized air to remove bacteria in the manufacturing process [68]. In 1947, a division of Sterling Drug developed a procedure whereby a sterile filling machine was used for bottling a solution in injectable preparations. This replaced a slow manual technique [109].

Sharp and Dohme employed public service advertising in 1947 to give information about the immunization of children and enhance the company's image [26]. Johnson & Johnson initiated a new training program for retail drug sales in 1949. The program recommended giving product information along with products, helping customers save money, and making them feel welcome [69].

In 1949, Merck and Company developed a method of packaging streptomycin that neared sterile perfection. Strict antiseptic conditions were set up in specially designed new buildings [110]. In 1954, Pfizer used sealed rooms and ultraviolet lights to ensure the purity of vials of Terramycin. Squibb's disposable injection units eliminated time-consuming preparation of syringe assemblies. Lederle and Sharp and Dohme created new labeling machines to reduce mislabeling [40]. Upjohn became the first company to use radiation sterilization in drug packaging [96].

Hoffman-LaRoche responded to public complaints about the prices of drugs by stating that a misunderstanding arose from the inability of pharmacists and the pharmaceutical industry to communicate facts to the public. The company began an educational campaign and urged the American Pharmaceutical Manufacturers Association to prepare a facts booklet that would be placed in prescription packages and doctors' waiting rooms [92].

In 1956, the consensus of pharmaceutical companies, such as Pfizer, Schering, Parke-Davis, Lederle, and Ciba, was that the industry had failed to give an accurate picture of itself to the medical industry. Physicians had not been adequately informed, as the companies emphasized selling techniques and tools. Schering's spokesman said advertisements had to be informative, make frank disclosures of drawbacks, and not knock competitors [34, p. 43].

Individual companies relied on public relations to combat the effectiveness of the 1959 Kefauver investigations. Companies, such as Upjohn, felt the hearings were held because the industry had insufficiently informed the general public about itself. The companies had to detail their contributions to advances in the prevention and curing of diseases at reasonable prices. Merck and Schering said drug firms were given little opportunity to present their side of the story at press briefings [91].

In 1959, Pfizer was questioned about its advertising techniques. While defending its practices, the company conceded one of its mailing pieces may have been misleading [85]. Merck used its research director to defend its promotion campaigns against Senate investigation and discuss doctors' confidence in branded drugs [103].

Winthrop Laboratories criticized generic legislation in 1961, and pointed to 24 key differences between branded and generic drugs. These variations could make a decisive difference in the strength, purity, and quality of drugs. A Sterling spokesman said there would be no incentive for pharmaceutical research, since innovative manufacturers would be unable to use their own labels [59].

Many drug manufacturers protested medicare programs in 1962, fearing controlled drug prices and troubles with a demoralized medical profession [34]. By 1963, a number of companies began to feel pressured by excessive government regulations. For example, Eli Lilly said the public suffered through unreasonable delays and roadblocks in the introduction of new medicines because of over-regulation. Prescription costs increased without tangible benefits. Lilly believed consumer safety lay in the reliability of the manufacturer and its willingness to stake the company reputation upon the quality of products and services [37].

During recent years, individual company responses to major issues have been rare, as the companies have relied upon their trade associations to take positions or stands that are representative of the industry and its members. Company executives frequently act as officials within trade associations. When they speak out on an issue, it is usually to present the association's view, not necessarily that of the company with which they are affiliated.

Only one specific company action was found in the literature of the 1970s. In 1977, the makers of Librium and Darvon said generics differed quantitatively from these products and did not carry expiration dates. The companies noted other differences as well, when addressing the medicaid program's Pharmaceutical Reimbursement Advisory Committee [14].

Company Responses to Primary Study

A mail survey on consumerism in the pharmaceutical industry was sent to seven drug manufacturers and four drug chains. Four manufacturers responded: Bristol-Myers (BM), Eli Lilly (EL), Hoechst-Roussel Pharmaceuticals (HRP), and U.S.V. Laboratories (USVL). Three of the manufacturers and all four of the retailers did not reply, despite two requests: Beecham Laboratories, Marion Laboratories, and Pfizer Laboratories; and Genovese Drug Stores, Hook Drugs, Jack Ekerd, and Walgreen Drug Stores.

All of the companies have customer complaint policies, despite their limited interface with final consumers. None has an in-house consumer advocate, but three express interest in consumers through their trade associations or other means. Two of the companies explain their use of educational programs. Three companies provide product-related information to the medical profession, not directly to final consumers. One company publishes a product information booklet. Two companies adapt their products to consumer desires; two do not answer this question. Three of the companies state that quality assurance is quite important. All the companies feel a wide range of legislation affects them, both federal and state. All companies say they are sensitive to consumer pressure. Three companies evaluate the overall impact of consumerism, stating that consumerism has had a positive effect.

The companies recognize the growing influence of consumerism and have begun or continue to make provisions to evaluate and deal with it.

The individual responses of the participating companies appear in Table 9.2. The answers were condensed and categorized by the author. All questions were not answered by each company.

THE OVERALL EFFECTS OF CONSUMERISM

The impact of consumerism on the pharmaceutical industry and an evaluation of consumerism in this area follow.

Impact of Consumerism

Consumerism has had a significant impact on the pharmaceutical industry for more than 75 years, ever since consumer groups supported pure food and drug legislation in 1902. A long line of consumer issues and government laws or regulations has followed.

In many instances, industry organizations opposed government legislation prior to enactment. However, they cooperated after the laws became effective. For example, in 1948, ten years after passage of the Food, Drug, and Cosmetic Act, industry representatives praised the law for its accomplishments.

The 1950s were difficult for the industry because the Kefauver hearings generated a lot of negative publicity, particularly about pricing practices. In the 1960s, legislation was enacted in several

TABLE 9.2

Pharmaceutical Company Responses to the Study

Question 1	The Consumer: What type of policy do you have for handling complaints? Does the company have a consumer complaint department? Is there a consumer advocate in-house? Do you have or participate in any educational programs?
BM	All complaints are recorded and responded to by individual divisions, and monthly reports filed with the corporation. Trends are examined. Each division has a customer complaint department. Divisional and corporate departments act as "early warning" systems to help deal with problems when they reach crisis proportions. There is no formal in-house advocate, but Bess Myerson serves as a consultant. She reviews the consumer complaint machinery, advertising plans, packaging, and other information of interest to consumers. Educational programs are not mentioned in the response.
EL	Four registered pharmacists monitor and answer all product complaints. Therapeutic complaints are answered by the medical staff. Reports are made directly to one of two vice-presidents. Complaints are handled through the technical services department. There is no individual in-house consumer advocate, but the functions of an advocate are found in the public relations services department and the public affairs division. Publications and individual diet charts are prepared. Information about diseases is published. Educational materials are provided to teachers, students, the medical profession, and the general public.
HRP	Interfaces with final consumers are rare, since ethical pharmaceuticals are produced. The few complaints received are processed by the customer communications department. The views of the National Pharmaceutical Council, which employs a consumer advocate to guide members, are supported. Educational materials are disseminated through a speakers bureau, which discusses the economic aspects of medical care and therapy and provides health care instruction.

(continued)

Table 9.2 (continued)

USVL   Customer inquiries are handled through a service department. Most company contact is with pharmacists and other members of the health care delivery system. A formal complaint department is not needed. An in-house consumer advocate is not employed. Educational programs are not addressed in the response.

Question 2   The Product: What types of product-related information are made available to the public? Are you modifying your products in response to consumerism? What type of procedures do you follow to ensure product quality?

BM   One of the most useful pieces of information is The Bristol-Myers Guide to Consumer Product Information, edited by Bess Myerson. Each division has a quality control department. A good manufacturing practices department oversees manufacturing practices throughout the company.

EL   Information about pharmaceutical products is directed only at the health profession. There is great sensitivity to product modification suggestions from consumers. The consumer preference laboratory runs a myriad of tests on all aspects of products, from the type of bottle cap to package size to appearance and taste. Quality control groups monitor the entire manufacturing process. Good manufacturing practices include building condition, equipment, storage, and personnel capabilities. An ongoing quality awareness training program is provided to employees.

HRP   Product-related information is provided to consumers through physicians. Until now, there has been no need to modify the marketing approach in response to consumerism. The company is sensitive to consumer needs and has improved packaging to minimize unintentional pediatric overdosing.

USVL   Patient-aid information is provided to the medical profession, not to the public. Quality control and quality assurance departments verify products during every step of manufacturing. Products are subjected to rigid examinations.

(continued)

Question 3	Outside Influences: What type of consumer regulations affect your operations? How does your company respond to outside consumer pressure? How do you evaluate the effect of consumerism on your company?
BM	The company is regulated by literally scores of government organizations, including perhaps a dozen at the federal level and others on state and municipal levels. All serious consumer letters are answered by a company officer. When consumer requests are of substance, they are acted upon. Consumerism has had a healthy effect. An informed consumer is usually a satisfied customer. The net effect of consumerism appears to be in the area of consumer information.
EL	The Environmental Protection Agency, drug substitution legislation, and package inserts have affected company operations. The company gives thoughtful consideration to consumer-related issues, and comments at public forums. The views of management are gladly provided to legislators and agency administrators.
HRP	Any consumer action that influences legislation, such as the repeal of antisubstitution laws and the establishment of state formularies, affects the company. The firm wishes to operate in concert with consumer needs, maintaining the philosophy that all are ultimately consumers.
USVL	The pharmaceutical industry is subject to procedures and laws from federal and state governments. These regulations are followed for legal, moral, and ethical reasons.

Source: Compiled by the author.

areas: certification of the safety and efficacy of insulin and penicillin, the jurisdiction of the FDA from manufacturer to sale to the ultimate consumer, labeling of drugs for prescription use only, drug safety, new drug clearance procedures, and honest and informative packaging.

As consumer demands increased, the industry improved its responsiveness. There has been intense concern for product quality, reasonable prices, reliability, communication and information, and safety. Previously, the industry concentrated its efforts on satisfying and communicating with the medical profession, not final consumers.

Individual companies have had to change their policies, products, and organization structures in response to consumerism. Frequently, the companies have expressed their views through their trade associations. A number of companies have worked hard to improve their operations and images to the public by: upgrading plant sterilization, developing innovative advertising and training programs, introducing new drugs, and utilizing education programs.

In recent years, legislation in several areas has been, and in some instances still is, opposed by trade associations and companies. Such legislation includes generic drugs, price posting, and the delay in new drug certification.

At present, consumer groups are most active in promoting legislation involving pharmacy ownership, generic substitution laws, product information for consumers, drug price advertising, and price posting. Consumer groups continually monitor industry practices and consumer legislation. They testify at congressional hearings, propose new bills at all levels of government, lobby for their demands, and bring pressure on industry members who do not comply with requests.

Evaluation of Consumerism

Consumerism has touched every aspect of the pharmaceutical industry and often obtained changes in industry practices. Many of the changes have proven to be beneficial to the consumer and industry alike. Product quality, safety, and industry marketing practices have improved.

Responsible manufacturers have cooperated with consumers and government in working out compromises to regulate the industry. They also have sanitized their plants, educated consumers, and otherwise upgraded operations. The pharmaceutical industry has been subjected to intensive government scrutiny because of its important role in the public's health.

Some regulations have hampered the industry and yielded debatable results for consumers. For example, the controls on new drug introductions have delayed needed medication from reaching consumers as well as assuring product safety. Demands for generic prescriptions may lead companies to cut back on their large research and development expenditures, since they will not benefit from name identification with major new drugs.

It is necessary to recognize the vital role government regulation has played in restricting flagrant abuses and preventing fraudulent and dangerous drugs from reaching the public. However, consumer safety also lies in the reliability of manufacturers and their willingness to stake reputations on product and service quality. Government regulation and industry self-regulation provide a powerful force for the consumer's interest.

Various pieces of consumer legislation should lead to increased competition, thereby lowering prices. These include open pharmacy laws, price posting, and advertising of pharmaceutical prices. On the other hand, package inserts and antibiotic batch certification require higher manufacturers' costs. Consumerists need to weigh the benefits of these laws against their dollar costs to consumers.

FUTURE OUTLOOK

There is little doubt that consumerism will continue to influence all aspects of the pharmaceutical industry. Manufacturers will be pressed to revise processes and procedures in order to ensure product safety and effectiveness. New product development and certification will be time-consuming. Greater interest will be taken in communicating directly with final consumers. Distributors and pharmacists will become more involved with pricing, product information, and generic drugs. Restrictive pharmacy ownership laws will be repealed, and large chain and discount drug stores will continue to grow. Problems will arise for pharmacists, since new generic drug laws will not protect them against liability claims.

Consumer groups will grow in number and in strength, particularly specialized groups like those comprised of senior citizens. Women's groups will demand information about the side effects and risks of birth control pills and other medication. Small, local consumer groups will band together to form larger federations and exert greater power. Important issues will be prices, safety, information, production impact on the environment, and advertising. Consumer groups will first ask for voluntary industry compliance with their requests. Then, they will utilize boycotts, picketing, and court action. Finally, new legislation will be sought.

The government will continue as an intermediary between consumers and the pharmaceutical industry. Federal agencies, especially the FDA and FTC, will seek to expand the implementation of current legislation and establish new regulations. Hearings will be held frequently to gain industry and consumer input, and proposals will be revised to reflect these views. State governments will work to resolve antisubstitution and restrictive ownership issues.

The pharmaceutical industry will consider increased government controls and consumer actions as threats to its survival. The industry will react negatively to pressure, and lobby to prevent or revise legislation. Public relations campaigns will be used to enhance the industry's reputation. The industry also will acknowledge the importance of consumerism and seek to voluntarily implement progressive policies toward responsible consumer issues. Open communication will be encouraged. Involvement in community services will be expanded.

Individual companies will be most affected by consumerism, since they represent a focal point for consumer demands and government legislation. Companies will restructure internal organizations to improve communication with final consumers, broaden complaint policies and departments, offer educational programs, employ consumer affairs specialists, participate in community service, and provide instruction in proper health care. Companies will continue to have associations speak for them, and support the associations' opposition to new regulations.

RECOMMENDATIONS

Recommendations are made for consumer groups, government, the industry, and individual companies.

Consumer Groups

Past experience has indicated that many industry practices will not be altered without outside pressure. This belief places consumerism on the offensive, as an opposing force to the pharmaceutical industry, when the two should complement each other. The avenues of communication must be kept open. This requires responsible listening as well as recommendations for industry improvements. Consumer groups must weigh the costs of their proposals against the benefits. This is difficult to do in the health field, because the value of human life cannot be measured.

Government

There is a delicate balance between government regulation in the consumer's interest and overregulation to the industry's detriment. Government action should concentrate on halting harmful industry activities, while using a positive approach of offering incentives for compliance with existing laws and regulations. Company research and development should be promoted. Actions tending toward socialized medicine should be deferred, since stimulation for new products would be removed. The industry should be encouraged to interact with the government and pursue a meaningful program of self-regulation.

The Industry

It is essential that the pharmaceutical industry gain insight and understanding of consumerism and its demands. Increased time and finances must be spent on the study of consumer needs, wants, behavior, and expectations. Information and public relations must be geared to final consumers. Industry representatives must continue to present opinions at government meetings; they also should seek to cooperate and compromise. Self-regulation should be undertaken before government legislation is needed. Trade associations must foster a spirit of cooperation with consumer groups, and inform members of consumer desires and requests. The associations also should function as clearinghouses for their members and the public. Community activities should be expanded. The industry must always act to protect consumers and generate a positive image.

Companies

Companies must exhibit a real interest in consumer needs through the study, planning, and execution of consumer programs. Skilled and trained personnel should be employed to interpret and react to consumer issues. Product information and consumer education must be improved. Policies also should be established for environmental protection, conservation, and restoration. Failure to respond to consumerism will heighten pressure on specific companies and their products.

BIBLIOGRAPHY

1. Aaker, David A., and Day, George S. Consumerism: Search for the Consumer Interest. New York: Free Press, 1971.

2. ____. Consumerism: Search for the Consumer Interest, 2d ed. New York: Free Press, 1974.

3. "Ad Ethics under Fire in Senate Drug Probe." Advertising Age 33 (February 5, 1962), pp. 1ff.

4. "ADMA Protests New Drug Publicity Plan." Oil Paint and Drug Reporter 154 (November 8, 1948), pp. 4ff.

5. "ADMA Views Federal Control As Threat to Scientific Progress." Oil Paint and Drug Reporter 157 (April 3, 1950), pp. 5ff.

6. "Advertising and Tugwell." Business Week (October 28, 1933), pp. 13-14.

7. "AMA Urges MDs to Fight Substitution Moves." American Druggist 168 (September 15, 1973), pp. 64ff.

8. "APHA and NARD Leaders Assail Differential Pricing." American Druggist 171 (May 15, 1975), p. 32.

9. "Arkansas Law Relaxes Curbs on Substitution by RPh's." American Druggist 171 (April 1, 1975), p. 19.

10. "Battle Over Florida Mandatory Substitution Law May Have National Repercussions." American Druggist 175 (February 1977), pp. 17ff.

11. "Bromide Backfire." Business Week (September 31, 1942), pp. 22ff.

12. Burton, L. V. "Battle of the Copeland Bill." Food Industries 5 (April 1934), pp. 150-52.

13. Cain, R. M. "Detailing the Physician." Oil Paint and Drug Reporter 115 (May 13, 1929), p. 55.

14. "Can Librium, Darvon Be Easily Replaced by Generics?" Drug Topics (November 1, 1977), pp. 18ff.

15. "Capper Bill and Advertising of Medicines and Cosmetics." Printer's Ink 164 (August 2, 1933), pp. 33, 36-37.

16. "Chains Rally Consumerists to Fight Bills on Ownership." American Druggist 171 (January 1975), pp. 16ff.

17. "Church Group May Seek Ban on All Drug Advertising." American Druggist 167 (April 15, 1973), p. 76.

18. Congressional Quarterly. Washington Information Directory 1977-78.

19. "Consumer Federation Advocates 'Strong Medicine'." American Druggist 168 (September 15, 1973), pp. 36ff.

20. "Consumer Protection from Producers Angle." Printer's Ink 166 (March 15, 1934), pp. 80-81.

21. "Copeland Bill Is Introduced: Its Full Text." Comments by J. F. Hoge. Printer's Ink 170 (January 10, 1935), pp. 12-14ff.

22. "Copeland Bill Slated for Quick Passage." Printer's Ink 166 (February 15, 1934), pp. 21, 24-25.

23. Copeland, Royal S. "A Food and Drug Bill Finally Passes." Advertising and Selling 31 (July 1938), pp. 17-19.

24. ____. "Protection for the Public." Scientific American (February 1938), pp. 88-89.

25. Dameron, Kenneth. "How Advertising Can Help the Consumer Education Movement." Printer's Ink 190 (March 29, 1940), pp. 13-15.

26. Dever, E. J. "Health Ed Campaign Is Good Public Relations." Printer's Ink 218 (March 14, 1947), pp. 44-45.

27. "Drug Act Tests." Business Week (November 9, 1946), pp. 64-65.

28. "Drug Ads Assure Public of High Quality." Advertising Age (February 22, 1960), p. 44.

29. "Drug Ads: Honesty Pays." Chemical Week 78 (May 1956), pp. 56ff.

30. "Drug Advertising Jurisdiction Transfer Recommended." Oil Paint and Drug Reporter 155 (March 14, 1949), pp. 3ff.

31. "Drug Bill Friends Shift Tactics." Business Week (November 1936), pp. 19-20.

32. "Drug Industry Reaches Accord on Durham Bill on Prescription Refills." Oil Paint and Drug Reporter 160 (July 30, 1951), p. 3.

33. "Drug Industry's Future Is Seen Dependent upon the Doings of the FDA." Oil Paint and Drug Reporter 185 (April 13, 1964), p. 4.

34. "Drug Makers Frown on Medicare." Chemical Week 90 (June 1962), pp. 43-44.

35. "Drug Manufacturers Gain Point as House Approves Durham Bill." Oil Paint and Drug Reporter 160 (August 6, 1961), pp. 4ff.

36. "Drug Men Lose Another Round; Package Insert Rule Will Stand, With Six Months for Compliance." Oil Paint and Drug Reporter 180 (September 4, 1961), pp. 3ff.

37. "Drug Over-Regulation Seen Hurting Public by Impeding Medical Progress." Oil Paint and Drug Reporter 183 (June 3, 1963), pp. 43ff.

38. "Drug Sales Suggested for Consumer Benefit." Oil Paint and Drug Reporter 194 (December 2, 1968), p. 7.

39. "Drug Plant Sanitation Principles Set." Oil Paint and Drug Reporter 154 (October 4, 1948), pp. 5ff.

40. "Drugs: Packaged with Life and Death Exactitude." Modern Packaging 47 (August 1954), pp. 92-99ff.

41. Dunbar, Paul B. "Enforcement of Food and Drug Act." Oil Paint and Drug Reporter 110 (November 1, 1926), pp. 22ff.

42. Dunn, Charles Wesley. "Food and Drug Legislation in the U.S." Oil Paint and Drug Reporter 110 (November 1, 1926), pp. 22ff.

43. ____. "How S.5 Will Work." Printer's Ink 184 (July 7, 1938), pp. 44, 46-49.

44. "Ethical Drug Ads Would Be Curbed Under FDA Rule." Chemical Marketing Reporter 202 (August 28, 1972), pp. 4ff.

45. "FDA Needs an Overhauling, But Larrick Can Do the Job: Citizens Advisory Committee." Oil Paint and Drug Reporter 182 (October 29, 1962), pp. 3ff.

46. "FDA Reveals Policies on Prescription Refills." Oil Paint and Drug Reporter 154 (December 20, 1948), p. 3.

47. "FDA to Screen Promotion for New Drugs." Advertising Age 31 (July 25, 1960), p. 3.

48. "Federal Drug Law Controls Retail Sales." Oil Paint and Drug Reporter 153 (January 26, 1948), pp. 3ff.

49. Federal Register 41 (December 7, 1976).

50. Fisk, Margaret. Encyclopedia of Association, vols. I & II. 1977.

51. "Food, Drug and Cosmetic Act at End of Its First Decade." Oil Paint and Drug Reporter 153 (June 21, 1948), pp. 5ff.

52. "Food and Drug Bill Passed at Last." Business Week (June 18, 1938), pp. 36–37.

53. "FTC: Base Rx Reimbursement on Usual and Customary Charge." American Druggist 171 (May 1, 1975), pp. 15ff.

54. "FTC on the Pan." Business Week (May 29, 1943), pp. 90ff.

55. "FTC Plans to Preempt State Curbs on Rx Price Advertising." American Druggist 171 (June 15, 1975), pp. 19–20.

56. "FTC Price Probe Called a 'Sham'." American Druggist 173 (January 1976), p. 18.

57. "FTC Report Urges Time Limit on Exclusive Use of Drug Brand Names." American Druggist 176 (June 1977), pp. 15ff.

58. "Generic Name Issue." Oil Paint and Drug Reporter 192 (October 23, 1967), p. 3.

59. "Generics Called Menace." Oil Paint and Drug Reporter 179 (May 29, 1961), pp. 7ff.

60. Giacinto, V. "Quality Must Be Deep Rooted: Merck's Quality." Chemical and Engineering News 35 (May 6, 1957), p. 38.

61. Hecht, Annabel. "Informing Patients on Prescription Drugs." FDA Consumer (March 1976).

62. ____. "What Drug Price Ads Must Tell." FDA Consumer (March 1976).

63. "HEW Eyes Kansas Variable Fee As Answer to MAC-AAC Protests." American Druggist 171 (March 1, 1975), pp. 14ff.

64. "HEW Seeks Ways of Estimating Pharmacies' Acquisition Cost." American Druggist 171 (April 15, 1975), pp. 15-16ff.

65. "Insert Rule to Up Cost of Drugs." Oil Paint and Drug Reporter 180 (September 11, 1961), p. 5.

66. "Is FTC Planning to Call for Repeal of Anti-Substitution Laws?" American Druggist 172 (December 1975), pp. 16-17.

67. "Is Over Cautious FDA Depriving Americans of Vital New Drugs?" American Druggist 165 (May 15, 1972), p. 21.

68. Jackson, H. C. "Sterilized Air Cuts Illness, Gives Us Better Products: Bristol-Myers Co." Factory Management and Maintenance 99 (December 1941), pp. 81-82.

69. "Johnson and Johnson Trains Retail Drug Sales People to 'Sell As Customers Like It'." Sales Management 62 (May 20, 1949), pp. 82ff.

70. "Kefauver Attack on Drug Industry Unjustified: PMA." Oil Paint and Drug Reporter 180 (July 3, 1961), pp. 3ff.

71. "Kefauver Drug Probers Are in with Verdict on the Industry: Guilty of Extraordinary Profits." Oil Paint and Drug Reporter 180 (July 3, 1961).

72. "Legislation and Legal Matters Pertaining to the Drug Industry." Oil Paint and Drug Reporter 115 (June 10, 1929), p. 42B.

73. "Liggett Wins in Supreme Court." Printer's Ink 145 (November 22, 1928), p. 80.

74. Lund, J. Y. "Drug Men Should Pay More Attention to the Consumers." Oil Paint and Drug Reporter 185 (April 20, 1964), p. 43.

75. Mason, Harry B. "Advertising to Physicians: A Consumer Market for Medicinal Agents." Printer's Ink 112 (July 22, 1920), pp. 73-74ff.

76. McClellan, Grant S. The Consuming Public. H. W. Wilson, 1968.

77. "Mixed Reaction Greets FTC Complaints Against Three Drug Advertisers." Printer's Ink 259 (April 5, 1957), p. 34.

78. Morehouse, P. G. "After Two Years of Wheeler-Lea." Advertising and Selling 32 (May 1940), pp. 22-23.

79. "NACDS Reaffirms Stand Against Substitution." American Druggist 176 (June 1977), pp. 27ff.

80. Neal, Harry Edward. The Protectors. New York: Julian Messner, 1968.

81. Nelson, G. "Rx Drug Prices: The Investigators Get Busy Again." Oil Paint and Drug Reporter 191 (January 9, 1967), pp. 3ff.

82. "New Highlights." FDA Consumer (March 1976).

83. Nichols, G. A. "Beat the Tugwell Bill." Printer's Ink 165 (November 2, 1933), pp. 10-11ff.

84. "Ownerships Rally Consumerists to Fight Bills on Ownership." American Druggist 171 (January 15, 1977), pp. 16ff.

85. "Pfizer Admits Ad Hit by Magazine May Have Misled." Advertising Age 30 (January 19, 1959), pp. 1ff.

86. "Plant Inspection Backed by Trade: Lawmakers Want Checks on Power." Oil Paint and Drug Reporter 163 (May 25, 1953), pp. 3ff.

87. "PMA Criticizes AphA Move to Do Away with Brand Names." American Druggist 170 (September 15, 1974), pp. 46-47.

88. "PMA Speaks Out on Substitution." American Druggist 165 (April 17, 1972), pp. 38-39.

89. "PMA Tells Public Generic Savings Claims Are 'Illusion'." American Druggist 164 (October 4, 1971), p. 23.

90. "PMA Told Retail Druggists Oppose Compulsory Prescribing of Generics." Oil Paint and Drug Reporter 191 (April 10, 1967), pp. 43-44.

91. "PR Brains Working to Combat Kefauver." Editors and Publishers 92 (December 26, 1959), p. 39.

92. "Prescription for Druggists." Chemical Week 74 (May 22, 1954), pp. 21-22.

93. "Prescription Refilling Policies of FDA Hit." Oil Paint and Drug Reporter 158 (September 11, 1950), pp. 5ff.

94. "Probe Drug Prices." Business Week (July 20, 1940), p. 44.

95. "Protest New Drug Regulations." Business Week (November 5, 1938), pp. 36-38.

96. "Radiation Sterilization At Work." Modern Packaging 29 (September 1955), pp. 144-47ff.

97. "Report of Committee on Legislation." Oil Paint and Drug Reporter 115 (June 10, 1929), p. 42C.

98. "Report of NWDA Committee on Legislation." Oil Paint and Drug Reporter 116 (October 9, 1929), pp. 23, 25.

99. "Report of NWDA Committee on Quality of Medicinal Products." Oil Paint and Drug Reporter 112 (October 6, 1927), pp. 25ff.

100. "Reveal Formulas." Business Week (September 13, 1941), pp. 42ff.

101. Russell, Otis E. "Keep the Piping Clean." Heating and Piping and Air Conditioning 12 (July 1940), p. 434.

102. "Rx Insert Rule to Up Cost of Drugs: PMA." Oil Paint and Drug Reporter 180 (September 11, 1961), pp. 5ff.

103. "Senate Probers May Look At Drug Promotion Next." Advertising Age 30 (December 14, 1959), pp. 1ff.

104. "Serious Label Jam." Printer's Ink 186 (March 16, 1939), pp. 33-34ff.

105. Simmons, Henry E. "Brand vs. Generic Drugs: It's Only a Matter of Name." FDA Consumer (March 1973).

106. Smith, Alfred E. "Al Smith on the Tugwell Bill." Printer's Ink 166 (January 4, 1934), p. 32.

107. State Education Department. Handbook II: Pharmacy Law Rules Information, Supplement. 1975.

108. "States Get 'EAC' Data on Drugs from HEW." American Druggist 173 (April 1976), pp. 25-26.

109. "Sterile Filling." Modern Packaging 20 (January 1947), pp. 134-35.

110. "Streptomycin: Showplace Packaging Plant at Merck." Modern Packaging 22 (March 1949), pp. 82-85.

111. "Substitution Laws Seen Curbing RPh's Freedom." American Druggist 175 (January 15, 1977), p. 42.

112. "Supreme Court Removes Ban on Drug Price Ads." NYS Consumer Protection Board (June-July 1976).

113. "Trade Associations Aiding in Drug Law Simplification." Chemical and Engineering News 28 (October 9, 1950), p. 3,501.

114. "Tugwell Bill Assailed by Bristol As Unfair." Oil Paint and Drug Reporter 124 (November 27, 1933), pp. 15ff.

115. U.S. Department of Health, Education, and Welfare. "A Primer on New Drug Development." FDA Consumer Memo, HEW Publication no. (FDA) 74-3021.

116. ____. "Fair Packaging and Labeling Act." FDA Consumer Memo, HEW Publication no. (FDA) 74-1019.

117. ____. "Milestones in U.S. Food and Drug Law History." HEW Publication no. (FDA) 75-1005.

118. ____. "We Want You to Know About the Laws Enforced by the FDA." HEW Publication no. (FDA) 75-1007.

119. ____. "We Want You to Know About Today's FDA." HEW Publication no. (FDA) 77-1021.

120. Van Avery. Public Health. New York: W. H. Wilson, 1959.

121. "We'll Back Substitution . . . If You Accept Price Posting." American Druggist 167 (April 15, 1973), p. 21.

122. "Where Congress' Drug Industry Probe Leads." Business Week (December 19, 1959), pp. 30-31.

10

CONSUMERISM AND THE PROFESSIONS

Lisa Chiranky

INTRODUCTION

The legal and medical professions are both self-regulatory. They set rules and regulations for membership in their professions, discipline nonconforming members, provide services to consumers, and have little government interference. Both professions possess powerful trade associations that traditionally have defended their rights to self-regulation and free enterprise.

As consumerism grows as an important force, the legal and medical professions will be more affected. In recent years, malpractice suits have skyrocketed, advertising has been approved for professionals, consumers have requested a lot of information, and the use of second opinions has increased. These actions will continue in the future.

In this chapter, consumerism in the legal and medical professions is detailed. For each profession, the history of consumerism, consumer groups, government actions, and the responses of the industry and individual practitioners to consumerism are investigated.

THE HISTORY OF CONSUMERISM IN THE PROFESSIONS

The Legal Profession

One of the earliest legal organizations was the New York Law Institute, established in 1828. Its sole function was to provide a legal library service for members. Later organizations, such as the New York Bar Association, Boston Bar Association, and American Bar Association (ABA), stated their objective as the upgrading of professional requirements.

315

Prior to 1846, admission to the bar in most states required several examinations spread out over a ten-year period. An individual progressed from attorney to solicitor to counsellor. As of 1846, any male citizen who was at least 21 years of age, had good character, and completed learning qualifications was entitled to admission to practice law in court [74].

At this time there was criticism of the legal profession by writers like Alexis de Tocqueville, who said in <u>Democracy in America</u> that lawyers were hostile to the mass public, conservative, antidemocratic, and interested in private gain. In 1868, the political involvement of judges and lawyers in the struggle over control of the Erie Railroad became public knowledge when the issuance of illegal injunctions leaked out.

The New York Bar Association recognized in the 1870s that it had to aid the courts in the punishment of lawyers guilty of unprofessional conduct. It created two committees to deal with conduct. One committee concentrated on the qualifications of judicial candidates and judicial misconduct. The second committee dealt with attorneys suspected of misconduct. Records were not kept until 1897, but a review of the data from 1897 to 1920 showed a large increase in complaints, while penalties remained small. In 1901, for example, there were a total of 63 complaints and three disbarrings and two suspensions. In 1920, there were 940 complaints and 15 disbarrings, two suspensions, and one censure [74, p. 366].

In 1876, the American Bar Association was formed as a national organization consisting of several local bar associations. The ABA sought to institute uniform goals and actions, which had not been possible with unaffiliated local bars. The ABA had an exclusive membership policy for many years and tried to prevent Louis Brandeis, a Jewish lawyer, from obtaining a seat on the Supreme Court. The ABA also considered negligence lawyers to be unprofessional and constantly chastised them as ambulance chasers [14].

During the 1930s and 1940s, a few lawyers were quite active politically. Politico-lawyers appeared and worked for special interest groups. They had large earnings, due to real or contrived influence with federal officials. The legal profession, as well as the government, openly discouraged the activities of politico-lawyers [90].

The ethics of two-fee arrangements received considerable discussion in the 1940s. Under the retainer fee, a lawyer agreed to take care of certain nominal legal services over a period of time for a fixed fee. The retainer fee was criticized because of its size and exclusions. Under the contingency fee, a lawyer received from one-fourth to one-third or more of what was recovered as a result of litigation; no fee was charged if nothing was recovered. The contingency fee most often was used in personal injury cases, small debt collections, will contests, and negligence suits. This fee generated controversy because of the large percentage charged and the lack of time a lawyer would spend on a case with a low probability of winning [33]. The ABA did not devise solutions or alternatives to these fee plans, and there was little discussion of legal care for clients who could not afford attorneys.

The American Civil Liberties Union (ACLU), formed in 1920, became active in cases involving racial discrimination during the 1950s. The ACLU was interested in protecting the rights of individuals to freedom of speech, due process, and racial and religious equality before the law. It brought test cases to court, testified before legislative bodies, and publicly protested civil rights violations. It also worked with government officials to prevent legislation that might infringe on civil liberties [58].

In 1964, the Economic Opportunity Act set up offices throughout the country to deal with consumer problems, including substandard housing, urban poverty, inadequate education, and the inability of consumers to purchase legal and medical services. For the first time, the federal government directly subsidized legal aid for the poor. The Criminal Justice Act of 1964 provided funds for public defenders. The Office of Economic Opportunity created an Office of Legal Services to offer free legal aid to individuals in civil matters. The ABA discussed and debated the pros and cons of legal aid at great length, but changed no policies. In addition, lawyers were not encouraged to participate in legal aid programs. Many ABA members expressed concern that legal aid would create competition [14].

During the 1960s, the ABA reexamined professional ethics. In 1964, a committee was established to propose revisions to the 1908 Canon of Ethics. This action was in response to Supreme Court decisions that had lessened the self-regulatory powers of the association. The Canon of Ethics was revised in 1969 and renamed the Code of Professional Responsibility. The new code stated aspirations and specific disciplinary rules [14].

The modern legal disciplinary system has evolved during the latter part of the twentieth century. Currently, admission to the practice of law and lawyer discipline are functions of the highest court in a state. An investigation begins after a complaint against a lawyer is received from a dissatisfied client, information in the media, or some other means. The complaint is investigated by a lawyer member of a committee created for this purpose, a professional investigator, or a staff lawyer of the local ABA. Findings are reported to an inquiry panel, which reviews the report and determines if the complaint should be dismissed, an informal warning imposed, or formal charges filed [110].

The issue of attorney advertising has been debated for the last several years, with the ABA backing its traditional practice of banning lawyers from soliciting business. In 1976, two Arizona lawyers advertised in a local newspaper. The state bar association brought charges against them and suspended them from practice for one week. The Supreme Court reversed lower court decisions and gave lawyers the right to advertise their services in 1977 [111].

The expansion of no-fault insurance laws has been controversial. Many lawyers oppose no-fault automobile insurance laws and other proposed no-fault laws, stating that consumer rights are lessened. They need not add that no-fault laws also decrease the use of lawyers and their fees [112]. No-fault laws have not proven to be as effective in lowering legal costs as predictions had indicated.

Other consumer issues also have arisen or grown in recent years: legal aid, fee-setting, changes in and enforcement of disciplinary rules, self-regulation versus self-interest, effectiveness of self-regulation, and the activities of the ACLU.

The Medical Profession

In the nineteenth century, the medical profession consisted not only of conventional medical practitioners but of homeopaths, eclectics, faith healers, and other cultists. A small group of practitioners, concerned with the state of the medical field, established the American Medical Association (AMA) in 1848. The purposes of the AMA were to raise standards within the profession and rid medicine of its diverse and medically questionable sects. Today, the AMA is a national organization comprised of state, territorial, and county societies. To be a member of the AMA, a doctor must have membership in a county or district society. Each society sets its own qualifications for membership. The AMA has been able to use its powers to keep the medical profession cohesive. AMA powers include controlling the quantity of physicians, setting requirements for training and hospitals, certifying medical schools, and controlling state medical examining boards [20].

During the middle and late 1800s, the number of medical colleges expanded rapidly; educational standards were lax. Standards were so low that even the best schools did not provide quality medical training. The AMA partially attributed this to the low caliber of medical journalism. Most of the several hundred periodicals on health and disease had little scientific merit and carried excessive amounts of advertising. In 1883, the Journal of the American Medical Association (JAMA) appeared. JAMA did more to enhance the image of the AMA than any other action in the nineteenth century. It enabled the AMA to fight questionable medical sects, disseminate knowledge about advances in medical science, and publicize association activities. The circulation of JAMA quadrupled between 1883 and 1900 [20].

The AMA appointed a committee to devise a framework for ethical standards in May 1903. The principles of ethics pertained to: duties of physicians to each other, duties to the public, compensation, the responsibility of reporting charlatans, and informing the public about dangers. Public advertising was considered incompatible with good standing in the profession. These ethical standards made medical practice more uniform.

For many years the AMA led the battle against patent medical frauds and nostrums. It joined with private crusaders, including Samuel Adams, author of Great American Fraud, in seeking food and drug legislation. JAMA kept readers informed of the association's positions and helped increase support for federal legislation. The Pure Food and Drug Act was passed in 1906 [62].

The administration of Franklin Roosevelt brought the medical profession into a new era, as medicine became a target of government reform. In 1938, Roosevelt called a National Health Conference. It recommended greater government participation in the field of public health. Several issues were brought to the attention of the public: the high costs of medical care, national health insurance, the effectiveness of self-regulation, malpractice and unnecessary surgery, fee-splitting, and licensing methods [53].

During the 1940s, the medical profession basically was uninvolved with consumerism. The major interest was increasing the supply of doctors needed for World War II. The AMA encouraged accelerated programs by medical schools, and was not concerned about lowered educational standards [62].

The growth and expansion of group medical practice was a major factor throughout the 1950s. Under group practice, several doctors, each with a different specialty, practiced in the same office. Group practice was a way of holding down costs and giving consumers complete medical care at reasonable prices.

At this time, the AMA conducted a number of surveys and found that as many as 30 percent of practicing physicians took little or no part in formal or semiformal educational activities to keep current with new medical knowledge. Despite this, no policy changes occurred [62].

In 1959, the AMA ended its long opposition to medical plans, particularly those sponsored by unions. Before, doctors who participated in such plans were considered unethical. The removal of the ban by the AMA signaled to many doctors that they could participate in plans without being stigmatized [62].

President John Kennedy presented to Congress in the early 1960s a broad program of federal medical insurance for the elderly. He also suggested several measures the federal government could take to help consumers deal with the consequences of illness. The AMA did not support these proposals, and worried about socialized medicine.

The shortage of doctors became a serious problem in the late 1960s. Hundreds of small towns and big city slums had few, if any, general practitioners. In 1967, it was estimated that the shortage of physicians was approximately 50,000. The ratio of physicians in private practice who devoted themselves to family medicine dropped from 76 per 100,000 people in 1950 to 50 per 100,000 people in 1967. The trend continued into the 1970s [62, p. 238]. Further, U.S. medical schools faced serious financial problems and a lack of facilities.

Thousands of foreign physicians immigrated to the United States between 1967 and 1970. During 1967 alone, about 45,000 doctors trained in foreign medical schools set up practices in the United States. This influx has continued over the last decade. As many as 5,000 foreign-trained doctors have been unable to pass tests of basic medical knowledge and currently practice medicine without licenses [62, p. 239]. Because of the acute shortage of physicians, a number of regulatory groups have not moved against unqualified, foreign-trained doctors.

The growing awareness of consumers about their medical rights and the influx of foreign-trained physicians led to an increase in malpractice litigation. In 1970, one of every six doctors was sued for medical malpractice [62, p. 245]. A great deal of debate took place over alternative plans to gain stricter quality control of medical services. The government set up the Professional Standards Review Organization in 1973 to regulate physicians better.

Since 1974, the medical profession has been monitored closely by consumer activists and physicians. Some highly critical statistics have been generated. In 1976, for example, it was estimated that as many as 16,000 of the 320,000 licensed doctors in the United States (about 5 percent) were unfit or incompetent. These 16,000 doctors treated 7.5 million patients per year. A total of nearly 2.4 million unnecessary operations were performed each year, and this resulted in 11,900 deaths. Each year 10,000 U.S. patients died or suffered potentially fatal reactions following the administration of unneeded antibiotics. An estimated 260,000 women underwent needless hysterectomies each year [62, p. 267].

Consumerism now focuses on the effectiveness of self-regulation, the role of the federal government in health care, the increase in malpractice and unnecessary surgery, the ethics of fee-splitting, the costs of health care, and licensing methods.

ACTIVE CONSUMER GROUPS

The Legal Profession

There are virtually no consumer organizations that function as watchdogs for the legal profession. Well-known consumer groups, such as Ralph Nader's, generally do not deal with the legal profession.

Local consumer affairs departments have no jurisdiction over legal complaints and refer them to the bar association in the area. Various legal organizations, such as the National Legal Aid and Defender Association, the Legal Services Corporation, and the American Civil Liberties Union, provide legal services to low-income and other individuals.

The Medical Profession

The number of consumer groups dealing with the medical profession is small, since consumerism in this field has developed very recently and local consumer agencies refer complaints to area AMA chapters.

The Public Citizens Health Research Group, a Ralph Nader organization, is the major consumer organization that deals exclusively with the medical profession. The group publicizes aspects of the medical field that require investigation and public attention, conducts and publishes studies, and appears before Congress. The Health Research Group is most involved with: national health insurance, doctor accountability, medical device legislation, medical malpractice, unnecessary surgery, and the quality of medical care [120].

The National Center for Health Statistics, funded by the Department of Health, Education, and Welfare (HEW), is not a consumer group per se. However, it aids consumerists by providing them with statistics to support their assertions [62].

GOVERNMENT

The Legal Profession

Government involvement with the legal profession was negligible until the 1960s and 1970s. During the 1960s, the Office of Economic Opportunity (OEO) and free legal aid were established. Sargent Shriver, the head of OEO, pledged it would not adversely affect the bar. Bar associations did not give a reciprocal pledge about their dealings with OEO [14].

Intense professional opposition to OEO occurred at the local level, where individual and small-firm lawyers feared a loss of business to legal aid attorneys. This opposition has continued. For example, in late 1977, the Nassau County Bar Association and the Legal Aid Society of Nassau County argued about the screening of legal aid applicants. The bar claimed that legal aid, free legal service for indigent criminal defendants, was helping clients who did not qualify because their incomes were above allowable levels [36].

Most government action toward the legal profession has concerned lawyer discipline. In 1970, an ABA committee, created because of government pressure, completed a three-year study of lawyer discipline throughout the country. The committee was headed by retired Supreme Court justice Tom Clark and reported:

> the existence of a scandalous situation that requires the
> immediate attention of the professions and courts. . . .
> with few exceptions, the prevailing attitude of lawyers
> towards disciplinary enforcement ranges from apathy
> to outright hostility. Disciplinary action is practically
> non-existent in many jurisdictions; practices and pro-
> cedures are antiquated; many disciplinary agencies
> have little power to take effective steps against male-
> factors [110, p. 10].

As a result of the Clark Report, several state courts took actions to upgrade the legal profession, make it more responsive to the needs of consumers, and enact more stringent disciplinary rules. Table 10.1 summarizes the Clark Report recommendations and the percentage of state jurisdictions that adopted them as of 1976 [69].

Several state jurisdictions instituted reform measures in the early 1970s. For example, California, Colorado, Georgia, Idaho, Indiana, Maine, Michigan, Minnesota, Nebraska, New Hampshire, Washington, and Wisconsin added nonlawyers to their disciplinary boards, since the public wanted to know more about the inner workings of the legal profession. This opened the system of rules, regulations, and punishment to public scrutiny. Other states were hesitant to allow nonlawyers to participate, feeling that: nonlawyers did not understand the intricacies of the legal process, lawyer members of the board would be too influential, and review by the highest state court ensured due process to the public [110].

Specific procedures to verify or audit lawyers' trust accounts were instituted by various states, including Delaware, Florida, Iowa, Maryland, New Mexico, and New Jersey. The purpose of

TABLE 10.1

State Adoptions of Clark Report Recommendations

Recommendations	Percentage of State-Level Disciplinary Jurisdictions Adopting Rules Similar to Those Recommended
Centralization of disciplinary enforcement	87
Rotation of membership of disciplinary boards	87
Initiation of investigations without complaints	92
Centrally located records of complaints	81
Informal admonition of minor misconduct	79
Resignation without prejudice while under disciplinary investigation	72
Suspension for incapacity	83
Reciprocal discipline	66
Suspension on conviction of serious crime	79
Conviction—conclusive evidence of guilt for disciplinary proceedings	87
Protection of clients when attorney disciplined, died, or disappeared	51
No rapid reinstatement after disbarment	83
Required accounting for client funds	55
Audit of attorneys' trust funds	14

Source: National Center for Professional Discipline, American Bar Association, Chicago, Illinois, November 15, 1976.

such procedures was to keep attorneys aware of their obligations regarding the proper maintenance of trust accounts [110].

Fee dispute arbitration systems were established by the highest state courts in many states, such as Alaska. These systems enabled fee disputes to be settled more easily and efficiently [110].

The state of Michigan developed a variety of reforms. On January 8, 1970, the State Bar Grievance Board was created by the state supreme court. The board was composed of three lawyers appointed by the state bar, two lawyers appointed by the state supreme court, and two laymen appointed by the state supreme court. Arbitration of fee disputes could be handled by one board-designated ombudsman, when both parties to the dispute agreed with this. No fee was charged for the service. In 1972, an amendment made the failure to answer a request for investigation or a formal complaint liable to disciplinary action [80]. During its first few years, the Michigan system increased disciplinary actions by 400 percent [85, p. 58].

Federal activity continued with the enactment of the Legal Services Corporation Act of 1974. The act provided legal assistance to the poor in civil matters [86]. The Senate established the Subcommittee on Citizens Interests in 1975. Previously, no federal agency or congressional committee had the primary mission of regulating or overseeing the legal profession. The subcommittee was to study the legal profession, make recommendations, and implement programs. However, in 1976, a Nader report criticized the subcommittee, concluding that:

> the result of this subcommittee's activities has been a federal policy of benign neglect. Virtually exclusive control over lawyers' conduct remains vested in the ABA and a network of state and local bar associations, that promulgate rules of professional conduct for lawyers as well as standards for accreditation of law schools, admission to practice and disciplinary procedures [85, p. 297].

To date, no program or changes have been instituted on a national level to change the self-regulatory nature of the legal profession.

In June 1977, the Supreme Court ruled that lawyers could legally advertise. As a result, the ABA adopted a code of guidelines for lawyers who wished to advertise to the public.

The Medical Profession

The medical profession was relatively free of government action until the New Deal era of Franklin Roosevelt. Then a 1935-36

National Health Survey confirmed prior suspected conditions: a large proportion of the population could not afford medical care. As a result, many legislators became interested in the health profession and its performance [62].

On July 31, 1938, the attorney general announced charges against the AMA and several affiliated societies. They were accused of violating the restraint of trade provision of the Sherman Act by attempting to crush a plan launched by the nonprofit Group Health Association. Group Health provided hospitalization and medical services for employees of the Home Owners Loan Corporation and their dependents. The government said AMA officials had threatened to expel any physician who served on the staff of Group Health and tried to close hospitals to these doctors. In 1943, the AMA was convicted of violating the Sherman Act, and fines were imposed. After this, the AMA retained its attitude toward group health plans and the doctors who participated in them, but it was much more subtle [20].

It took the government about 30 years to enact a national health insurance plan. The first congressional bill, dealing with a federally subsidized system of state health insurance, was introduced in 1936. It did not pass. Other legislation was proposed in 1939 and 1959. These laws also were defeated. In 1960, Kerr-Mills, which gave federal assistance to states in meeting the medical costs of the aged, was approved. But in 1961, a bill covering hospitalization benefits for the aged was turned down. Medicare, a plan of medical insurance combining all previous legislative efforts, finally was established in 1965. In effect, this was the first consumer-oriented program regarding the medical profession. The AMA was able to lobby successfully for 30 years [93].

The Department of Health, Education, and Welfare was given cabinet status in 1953. Despite its title, HEW was not created to regulate the medical profession. Two HEW agencies, the Public Health Service and the Food and Drug Administration (FDA), concentrate on medical issues. The Public Health Service handles medical research and improves methods of disease control. The FDA enforces food and drug laws. It certifies new drugs, determines which drugs require prescriptions, sets standards for labeling, and can recall drugs. In 1969, the Supreme Court stated that medical devices could be legally treated as drugs by the FDA. The Kennedy Medical Device Bill of 1973 expanded the authority of the FDA to include safety and effectiveness testing of devices [62].

In 1973, the government established a policy for Professional Standards Review Organizations (PSRO), and made it clear that the failure of this opportunity to self-regulate would lead to increased federal regulation. PSROs were to set standards of care or norms for the treatment of different illnesses, review doctors' payment requests under medicare and medicaid, compare norms with actual requests, and deny excessive claims. Local PSROs were comprised of area doctors who agreed to follow certain guidelines and formulate care standards. PSROs were intended to improve medical care while holding down costs by this system of peer review [76]. According to legislation, the PSRO system was to have been operationalized and effective by 1976 or doctors would lose control of the program [79]. Although there is controversy about the effectiveness of the PSRO program, it is presently controlled by physicians.

Government action also occurred in response to various incidents. For example, a surgery scandal arose in Suffolk, New York, during fall 1977. Several doctors were accused of allowing non-medically-trained sellers of surgical equipment to participate in surgical procedures. As a result of the disclosures, HEW and the state medical licensing agency created a special task force to examine this practice and investigate charges of misconduct [100].

Recently, doctors have been allowed to advertise. Thus far, few physicians have begun to use this tool. Many believe advertising is unprofessional, and prefer to list their names, addresses, and specialties in directories.

INDUSTRY RESPONSES TO CONSUMERISM

The Legal Profession

The responses of the legal profession to consumerism are available in the published literature and through a survey of major trade associations.

Responses of the Legal Profession
As Reported in the Literature

In the 1920s, the ABA created a Standing Committee on Legal Aid and recommended that every state bar association appoint a similar committee. At that time, like today, many members supported legal aid societies, but did not feel personal obligations to represent the poor [85]. The legal profession as an entity has been supportive of legal aid only within the last few years [86].

Since the mid-1960s, ABA leaders have affirmed explicitly the duty of the association to make legal services available regardless of a client's ability to pay. However, their statements have been ambiguous because for many years the ABA did not say whether the obligation to give free legal services was the responsibility of the collective bar or individual lawyers [85].

The ABA approved an ethic of personal obligation in August 1975. It adopted the position that public service was a professional obligation of each lawyer. Several ABA leaders advocated the imposition of a requirement that each lawyer perform public service work. As a voluntary organization, however, the ABA was limited in its enforcement demands [85].

The Clark Report, cited earlier, was published by an ABA committee investigating the legal profession. It recommended drastic reform measures and urged the ABA to take the lead in helping individual state courts and organizations adopt the measures. In 1973, the ABA established a Standing Committee on Professional Discipline and a National Center for Professional Discipline to promote and direct efficient disciplinary enforcement in the United States. The coordinated activities of the two groups provided professional training programs and consulting services to disciplinary agencies and individual lawyers, and course and informational materials on lawyer discipline. Chief Justice Warren Burger stated in his 1976 year-end report on the judiciary that the bar was increasingly recognizing its obligation to discipline lawyers who betrayed professional trust. Disciplinary action increased 85 percent from 1973 to 1976 [69].

Through the National Center for Professional Discipline, a data bank enabled states to exchange information on lawyers guilty of unprofessional conduct. The center also disseminated information to the public on the effectiveness of self-regulation, including the number of complaints processed and their disposition.

The ABA formed a Commission on Advertising in August 1977. This commission developed a set of guidelines for lawyers who chose to advertise. These guidelines specified advertising content limitations and made violators subject to disciplinary hearings [28]. The commission is composed of seven members, including representatives from the media, consumer groups, the advertising industry, and lawyers.

The Commission on Advertising is responsible for assessing developments in legal advertising, assisting bar associations in implementing court decisions regarding advertising, and making suggestions about advertising programs [32]. The commission has established a national clearinghouse to gather information on advertising and generate future guidelines [28].

Legal Association Responses to Primary Study

Three major legal associations were sent a mail survey on consumerism. Two responded: American Bar Association (ABA) and Legal Services Corporation (LSC). A third organization, the National Legal Aid and Defender Association, did not reply, despite two requests.

The replies of the cooperating associations were quite brief. Both chose not to answer several questions. A summary of their responses appears in Table 10.2.

The Medical Profession

The reactions of the medical profession to consumerism are described in the literature and through a primary study.

Responses of the Medical Profession
As Reported in the Literature

The AMA has been extremely active as a lobbyist. It has sought to defeat health insurance programs, minimize government controls, and maintain the level of physician fees.

Beginning in 1943, the AMA spent approximately $3 million to distribute literature directing members to oppose the Wagner-Murray-Dingell Bill. By 1949, the AMA already had spent $1.5 million for lobbying against national health insurance [53]. Currently, advertisements in major newspapers across the country advocate the AMA's positions on a variety of issues. These cost millions of dollars each year.

County medical societies still review patient and colleague charges of malpractice. As their actions are secret, data on the number of complaints and the disposition of them are unavailable. The societies do not employ agents to look for violations, inspect or review everyday behavior, or instigate charges on behalf of the public. Formal screening and review procedures are lacking. According to the AMA, patient confidentiality precludes any formal review procedure [48].

Self-regulation consists of sanctions being placed on offending physicians by their peers. The first step is for one physician to pinpoint the unprofessional conduct of another. Then, the physicians discuss the questionable behavior among themselves, with the accuser hoping the poor practice will be ended by the guilty party. If this fails, referrals are ended as an economic sanction. Boycotts and refusals to work with a poor practitioner may result. Rarely do sanctions go beyond this point, or doctors press formal charges against colleagues they feel are guilty of poor practices [48].

In addition to its battle against federal health insurance, the AMA has opposed the idea of contract practice, where a physician agrees to work for a specified time for a salary. Many group insurance plans tried to obtain physicians on a yearly basis for straight salaries, as the plans sought to give low-cost medical care for mem-

TABLE 10.2

Legal Association Responses to Consumerism

Question 1   Generally speaking, how does your association feel
             about the consumer movement?
ABA   A response to this question is not indicated.
LSC   A response to this question is not indicated.

Question 2   How has the consumer movement affected the members
             of your association in regard to ethics, discipline,
             etc.?
ABA   Advertising by attorneys is now permitted.
LSC   A response to this question is not indicated.

Question 3   Has the association created a position, panel, or
             department to deal with the effects of the consumer
             movement?
ABA   A Commission on Advertising has been created.
LSC   The organization was formed to help poor people who
             could not afford legal services.

Question 4   Does the association provide representatives to appear
             before government committees examining consumer
             issues?
ABA   A response to this question is not indicated.
LSC   Representatives are provided.

Question 5   Does the association provide speakers to appear
             before national and/or local consumer groups?
ABA   A response to this question is not indicated.
LSC   A response to this question is not indicated.

Question 6   What do you perceive to be the long-term impact of
             consumerism on the profession you represent?
ABA   Advertising will have a vital impact. It will give the
             public more information concerning legal needs and
             the availability of legal services.
LSC   Consumerism exposes the need for better legal services
             for the poor.

Source: Compiled by the author.

bers. These plans were fought by the AMA, which said they offered a definite amount of payment for an indefinite amount of work. This resulted in retail medical services at wholesale prices. The AMA considered any system unethical if it compensated physicians at a rate below that usually charged by the profession or at a level that precluded competent service. The AMA also felt contract practice would encourage physicians to underbid for contracts, and lead to the solicitation of patients and unfair competition. The association feared prepaid health plans and national health insurance would cause doctors to lose professional status and take away the rights of patients to choose their own physicians [20].

Once the AMA realized it could not deter group health plans, it switched tactics. The AMA supported the plans so it could gain greater control over them. In addition, the association realized voluntary health plans were preferable to federal legislation, which would be more restrictive if the AMA did not back group health plans [20].

Recently, new organizations have formed within the medical profession. These organizations are comprised of physicians who no longer agree with AMA policies. Many feel the AMA is not concerned with the welfare of the individual patient and/or public. The new groups stress consumer-oriented positions [62].

"New Left" organizations accuse the AMA of preventing health programs rather than developing them, thus causing a shortage of medical manpower at reasonable prices. These organizations include the Medical Committee for Human Rights, Health Policy Advisory Center, and Medical Resistance Union.

A small group of residents and interns belonging to the AMA have established the National Staff Conference. Their objective is to create a new national medical organization that would be more responsive to the needs of the public. One conference member said: "Frankly, I am sort of ashamed to admit that I belong to the AMA. It has opposed everything without offering viable alternatives" [62, p. 252].

On the other side are physicians who feel the AMA is too consumer-oriented. These doctors have formed the National Council of Medical Staffs, an extreme right-wing group. The organization opposes government health plans and is concerned with the increasing amount of government action toward the medical profession [62].

Medical Association Responses to Primary Study

Six medical associations were sent a mail questionnaire on consumerism. Three sent responses: American Medical Association (AMA), the consumer-run and federally funded Consumer Commission

on the Accreditation of Health Services (CCAHS), and the local
Suffolk County Medical Society (SCMS). Two associations did not
reply, after two mailings: American College of Obstetricians and
Gynecologists, and American College of Physicians. One organization, the American Academy of Family Physicians, asked for a
detailed explanation of the study; this was done, but no additional
reply came from the academy.

The responses of the three cooperating groups are shown in
Table 10.3. Answers were summarized and categorized by the
author.

INDIVIDUAL RESPONSES TO CONSUMERISM

The Legal Profession

The responses of individual members of the legal profession
to consumerism, as reported in the literature and through a primary
study, are limited.

Individual Responses As Reported in the Literature

Lawyers and law firms generally have not taken any positions
or initiatives on consumer issues. They have chosen to follow the
rules and standards determined by the ABA or court decisions.

In 1974, congressional funds to pay attorneys appointed to
represent indigent defendants in federal cases were cut in half.
Members of the Washington, D.C., bar were notified that money
would not be available to pay attorneys who defended indigents under
the Criminal Justice Act. The judges of the Washington Superior
Court initiated a program whereby lawyers would still be appointed,
although not compensated. The criminal lawyers in Washington filed
a lawsuit to compel funding and enjoin the appointment of inexperi-
enced counsel in criminal cases. In addition, experienced trial
lawyers refused to accept further appointments [85].

Consumer-conscious attorneys have been ostracized by fellow
lawyers. For example, Philip Hirchkop has been subjected to numerous disciplinary actions. His supporters feel Hirchkop has been
ostracized because of certain activities. He was cofounder of the
Virginia American Civil Liberties Union (ACLU), a member of the
National Board of the ACLU, and widely known for his writings and
teaching in the field of civil rights and civil liberties [85].

After the 1977 Supreme Court ruling that permitted lawyers
to advertise, two Edinburgh University law professors asked people
if they would resent approaches by attorneys. Less than 2 percent

TABLE 10.3

Medical Association Responses to Consumerism

Question 1	Generally speaking, how does your association feel about the consumer movement?
AMA	The association agrees with consumerists that consumers should have more influence in the medical care system.
CCAHS	The commission is part of the consumer movement. A study on the need for a national consumer network is being completed.
SCMS	There is no official position.
Question 2	How has the consumer movement affected the members of your association in regard to ethics, discipline, etc.?
AMA	A response to this question is not indicated.
CCAHS	The consumer movement has had little effect on the medical profession in regard to ethics and discipline.
SCMS	The peer review program has been made mandatory. Peer review was begun in Suffolk before the popularity of consumerism.
Question 3	Has the association created a position, panel, or department to deal with the effects of the consumer movement?
AMA	A department of consumer affairs will be established shortly.
CCAHS	A response to this question is not indicated.
SCMS	A response to this question is not indicated.
Question 4	Does the association provide representatives to appear before government committees examining consumer issues?
AMA	Representatives appear before government committees.
CCAHS	Representatives are sent, but a lack of funds and staff prevents full-time participation.
SCMS	A response to this question is not indicated.

(continued)

Question 5	Does the association provide speakers to appear before national and/or local consumer groups?
AMA	A response to this question is not indicated.
CCAHS	On occasion, speakers appear before consumer groups.
SCMS	Attempts are willingly made to provide speakers when requests are made by various organizations.

Question 6	What do you perceive to be the long-term impact of consumerism on the profession you represent?
AMA	A new department of consumer affairs will help to determine the future impact of the consumer movement.
CCAHS	A response to this question is not indicated.
SCMS	This is a difficult question. There are too many variables involved to reply.

Source: Compiled by the author.

responded yes. People with minimal educations were the most receptive to solicitations by attorneys [85].

A number of law firms and individual lawyers feel advertising is unprofessional and will not advertise. Some lawyers do advertise and view it as a mechanism to maintain or increase business. Others advertise and envision it as a step toward making lawyers more sensitive to the needs of the consumer [28].

Individual Responses to Primary Study

A mail survey on consumerism in the legal profession was sent to five New York area firms. Four firms did not respond at all, despite two letters: Ford, Marrin, Esposito, Witmeyer, and Bergman; Rubin, Baum, Livin, Constant, and Friedman; Sachs, Montgomery, Molineaux, and Pastore; and Wolf, Haldenstein, Adler, Freeman, Herz, and Frank. One firm did reply, but answered no or none to all questions: Friedlander, Gaines, Cohen, Rosenthal, and Rosenberg.

The Medical Profession

The responses of individual members of the medical profession to consumerism, as reflected in the literature and a primary study, are limited.

Individual Responses As Reported in the Literature

The development of group practices by members of the medical profession has led to positive and negative effects on consumers. The move toward group practices, although officially opposed by the AMA, began in the 1920s and peaked during the 1950s and 1960s. On the positive side, group practices combined the skills of a panel of specialists, reduced costs, and serviced large groups. The negative factor was that group practices led to the demise of the general practitioner, and many consumers complained of impersonal treatment [62].

A few famous doctors, such as William Mayo, have been outspoken about the physician's responsibility to the patient. In 1937, a committee of internationally known physicians and 430 well-known members of the AMA declared their independence from the AMA. They adopted principles and proposals that had been overwhelmingly rejected by the AMA. The committee stated that health was a direct concern of government, a national public health policy aimed at all people should be formulated, and medical care was not related to economics. Shortly after the positions of the unnamed committee were made known to the AMA, it disbanded [62].

Today, several individual doctors actively stress the physician's responsibility to the consumer and disagree with AMA policies. However, the AMA remains a strong, pervasive entity. The private nature of the medical profession makes it difficult to assess individual behavior.

Individual Responses to Primary Study

A survey on consumerism in the medical profession was mailed to four New York area physicians. One, Fredric Daum of North Shore University Hospital, responded. Two did not reply at all, after two letters: Marvin Belsky and Samuel Pacher. One, Stevan Jonas, said he did not wish to participate.

Dr. Daum handles complaints personally or refers them to an associate. Patients are educated on a one-to-one basis. Services are modified or changed to meet the needs of patients. Personal integrity is the safeguard to quality service. Consumerism has had a limited effect on Dr. Daum personally. The threat of malpractice has affected some doctors by making them more aware of their responsibility to provide quality service. Dr. Daum and his associates believe they have always offered quality service.

THE OVERALL EFFECTS OF CONSUMERISM

The Legal Profession

The impact of consumerism on the legal profession and an evaluation of consumerism in this field follow.

Impact of Consumerism

The American Bar Association, as the major trade association of the legal profession, has the sole responsibility for regulating its members. It sets rules for admission to the profession, establishes guidelines for conduct, and disciplines practitioners who violate legal or ethical standards. The power of the ABA has changed little over the past 100 years.

No meaningful consumer groups have developed. In most jurisdictions, consumer complaints addressed to consumer affairs departments are forwarded to the local bar associations. The government, mainly through court decisions, has had some impact, such as allowing advertising.

The ABA recently has improved its efforts toward consumers, partly because of the general impact of consumerism and the realization that the image of the profession was not good. During the 1960s, several polls were taken of the public's attitude toward lawyers.

These yielded negative findings. Indications were that the image of the profession could be improved if the quality of legal services was upgraded, disciplinary proceedings made more meaningful, and responsibility to the public was heightened [19].

In an attempt to upgrade the legal profession and improve the behavior of its members, the ABA formed the Clark Committee and followed its recommendations. The Clark Report of 1970 was highly critical of the self-regulatory performance of the profession. As a result of the Clark Report, the ABA set up permanent disciplinary committees, helped state court systems establish improved disciplinary procedures, and enacted a central clearinghouse for the enforcement of rules and regulations.

Within the last few years, the ABA also has changed its position regarding legal aid. The association now states that it is the responsibility of the profession to provide legal services to those who cannot afford to purchase them. However, the ABA has not created any guidelines or requirements for public service by attorneys.

Evaluation of Consumerism

It can be concluded from the history of the legal profession that lawyers have not always been responsive to the needs of consumers. Despite this, the formal consumerism movement, meaning consumer groups and government, has not taken an active leadership role in correcting deficiencies in the legal system. Whatever codes of ethics, standards of professional conduct, and disciplinary procedures that do exist have been developed by the profession, notably the ABA.

All the reforms of the profession have been generated from within. Lawyers, through the ABA, subjected themselves to a critical appraisal in 1970 and reacted well to it. Many consumer-oriented practices were adopted. Rather than wait for federal legislation, the profession has sought to improve the quality of legal services on its own initiative. This process has occurred only in the last decade and will expand sharply in the next decade.

The Medical Profession

The effects of consumerism on the medical profession and an analysis of consumerism are detailed below.

Impact of Consumerism

The growth of consumerism has led to various policy changes on the part of the American Medical Association, which continues to exert tremendous control over all aspects of the medical process. For example, the AMA no longer opposes salaries for physicians working for medical plans or considers these doctors unethical. It now recognizes that patients have as much right to join a medical plan as to select an individual doctor. The AMA also has ended its struggle against national health insurance, and willingly cooperates in setting up PSROs to review the treatment of medicare and medicaid patients and reimbursement payments for physicians. After long opposition and costly lobbying campaigns, the AMA now states that government has a proper role to play in medicine, and it is the duty of the AMA to see that the role is undertaken responsibly.

Consumerism has brought certain medical activities, such as fee splitting, to the attention of the public. Under fee splitting, a physician receives a payment for making a referral to a colleague. The AMA and other medical organizations forbid this practice, which exists on a large scale. There also has been public disclosure of information and statistics regarding incompetent physicians, unnecessary surgery and/or prescription drugs. Consumer groups, medical boards, and individual consumer activists are working to prevent these occurrences.

Malpractice litigation and, subsequently, malpractice insurance rates have increased substantially in the last few years. Some jury awards have been in the million-dollar-plus category.

Physicians have left the AMA in large numbers. In 1962, 61 percent of the medical doctors in the United States belonged to the AMA. This dropped to 50.3 percent by early 1971. The decline has continued to the present [62, p. 252]. To many non-AMA physicians, the organization is archaic, irrelevant, and doctor-oriented. New liberal and conservative medical groups have been formed by AMA defectors. Some polarization is taking place in the profession.

Evaluation of Consumerism

The consumer movement is just beginning to have a major impact on the medical profession. The development of the PSRO program is a step toward making the profession more responsive to consumer needs. In the past, there were virtually no formal review procedures for the discipline of physicians guilty of unprofessional conduct. Today, mechanisms exist only when health insurance payments are involved.

The AMA has not been very consumer-oriented. Policy changes have occurred when government intervention seemed inevitable, not before. Although the AMA is aware that medical abuses and incompetent physicians exist, it has made no voluntary effort to establish formal disciplinary mechanisms. The PSRO program was initiated by the government.

Since the AMA is so powerful, consumer-oriented medical policies cannot and will not be generated unless the AMA pushes for them. Spin-off groups, no matter their intentions, can have only a limited influence on the profession.

Consumer groups and government have not been assertive enough. Consumer groups have not lobbied effectively or publicized their concerns. Their overall efforts have been negligible. On the other hand, many government officials have proposed legislation or regulations to improve medical practices. These endeavors, however, have been overpowered by the AMA.

FUTURE OUTLOOK

The Legal Profession

New legislative restrictions on the legal profession, at the federal and state levels, are unlikely. Lawyers form the biggest bloc of elected government officials, and many retain their membership in law firms. Voluntary self-regulation will expand and become more effective.

Many states will create independent agencies to preside at disciplinary hearings. The agencies will have a majority of non-lawyers and a minority of lawyers. They will investigate a range of matters and have a staff for research purposes. As of 1975, seven states had added nonlawyers to their grievance boards [85].

Another factor will cause the legal profession to voluntarily become more consumer-oriented: competition. Over the next several years, there will be more graduates of law schools than available positions. The increased competition for clients will lead to quality legal services at reasonable prices.

The Medical Profession

The medical profession will have to resolve important issues in the near future, including: how to hold down costs, which treatments should be covered by government medical plans, how to deal with euthanasia, how to fund expensive treatments, and when to require second opinions.

A preventive medical plan, aimed at diagnosing and minimizing illnesses before they develop, will be established. At first, this will be done with voluntary health groups. The plan will reduce costs significantly. A national health care system probably will be enacted by 1990, but its form and coverage cannot be predicted now.

Consumers will insist on open and informed health care. Physicians will be asked to explain treatments, operations, and prescriptions. Alternative treatments will be explained, and patients will be given greater choice in the selection process. Doctors will not be allowed to hold back on information.

Malpractice suits will increase as consumers seek reparations for malpractice or unsatisfactory results not based on negligence. The suits will seek substantial monetary awards. Malpractice insurance premiums will rise, and doctors will pass the increase on to consumers. In addition, doctors will conduct more time-consuming and expensive tests prior to treatments or operations in order to reduce their liability. Because of this, some states will change their malpractice laws and court procedures.

Consumer groups and government will be more assertive. Consumers will protest hospital closings, high costs, poor medical practices, and the shortage of general practitioners. The government will enact legislation to hold down hospital costs and provide health care for all.

On a voluntary basis, the AMA will seek to upgrade doctor performance and knowledge. Individual specialties will tighten certification standards. Attendance at ongoing educational seminars and periodic testing will be required of all physicians. More doctors will become consumer-oriented.

RECOMMENDATIONS

The Legal Profession

Consumer-oriented practices in the legal profession, such as those initiated in Michigan, must be expanded. Disciplinary boards should include majority, not minority, representation from the public. State boards of professional responsibility should assume rule-making functions and focus on the costs and availability of legal services. Disciplinary hearings should be open to the public and reduce the secrecy that has existed. A fair way to accomplish this would be to publicize only those cases supported by substantial evidence. This would be analogous to closed grand jury proceedings and open trials.

Arbitration panels should be set up to resolve fee disputes. The panels would reduce the need for litigation, speed up the process, and free disciplinary boards to concentrate on lawyer conduct.

The ABA should create a mechanism for legal aid by requiring attorneys to devote specified periods of time with indigent clients. This requirement should become part of licensing provisions. An alternative would be the funding of legal aid by attorneys who do not wish to devote their time.

The government can improve the legal system by reducing the need for lawyers in routine transactions. Intensive citizen education about the law is essential. Federal and state funding should improve, or enact: small claims courts, mediation and arbitration panels, and consumer complaint departments. These resources should be accessible, quick, inexpensive, and function without attorneys. Non-legal and paralegal personnel should serve the same purpose. Procedures for items such as wills and mortgages should be simplified. The government also should subsidize judicare, free legal service for the poor and elderly [19].

The profession must continue to increase its responsiveness to consumer needs. This, combined with government regulations, would lead to a true consumer orientation.

The Medical Profession

Steps must be enacted to aid the medical profession in becoming more consumer-oriented. Consumers must be educated about available medical services, their costs, their benefits, and their risks. In addition, a program of preventive medicine should be instituted by the government or the profession, thereby diagnosing health problems before they get out of hand.

Consumers should be taught to seek second opinions and read product information for drugs and medical devices. Many insurance companies are developing second opinion programs. For example, Blue Cross/Blue Shield in New York now provides a service by which eligible subscribers can visit any of 2,000 board-certified surgeons who have agreed to participate in the program, after their original physician has recommended surgery. Blue Cross pays for the second opinion [121]. Some doctors and other critics say this program adds costs and delays crucial surgery. Blue Cross comments that 15 percent of surgery is not necessary. In New York, a 1976 law requires all health insurance firms to offer second opinion programs. Certain medicaid payments will not be made unless two opinions recommend surgery.

At present, doctors are licensed for life and are not mandated to keep up with advances in the field. Physicians should be relicensed periodically and required to participate in continuing education programs. Further, doctors should have to become certified in the use of a new medical device or technique before they could employ it. Medical salesmen also should be licensed and better trained. They should not be permitted to participate in operations.

Medical records of hospitals and individual doctors should be examined on a regular basis. From this, normative data should be generated, and the performance of hospitals and doctors compared to it.

In 1970, the Carnegie Commission report on medical education concluded that all medical schools had followed the Flexner model of education since 1910. This model calls for emphasis on biological research and science. It largely ignores health care issues and societal questions. Medical schools should include physician responsibility, community needs, ethics, and other social factors in their curricula. Currently, about three-fourths of the medical schools in the United States have some type of course in ethics, but only half require ethics training. This must be increased.

A better and more efficient system for compensating victims of medical malpractice must be created, thus reducing insurance and medical costs. One alternative is a limited form of no-fault insurance. Another is the use of voluntary or mandatory arbitration to slow down the growth of court cases. A third recommendation is to place limitations on awards. Fourth, several states have established patient compensation funds to spread the risk of large malpractice settlements among a large number of doctors and hospitals. In Indiana, for example, this policy resulted in a drop of malpractice insurance rates for orthopedic surgeons from $13,250 in 1975 to $3,380 in 1977 [99, p. 10]. A fifth means for improving the handling of malpractice is channeling, under which claims would be channeled to hospitals and multiple-party lawsuits would not be permitted. Hospitals would be made legally responsible for the actions of doctors practicing within their walls.

Come-and-go surgery is a method of reducing costs. Under this technique, patients do not enter a hospital or stay overnight in a facility. They make appointments at surgical centers, have minor surgery, and go home the day of the surgery. Costs are half of similar operations in hospitals [31].

A medical superagency, governmental not self-regulatory, should be established in each state. The superagency would devise and enforce statewide rules for treatment in hospitals and doctors' offices. It also would work to enact stricter regulations for licensing, supervision of performance, cost controls, and health insurance companies.

Government, consumerists, and physicians must work together to define the goals of the medical profession, its responsibilities to the public, and long-run direction.

BIBLIOGRAPHY

1. "Adamant Against Ads." Time 107 (March 1, 1976), pp. 40-41.

2. "Additions to the Medical Profession." Science 96 (July 3, 1942), p. 8.

3. "Admission to Medical Practice: Statistics of the State Medical Licensing Boards for 1942." Education for Victory 2 (July 1, 1943), p. 8.

4. "AMA Goes Political." Christian Century 78 (August 9, 1961), p. 49.

5. "AMA Indicted." Time 33 (January 2, 1939), p. 18.

6. "AMA: Issues with Which It Is Confronted." Fortune 18 (November 1938), pp. 88-92.

7. "AMA Lobby Buys $1,110,000 Worth of Ads." Consumer Reports 15 (October 1950), pp. 454-55.

8. "AMA on Trial." Nation 148 (December 31, 1938), p. 4.

9. "AMA Reorganization." Newsweek 28 (December 23, 1946), p. 28.

10. Andrews, C. S. "Medical Practice and the Law." Forum 31 (July 1901), pp. 542-51.

11. "Anti Trust Charges Hits MD's." Business Week (August 6, 1938), p. 36.

12. "Anti Trusts Hits The Professions." Business Week (December 8, 1973), p. 67.

13. "Appeal to History: Step Toward Ending Discrimination in the Ranks of Organized Medicine." Newsweek 72 (July 1, 1968), p. 60.

14. Auerback, Jerold S. Unequal Justice. New York: Oxford University Press, 1976.

15. "Bar Association and the Negro." Outlook 102 (September 9, 1912), pp. 1-2.

16. "Bar's Ban: To Admit More Negroes." Newsweek 22 (September 6, 1943), pp. 758-59.

17. Beatty, J. "Lawyers on the Loose; Bar Needs Regulation." Forum 93 (June 1935), pp. 372-74.

18. Berman, D. M. "Voice of the American Bar." Nation 188 (March 21, 1959), pp. 247-50.

19. Bloom, Murray. The Trouble with Lawyers. New York: Simon and Schuster, 1968.

20. Burrow, James G. AMA: Voice of American Medicine. Baltimore, Md.: Johns Hopkins Press, 1963.

21. "Campaign to Defeat Compulsory National Health Insurance." Nation 171 (July 28, 1950), p. 21.

22. Carlin, Jerome E. Lawyers Ethics: A Survey of the NYC Bar. New York: Russell Sage Foundation, 1966.

23. "Changes in the Legal Profession." Nation 97 (August 28, 1913), pp. 182-83.

24. "Character Bar: Plan to Raise Standards of Ethics and Discipline." New Republic 166 (June 17, 1972), p. 9.

25. "Charges of Rape Against Doctor Are Dismissed." Newsday (December 30, 1977), p. 22.

26. "Checking Up on Lawyers." Saturday Evening Post 207 (May 11, 1935), p. 22.

27. Clark, M. "Health Plan Battle: The AMA or JFK?" Newsweek 57 (May 8, 1961), p. 98.

28. "Code of Advertising Is Adopted by ABA." Newsday (August 11, 1977).

29. Coggeshall, L. T. "Government Interest in Medicine and Health." Vital Speeches 28 (August 1, 1962), pp. 629-31.

30. Cohen, J. H. "Code of Ethics for Lawyers." Independent 62 (April 18, 1907), pp. 908-10.

31. "Come and Go Surgery." Time (October 10, 1977), p. 96.

32. Correspondence with Susan O'Neill, Staff Assistant of ABA (March 3, 1978).

33. Dawson, M. "How Bad Are Lawyers?" American Mercury 63 (July 1946), pp. 14-20.

34. Denenberg, Herbert. How to Keep Them Honest. Emmaus, Pa.: Rodale Press, 1974.

35. "Dirty Work by the Doctors: Attempt to Kill the Pending Wagner-Murray Bill." New Republic 109 (August 30, 1943), p. 272.

36. "Dispute Over Legal Aid Screening." Newsday (November 28, 1977), p. 3.

37. "Doctors Oppose the Wagner Health Bill." Christian Century 96 (December 6, 1969), p. 694.

38. "Doctors to Watch Doctors: Peer Review System." Science News 96 (December 6, 1969), p. 524.

39. Drew, E. "Rule of Lawyers." New York Times Magazine (October 7, 1973), pp. 16-17.

40. Drinker, H. S. "Legal Ethics." Annals of American Academy of Political Science 297 (January 1955), pp. 37-45.

41. "Federal Health Programs and the AMA." Science News 88 (September 23, 1938), pp. 275-76.

42. Fitts, W. T. "Ethical Standards of the Medical Profession." Annals of American Academy of Political Science 297 (January 1955), pp. 17-36.

43. Flower, B. O. "Menace of Medical Monopoly in U.S." Arena 9 (February 1894), pp. 400-16.

44. ____. "Restrictive Medical Legislation and the Public Weal." Arena 19 (June 1898), pp. 781-809.

45. Forbes, E. A. "Is the Doctor a Shylock?" World's Work 14 (May 1907), pp. 8,892-96.

46. Foshay, P. M. "Organization of the Medical Profession." Forum 32 (October 1901), pp. 166-71.

47. Fostlick, J., and Howard, L. "Advertisers At Law: Supreme Court Decision." Newsweek 90 (July 11, 1977), pp. 47-48.

48. Friedson, Eliot. Profession of Medicine. New York: Dodd, Mead, 1971.

49. Galton, L. "Doctors Debate Fee Splitting." New York Times Magazine (March 4, 1962), p. 19.

50. Gilb, Corinee Lathrop. Hidden Hierarchies. New York: Harper and Row, 1966.

51. Greenberg, S. "Decline of the Healing Art." Harper 221 (October 1960), pp. 135-36.

52. "Growing Idea: Standard Fees for Doctors." U.S. News 47 (July 13, 1959), p. 4.

53. Harris, Richard. A Sacred Trust. New York: American Library, 1966.

54. "Has the Profession of Law Been Commercialized?" Forum 18 (February 1895), pp. 679-85.

55. Heffenger, A. C. "Medical Fees: Are They Excessive?" North American Review 188 (November 1908), pp. 756-60.

56. "Hospital vs. Organized Medicine." America 93 (June 18, 1955), p. 303.

57. Howland, H. E. "Practice of Law in New York." Century Magazine 62 (October 1901), pp. 803-25.

58. "How to Make the Legal Profession Civically Responsible." Christian Century 74 (January 30, 1957), pp. 125-27.

59. Hull, K. "Position of Radical Lawyers in America." Christian Century 89 (December 13, 1972), pp. 1,268-71.

60. "Insuring Health: AMA Establishes Standards." Business Week (March 9, 1946), p. 20.

61. "Improvements for the Medical Device Bill." Health Research Group (November 1973).

62. Jarcho, Saul, et al. Medicine and Health Care: The Great Contemporary Issues. New York: New York Times, 1977.

63. Johnson, G. W. "Medical Politics." New Republic 52 (March 6, 1965), pp. 35-36, and (February 13, 1965), pp. 11-12.

64. Jones, Kenneth L., et al. Consumer Health. San Francisco: Canfield Press, 1971.

65. Keim, W. P. "What the AMA Really Fears." New Republic 52 (March 6, 1965), pp. 35-36, and (February 13, 1965), pp. 11-12

66. Kime, Robert E. Health: A Consumer's Dilemma. Belmont, Calif.: Wadsworth Publishing, 1970.

67. Langer, E. "AMA: Some Doctors Revolt, But Not a Revolution." Science 157 (July 21, 1967), pp. 285-88.

68. "Lawyers and Lobbyists." Fortune 45 (February 1952), pp. 127-30.

69. Lawyer Discipline. Chicago, Ill.: ABA Center for Professional Discipline, 1977.

70. "Lawyers Behind the Times." Nation 83 (August 26, 1906), pp. 137-38.

71. "Lawyers on Trial: Problems of Competence of American Trial Lawyers." Newsweek 82 (December 10, 1972), p. 75.

72. Levin, Tom. American Health: Professional Privilege vs. Public Need. New York: Praeger, 1974.

73. Lieberman, Jethro K. The Tyranny of the Experts. New York: Walker and Co., 1970.

74. Martin, George. Causes and Conflicts: The Centennial History of the Association of the Bar of the City of New York. Boston: Houghton Mifflin, 1970.

75. Maurer, H. "M.D.'s Are Off Their Pedestal." Fortune 49 (February 1954), pp. 138-42.

76. McGarral, Robert E., and Kenney, Patricia. "PSRO: Doctor Accountability or Consumer Disaster?" Health Research Group, Washington, D.C.

77. McMurtry, L. S. "American Medical Association: Its Origins, Progress and Purpose." Science News 22 (July 28, 1905), pp. 97-105.

78. Means, D. M. "Responsibility of Lawyers As Citizens." Nation 69 (July 20, 1899), p. 45.

79. Means, J. H. "Doctors Lobby." Atlantic Monthly 186 (October 1950), pp. 57-60.

80. "Michigan Supreme Court Rules for the State Bar Grievance Board." State Bar Grievance Board, Michigan (July 1977).

81. Moley, R. "Politics Is in the Picture." Newsweek 33 (June 20, 1949), p. 92.

82. Moore, Wilbert E. Roles and the Professions. New York: Russell Sage Foundation, 1970.

83. "More Trouble for Doctors and Lawyers." Business Week (April 25, 1977), p. 102.

84. "Must It Be Socialized Medicine? What the Profession Must Do to Preserve Its Freedom." Commonweal 40 (September 29, 1944), pp. 558-63.

85. Nader, Ralph, and Green, Mark. Verdicts on Lawyers. New York: Thomas Y. Crowell, 1976.

86. "News." Legal Services Corporation, Washington, D.C. (April 1977).

87. Owens, P. "Jury of His Clubmates." Nation 209 (November 3, 1969), pp. 462-64.

88. "Physicians War About Incompetent Doctors." U.S. News 60 (January 3, 1966), p. 10.

89. Pilpil, H. F. "Job the Lawyers Shirk." Harper 220 (January 1960), pp. 67-71.

90. "Politico Lawyers Say Goodbye to Their Politics And . . . ." *Newsweek* (January 27, 1934), p. 8.

91. "President Frowns on Politico Lawyers." *Literary Digest* 117 (January 27, 1934), pp. 10-11.

92. "Public Opinion About Doctors." *America* 92 (December 11, 1954), p. 294.

93. Rayack, E. "AMA: The Restrictive Power." *Nation* 200 (May 3, 1965), pp. 470-79.

94. "Reform or Facesaving?" *Newsweek* 28 (July 15, 1946), p. 60.

95. Reed, C. A. L. "Address of the Pres. of the AMA." *Science News* 13 (June 14, 1901), pp. 924-38.

96. "Rewards and Responsibilities of Medical Practice." *Living Age* 189 (June 13, 1891), pp. 659-72.

97. Rinehart, S. M. "High Cost of Keeping Alive." *Saturday Evening Post* 198 (January 9, 1926), p. 39.

98. Rogers, E. S. "Relationship between the Medical Profession and Government." *American Journal of Public Health* 34 (March 1944), pp. 285-87.

99. Rosenfeld, Neill. "Bugs in Malpractice Compensation." *Newsday* (December 28, 1977), p. 9.

100. ____. "HEW Joins Surgery Investigation." *Newsday* (November 4, 1977).

101. ____. "Medical Ethics Brought into Focus." *Newsday* (December 5, 1977), p. 3.

102. ____. "Patient's Misunderstanding Is No. 1 Reason for Lawsuit." *Newsday* (December 28, 1977), p. 9.

103. ____. "Task Force Suggests Medical Superagency." *Newsday* (January 1, 1978), p. 8.

104. Silverman, M. "Doctors Who Crackdown on Doctors." *Saturday Evening Post* 227 (February 12, 1955), pp. 32-33.

105. Stinch, F. H. "Attack on the Legal Profession." Vital Speeches 4 (October 15, 1937), pp. 27-29.

106. Stratton, G. M. "Lawyers and Physicians: A Contrast." Atlantic Monthly 111 (January 13, 1910), pp. 4ა-52.

107. "Supreme Court and the ABA: Selecting Supreme Court Nominees." Time 96 (August 10, 1970), p. 43.

108. "Talks and Reports on the Professions' Plight." Newsweek 3 (June 16, 1934), p. 3.

109. Tancredi, Lawrence R., ed. Ethics of Health Care. Washington, D.C.: National Academy of Sciences, 1974.

110. The Lawyer Disciplinary Process. Chicago, Ill.: ABA Center for Professional Discipline, 1977.

111. "The Selling of the Law." Newsday (September 29, 1977).

112. "Those Lawyers." Time 111 (April 10, 1978), pp. 56-66.

113. Tuck, Miriam, and Gradner, Arlene B. Consumer Health. Dubuque, Iowa: William Brown, 1972.

114. Vaillant, G. E. "Physicians: What Ails Thee?" Newsweek 78 (October 18, 1971), p. 84.

115. Vaugn, V. C. "Future of the Medical Profession." Science News 31 (January 28, 1910), pp. 127-37.

116. Viorst, M. "Washington's Influential Lawyer Lobbyists." Dun's Review 91 (January 1968), pp. 32-33.

117. "When Two Lawyers Ran Afoul of Ad's Rules." U.S. News 80 (January 26, 1976), p. 62.

118. Wilder, A. "Medical Freedom and Medical Legislation." Arena 26 (December 1901), pp. 631-41.

119. Williams, G. "Truth About Fee Splitting." Reader's Digest 53 (July 1948), pp. 129-31.

120. Wolf, Sidney. "House Subcommittee on Oversight and Investigations on Unnecessary Surgery." Public Citizens Health Research Group (July 15, 1975).

121. Zinman, David. "Insurers Stick with Plan for Second Opinion Before Surgery." Newsday (October 10, 1977), p. 7A.

11

CONSUMERISM AND RETAILING

Charles A. Casale

INTRODUCTION

Consumerism has had a substantial impact on all aspects of retailing. In this chapter the focus is on department-store retailing. Department stores are defined as having annual sales in excess of $5 million, 25 or more employees, and diverse product lines. They have prospered since the beginning of the twentieth century and are important shopping places for consumers of all types. In most cases, department stores have a main location and branch stores to accommodate their customers. Several large groups own a number of department stores. For example, Federated Stores owns Abraham & Straus, Bloomingdale's, Burdine's, Rich's, and other chains. It is department stores, because of their size, that have borne the brunt of consumerism in retailing.

Today, annual department-store sales are greater than $70 billion and account for more than 10 percent of total retail-store sales. The largest retailer in the world, Sears Roebuck, generates the majority of its sales from department-store operations.

The history of consumerism, active consumer groups, government activity, and industry and company responses to consumerism in retailing are detailed in the following sections.

THE HISTORY OF CONSUMERISM
IN RETAILING

At the beginning of the twentieth century, the general store was the major type of retail outlet. Shortly thereafter, the specialty store, and then the department store, evolved [40]. The objective of the department store was to combine various lines of soft and hard goods, profitably and conveniently, under one roof. The consumer would benefit since interstore travel was reduced.

As early as 1909, it was reported that department stores were lacking in their attention to consumer needs [40, 71]. An important complaint involved ineffective salesmanship. Sales clerks were considered crude, disinterested, discourteous, and ignorant of the stock carried by the store. Many chewed gum while conversing with customers [196].

Improvements in advertising were cited during the early 1900s. For example, the first sentence of an advertisement made clear what was being offered for sale, instead of stating an irrelevant catch phrase [196]. However, problems in advertising did exist. Merchandise did not always meet generally accepted standards. As an example, Smith and Company had an advertisement for wash silk; the product was neither wash nor silk [40]. Advertising in newspapers included errors, such as inappropriate pictures, denials of facts, and exaggerations [71, 196].

After 1910, the emphasis of the consumer movement was on the service differential of a small store versus a department store, the effects of World War I shortages on consumers, and the beginning stages of analyzing consumer needs as a science.

Small stores argued that their knowledge of consumers was greater than department stores, since many small stores kept detailed records on consumer sizes and preferences. They used the records to help shoppers and develop meaningful mail advertising [51].

World War I created merchandise shortages for consumers. Some retailers downplayed shortages, under the assumption that customers would not miss or ask for items that were not advertised or displayed. A number of department stores employed a different strategy. They printed newspaper advertisements explaining why merchandise shortages existed [147].

During this time, psychology was used by department stores to analyze customers. Retailers realized specific differences existed between male and female shoppers. The stores used sensory appeals for women, and price and durability appeals for men [136, 147]. In the 1920s, consumer studies were further utilized; department-store strategies were enacted to exploit consumer behavior [125, 126].

Consumers faced renewed and new problems in the 1930s. The problem of false advertising reemerged. Consumers were highly suspicious of comparative-price advertising. Shoppers commented that department stores brought in merchandise, marked it at artificially high prices for a short time, and then placed low prices on it [184, 1]. Consumers also were concerned about product quality, overcharges, and short-weighting [177]. Less and less wearing apparel was made at home. Difficulties arose because merchants provided no guidance about the quality of their apparel, and wearability tests were not available.

To ease consumer worries, the Better Business Bureau of New York suggested that each major department store have a committee consisting of typical consumers. The committee would voice consumer viewpoints to the store. Several New York area department stores started these committees [177].

On April 20, 1937, the National Retail Dry Goods Association proposed a program for coordinated standards, grades, and labels among manufacturers, retailers, and government. The goal was to make consumer goods uniform. The program had eight principal activities: elimination of misleading information in any form; development of a plan for truthful and factual information; cooperation among manufacturers, retailers, and consumer representatives in developing standard terminology; cooperation in the generation of standards for performance, durability, measurement, composition, and fiber content; definition of advertising practice standards by the National Retail Dry Goods Association; encouragement of manufacturer standards; independent certification of tested materials; and full cooperation with a proposed Consumer-Retailer Relations Council [180, p. 36].

The National Consumer-Retailer Council was formed in the summer of 1937. Its purpose was to improve relations between consumers and retailers to their mutual advantage. The council believed informative labeling, advertising, and merchandising were essential to retailer success [68, 64]. During the 1940s, the council played an important role in advancing informative labeling, selling, and consumer relations [94].

As retailers began to understand the objectives of the consumer movement, they found that changes in business practices could reduce costs, increase profits, and expand goodwill. For example, a program entitled "Informative Selling—A Store Guide for Consumer Cooperation," showed retailers how to improve their businesses in a consumer-oriented manner. This program was planned by the National Consumer-Retailer Council [187].

During the 1950s, informative labeling was again a prominent topic. Department stores complained that manufacturers' labels were sales-producing and not informative. Tags generally were devoted to puffery and were removed by retailers. Department stores wanted to combine advertising with factual labeling [129].

Consumer refunds and damages were discussed in the 1950s, as sellers realized they had to go beyond truthfully answering questions prior to purchases. The courts ruled that buyers purchased new merchandise with the expectation it was sound and free from defects. Formerly, consumers were protected only if they incurred injuries from inherently dangerous products [185].

Consumer credit emerged on a large scale during the 1950s, as stores sought to increase sales and make transactions easy for customers. A variety of credit plans were expanded or introduced, including revolving credit and 30-day accounts. In-house credit departments were established by large retailers. States passed legislation restricting interest charges, usually to 1.5 percent per month on unpaid balances up to $500 [77].

The 1960s were turbulent for retailers. A variety of practices were challenged, including: standards used for store purchases of merchandise, informative labeling, consumer credit, invasion of privacy, and deceptive advertising. An examination of the most important of these issues follows.

Consumer credit was assessed by both consumerists and retailers in the 1960s. Consumerists backed, and were successful in passing, a truth-in-lending bill. They suggested usury and fraud existed in credit transactions, and felt poor people were being preyed on. Consumer advocates also said consumers were confused about credit charges, and successfully pressed for a full disclosure law. This law had a special provision for revolving accounts, requiring interest rates to be stated as monthly percents on unpaid balances [111].

Department stores countered the claims of exorbitant interest rates by publicizing a 1968 study by the National Retail Merchants Association, which showed the average cost of granting credit was 3.41 percent of credit sales. It cost department stores more to issue credit than they received from credit payments, and the cost rose from 1963 to 1968 [106].

Congressman Wright Patman, a supporter of truth-in-lending, said "retailers sell merchandise at cost and make their money on credit" [56, p. 16]. Other truth-in-lending supporters called for a lower ceiling on retail credit charges. The National Retail Merchants Association replied that cash customers would have to subsidize credit customers if the ceiling was reduced.

As credit bureaus became more active in investigating applicants, the issue of invasion of privacy arose. Consumers were concerned about the accuracy and currency of information in their files, as well as its access to others. In 1968, safeguards were adopted to ensure confidentiality and the deletion of dated material [56].

In the 1960s, consumerists complained of deceptive advertising. They believed advertisements were confusing and misleading rather than informative and straightforward. Some appliance manufacturers recognized the problem between retailers and consumers, and redesigned their specification sheets into easy-to-comprehend, point-of-purchase aids. For instance, Frigidaire introduced Information Tags in 1968. These tags explained capacity and performance limitations, operating procedures, option features, and the warranty in effect [111]. Retailers began to distinguish among advertising, consumer information, and consumer education. The purpose of advertising was to sell. Consumer information provided product characteristics. Consumer education stressed training shoppers [197].

In the 1970s, retailers faced a number of consumer issues. Tris, the flame retardant used in children's nightclothes, was suspected of having a link to cancer in April 1976. The Consumer Product Safety Commission (CPSC) banned the sale of Tris-treated items in April 1977. Retailers had to remove all affected garments from their inventories. This caused difficulties with manufacturers over what items were returnable, and consumers were confused as to which garments had Tris [69].

New York removed Sunday blue laws in June 1976. Prior to that time, the laws were not enforced unless formal complaints were made. The immediate response of retailers was mixed. From a monetary standpoint, the New York economy was stimulated by the creation of jobs and higher sales tax payments. However, many labor unions, small retailers, and consumers favored the reinstatement of blue laws to allow one day of rest [7].

Recently, retailers turned their attention to urban problems. A number of department stores established corporate offices of urban affairs. Heavy emphasis was placed on employment opportunities for minorities. Many stores enacted broad consumer-education programs. There were experiments with unit pricing and explaining credit purchases to low-income consumers [79]. Retail management had meetings with community leaders before selecting store locations. Pollution control was tightened [34].

Some problems were not completely resolved. Consumers continued to complain of delayed deliveries, improper billings, and unsatisfactory return policies [127]. By 1977, a large number of department stores had appointed top-level executives to posts that dealt exclusively with consumer affairs. They often worked to resolve complaints [47].

ACTIVE CONSUMER GROUPS

All available sources of information, including Consumer Federation of America and various trade associations, were examined or contacted in an attempt to identify and describe relevant consumer groups. On the basis of this search, it is concluded that no active consumer groups exist in the retail industry.

GOVERNMENT

Government Institutions

Two agencies and one cabinet-level department have the greatest influence on retailing: Federal Trade Commission (FTC), Consumer Product Safety Commission, and the Department of Health, Education, and Welfare (HEW).

The Federal Trade Commission, created in 1914 and amended in 1938, ensures open competition and honest business practices. It sees that prices paid by retailers follow the provisions of the Robinson-Patman Act and that advertisements conform to various laws.

The Consumer Product Safety Commission, founded in 1972, protects consumers against unsafe or dangerous products. It can issue recalls and determine how they are to be handled. As intermediaries between manufacturers and consumers, retailers are involved with product safety and liability.

The Department of Health, Education, and Welfare is a cabinet-level department. Its Office of Consumer Affairs analyzes and coordinates implementation of all federal activities in the area of consumer protection, and recommends ways in which government consumer programs may be made more effective [101].

Important Legislation

Several pieces of federal legislation have the greatest impact on retailing: Sherman Anti-Trust Act, Robinson-Patman Act, Wheeler-Lea Amendment, Anti-Merger Act, Flammable Fabrics Act, Federal Hazardous Substances Act, Truth-in-Lending Act, and Magnuson-Moss Warranty Act. Another law, Miller-Tydings Act, regulated fair trade (resale price maintenance); it was repealed in the mid-1970s. In addition, a multitude of state and municipal laws control zoning, store hours, prices, delivery, advertising, and so forth. The federal laws are outlined in Table 11.1.

Major Actions

Federal, state, and local governments have been active in several areas concerning retailing: full disclosure, consumer credit, blue laws, price-fixing, and product safety.

TABLE 11.1

Federal Legislation Affecting Retailing

Legislation	Year Enacted	Key Provisions
Sherman Anti-Trust Act	1890	Makes restraint of trade illegal
Robinson-Patman Act	1936	Eliminates price discrimination in sales to retailers, regulates discounts and allowances
Wheeler-Lea Amendment	1938	Gives FTC powers to protect consumers, restricts deceptive practices
Anti-Merger Act	1950	Prevents mergers that would lessen competition
Flammable Fabrics Act	1953	Sets standards for flammability, bans products not meeting standards
Federal Hazardous Substances Act	1960	Prevents the sale of hazardous substances, requires labeling of dangerous products
Truth-in-Lending Act	1968	Mandates disclosure of interest rates and other aspects of consumer credit
Magnuson-Moss Warranty Act	1975	Strengthens and clarifies provisions of warranties

Source: Compiled by the author.

Full Disclosure

On January 17, 1966, Esther Peterson, Special Assistant for
Consumer Affairs under President Lyndon Johnson, warned retailers
that the government would provide consumers with information about
products and purchase terms if the retailers did not [162].

In 1968, Senator Warren Magnuson introduced a full-disclosure
bill for guarantees. Under the bill, the guarantor had to be specified,
as well as the provisions of the guarantee. After seven years, the
law was passed as the Magnuson-Moss Warranty Act of 1975 [111].

Consumer Credit

The FTC investigated abuses with charge customers in 1970.
It instituted new procedures in an attempt to warn retailers that they
had to follow guidelines or be subject to FTC intervention. The new
rules covered two provisions. First, stores were required to mail
bills at least 21 days before they were due and note payments on the
same day they arrived. Bills had to include descriptions of the
merchandise purchased. Second, disputed items could not be billed
until the dispute was settled. If the consumer won, there could be
no interest charges for the time during the conflict. In addition,
consumers had to be informed when credit bureaus were employed.
Each bill had to contain the name and phone number of a store employee who was able to answer questions [105].

Blue Laws

Sunday blue laws have been handled differently throughout the
United States. The Association of General Merchandising Chains
listed 30 states that had some form of Sunday selling laws as of 1975.
Usually, the laws were coupled with restrictions on working on Sunday. Enforcement ranges from strict in Mississippi (95 percent)
and Louisiana to sporadic and spotty in Indiana, Oklahoma, and South
Carolina. In practice, blue laws have led to confusion because of
varying standards and applications. For example, it was permissible
in Arkansas to sell film, flashbulbs, and batteries, but not cameras
or projectors. In New Jersey, some counties allowed the sale of
golf jackets, tennis shorts, ski pants, and fishing boots, but not
shirts, dresses, or regular shoes. However, 11 New Jersey counties forbade all Sunday selling [127].

New York blue laws were based on the Bible. Its edict against
work on Sunday was "an act against profanation of the Lord's Day,
called Sunday, or an act for suppressing immorality" [99, p. 1].
In 1976, the U.S. Supreme Court upheld Sunday closings in principle,
saying that while most were originally based on religious precepts,

a common day of rest could be regarded as in the public interest [122].

The events in New York offer an interesting example of the blue law controversy. In New York City, police refrained from enforcing blue laws after 1970, unless formal complaints were made [21]. During 1975, the New York State Court of Appeals expressed grave dissatisfaction with the laws, but upheld their constitutionality [122]. However, in 1976, the Court of Appeals unanimously declared the section of the state blue laws that prohibited the sale of most items on Sunday to be unconstitutional [21].

After the court ruling, the 5,000-member New York State Council of Retail Merchants and some labor unions began to press for new state legislation to keep stores closed on Sundays. The president of the United Store Workers said Sunday openings would result in "sales divided among seven days instead of six and a costly disaster for companies" [189, p. 18]. The Metropolitan New York Retail Merchants reported its 21 major members to be split on the issue. The Fifth Avenue Association opposed Sunday openings.

Sunday openings of department stores in New York began in late August 1976. The first to open were Macy's, Korvettes, and Alexander's. When a bill was introduced in the legislature to reinstate Sunday closings, Macy's was against it and detailed statistics showing increases in revenues and employment [7]. In July 1977, Governor Hugh Carey announced he would veto any attempt to revive blue laws in New York [102].

Price-Fixing

A federal grand jury investigated alleged price-fixing by at least seven New York stores in May 1973. The probe covered a wide range of apparel-pricing practices, as well as social meetings by leading merchants. The seven New York stores were: B. Altman, Henri Bendel, Bergdorf Goodman, Bloomingdale's, Bonwit Teller, Lord & Taylor, and Saks Fifth Avenue. Possible Sherman antitrust violations were explored [25].

The investigation began when a maternity clothes manufacturer and a men's slacks producer complained to the antitrust division of the Justice Department that they faced discrimination due to retail price-fixing. By June 1974, the investigation centered on past store pricing practices, the dissemination of an apparel price list, and the records of a defunct trade association [24].

On October 8, 1974, Saks, Bergdorf Goodman, and Bonwit Teller were indicted for conspiracy to fix the prices of women's clothing. Two executives, one from Saks and one from Bergdorf Goodman, also were indicted [18]. In February 1975, a federal judge imposed the maximum antitrust fine of $50,000 on each of the three stores, after the stores pleaded no contest [19]. The two executives were fined $15,000 and $25,000 respectively [20, 30].

During 1976, the three stores offered $5.2 million to settle seven class-action suits brought by credit customers [1]. By late 1976, 57,000 charge customers had applied for refunds [11]. In December 1976, the Justice Department filed a consent judgment that forbade the stores and their parent companies from agreeing with anyone to fix women's retail clothing prices. It also banned the stores from trying to influence the prices of other retailers and clothing manufacturers [53].

Federated Department Stores and Saks were indicted by a federal grand jury in April 1976 because of an alleged conspiracy to fix prices on women's apparel in the San Francisco Bay area from 1963 to 1974 [12]. The action was brought by area consumers. In June 1976, both companies filed no-contest pleas and were each fined the maximum of $50,000 [31].

Product Safety

The debate over the flame-retardant Tris began in April 1976, when a possible link between children's pajamas and cancer was uncovered. Evidence indicated Tris was mutagenic, meaning it had the capability of altering the genetic material in living cells. Prior to 1976, it appeared Tris was an effective flame retardant. Yearly deaths of young children had declined from 47 in 1970-71 to 24 in 1973-74 [37].

The Consumer Product Safety Commission prohibited the sale of an estimated 20 million garments in retail inventories and halted further production of Tris-treated clothing in April 1977 [193]. The CPSC rejected a recall of all items that had been previously sold, which came to about 120 million garments, but it gave the public the right to request refunds on all garments that had not yet been laundered [38].

The American Apparel Manufacturers Association called the ruling an injustice and contended it would drive many sleepwear manufacturers out of business. The association asked a federal court to halt $200 million in consumer refunds until the government better defined who would pay them. It told the court that the manufacturers of raw fibers should bear the costs, since the material was already hazardous when it reached manufacturers. At the same time, the Environmental Defense Fund went to federal court to force the CPSC to require retailers to repurchase all Tris-treated sleepwear in the hands of consumers. The Environmental Defense Fund disagreed with the CPSC's assertion that washing garments would make them safe [141].

In May 1977, a federal court ordered chemical companies, garment manufacturers, and retailers to share the $200 million in refunds. Any unwashed garment could be returned by the consumer to the retailer for the full purchase price. The retailer would then collect the purchase price from the manufacturer, who collected its purchase price from the mill, which collected its purchase price from the chemical company [49]. However, in June 1977, a federal district judge stayed the refund process on the request of Spring Mills [117]. After losing an appeal, the CPSC issued a new warning forbidding the continued sale of Tris [54].

The Environmental Defense Fund found 18 percent of the stores it checked in a July 1977 survey were still selling Tris. The CPSC charged F. W. Woolworth with violating the ban. The company denied the charge, but agreed to a court order prohibiting any violation of the ban [188]. The following month, a federal district judge ordered Macy's to stop selling Tris-treated clothes. Macy's said only ten garments, inadvertently left on the shelves, were found by the CPSC after checking 76 stores [140]. In September 1977, Federated Stores agreed to a consent order forbidding the sale of Tris-treated clothes [88].

Material treated with Tris is still widely used in products, such as toys, doll's hair, draperies, and upholstery. The CPSC has stated that in the absence of a single known death, there is no reason to ban the use of Tris in items other than clothes [37].

The Carter Administration

Under the Carter administration, FTC Chairman Michael Perschak noted that commission activities were likely to concentrate on mergers (particularly in the supermarket industry), shopping center leases, economic power, advertising practices, labeling, distribution of merchandise, and manufacturing. Performance testing would be conducted under conditions of competitive shopping [42].

INDUSTRY RESPONSES TO CONSUMERISM

This section examines the reactions of the retail industry to consumerism, and is divided into two sections: industry responses based upon the literature and trade association replies to a primary study.

Industry Responses As Reported in the Literature

During the early 1900s, the retail industry was concerned with false advertising and its impact on consumers. However, it was not until the 1930s, when the Better Business Bureau of New York campaigned against false advertising, that retailers showed real improvement in this area [184, 1]. The bureau conducted investigations of individual stores to monitor price claims:

> Solutions to the problem of misleading comparative
> price claims in retail advertising lie in the thorough
> investigation and correction of abuses on the basis of
> individual facts [184, p. 9].

The Better Business Bureau of New York started a drive to inform the public of the validity of comparative price advertising. The bureau looked at the good values of merchandise sold by respected stores, and hoped other retailers would also sell good products at fair prices. It wanted all stores to purchase reputable merchandise, place a reasonable markup on it, tell the public about their procedures, decide on standard practices, and advertise honestly [184].

In 1940, the National Consumer-Retailer Council worked on several projects to aid consumers. It set up a committee on informative labels, which worked with manufacturers and retailers, and sought the type of information needed for commodity goods labels. A committee on standards was established. This committee tried to promote standards and agreement among manufacturers, retailers, and consumers. Another project dealt with improving techniques of selling and customer relations. By the late 1940s, the council had developed several plans to facilitate buyer and seller relationships. It also distributed unbiased materials on consumption and distribution and provided a meeting place for consumers and retailers [94].

The National Retail Merchants Association (NRMA) embarked on a program to upgrade the relative standing of retailing and gain recognition for retail management as a profession in 1960. The goal of the NRMA was to make the public more aware of retailing and its contributions. The association felt consumers knew retailers by their physical stores, fixtures, display windows, merchandise, and advertising. They did not know the economic and social roles of retailing. The NRMA's program emphasized that retailing employed up to 20 percent of a local labor force, carried the heaviest burden of local taxes, and was the major source of income for local newspapers. Retailers spent as much in newspaper advertising as they made in net profits after taxes [86].

At the 1967 annual NRMA convention, William O. Batten, then chairman of J. C. Penney, stated that retailers had to inform and educate the public. He warned that the government would take this responsibility if retailers did not [26]. Batten discredited statements about the "market power" of department stores, saying con-

sumers were too competent for this to occur and competition was
intense [34].

A 1967 study by the New York Better Business Bureau analyzed
consumer complaints in department stores. It found more than 50
percent of the complaints involved matters other than merchandise
misrepresentation or fraud. The bulk of the complaints referred to
nondelivery or partial delivery of goods, loss of merchandise, unsatisfactory workmanship, poor installation, and ineffective service.
The study showed consumer attitudes toward department stores to
be generally favorable. Consumers saw no pressing need for extensive legislation [82].

The Consumer Affairs Committee of the NRMA stated in 1977
that the Carter administration was trying to be responsive to consumers and would be very sensitive to retailing. The committee
believed consumers had legitimate problems and objectives that
needed to be achieved, but not at the expense of retailing. At this
time, the committee was instructed to offer policy suggestions to
NRMA members on energy, electronic funds transfer, and consumer
protection. The chairman of the committee commented "that the
proposed Agency for Consumer Advocacy was the focus of the committee's attention" [44, p. 26].

Trade Association Responses to Primary Study

A mail questionnaire on consumerism in retailing was sent to
seven major trade associations. Three responded to the study:
American Research Merchandising Institute (ARMI), National Retail
Merchants Association (NRMA), and Retail Advertising Conference
(RAC). One association, American Retail Association of Executives,
said to contact the NRMA. Three associations did not reply at all,
after two letters: American Retail Federation, Independent Retail
Businessman's Association, and National Mass Retailing Institute.

Overall, the participating associations indicate an awareness
of the consumer movement and its importance to retailers. The
associations favor consumerism, but feel its effect on member companies has been marginal. They attribute this to the lack of organized
consumer groups in the retail industry.

The trade associations do provide representatives to appear
before various government committees examining consumer issues.
They feel they could do more for consumers, if called on to do so.
None of the associations has a formalized speakers program, but
two would supply speakers upon request. The associations think
the long-term impact of consumerism will be the development of a
more informed consumer. They warn that overzealous consumerism
may be counterproductive.

Table 11.2 contains the responses of the three cooperating trade associations. The answers have been condensed and categorized by the author.

COMPANY RESPONSES TO CONSUMERISM

This section examines the reactions of retail firms to consumerism, and is divided into two sections: company responses based upon the literature, and company replies to a primary study.

Company Responses As Reported in the Literature

Individual retailers showed their first concern for consumer issues in the 1920s. At that time, standards, grades, and labels were important. On August 22, 1927, Macy's established a Bureau of Standards. The purpose of the bureau was to test merchandise from the consumer's perspective. Previously, Macy's, Sears Roebuck, Eatons of Canada, and other retailers tested merchandise from the vantage point of their own interests as buyers [36].

At an Abraham & Straus laboratory luncheon in 1937, the chairwoman of the fabric and ready-to-wear section of the fashion group told her employees that "merchandise labeling" would be important in the future. Labeling, she commented, had to be simple and standardized, and broken into three separate types: fiber-content labels, quality labels, and use labels. There was an increasing need to inform consumers of what they were buying when they purchased merchandise [52].

No responses of individual retailers to consumerism were found in the literature between 1938 and 1970, when informative labeling resurfaced as an issue. Federated Department Stores conducted a study on informative labels at its Lazarus stores in Columbus, Ohio. It wanted to determine whether more point-of-sale information was necessary and if scientific studies were required to determine exact customer information needs. The answer to both questions was yes. Federated's study showed meaningful information was found on product packages, but it was often hard to understand. Products with information tags lacked uniformity and were too technical. Federated determined that the responsibility for informative labeling was with manufacturers, since it would be impossible for retailers to prepare and attach appropriate information to each item they sold [172].

During 1970, J. C. Penney aided the education of the surrounding community. It had a separate educational-relations department

TABLE 11.2

Retail Trade Association Responses to Study

Question 1	Generally speaking, how does your association feel about the consumer movement?
ARMI	The consumer movement is considered healthy.
NRMA	Consumerism is recognized as developing more knowledgeable consumers, who are able to make better-educated buying decisions. Retailers have a growing awareness that they must anticipate and be responsive to consumer needs.
RAC	Consumerism is favored. Member firms realize and appreciate the need for a variety of customer relations, and have done so for a long time.

Question 2	How has the consumer movement affected the companies that belong to your association, in regard to retailing?
ARMI	There has been no effect.
NRMA	The association's Consumer Affairs Committee studies consumer issues, movements, and legislation, and translates this information into practical advice for member firms.
RAC	Other than emphasizing the importance of customer relations, the impact has been limited.

Question 3	Has the association created a position, panel, or department to deal with the effects of the consumer movement?
ARMI	There is no position, panel, or department.
NRMA	The Consumer Affairs Committee analyzes consumer issues and makes suggestions to members.
RAC	Speakers comment on the consumer movement, its recognition, and importance. The wiser the shopper, the more critical and discriminating he or she is.

| Question 4 | Does the association provide representatives to appear before government committees examining consumer issues? |

(continued)

Table 11.2 (continued)

ARMI	The association works with the National Association of Wholesalers in this area.
NRMA	Representatives frequently testify before congressional committees and government agencies on a variety of consumer-oriented issues.
RAC	The association has not been invited, but would send representatives if asked.
Question 5	Does the association provide speakers to appear before national and/or local consumer organizations?
ARMI	No speakers are provided.
NRMA	An informal relationship is maintained with many well-established national consumer organizations. The Consumer Affairs Committee is active.
RAC	The association has not been invited to send speakers, but would do so if invited.
Question 6	What do you perceive to be the long-term impact of consumerism on the industry you represent?
ARMI	If consumerism does not become overzealous, it will remain productive; otherwise, it will be counter-productive.
NRMA	In general, the consumer movement will have beneficial long-term effects on the retail industry, since the population will be more informed.
RAC	There will be increased skill in shopping, and the need for retailers to continue to recognize that fact. Good morals represent good business practices.

Source: Compiled by the author.

that published a free magazine called Forum for home-economics teachers, and distributed other educational materials at cost. The department established an experimental program to teach poor minority groups [79]. It presented annual programs on professional enrichment for local educators, sponsored by Penney store managers. The department also organized educational programs for consumers at local stores [161].

At this time, J. C. Penney used a consumer affairs department to add a consumer perspective to corporate policymaking. The department included a consumer advocate, who had the authority to disagree publicly with Penney management on consumer issues. While Penney saw public credibility in retailers declining, it believed that through increased sensitivity retailers could cause customers to be more responsive [161].

In the 1970s, Sears based its educational materials on two premises. One, the children of today are consumers of today as well as tomorrow. Two, informed customers were likely to be satisfied customers. Operating under these guidelines, Sears geared its educational efforts toward home-economics classes, extension programs, 4-H Clubs, distributive education, social studies, and business courses. The objectives of Sears' education program were to: inform consumers of hidden values in contemporary merchandise; show how personal satisfaction with purchases directly related to wise decision making in the marketplace; and help students develop the proper knowledge, skills, and attitudes to become competent consumers. In addition to its educational programs, Sears distributed booklets on products and their usage, assured consumers of the accuracy and descriptiveness of catalog copy, used permanent care labels, and reviewed purchases of private-brand products [58].

Hess Department Stores of Pennsylvania has considered consumer affairs an important aspect of business. For 1976, returns were less than 1 percent and unreasonable complaints were less than 0.1 percent of sales. These figures reflected Hess's use of personal relations and consumer-oriented promotions, and a deep involvement by the store and officials in community affairs. Hess stressed the quality of its sales staff, continuous training, and the development of sales specialists. During 1977, the store introduced a "Consumer Expo," at which presidents of manufacturing companies were invited to demonstrate and sell their products. This event was well received by consumers and manufacturers. Hess also sponsored a series of ethnic promotions, which involved various community leaders in forums and programs.

In 1977, Federated Department Stores reiterated that its job was to give consumers what they wanted, when they wanted it. Customer satisfaction had to be based on consumer beliefs, not those of management. The money-back guarantee was a significant policy, used by all Federated units. A consumer could return a product after its purchase, for any reason, and receive a refund or credit. In addition, all Federated stores trained their sales personnel to consider customer service as the number-one priority, stressing the bond between the consumer and the store. For example, the Gold Circle discount-store division used interview sessions and surveys, which led to changes in visual merchandising and department delineation. Burdine's used consumer advisory boards to aid in departmental planning. Bullock's hired consumer affairs professionals to work on product safety and other problems. Abraham & Straus and Lazarus offered expanded labeling programs to provide additional product information [47].

Company Responses to Primary Study

A mail questionnaire on consumerism in retailing was sent to 12 major department stores and parent companies of department stores. Six answered the questions in the survey: Gimbel Brothers, Macy's, Marshall Field, Montgomery Ward, J. C. Penney, and Sears. Five companies did not reply at all, despite two requests: Alexander's, Allied Stores, Dayton-Hudson, K-mart, and Mercantile Stores. One firm, Federated Department Stores, stated that it was impossible to make any generalizations since responses to consumerism differed by division. Federated suggested that each division be contacted directly; this was not done.

Generally, the responses of the cooperating retailers acknowledge the significance of consumerism and its impact on operations. They recognize the importance of handling consumer complaints in a timely manner. All are willing to accept merchandise for refunds if consumers are dissatisfied. Customer service departments are utilized to assist consumers with merchandise and/or service problems.

Many stores have a separate division of consumer affairs that reports to senior management. The division usually has input into all areas that affect consumers and is responsible for educational programs. All the companies rate safety very highly. This has led to the publication of literature and demonstration sessions on the proper use of products.

The stores view the consumer movement as a mechanism for consumer protection. They agree that if retailers do not protect consumers, the government will. In many instances, the companies constantly review procedures to ensure their consistency with consumer goals. They find no need for new government legislation as long as retailers are responsible in dealing with consumers.

Table 11.3 contains the replies of the participating retailers to each question in the survey. Answers have been summarized and categorized by the author.

TABLE 11.3

Retail Company Responses to Study

Question 1	The Consumer: What type of policy do you have for handling complaints? Do you have a consumer complaint department? Is there a consumer advocate in-house? Do you have an educational program or participate in educational programs for consumers?
Gimbels	A customer service department handles mail, phone, and in-person inquiries and complaints. The director of Consumer Affairs heads the Consumer Affairs Department. The director is a consumer advocate. The company is also associated with the Better Business Bureaus in all communities it serves, various trade organizations, and the Society of Consumer Affairs Professionals in Business (SOCAP).
Macy's	Consumer complaints are adjusted in a timely manner and result in satisfied customers. A vice-president for Customer Service supervises four customer service areas: bill adjustments, furniture/television, floor coverings, and all other merchandise. This vice-president acts as a consumer advocate. No formal consumer education programs are provided.
Marshall Field	The basis of the policy for handling consumer complaints is that the consumer is always right. There are no in-house consumer advocates or educational programs for consumers.
Montgomery Ward	Complaints are handled at the store level by store managers. A customer complaint department is headed by the Corporate Director of Customer Relations. There is no specific in-house advocate. However, people in several departments spend most of their time working on consumer issues and on behalf of consumer interests: Consumer Information Services, Corporate Customer Relations, and Regional Public Relations. The Consumer Economics Forum, a series of courses for teachers, was launched in 1973 in

---

(continued)

Table 11.3 (continued)

	cooperation with the Chicago Better Business Bureau and the Chicago Board of Education. The forum fosters dialogue among educators and business, consumer, labor, and government representatives. Distributive education seminars are held throughout the country.
Penney	Consumers are encouraged to take their complaints directly to store managers. The Consumer Affairs Department, which has a resident consumer advocate, works to influence management decisions. The Educational Relations Department has a staff of five field representatives who work throughout the United States to help Penney stores present annual programs for educators.
Sears	All consumer complaints are handled in the store in which they occur. The Customer Relations Department reestablishes lines of communication between complainants and local store managers. There is no consumer advocate in-house. The Consumer Information Services Department has developed multidisciplinary print and audiovisual programs to aid consumers.
Question 2	The Product and Service: What type of product-related information is made available to the public? Are you modifying or changing your products in response to consumerism? What procedure do you follow to ensure product and service quality?
Gimbels	Product-related information is made available through advertising. The Consumer Affairs Department checks all merchandise, in reference to price claims, fabric contents, and manufacturers' efficiency claims. This assures truthful and exact information for consumers.
Macy's	Educational and informational brochures are distributed to consumers in the appropriate departments. Product modification occurs in response to an analysis of consumer desires, and is unaffected by outside influences. Three basic tools

(continued)

	ensure quality: vendor performance reviews, bureau of standards, and furniture quality control.
Marshall Field	Product information on material or fiber content and about the care and uses of items are readily available to consumers on request. A company-owned testing laboratory certifies product quality.
Montgomery Ward	Product-related information is made available via store demonstrations and through point-of-sale literature and films. School programs emphasize energy conservation, good buymanship, and the wise use of credit. Products are changed and modified in response to the changing needs, demands, attitudes, and life-styles of consumers. Merchandise departments work closely with manufacturers to be sure that product specifications and quality meet maximum standards. These departments also use laboratory facilities to test new merchandise and develop new products and specifications. The Merchandise Procurement and Development Department includes merchandise comparison, merchandise development, quality assurance, and a testing laboratory.
Penney	The Consumer Affairs Department gives complete information to consumers to help them as much as possible. Consumer research, coordinated with manufacturers, determines customer wants. Continued testing and retesting ensure product and service quality.
Sears	At each store outlet, product-related information is available upon request. After constant surveys of consumer needs, product lines are modified to reflect these needs. Sears Laboratories ensure product and service quality.
Question 3	Outside Influences: What type of consumer regulations affect your operations? How do you respond to outside consumer pressures? How do you evaluate the effect of consumerism on your company?
Gimbels	Consumer regulations affect operations.

(continued)

Table 11.3 (continued)

Macy's	Truth-in-Lending, Fair Credit Billing, and the Magnuson-Moss Warranty laws have the most effect on operations. If a company practice is questioned by any individual or group, the practice is evaluated against Macy's standards; the practice would not be changed if it is determined to be proper and fair. Consumer groups help Macy's to focus on its goals of proper merchandise assortment, ambience, service, quality, and value.
Marshall Field	The company is affected by government regulations. It responds to consumer questions by listening. The impact of consumerism is not substantial at this time, but it is growing.
Montgomery Ward	Many consumer regulations influence operations. The company works closely with federal, state, and municipal regulatory groups on such topics as safety, credit, warranties, advertising, energy, and ecology. Each consumer pressure is analyzed on its merits to determine appropriate action. Montgomery Ward cooperates and participates with the consumer movement to achieve mutual understanding and sound solutions to problems and issues. The retailer who does not react to consumerism will not survive.
Penney	Penney has responded to consumerism by creating the Consumer Affairs Department. The department provides leadership in the development of a coordinated corporate strategy for recognizing consumer interests.
Sears	Most consumer regulations affect store operations.

Source: Compiled by the author.

THE OVERALL EFFECTS OF CONSUMERISM

The effects of consumerism upon retailing and an evaluation of consumerism in this area are presented below.

Impact of Consumerism

Consumer issues in retailing first arose in the early 1900s. However, the retail industry did not offer a meaningful reply until the 1930s. Then, the National Retail Dry Goods Association aggressively pushed for consumer goods standardization. During the 1940s, the National Consumer-Retailer Council sought increased utilization of informative labeling to aid consumers and retailers. This was the first organization to try actively to improve relations between retailers and consumers.

Consumerism turned to consumer protection in the 1950s, as the courts safeguarded shoppers against harmful products. At this time, consumer credit increased retail store sales and made it easier for people to buy. Problems emerged from new types of credit agreements, and questions were raised about interest charges and credit limits.

The 1960s saw the start of the modern era of consumerism in the retail industry. Retailers attempted to gain customer confidence, while consumers thought stores were unconcerned about them. There were criticisms of merchandise standards, informative labeling, usury, fraud, and deceptive advertising. Consumer activists were successful in obtaining truth-in-lending and other government legislation. Retailers came to realize that consumerism was not a passing fad.

In the 1970s, retailers faced urban community problems and established community relations departments to resolve them. Broad consumer education programs evolved. Consumer activism was most concerned with full disclosure, consumer credit, blue laws, price-fixing, and product safety.

Due to consumerism, retailers now provide free educational material to the community, conduct consumer research before introducing new policies or modifying old ones, employ consumer affairs personnel, adhere to liberal money-back guarantee practices, and interface with government and consumer groups. Most retailers acknowledge that their success is dependent on customer satisfaction.

At present, consumerism in retailing appears to be at a major crossroads. On one side, government agencies and consumers are pushing for further legislation. On the other side, retailers feel overburdened by the amount of existing legislation, at all levels of government, that affects operations.

Evaluation of Consumerism

Consumerism has benefited consumers by requiring retailers to treat the consumer's rights and satisfaction as a top priority in store operations. Threatened with the possibility of government intervention, retailers have taken it upon themselves to educate consumers and respond to their complaints.

The cost of consumerism has been substantial. For example, the children's wear industry estimated that in 1976 federal legislation alone resulted in $25 to $50 million in higher prices for consumers [58].

In some cases, regulation seems to overprotect consumers at the expense of both consumers and retailers. As an illustration, a California state statute on children's flammable garments mandated that all children's clothing, not just nightwear, had to be flame retardant by 1979. As of 1976, only 5 percent of children's clothing, other than sleepwear, was made of flame-retardant fabrics, because a flame retardant for polyester-and-cotton blend materials was not yet invented. If California stores are forced to abide by this law, all children's clothing would be made of 100-percent polyester or cotton fabrics. In general, parents do not like these expensive and nondurable fabrics [58].

State and municipal legislation is particularly restrictive for national retailers, since they must adhere to different laws in each location they operate. Product lines and inventories are large because of this, and prices are higher.

Legislators must take into account the total impact of laws on consumers and retailers before enacting them. By and large, retailers, because of their close link with consumers, have been consumer-oriented and focused on consumer problems. Any consumer protection that is enacted should be on the national level to minimize costs, conflicts, and confusion. National legislation also would receive greater acceptance by consumers and retailers.

FUTURE OUTLOOK

Consumerism will be moving into a new phase that is less active and confrontational, but more sophisticated and discerning. Consumers now realize governmental intervention is not always the best and most effective remedy. Just as retailers will be more inclined to work with consumers to solve their problems, consumers will be interested in cooperating with retailers.

There will be an influx of specialized consumer groups that will be active in limited regional areas and oriented toward the resolution of specific issues. Retailers will be quite responsive to these groups; therefore, a national retail consumer group will not develop. Consumers will expect retailers to provide more information about the products they sell and the prices they charge. Consumers also will want retailers to research their needs and desires.

Government action will be reduced as retailers and consumers cooperatively reconcile their differences. The most probable areas of government involvement are price-fixing, credit disclosures, delivery, and advertising. These issues have not been adequately resolved as yet.

The primary consumerism challenge facing retailers will be the establishment or reestablishment of consumer confidence. In an effort to generate confidence, retailers will spend more time and money on consumer education and public relations. The role and contribution of retailing will be publicized extensively. Trade associations and individual retailers will work together in this effort.

Retailers also will put pressure on suppliers and manufacturers to provide the quality, information, and value that final consumers demand. Channel members will work together to accomplish these objectives, as they all come to realize that positive responses to consumerism will yield many sales and image benefits.

RECOMMENDATIONS

Recommendations are offered for consumer groups, government, the industry, and individual retailers.

Consumer Groups

Local consumer groups must become more involved with retailing and retail business practices. The groups should monitor area retailers and educate consumers about their rights and recourses. The groups should strive to interact with retailers. Where possible, consumer groups should try to place representatives on retailers' consumer affairs panels. Since many retailers have done a solid job of addressing consumer issues, legislation should not be pressed by consumer groups until after the retailers have proven unresponsive or ineffectual.

Government

Further government action should be restrained. The costs, as well as the benefits, for consumers and retailers alike should be

carefully assessed before new legislation is enacted. Legislation
should be balanced to protect both consumers and retailers. National
laws, which encourage uniform practices for national and regional
retailers, are preferred over narrow municipal laws that require
different and conflicting methods of operation. When evaluating regulations, government must receive input from consumers and retailers.

The Industry

The retail industry must promote a better understanding between consumers and member firms. Trade associations must continue to advise retailers, educate consumers, develop more efficient
business practices, cooperate with government, participate in community affairs, and research the changing social and economic environment. Standards of ethics and guidelines for store operations
must be proposed by the industry and promulgated by retail firms.
Open forums should be encouraged.

Companies

Individual retailers have worked hard to gain customer confidence and minimize government intervention. They must sustain
these efforts. Several areas need considerable improvement,
including delivery, informative labeling, deceptive advertising, and
price-fixing. Retailers should strive to obtain national, uniform
self-regulatory and government rules. They must upgrade consumer
affairs and customer service departments. Consumer education
regarding store policies and products is essential if retail image is
to improve. Cooperation with consumers and government is necessary.

BIBLIOGRAPHY

1. "Ads and Consumers: Buying Movements Analyzed as A.F.A.
    Convention Closes." Newsweek 14 (July 3, 1939), p. 38.

2. "After the Marathon: Violations of Clayton Act." Time 87
    (March 24, 1966), pp. 80ff.

3. "Another Nightwear Chemical Causes a Safety Controversy."
    New York Times (October 15, 1977), p. 24.

4. "And Now the Sunday Green Laws." New York Times (July 6, 1977), p. 18.

5. "Balky Consumer." Business Week (September 23, 1933), pp. 3-4.

6. "Ban Asked on Children's Wear with Flame Retardant." New York Times (February 9, 1977), p. 25.

7. Barmash, Isadore. "Albany Bill Heats Sunday Trade Issue." New York Times (May 26, 1977), pp. 1, 7.

8. ____. "Credit Due 55,000 in Price-Fixing Case." New York Times (June 28, 1977), p. 39.

9. ____. "Discounters' Group Hears a Prediction of Wave of Payoffs." New York Times (May 23, 1972), pp. 53ff.

10. ____. "Educate Public, Merchant Asks." New York Times (January 10, 1967), p. 53.

11. ____. "57,000 Ask Refunds of 3 Sued Stores." New York Times (October 21, 1976), p. 31.

12. ____. "Flame-Resistant Fiber at Hoechst." New York Times (October 26, 1977), p. 3.

13. ____. "FTC Is Studying Bloomingdale Links." New York Times (August 23, 1977), p. 49.

14. ____. "Lawyers to Get 30% of Store Refunds in Overcharge Suit." New York Times (October 27, 1977), p. 3.

15. ____. "Macy's Confirms Reports of Sunday Operations." New York Times (July 28, 1976), p. 47.

16. ____. "Price-Fixing Case on Stores Widens." New York Times (May 17, 1973), pp. 1ff.

17. ____. "Retail Meeting Warned on Consumers." New York Times (January 11, 1972), p. 49.

18. ____. "Saks, Bergdorf and Bonwit Accused as Price-Fixers." New York Times (October 8, 1974), pp. 1ff.

19. ____. "Saks, Bergdorf and Bonwit Fined." New York Times (February 28, 1975), pp. 43ff.

20. ____. "Saks Executive Fined $15,000 on Price-Fixing Plea of Guilty." New York Times (May 1, 1975), p. 59.

21. ____. "State Hearings Set on Sunday Stores." New York Times (September 1, 1976), p. 49.

22. ____. "3 Big Stores in New York Plan to Open on Sundays." New York Times (July 23, 1976), pp. 1ff.

23. ____. "3 Stores Offer to Settle Suits." New York Times (July 10, 1976), pp. 1ff.

24. ____. "U.S. Charges Pend in Apparel Pricing." New York Times (June 13, 1974), pp. 65ff.

25. ____. "U.S. Paid to Widen Store Price Case." New York Times (May 14, 1973), pp. 45ff.

26. Batten, W. M. "Retailing Must Inform and Educate the Public." Stores 49 (February 1967), pp. 11-12.

27. ____. "Responsible Retailing." Dun's Review 89 (March 1967), pp. 83-86.

28. Becker, B. W. "Consumerism: A Challenge or a Threat?" Journal of Retailing 48 (Summer 1972), pp. 16-28.

29. Bender, W. C. "Consumer Purchase Costs: Do Retailers Recognize Them?" Journal of Retailing 40 (Spring 1964), pp. 1-8.

30. "Bergdorf Executive Fined $25,000 in Fixing of Prices." New York Times (August 13, 1975), p. 45.

31. Berry, L. L. "Improving Retailers' Capability for Effective Consumerism Response." Journal of Retailing 52 (Fall 1976), pp. 3-14.

32. Blankertz, D. F. "Customers' Patronage of a Parent and a New Branch Store." Journal of Home Economics 44 (April 1952), p. 294.

33. Blood, J. "Credit Purchases Now 60% of Big Store Sales, NRMA Told." Merchandising Week 105 (September 17, 1973), p. 3.

34. _____. "New Generation Offers Retailers New Opportunities." Merchandising Week 105 (November 12, 1973), pp. 1ff.

35. Bogart, L. "Future of Retailing." Harvard Business Review 51 (November 1973), pp. 16-18ff.

36. Brightman, H. W. "Growth of Consumer Influence in the Retail Field." Journal of Home Economics 29 (October 1937), pp. 505-11.

37. Brozan, Nadine. "Flame-Retardant Sleepwear: Is There a Risk of Cancer?" New York Times (April 10, 1976), p. 32.

38. _____. "U.S. Bans a Flame Retardant Used in Children's Sleepwear." New York Times (April 18, 1977), p. 14.

39. Buc, N. L. "Retailers Liable for Ads Prepared by Resources." Stores 57 (December 1975), p. 26.

40. Burgess, G. "Trials of a Department Store Critic." Collier's National Weekly 44 (November 6, 1909), p. 20.

41. "Business Leaders Told to Counter Consumerism." Merchandising Week 102 (April 13, 1970), p. 18.

42. "Carter Team and Retailing." Chain Store Age Executive 53 (June 1977), pp. 21-26.

43. "Cash-Carry Plan Gains in Retailing." New York Times (November 13, 1932), p. 9.

44. "Chains and Consumerism: New Directions Necessary?" Chain Store Age Executive 53 (June 1977), pp. 26-28

45. "Chain Stores Organize to Build Good Will, Fight Sales Tax." Business Week (October 15, 1930), p. 10.

46. Chapman, P. "Consumer Affairs: Retailer Responsibility Extends to New Areas." Stores 59 (April 1977), p. 43.

47. _____. "How Two Companies Handle Consumer Affairs (Federated and Hess's)." Stores 59 (May 1977), pp. 45-46.

48. "Charge Accounts Aren't What They Used to Be." Business Week (June 1, 1932), p. 8.

49. Charlton, L. "The Facts About Tris Don't Leave Much Choice." New York Times (July 3, 1977), p. 3.

50. Collazzo, C. J., Jr. "Effects of Income upon Shopping Attitudes and Frustrations." Journal of Retailing 42 (Spring 1966), pp. 1-7.

51. Colson, W. F. "How I Hold My Customers." Systems 24 (October 1913), pp. 367-71.

52. Conroy, Thomas F. "Standards Action Is Gaining Rapidly." New York Times (April 25, 1937), p. 9.

53. "Consent Judgment Sought for 3 Large Stores." New York Times (December 17, 1976), p. 11.

54. "Consumer Agency Issues New Warning on Tris." New York Times (August 20, 1977), p. 8.

55. "Consumer Credit and Shoddy Goods." U.S. News 71 (October 4, 1971), p. 59.

56. "Consumer Has the Right to Know." Stores 51 (February 1969), p. 16.

57. "Consumerism." Journal of Retailing 48 (Winter 1972-73), pp. 3-100.

58. "Consumerism at Sears: Education Is a Big Effort." Stores 55 (September 1973), p. 3.

59. "Consumerism: Fighting Back." Merchandising Week 102 (February 23, 1970), p. 6.

60. "Consumerism in 1975: Threat or Challenge?" Stores 57 (March 1975), pp. 26ff.

61. "Consumerism Is Good Business." Stores 56 (June 1974), p. 64.

62. "Consumer Keeps Right on Buying." Business Week (February 6, 1954), pp. 42ff.

63. "Consumer King." Fortune 59 (March 1959), pp. 44ff.

64. "Consumer-Retailer Alliance." Journal of Home Economics 36 (December 1944), p. 650.

65. "Consumers Are Voters, Too; Robinson Bill for Regulation of Chain Stores and Other Large-Scale Distributing Organizations." Collier's National Weekly 97 (May 23, 1936), p. 74.

66. "Consumer Slowdown." Time 71 (April 14, 1958), p. 88.

67. "Consumers: What They Think, What's True." Newsweek 50 (August 5, 1957), p. 69.

68. "Co-operation between Consumers and Retailers." Journal of Home Economics 32 (December 1940), pp. 688-90.

69. "Court Orders Chemical Concerns and Stores to Share Tris Burden." New York Times (May 4, 1977), p. 1.

70. Cox, R. "Consumer Convenience and Retail Structure of Cities." Journal of Marketing 23 (April 1959), pp. 344-62.

71. Crawford, H. "Ethics of a Big Store." Independent 67 (August 12, 1909), pp. 358-60.

72. Cunningham, R. M. "Customer Loyalty to Store and Brand." Harvard Business Review 39 (November 1961), pp. 127-37.

73. "Curbs on Selling Fought at Albany." New York Times (October 3, 1957), p. 29.

74. "Customers Help Run the Store at Mays." Business Week (January 19, 1952), pp. 140-42.

75. Dana, M. "Your Customers Want You to Know." Stores 50 (June 1968), p. 25.

76. "Denver Complaints Studied by Stores." New York Times (July 27, 1967), p. 57.

77. "Department Stores Play Banker; Revolving Credit Plan." Business Week (May 18, 1957), pp. 65-66ff.

78. "Department Stores Worry." Business Week (January 24, 1953), pp. 43-44ff.

79. Deutsch, C. "Retailers Face Urban Problems." Stores 52 (October 1970), pp. 4-5.

80. "Discussion." Journal of Marketing 39 (July 1975), pp. 64-68.

81. Dodge, R. E. "Selling the Older Consumer." Journal of Retailing 34 (Summer 1958), pp. 73-84.

82. Doherty, L., and Block, M. "Retailers Faced with Consumer Anger, Low Profits, SMI Hears." Advertising Age 46 (May 12, 1975), pp. 2ff.

83. Dornoff, R. L., and Tankersley, C. B. "Do Retailers Practice Social Responsibility?" Journal of Retailing 51 (Winter 1975-76), pp. 33-42.

84. Down, Arthur A. "Theory of Consumer Efficiency." Journal of Retailing 37 (Spring 1961), pp. 6-12ff.

85. Dubbs, E. "NRMA Will Stress Retailers' New Role in Changing Society." Merchandising Week 100 (January 8, 1968), pp. 1ff.

86. Engle, E. F. "Retailers Rely on Paper in Ambitious Public Relations Program." Editor and Publisher 93 (July 16, 1960), pp. 17-18.

87. "Federated and Saks Fined on Price-Fixing Charges." New York Times (June 10, 1976), p. 63.

88. "Federated Stores Consents to Order on Tris Garments." New York Times (September 1, 1977), p. 12.

89. Fisk, G. "Conceptual Model for Studying Customer Image." Journal of Retailing 37 (Winter 1961-62), pp. 1-8ff.

90. "Forgotten Customer." Living Age 356 (July 1939), pp. 477-78.

91. "FTC Cracks Down on Chains Ad Deals." Business Week (December 10, 1955), pp. 54ff.

92. "FTC Rules Against Gimbels Price Ads: Tells Advertisers to Respect Guides." Advertising Age 33 (August 20, 1962), pp. 1ff.

93. "FTC Says 200,000 Got Refunds by Store Chains." New York Times (October 21, 1976), p. 63.

94. Gertz, M. "Retailer and Consumer." Journal of Home Economics 32 (April 1940), pp. 213-18.

95. Gilkey, J. G. "Your Stake in Urban Affairs." Stores 52 (October 1970), pp. 7ff.

96. Gillespie, K. R. "Are Your Ads Guilty, As Charged?" Journal of Retailing 34 (Fall 1958), pp. 127-28ff.

97. "Gimbels Off-List Ads Not Deceptive, F.T.C. Officials Say." Advertising Age 33 (January 22, 1962), p. 2.

98. Goldman, A. "Churches Criticize Shopping on Sundays." New York Times (August 28, 1976), p. 1.

99. Goldstein, T. "New York Appeals Court Voids Sunday Sales Ban." New York Times (June 18, 1976), pp. 1ff.

100. Goodman, S. J. "Raising the Image of Business." Stores 56 (March 1974), pp. 11ff.

101. Government Manual, 1977/78. Office of the Federal Register, pp. 241-81, 479-80, 540-46.

102. Greenhouse, L. "Governor Is Opposed to Blue-Law Revival." New York Times (July 7, 1977), p. 6.

103. Greer, C. C. "Deciding to Accept or Reject a Marginal Retail Credit Applicant." Journal of Retailing 43 (Winter 1968), pp. 44-53.

104. Harris, R. P. "Grass Root Project: Consumer Buying." Journal of Home Economics 38 (December 1946), pp. 639-40.

105. "Hearing on Credit Bills to Air Retail Complaints." Merchandising Week 102 (November 9, 1970), p. 9.

106. "High Cost of Retail Credit Granting Goes Higher." Stores 51 (February 1969), pp. 14-15.

107. Hollander, S. C. "American Retailer: Subservient and the Public?" Journal of Retailing 34 (Fall 1958), pp. 143-53ff.

108. Hollander, S. C., and Roddewyn, J. J. "Retailing and Public Policy: An International Overview." Journal of Retailing 50 (Spring 1974), pp. 55-66ff.

109. Howard, M. C. "Government, the Retailer, and the Consumer." Journal of Retailing 48 (Winter 1972-73), pp. 48-62.

110. Hutchinson, B. "Consumer Protection Song: New Notes for Retailers." Merchandising Week 99 (November 6, 1967), p. 5.

111. ____. "Consumer Protection." Merchandising Week 100 (January 1, 1968), pp. 17-21.

112. "Improvements in the Position of the Consumer at Law." Consumer Bulletin 44 (June 1961), pp. 31-32.

113. "Industry Hears Definitive Plan on Consumerism." Merchandising Week 101 (November 3, 1969), p. 74.

114. Jackson, C. W. "Can Retailing React to Today and Lead the Way to Tomorrow?" Stores 51 (September 1969), p. 35.

115. Jolson, M. A., and Spath, W. F. "Understanding and Fulfilling Shoppers' Requirements: An Anomaly in Retailing." Journal of Retailing 49 (Summer 1973), pp. 38-50.

116. Judge, J. "Retailer Urged to Develop Greater Consumer Sensitivity." Chain Store Age Executive 53 (June 1977), p. 27.

117. "Judge Strikes Down Safety Ban on Tris." New York Times (June 24, 1977), p. 9.

118. Kahn, R. "Present Retailer Reaction to Consumerism—Death or Hope?" Journal of Retailing 49 (Spring 1973), pp. 3-9.

119. Kanner, Lee. "Customers Encounter Non-Response." New York Times (November 12, 1967), p. 14.

120. Kartz, D. L. "Public and Legal Constraints of the Retailer: A Changing Societal Environment." Journal of Retailing 47 (Fall 1971), pp. 73-78ff.

121. "Keen-Nosed Consumer Is Uncanny at Smelling Bargains These Days." Business Week (July 6, 1932), p. 9.

122. King, W. "Selling on Sundays Rising Despite Confusing Laws." New York Times (May 22, 1976), p. 1.

123. Kirsch, F. "Retailers Do Practice Consumerism." Stores 55 (July 1973), pp. 12ff.

124. _____. "Consumerism at Dayton's: A Consumer Information Center." Stores 55 (August 1973), pp. 2ff.

125. Kirstein, E. "Why We Know What the Public Wants." Systems 42 (August 1922), pp. 155-57.

126. Kisseberth, I. V. "Why We Always Have What Customers Want." Systems 46 (November 1924), pp. 567-70.

127. Kleeberg, I. C. "Department Stores and Consumerism." Stores 56 (October, November, December 1974), pp. 2ff., 4-5, 31-32.

128. Koshetz, H. "Korvettes Calls Sunday Pace Good." New York Times (August 17, 1976), pp. 43, 50.

129. "Label Held an Aid in Inducing Sales." New York Times (June 27, 1952), p. 37.

130. Lachman, L. "Discussion." Advertising Age 35 (April 27, 1964), p. 68.

131. Lazarus, R. "New Era of Community Service." Stores 56 (March 1974), p. 4.

132. Leblow, V. "Consumer Faces Retail Changes." Journal of Home Economics 41 (June 1949), pp. 291-94.

133. Lee, S. M. "Impact of Fair Trade Laws on Retailing." Journal of Retailing 41 (Spring 1965), pp. 1-6.

134. Lessis, V. P. "Consumer Store Images and Store Loyalties." Journal of Marketing 37 (October 1973), pp. 72-74.

135. Lichtenstein, Grace. "Business Bureau Backs Arbitration." New York Times (May 28, 1972), p. 79.

136. Liggett, K. "Some Things We Retailers Know About You Humans." American Magazine 84 (December 1917), pp. 47-48.

137. Linden, F. "Reading, Writing, and Retailing (Influence of Education on Consumer)." Conference Board Business Record 17 (October 1960), pp. 35ff.

138. Luchsinger, J. "Seven Shopping Days to Higher Costs." New York Times (January 23, 1977), p. 24.

139. MacLachlan, D. L., and Spence, H. "Public Trust in Retailing: Some Research Findings." Journal of Retailing 52 (Spring 1976), pp. 3-8.

140. "Macy Told to Stop Selling Clothes Treated with Tris." New York Times (August 21, 1977), p. 31.

141. "Makers of Children's Nightwear Ask Delay in Consumer Refunds." New York Times (April 21, 1977), p. 13.

142. "Mass Merchants Focus on Acquisitions, Consumerism." Merchandising Week 102 (April 20, 1970), p. 8.

143. "May Charge Interest on Overdue Accounts." New York Times (January 17, 1932), p. 18.

144. Mazur, P. "Future Challenges to Retailing." Chain Store Age (Adm. Ed.) 34 (January 1958), pp. 47-49.

145. McClure, P. J., and Ryans, J. K., Jr. "Differences between Retailers' and Consumers' Perception." Journal of Marketing Research 5 (February 1968), pp. 35-40.

146. McClure, T. H. "Retailers' Attitudes." Advertising Agency 51 (February 28, 1958), pp. 3-132.

147. Metcalfe, L. S. "Warning Customers of Merchandise Famines." Systems 30 (August 1916), pp. 186-91.

148. Millstein, I. M. "Retail Credit Cards—The Best Defense Is a Good Offense or Vice Versa." Stores 51 (June 1969), pp. 51-52.

149. Mitchell, J. "Consumer Gets a Break." New Republic 81 (January 30, 1935), pp. 324-26.

150. "Morris Pinpoints Top Priority: Legislation Affecting Retailing." Stores 59 (March 1977), pp. 45-46.

151. Moschis, G. P. "Shopping Orientations and Consumer Uses of Information." Journal of Marketing 52 (Summer 1976), pp. 61-70ff.

152. Moyer, M. S. "Consumerism in the Future: Complex Questions and Collaborative Answers." Business Quarterly 41 (Winter 1976), pp. 28-34.

153. "Nader Urges Retailer Push for Better Manufacturer Ads." Advertising Age 45 (February 25, 1974), p. 146.

154. "NARDA Symposium Psyches Out Consumer." Merchandising Week 102 (July 13, 1970), p. 61.

155. "New Ferment in Retailing." Dun's Review and Modern Industry 73 (January 1959), pp. 73-75.

156. "New Weapons: Installment Terms and Cash Discount Idea." Business Week (June 8, 1935), p. 14.

157. "New York Better Business Bureau Issues Booklet Outlining Retail Ad Standards." Advertising Age 32 (July 24, 1961), p. 48.

158. "No Fire Sale Now without a Permit." New York Times (January 6, 1937), p. 41.

159. "NRMA Convention Starts Tussling with 1966's Promise, Challenge." Merchandising Week 98 (January 10, 1968), p. 10.

160. Occhiograsso, J. A. "Consumerism: For Retailer, a Chance and a Challenge." Stores 54 (February 1972), pp. 16ff.

161. "Penney's As Consumer Educator." Stores 56 (January 1974), p. 25.

162. Peterson, E. "What Retailers Can, and Must, Do for Consumers." Merchandising Week 98 (January 17, 1966), p. 10.

163. Pfeiffer, P. L. "Where Do Your Customers Go?" Stores 55 (February 1973), p. 30.

164. "Presold Customers Strong on Quality Dealers Say." Merchandising Week 10 (August 18, 1969), p. 74.

165. "Rejections Increase Consumer Credit." Merchandising Week 107 (March 10, 1975), pp. 1ff.

166. "Retail Credit Overviews." Stores 57 (April 1975), pp. 8ff.

167. "Retailers' Riddles: Labor Problems and Customer Service." Business Week (January 24, 1942), pp. 42-44.

168. "Retail Implications of Wage-Price Controls." Journal of Retailing 47 (Winter 1971-72), pp. 3-4ff.

169. "Retail NRA Voted by Dry Goods Body." New York Times (June 15, 1937), p. 32.

170. "Retail Revolt Termed Likely." Editor and Publisher 102 (December 13, 1969), p. 16.

171. Richardson, E. L. "How to Restore Business-Consumer Trust." Commerce America 1 (March 29, 1976), pp. 4-5.

172. Rosenbaum, S. "Consumerism Is Here to Stay—Stores Do Something About It." Editor and Publisher 103 (February 28, 1970), pp. 16ff.

173. Rosenberg, L. J. "Retailers' Responses to Consumerism." Business Horizons 19 (October 18, 1975), pp. 37-44.

174. Rothberg, R. "Consumer-Retailer Loyalty." Journal of Retailing 47 (Winter 1971-72), pp. 72-82ff.

175. "Saks, Bergdorf Goodman and Genesco Are Sued." New York Times (December 11, 1976), p. 35.

176. Sauter, R. F., and Walker, O. C., Jr. "Retailers' Reactions to Interest Limitation Laws—Additional Evidence." Journal of Marketing 36 (April 1972), pp. 58-61.

177. Schmalz, C. N. "Retail Stores and Their Customers: A Suggestion for Better Relations." Journal of Home Economics 28 (May 1936), pp. 285-88.

178. "Sleepwear Makers Seek Relief in Recall." New York Times (April 25, 1977), p. 50.

179. Sloane, Leonard. "Retailers Are Scolded for Views That Put Women in Stereotype." New York Times (October 4, 1967), p. 63.

180. "Standards Program Drawn by Retailers." New York Times (April 20, 1937), p. 36.

181. "Store Chains Are Indicted." New York Times (April 29, 1976), p. 67.

182. "Store Complaints Studied by Stores." New York Times (July 27, 1967), p. 57.

183. "Stores Put Goods to Work Selling." New York Times (March 23, 1957), p. 25.

184. "Suggests Solutions to False Advertising." New York Times (June 5, 1932), p. 9.

185. Sykes, J. G. "Can You Get Your Money Back?" Reader's Digest 68 (June 1956), pp. 112-14.

186. Tarpey, L. X. "Who Is a Competing Customer?" Journal of Retailing 45 (Spring 1969), pp. 46-58ff.

187. "Third Annual Report: Summary." Journal of Home Economics 33 (January 1941), p. 39.

188. "Tris Ban Violation Laid to Woolworth." New York Times (May 18, 1977), p. 2.

189. "Unions and Some Retailers Oppose Sunday Openings." New York Times (June 18, 1976), p. 18.

190. United States Code Annotated. §§1-11. West Publishing, 1973.

191. United States Code Annotated. §§1115-1700. West Publishing, 1973.

192. United States Code Annotated. §§1701-End. West Publishing, 1973.

193. "Urge Cooperation in Labeling Goods." New York Times (April 29, 1937), p. 30.

194. "U.S. to Ease Restraints on Sleepwear Fabrics." New York Times (September 18, 1977), p. 26.

195. Walker, Q. F. "Retailer and Consumer under the New Deal." Annals of the American Academy of Political and Social Science (April 20, 1935), p. 24.

196. Warren, W. P. "Crudeness in Retail Stores." Collier's National Weekly 42 (February 20, 1909), pp. 25-26.

197. Weak, W. B. "Measuring the Customers' Image of a Department Store." Journal of Retailing 37 (Summer 1961), pp. 40-48.

198. Weiss, E. B. "That's a Heckuva Way to Run Bloomingdale's, Mr. Lachman." Advertising Age 35 (March 30, 1964), pp. 80ff.

199. ____. "Tradeism May Follow Consumerism Trend." Advertising Age 39 (October 16, 1968), pp. 70ff.

200. ____. "Is Anybody in the Store Listening?" Stores 51 (November 1969), pp. 31-32.

201. Williams, B. "Retailers, the Ghetto, and the Government: The Problem, the Promise, and the Potential." Merchandising Week 99 (December 11, 1967), pp. 6-7.

202. Williams, J. R. "NRMA President Tells Price Commission: Retailing Doesn't Need Controls." Stores 54 (May 1972), pp. 18-19.

203. ____. "Three Big Problems for Retailers." Stores 56 (August 1974), pp. 7ff.

204. Wolcott, R. "Which Way, Now, Consumer?" Journal of Home Economics 39 (October 1947), pp. 501-02.

12

AN INTER-INDUSTRY ANALYSIS
OF CONSUMERISM

Joel R. Evans

INTRODUCTION

The overall structure and impact of consumerism in the United States are discussed in this chapter. In addition, the similarities and differences of consumerism in the ten industries covered in the study are enumerated.

The order of presentation follows that of the preceding chapters: history of consumerism and major issues, consumer groups, government, industry responses, company responses, impact of consumerism, evaluation of consumerism, future outlook, and recommendations.

HISTORY OF CONSUMERISM

Each of the industries has gone through clearly defined eras of consumerism, as shown in Table 12.1. Most conform to the general trends of consumerism: late 1800s or early 1900s, 1930s through the 1950s, and 1960s to the present. All have experienced the major thrust of consumerism since the 1960s.

The first era of consumerism for banking, mail order, petroleum, pharmaceuticals, and the professions occurred in the nineteenth century. For major appliances, clothing, household products, and retailing, the first era began in the early 1900s. Lead, asbestos, and fluorocarbons had no interaction with consumerism until the late 1930s.

Generally, the initial consumerism era was propelled by business people, not consumers. Business people sought to improve their industries and eliminate undesirable competitors. Important issues were product purity, product quality, the threat of antitrust actions, safety, and behavior of personnel.

TABLE 12.1

History of Consumerism and Consumer Issues
by Industry

Industry	Consumerism Era	Consumer Issues
Major Appliances	1920s	Safety hazards
	1930s to 1950s	Safety hazards, brand proliferation, unwise spending, consumer education, repair services
	1960s to present	Sales-push money, warranties, servicing, product information, planned obsolescence, product safety, replacement parts availability
Banking	Mid- to late-1800s	Supervision of note redemption, oversubscription, need for a banking system
	1910s to 1950s	Federal Reserve Act, mortgages, bank failure, recovery from Depression, installment loans
	1960s to present	Impersonal nature of banks, credit availability, privacy, discrimination, truthfulness, disclosure, interest rates, mortgages, redlining, electronic funds transfers
Clothing	1900s to 1920s	Poor quality, designs, endangered animals
	1930s to 1950s	Designs, labeling, misrepresentation, quality, flammability, deceptive practices, endangered animals, performance standards
	1960s to present	Quality, performance, labeling, fashion, animal conservation, care labeling, safety

(continued)

Industry	Consumerism Era	Consumer Issues
Household Products	1900s to 1920s	Purity, safety, high prices
	1930s to 1950s	Information, safety, false advertising claims, monopoly power, price administration, shortweighting
	1960s to present	False advertising, dangerous packages, package sizes, ingredient listing, unit pricing, product safety
Lead, Asbestos, and Fluoro- carbons	1930s to 1960s	Occupational dangers of asbestos, lead poisoning, nonoccupational dangers of asbestos
	1970s to present	Content of lead in paint, lead poisoning, cancer from asbestos, fluorocarbon pro- pellants, consumer and public safety
Mail Order	1879 to early 1900s	Catalog distribution, rural- free delivery, reduced postal rates, package size, reduced prices, misleading advertise- ments, social pressure, credit sales, unordered merchandise
	Late 1930s to 1950s	Customer service, mailing lists, lotteries, contests, free merchandise, deceptive advertising, credit, real estate sales
	1960s to present	Fair trade, lotteries, contests, privacy, new uses of mail order

(continued)

Table 12.1 (continued)

Industry	Consumerism Era	Consumer Issues
Petroleum	1860s to 1890s	Pools, trusts, supplies, prices, antitrust
	1900s to 1950s	Price-fixing, corruption, stock manipulation, false earnings reports
	1960s to present	Company size, stock manipulation, hoarding, price-fixing, cartels, false advertising, manufacturer actions toward dealers, bribery, octane ratings, synthetic oils, shortages of fuel
Pharmaceutical	Late 1800s to 1910s	Preservatives, contents, purity, safety
	1930s to 1950s	Useless and dangerous medicines, deceptive advertising, information, pricing, monopoly practices, prescriptions, side effects
	1960s to present	Information, safety, generic drugs, new product approval procedures, advertising, efficacy, quality control, pricing, pharmacy ownership, government reimbursement
Professions (Legal and Medical)	Mid-1800s to 1900	Law: lack of concern for mass public, political involvement, unprofessional conduct; Medicine: professional standards, poor education and literature, drug frauds
	1930s to 1950s	Law: political involvement, fee arrangements, discrimination, legal aid; Medicine: national health, group practice,

(continued)

Industry	Consumerism Era	Consumer Issues
		medical plans, medical insurance
	1960s to present	Law: legal aid, professional ethics, disciplinary procedures, advertising, no-fault laws; Medicine: health insurance, shortage of doctors, malpractice, competence, unnecessary surgery, fees, national health care
Retailing	1900s to 1920s	Inattention to consumer needs, salesmanship, advertising, shortages, consumer research
	1930s to 1950s	Standards, informative labeling, advertising, consumer refunds, credit
	1960s to present	Standards, purchases by stores, labeling, credit, privacy, advertising, consumer education, blue laws, product safety, urban problems, unit pricing, delivery, billings

Source: Compiled by the author from information in Chapters 2 through 11.

During the 1930s to 1950s, major appliances, clothing, household products, mail order, pharmaceuticals, professions, and retailing were exposed to the second era of consumerism. Banking faced this era from the 1910s to 1950s, encompassing pre- and post-Depression practices by member firms. Lead and asbestos showed their first signs of consumer safety dangers during the 1930–50 period. Petroleum underwent a second era from the 1900s to 1950s, concentrating on anticompetitive practices.

Overall, the second consumerism era saw heightened activity as consumer groups formed and government legislation was passed. While most consumer issues were not resolved during the second era, a multitude of topics were brought into public view, including: safety, brand proliferation, repair services, mortgages, installment loans, labeling, misrepresentation, quality, flammability, deceptive practices, performance standards, information, monopoly power, price-fixing, shortweighting, stock manipulation, prescriptions, side effects, legal aid, medical insurance and plans, credit, and consumer refunds. This era was quite productive and paved the way for the strong actions and court cases of the modern movement.

The third era of consumerism, 1960s to the present, has operated for major appliances, banking, clothing, household products, mail order, petroleum, pharmaceuticals, professions, and retailing. Only lead, asbestos, and fluorocarbons, which have been investigated and regulated in the 1970s as their dangers to consumers and the general public became known, have not corresponded to this era.

In all cases, the modern era of consumerism has been substantially more intense than its predecessors. Consumer groups and government have pushed hard to enact legislation and tighten regulations. Industries and companies have instituted a myriad of consumer-oriented policies and fought against restrictions they believed to be excessive. Court decisions have resulted in numerous cease-and-desist orders, but few fines. The scope of consumerism during the current era has been quite wide, covering a variety of consumer issues, such as: warranties, servicing, product information, planned obsolescence, product safety, impersonal nature of business, credit availability, privacy, discrimination, disclosure, redlining, electronic funds transfers, product performance, labeling, care labeling, conservation, false advertising, dangerous packages, ingredient listing, unit pricing, hazardous substances, contests, mailing lists, stock manipulation, price-fixing, monopolies, fuel shortages, generic drugs, efficacy, quality control, legal aid, ethics, no-fault laws, health insurance, national health care, unnecessary surgery, consumer education, blue laws, unit pricing, and urban problems.

CONSUMER GROUPS

There are active consumer groups in almost all the industries examined, as revealed in Table 12.2. However, there are few specialized consumer groups. Most of the activities of consumer groups have come from a limited number of general interest groups. In fact, only one of the groups listed in Table 12.2, Petroleum Watchdog, confines itself to the practices of one industry. All the others cover a broader spectrum of issues. The consumer groups involved with the largest amount of industries are Consumers Union, Ralph Nader's organizations, and Consumers' Research.

The groups have had a certain level of success in achieving their goals. Nonetheless, both limited resources and lack of consumer participation have restricted them. As a result of the few active consumer groups, many issues have been publicized, books and articles written, legislation enacted, and industry and company practices revised.

GOVERNMENT

Government agencies, legislation, and court cases have had far more effect on business operations and practices than consumer groups. During the past 100 years, the government has played a continually greater role as the protector of consumers. Table 12.3 contains a listing of the government agencies, federal legislation, and court decisions that have had the greatest impact on each industry in this study.

While government intervention has increased in recent years, enforcement and penalties have not grown accordingly, with the exception of a few famous rulings like STP, Anacin, and Listerine. The government, usually the FTC, frequently has been willing to employ cease-and-desist orders rather than seek fines and jail sentences. Further, given the amount of legislation now in existence, court cases have been rare.

INDUSTRY RESPONSES

Industries have responded to consumer pressures since their inception. In many cases, industries have sought to improve themselves without any outside consumer influences. This has occurred as concerned industry representatives attempted to upgrade operating standards and eliminate deceptive practices. Until recently, business

TABLE 12.2

Important Current Consumer Groups
and Their Activities by Industry

Industry	Consumer Group	Activities of Group
Major Appliances	Consumers' Research	Publication of articles in <u>Consumers' Research Magazine</u>, promotion of certification programs by trade associations
	Consumers Union	Publication of articles in <u>Consumer Reports</u>, investigation of radiation exposure from color televisions and shock hazards of refrigerator-freezers
Banking	Consumer Federation of America	Testimony for credit legislation, support for education of federal auditors and a national consumer bank, opposition to variable mortgage rates
	Consumer Action	Publication of <u>Break the Bank</u> and <u>It's in Your Interest</u>, campaign for full disclosure, opposition to misleading advertisements, release of Federal Reserve data on interest rates
	Ralph Nader	Publication of <u>Citibank</u>, opposition to redlining, deceptive practices, secrecy
	Common Cause	Support for credit legislation, use of mass letter-writing campaigns
Clothing	Consumers' Research	Tests for flammability

(continued)

Industry	Consumer Group	Activities of Group
	Consumers Union	Tests for flammability
	National Fire Protection Association	Publication of information on fires and explosions
	Action for the Prevention of Burn Injuries to Children	Education about burn prevention and consequences of fire
	Environmental Defense Fund	Petition with CPSC to ban Tris
Household Products	Consumers' Research	Ratings of household products, such as nonphosphate detergents
	Consumers Union	Ratings of household products, like silver polish and deodorants
	Federation of Homemakers	Support for hazardous substances legislation
Lead, Asbestos, and Fluorocarbons	Ralph Nader's Center for the Study of Responsive Law	Studies on hazardous minerals and substances, publication of Vanishing Air and Bitter Wages
	Natural Resources Defense Council	Protection of natural resources and the environment, petitions with CPSC, FDA, and EPA to ban fluorocarbon propellants, petitions with CPSC to ban asbestos in wall-patching compounds
Mail Order	Consumers Union	Publication of articles on mail-order practices, suit against two companies over billing practices

(continued)

Table 12.2 (continued)

Industry	Consumer Group	Activities of Group
	Truth in Advertising	Formation of a mail-order committee
	Center for the Study of Responsive Law	Study on consumer problems, mail order rated third
Petroleum	Ralph Nader's Petroleum Watchdog	Monitoring of petroleum industry, suit against four firms on behalf of independent retailers
	Consumers Union	Suit against companies on the basis of deceptive and misleading advertising, suit on gasoline hoarding to drive up prices
	Sierra Club	Suit against several companies for forming a nuclear cartel
Pharmaceutical	Consumers' Research	Support for food and drug legislation, testing of pharmaceuticals
	National Council of Churches	Opposition to advertising of over-the-counter drugs
	Public Interest Research Group	Study of prescription drug prices
	Consumer Federation of America	Support for drug price competition and open ownership of pharmacies
	Consumers Union	Articles on pharmaceuticals, petition for warning labels
	Consumer Action for Improved Food and Drugs	Petition for warning labels, information on labeling and packaging

(continued)

Industry	Consumer Group	Activities of Group
Professions (Legal and Medical)	None in the legal profession	None in the legal profession
	Ralph Nader's Public Citizens Health Research Group	Publicity of health issues, support for national health insurance, doctor accountability, medical device legislation, opposition to medical malpractice, unnecessary surgery
Retailing	None in retailing	None in retailing

<u>Source</u>: Compiled by the author from information in Chapters 2 through 11.

TABLE 12.3

Major Government Agencies, Federal Legislation,
and Court Decisions by Industry

Industry	Government Agencies	Federal Legislation	Court Decisions
Major Appliances	Federal Trade Commission (FTC) Food and Drug Administration (FDA) Consumer Product Safety Commission (CPSC)	FTC Act Wheeler–Lea Amendment Magnuson–Moss Act Energy Conservation Act Radiation Control for Health and Safety Act Refrigerator Safety Act	General Electric consent order to stop false ads
Banking	Comptroller of the Currency Federal Reserve System FTC Federal Home Loan Bank Board Federal Deposit Insurance Corporation National Credit Union Administration	Federal Reserve Act Banking Act of 1933 Home Owners Loan Corporation Truth-in-Lending Act Fair Credit Reporting Act Equal Credit Opportunity Act Fair Credit Billing Act Real Estate Settlement Procedures Act Unfair and Deceptive Practices by Banks Act	Class action suits brought by consumers largely ineffective

(continued)

Industry	Government Agencies	Federal Legislation	Court Decisions
		Home Mortgage Disclosure Act	
Clothing	National Bureau of Standards FTC CPSC	Wool Products Labeling Act Fur Products Labeling Act Textile Fiber Identification Act Flammable Fabrics Act Permanent Care Labeling Rule	Many companies ordered to stop misbranding and deceptive advertising Removal of Tris-treated products from the market
Household Products	Department of Commerce FTC FDA Health, Education, and Welfare (HEW) Environmental Protection Agency (EPA) CPSC	Food, Drug, and Cosmetic Act Insecticide, Fungicide, and Rodenticide Act Air Pollution and Prevention and Control Act Hazardous Substances Labeling Act Fair Packaging and Labeling Act Poison Prevention Packaging Act CPS Act Magnuson-Moss Act	Cease-and-desist orders or judgments against Listerine, Carter's Pills, Colgate, and others

(continued)

Table 12.3 (continued)

Industry	Government Agencies	Federal Legislation	Court Decisions
		Toxic Substances Control Act	
Lead, Asbestos, and Fluoro-carbons	FDA Occupational Safety and Health Administration (OSHA) EPA CPSC	Food, Drug, and Cosmetic Act Hazardous Substances Act OSHA Clean Air Act Lead-Based Paint Poisoning Prevention Act CPS Act	None; petitions by consumer groups resulted in regulations and enforcement
Mail Order	FTC Post Office	Postal Fraud Statute Consumer Credit Protection Act Fair Credit Billing Act Equal Credit Opportunity Act	Many companies issued cease-and-desist orders involving deceptive or misleading practices Ban on obscene matter upheld, pornography convictions obtained
Petroleum	Justice Department Interstate Commerce Commission FTC	Clayton Act Sherman Act Robinson-Patman Act Anti-Merger Act	Pending divestiture suits Fines and corrective ads for STP

(continued)

Industry	Government Agencies	Federal Legislation	Court Decisions
	EPA Department of Energy National Petroleum Council		Suit for dumping violations
Pharma- ceutical	Agriculture Department FDA FTC	Food and Drug Act Wheeler-Lea Amendment Food, Drug, and Cosmetic Act Miller Amendment Durham- Humphrey Amendment Factory Inspection Amendment Kefauver- Harris Amendments Fair Packaging and Labeling Act	Upheld legis- lation and caused amendments FDA seizures allowed Ruled factory inspection law too vague, causing an amendment Safety not accepted as proof of effectiveness FDA allowed to be judge of safety and efficacy Approval of prescription drug price advertising
Professions (Legal and Medical)	Office of Economic Opportunity Legal Services Corporation	Legal Services Corporation Act Sherman Act Medicaid	Professionals permitted to advertise AMA con- victed and fined for

(continued)

Table 12.3 (continued)

Industry	Government Agencies	Federal Legislation	Court Decisions
	Subcommittee on Citizens Interests HEW FDA Public Health Service	Medicare Kerr-Mills Act Kennedy Medical Device Bill	restraint of trade FDA allowed to treat medical devices as drugs
Retailing	FTC CPSC HEW	Sherman Act Robinson- Patman Act Wheeler-Lea Amendment Anti-Merger Act Flammable Fabrics Act Federal Hazardous Substances Act Truth-in- Lending Act Magnuson- Moss Act	Blue laws abolished in some juris- dictions, maintained in others Price-fixing convictions and fines against major retailers Tris-treated clothing ban upheld

Source: Compiled by the author from information in Chapters 2 through 11.

did not improve itself because of a true consumer orientation, but to increase sales and profits. The self-centered nature of business also applies for consumerists, and is not meant in a derogatory manner.

A wide range of industry responses have been reported in consumer, business, general, government, trade, and company publications since the beginning of consumerism. Table 12.4 has a summary of major trade association responses by industry. Two important conclusions are drawn from this table. First, a large and powerful group of trade associations exists in virtually every industry. Second, some associations feel their role is almost exclusively to protect the rights of their members, not consumers. These associations have worked actively to defeat consumer legislation. The protector associations are most prevalent in banking, clothing, household products, pharmaceuticals, and the medical profession. Other associations feel that consumer satisfaction, education, safety, and desires are as important as the rights of members. Representative of this type of reaction are the associations in major appliances, mail order, and retailing.

A mail survey on consumerism was sent to 95 major trade associations. After two mailings, 38, or 40 percent, answered the questions. Table 12.5 breaks down the response rate by industry. The number of responses varied from two for mail order and the professions to seven for major appliances. While the total response rate is good for a mail survey, the individual response rates for several industries are quite disappointing. It is impossible to know if the nonrespondents are giving an opinion of consumerism, indifference, or are backlogged by other responsibilities. Readers must draw their own conclusions about this.

The replies to the survey are summarized in Table 12.6. Of the 38 associations participating in the study, 16 strongly support consumerism and 11 have mixed feelings. The latter feel consumerism has led to overregulation; nine others see limited effects. Seventeen of the associations have positions, panels, or departments to handle consumer issues; 15 say they do not. Twenty-six supply speakers for government hearings. Twenty send speakers to consumer groups. Twenty associations see consumerism causing an increased responsiveness to consumer issues by business. Seven think the major impact of consumerism will be higher costs and prices.

It appears that the participating trade associations are quite active. Many exhibit strong support for consumerism, have specific people to deal with consumer issues, and furnish speakers to consumer groups. However, a number also appear at government hearings, find consumerism too burdensome, and think there is

TABLE 12.4

Summary of Industry Responses Reported
in Literature by Industry

Industry	Trade Association	Response
Major Appliances	Association of Home Appliance Manufacturers	Product standards, testing, certification, Major Appliance Consumer Action Panel (MACAP), consumer pamphlets, training information
	National Electrical Manufacturers Association	Safety standards
	Electronic Industries Association	Safety standards, consumer affairs office, information pamphlets
	National Electronic Association	National examinations for service technicians
	National Association of Television and Electronic Servicers of America	Examinations on repairs, code of ethics, fair advertising, publications on servicing
	Gas Appliances Manufacturers Association	MACAP
	American Retail Federation	MACAP
	Better Business Bureau	Pamphlets on major appliances, arbitration panels
	National Appliance and Radio-TV Dealers Association	Training courses
Banking	American Bankers Association	Consumer communication, uniform industry actions, protection

(continued)

Industry	Trade Association	Response
		against crimes, legislative lobbying, opposition to laws, support of cost-benefit analysis for laws
	National Association of Mutual Savings Banks	Full disclosure for mortgages, criticism of burdensome laws
	Independent Bankers Association of America	Opposition to fair credit reporting bill
	Consumer Bankers Association	Criticism of laws as technical and costly
	Bank Marketing Association	Financial Advertising Code of Ethics
Clothing	United Infant's and Children's Wear Association	Opposition to wool products labeling
	National Association of Men's Clothing Manufacturers	Opposition to wool products labeling
	National Board of Fur Farming Organizations	Support for fur labeling
	Council of American Fur Organizations	Criticism of animal protection campaigns
	American Apparel Manufacturers Association	Opposition, then support, for flame-retardant deadlines, criticism of CPSC's rulings on Tris
	Textile Fabrics Association	Opposition to textile fabric identification
	Textile Quality Control Association	Promotion and exchange of information
Household Products	Toilet Goods Association	Opposition to cosmetic safety and labeling laws, support of packaging and jars in existence

(continued)

Table 12.4 (continued)

Industry	Trade Association	Response
	Chemical Specialties Manufacturers Association	Opposition to ban on fluorocarbon propellants, information on methods for improving products
	Grocery Manufacturers of America	Self-regulation of packaging and labeling
	Cosmetic, Toiletry, and Fragrance Association	Self-regulation of ingredient listing, petitions to amend legislation and warning labels, denial of cancer link to hair dyes
	Soap and Detergent Association	Losing court case on phosphates, FTC investigation for anticompetitive tactics
	Glass Packaging Institute	Favorable report on childproof tops
	Toiletry Merchandisers Association	Adherence to fluorocarbon ban
	Manufacturing Chemists Association	Challenge to aerosol ban
	Toiletry and Cosmetic Association	Ingredient safety review program
	Proprietary Association	Opposition to efficacy rules and warning labels
	Paperboard Packaging Council	Monitoring of EPA project
	American Paper Institute	Monitoring of EPA project
Leads, Asbestos, and Fluorocarbons	American National Standards Institute	Remarks on surprising success of consumerism

(continued)

Industry	Trade Association	Response
	National Paint & Coatings Association	Proposals for levels of lead in paint, research study on lead consumption effects, petitions with CPSC in support of its proposals, distrust of agencies
	Asbestos Information Association	Campaign in support of asbestos
	Cosmetic, Toiletry, and Fragrance Association	Mandate for excluding asbestos from cosmetic talc
	Chemical Specialty Manufacturers Association	Opposition to fluorocarbon ban, public relations campaign for aerosols, adherence to fluorocarbon ban
	Council on Atmospheric Sciences	Opposition to fluorocarbon ban, research on fluorocarbon propellants
Mail Order	Direct Mail/Marketing Association	Information, industry guidelines, special interest committees, consumer action line, mail preference service
	Mail Advertising Association International	Aid for members in meeting deadlines
	Mail Order Association of America	Testimony at FTC hearings on refunds and the 30-day rule
	Parcel Post Association	Testimony at FTC hearings on refunds

(continued)

Table 12.4 (continued)

Industry	Trade Association	Response
	Associated Third Class Mail Users	Requests for reduced mailing rates
	Mail Advertising Service	Requests for reduced mailing rates
	Better Business Bureau	Handling of complaints on mail orders and mail frauds, arbitration
Petroleum	American Petroleum Institute	Legislative lobbying, correction of stock abuses and deceptive advertising, support for STP, criticism of legislation
	National Petroleum Refiners Association	Correction of deceptive advertising, support for STP
	Pennsylvania Crude Oil Association	Support for STP
Pharmaceutical	National Wholesale Druggists Association	Information to members about compliance with laws, safety, and quality, support for multiple seizures
	Proprietary Association	Standards for plant sanitation, opposition to legislation, praise for Food, Drug, and Cosmetic Act ten years after enactment
	American Drug Manufacturers Association	Opposition to legislation
	American Pharmaceutical Manufacturers Association	Opposition to generic drugs, praise for Food, Drug, and Cosmetic

(continued)

Industry	Trade Association	Response
		Act ten years after enactment, standards for plant sanitation, criticism of inserts and Kefauver Report, agreement to cooperate with Kefauver after amendments
	American Drug Manufacturers Association	Criticism of excessive government intervention, support for factory inspection
	American Pharmaceutical Association	Opposition to restrictions on pharmacists, support for generic drugs
	National Association of Retail Druggists	Opposition to generic drugs, criticism of HEW reimbursement plan, opposition to price posting
	National Association of Chain Drug Stores	Support for open pharmacy ownership, opposition to generic drugs, modified position on inserts
Professions (Legal and Medical)	American Bar Association	Legal aid committee, public service for lawyers, professional ethics, national clearinghouse, advertising guidelines, self-regulation
	American Medical Association	Legislative lobbying, sustained opposition to health insurance and national health care laws, information via journals, self-regulation, opposition to contract practice,

(continued)

Table 12.4 (continued)

Industry	Trade Association	Response
		standards for professional conduct
Retailing	Better Business Bureau	Study on consumer complaints, campaign against false advertising, monitoring of price claims, information to the public
	National Consumer-Retailer Council	Committees on informative labels and standards, improvement of selling and customer relations practices, communications between retailers and consumers
	National Retail Merchants Association	Information to public, education of public, Consumer Affairs Committee, policy recommendations to members

Source: Compiled by the author from information in Chapters 2 through 11.

TABLE 12.5

Response Rates of Trade Associations
to Study by Industry

Industry	Number of Associations Contacted	Number of Participants	Percent Participating
Major Appliances	9	7	78
Banking	10	5	50
Clothing	10	3	30
Household Products	14	4	29
Lead, Asbestos, and Fluoro- carbons	8	3	38
Mail Order	10	2	20
Petroleum	8	2	25
Pharmaceutical	10	4	40
Professions	9	5	56
Retailing	7	3	43
Totals	95	38	40

Source: Compiled by the author from information in Chapters 2 through 11.

overregulation. In sum, the results to the primary survey are quite consistent with the reports in the literature: U.S. trade associations are dichotomous in their responses to consumerism; one group is industry-oriented, the other consumer-oriented.

COMPANY RESPONSES

Individual companies have let their trade associations represent them on the most controversial topics of consumerism. It has been rare for specific companies to oppose publicly consumer legislation or consumer issues. From the available information, it seems that many large companies have been consumer-oriented and instituted

TABLE 12.6

Trade Association Replies to Survey Questions by Industry

Industry	Number of Responses	Feelings about Consumerism	Effects of Consumerism	Association Department Created	Representatives to Government Hearings	Speakers for Consumer Groups	Major Long-Term Impact of Consumerism
Major Appliances	7	2-strong support 4-mixed feelings 1-not involved with consumerism	1-new staff position 2-over-regulation 2-limited effects	3-yes 1-no	3-yes 1-has not been asked	2-yes 2-no	1-increased responsiveness 4-higher costs and prices
Banking	5	2-strong support 3-mixed feelings	4-over-regulation 1-class action suits and awareness	1-yes 4-no	5-yes	4-yes 1-has not been asked	3-increased responsiveness 2-higher costs and prices
Clothing	3	1-strong support	1-over-regulation	1-yes 2-no	3-yes	2-yes 1-no	1-increased respon-

		1-no position 1-not involved with consumerism	2-limited effects				siveness 1-limited 1-unsure
Household Products	4	1-strong support 3-mixed feelings	1-improved communication 3-over-regulation	2-yes 2-no	3-yes	3-yes	2-increased responsiveness 1-higher costs and prices 1-unsure
Lead, Asbestos, and Fluorocarbons	3	2-strong support	3-self-regulation	2-yes 1-no	2-yes 1-no	2-yes 1-no	3-increased responsiveness
Mail Order	2	—	—	1-yes	2-yes	1-yes	—
Petroleum	2	1-mixed feelings	1-self-regulation 1-declining industry image	2-yes	1-yes 1-has not been asked	2-yes	1-increased responsiveness

(continued)

417

Table 12.6 (continued)

Industry	Number of Responses	Feelings about Consumerism	Effects of Consumerism	Association Department Created	Representatives to Government Hearings	Speakers for Consumer Groups	Major Long-Term Impact of Consumerism
Pharmaceutical	4	3-strong support	2-over-regulation 2-limited effects	1-yes 3-no	2-yes 2-no	1-yes 2-no	4-increased responsiveness
Professions (Legal and Medical)	5	2-strong support 1-no position	1-advertising permitted 1-peer review 1-limited effects	3-yes	3-yes	2-yes	2-increased responsiveness 2-unsure
Retailing	3	3-strong support	1-new staff position 2-limited effects	1-yes 2-no	2-yes 1-has not been asked	1-yes 1-no 1-has not been asked	3-increased responsiveness

Totals	38	16-strong support 11-mixed feelings 2-no position 2-not involved with consumerism 7-no response	12-over-regulation 4-self-regulation 2-new staff position 9-limited effects 1-class action suits and awareness 1-improved communication 1-declining industry image 1-advertising permitted 1-peer review 6-no response	17-yes 15-no 6-no response	26-yes 3-no 3-has not been asked 6-no response	20-yes 7-no 2-has not been asked 9-no response	20-increased responsiveness 7-higher costs and prices 1-limited 4-unsure 6-no response

Source: Compiled by the author from information in Chapters 2 through 11.

progressive programs. In the literature, citations of small company responses to consumerism are all but nonexistent.

Table 12.7 summarizes a cross-section of company responses to consumerism as reported in consumer, business, general, government, trade, and company publications. Each industry possesses individual companies that have supported consumer issues, such as: service training, complaint handling, consumer education, expanded warranties, customer relations, consumer publications, simplified documents, product safety, quality control, packaging, advertising, deceptive practices, labeling, hazardous substances, prices, full disclosure, delivery, credit, generic drugs, legal aid, ethics, and community relations. Opposition has concentrated on precise issues, including: truth-in-lending, labeling of clothing, ban on Tris, ban on phosphates, 30-day rule, restrictive pharmacy ownership, drug substitution, new product approval delays, and elimination of legal aid fees. In a few instances, companies have been taken to court on charges of misleading or deceptive practices. Usually, these cases have resulted in cease-and-desist orders; occasionally fines have been imposed.

A mail survey on consumerism was sent to 115 large companies in ten industries. After two mailings, 48 companies, or 42 percent, answered the questions. The response rates by industry are shown in Table 12.8. The number of responses ranges from two for clothing, mail order, and the professions, to nine for petroleum. Aside from clothing, mail order, and the professions, at least four responses were received in each industry. It is interesting to note that the response rate of individual companies approximates the rate for trade associations, despite the greater public role played by the associations on consumer issues.

A summary of the replies to the survey appears in Table 12.9. Of the 48 companies answering the questions, 43 report established complaint policies. Twenty are centralized and 23 are decentralized. Twenty-five companies do not employ an in-house consumer advocate; 16 do. Thirty-two companies mention some form of consumer education. Eighteen offer a broad variety of education programs; nine emphasize brochures; four utilize seminars; and one concentrates on public relations. Twenty-nine companies use brochures as their primary source of product or service information. Thirty-four companies modify their products or services to satisfy company needs. Many firms point out that they do not make modifications to please consumerists. Thirty-nine companies describe rigorous programs to ensure product or service quality. Thirty-four firms feel a wide range of consumer regulations affect their operations; 11 others do not answer this question. Thirty-four firms believe consumerism has resulted in increased responsiveness to consumer needs and

TABLE 12.7

Summary of Company Responses Reported
in Literature by Industry

Industry	Company	Responses
Major Appliances	RCA	Consumer affairs office, service training
	Whirlpool	Consumer affairs office, Tech-Care program, Warranty Service Central, service training, Cool-Line, Consumer Buying Guide
	Zenith	Complaint letters reviewed by chief executive, service training, complaint-resolution system
	Tappan	Corporate director of consumer relations, consumer education materials
	Motorola	Office of Consumer Affairs, complaint-resolution system
	Maytag	Red Carpet Service, expanded warranties, service training
	White-Westinghouse	Sure Service program
	Frigidaire	Service Department, service training
	General Electric	Complaint-resolution system, free educational materials
Banking	Irving Trust	Praise for legislation expanding services
	Bowery Savings Bank	Praise for legislation expanding services
	Citibank	Opposition to truth-in-lending, publications supporting consumerism, legislative lobbying, cooperation with consumer programs, consumer affairs department, simple documents
	Bank of America	Consumer-oriented philosophy, full disclosure

(continued)

Table 12.7 (continued)

Industry	Company	Responses
	Ohio National Bank	Action Center
	Chase Manhattan Bank	Consumer affairs department
	Crocker National Bank	"People hours," free checking to elderly, simple documents
	Continental Illinois Bank	Simple documents
Clothing	Bamberger	Opposition to wool labeling
	J. C. Penney	Flame-retardant children's sleepwear, quality control
	Montgomery Ward	Care labeling, flame-retardant children's sleepwear, quality control
	Sears	Care labeling, flame-retardant children's sleepwear, quality control
	Hollywood Needlecraft	Criticism of Tris ban
	Cassie Cotillon	Criticism of Tris ban
	Monsanto	Wear-Dated program
Household Products	Bristol-Myers	Honesty in packaging, support for fluorocarbon ban, opposition to regulations on hair dyes
	Warner-Lambert	Honesty in packaging, consent order and corrective advertising for Listerine
	Colgate Palmolive	Removal of allegedly deceptive advertising and false claims, recall of laundry detergent, opposition to phosphate ban
	Purex	Improvement in advertising honesty
	Procter & Gamble	Removal of alleged deceptive advertising, opposition to phosphate ban
	Merck	Consent order for Sucret's advertising

(continued)

Industry	Company	Responses
	Lever Brothers	Opposition to phosphate ban
	Miles Laboratories	Changes in labeling and advertising of Alka-Seltzer
	Gillette	Recall of two deodorants
	S. C. Johnson & Company	Removal of fluorocarbons from furniture wax
Lead, Asbestos, and Fluorocarbons	DuPont	Voluntary discontinuation of lead paints
	Glidden-Durkee	Support for lead removal from paint
	PPG	Voluntary reduction in lead in paint levels
	Sherwin-Williams	Voluntary reduction in lead in paint levels
	Johnson & Johnson	Voluntary elimination of asbestos from talc
	Bristol-Myers	Studies on substitutes to fluorocarbon aerosols, introduction of pump spray products
	Gillette	Introduction of alternatives to fluorocarbon aerosols
	Alberto-Culver	Carbon dioxide replacing fluorocarbon propellant
	Clairol	Elimination of fluorocarbons
	Avon	Introduction of pump sprays
	Johnson & Sons	Hydrocarbons replacing fluorocarbon propellants
Mail Order	Montgomery Ward	Quality, low prices
	Sears	Inspection then payment policy, opposition to initial 30-day rule
	Book-of-the-Month Club	Market segmentation, support for negative-option rule
	Sunset House	Support for 30-day rule, support for honest sweepstakes
	Popular Services	Opposition to initial 30-day rule
	Columbia House	Opposition to initial 30-day rule
	Prentice-Hall	Opposition to initial 30-day rule

(continued)

Table 12.7 (continued)

Industry	Company	Responses
	Time, Inc.	Opposition to full disclosure for time-of-order processing
	Grolier	Consent order for misrepresented practices
	Fingerhut	Payment of fine for misleading advertising
	Gulf Oil	Full disclosure of credit charges
	Spiegel	Elimination of suing delinquent customers outside where they lived
	American Express	Testimony on privacy, voluntary compliance with requests for removals from mailing lists
	Reader's Digest	Statement of odds of winning its contest
Petroleum	Exxon	Early opposition to foreign dumping, information on pricing to the public, congressional testimony, disclosure of earnings, statements on additives, ads during oil embargo, proposal for national energy policy, discussion of nuclear reactors
	Mobil	Disclosure of earnings, statements on additives, ads during oil embargo, proposal for national energy policy
	Shell	Statements on additives, ads during oil embargo, proposal for national energy policy
	Conoco	Discussion of nuclear reactors
Pharma-ceutical	Parke-Davis	Defense of advertising
	Liggett	Opposition to law on restrictive pharmacy ownership

(continued)

Industry	Company	Responses
	Bristol-Myers	Criticism of Tugwell Bill and Copeland Bill, sterilized air to remove bacteria in manufacturing process
	Colgate Palmolive	Criticism of Copeland Bill
	Sterling Drug	Sterile bottling, criticism of generics
	Sharp and Dohme	Public service advertising on immunization of children
	Johnson & Johnson	Consumer-oriented training program
	Merck	Sterile packaging, criticism of Kefauver hearings, defense of advertising
	Pfizer	Purity of Terramycin, defense of advertising
	Squibb	Disposable injection units
	Upjohn	Radiation sterilization, criticism of Kefauver hearings
	Hoffman-LaRoche	Education campaign
	Schering	Informative advertising, criticism of Kefauver hearings
	Winthrop Laboratories	Criticism of generics
	Eli Lilly	Criticism of delays in new product approvals
Professions (Legal and Medical)	Washington, D.C. bar members	Opposition to cuts in payments for legal aid services
	Philip Hirchkop	Consumer-oriented lawyer ostracized by peers
	William Mayo	Early support for patients and their rights

(continued)

Table 12. 7 (continued)

Industry	Company	Responses
Retailing	Macy's Federated Department Stores	Bureau of Standards Employee training, actions of individual stores, study of informative labeling and responsibility of manufacturers, customer-orientation, money-back guarantee
	J. C. Penney	Education of surrounding community via education relations department, consumer affairs department, consumer advocate
	Sears	Educational materials and programs, accuracy of catalogs, permanent care labels, private brands
	Hess Department Stores	Personal relations and consumer-oriented promotions, involvement in community, employee training, Consumer Expo, ethnic promotions

Source: Compiled by the author from information in Chapters 2 through 11.

TABLE 12.8

Response Rates of Companies to Study by Industry

Industry	Number of Companies Contacted	Number of Participants	Percent Participating
Major Appliances	15	5	33
Banking	11	7	64
Clothing	10	2	20
Household Products	10	5	50
Lead, Asbestos, and Fluoro-carbons	13	6	46
Mail Order	10	2	20
Petroleum	14	9	64
Pharmaceutical	11	4	36
Professions (Legal and Medical)	9	2	22
Retailing	12	6	50
Totals	115	48	42

Source: Compiled by the author from information in Chapters 2 through 11.

wants; 12 do not reply to this question. When asked to evaluate consumerism, 18 firms decline to comment. Fourteen firms show a strong support for consumerism; 12 have mixed feelings.

From the survey, two points stand out. First, a majority of companies are consumer-oriented and employ a variety of responsible strategies. They utilize complaint policies, education programs, product information, product or service modification strategies, strong quality control programs, and in a number of cases, in-house consumer advocates. Second, consistent with the results of the literature search, when companies have nothing good to say about consumerism, they say nothing. For example, almost 40 percent of the companies do not evaluate the impact of consumerism.

TABLE 12.9

Company Replies to Survey Questions by Industry

<hr>

Major Appliances Industry

Number of Responses	5
Complaint Policy	2 centralized 3 decentralized
In-House Consumer Advocate	3 yes 2 no
Education of Consumers	3 broad variety of programs 1 public relations material
Product- or Service- Related Information	3 broad variety of information 1 brochures
Modifications for Consumers	4 yes
Quality Control Policy	5 rigorous programs
Consumer Regulations Affecting Operations	4 wide range
Reaction to Consumerism	4 increased responsiveness
Evaluation of Consumerism	2 strong support 1 mixed 1 unsure

Banking Industry

Number of Responses	7
Complaint Policy	3 centralized 4 decentralized
In-House Consumer Advocate	2 yes 4 no
Education of Consumers	3 seminars 2 brochures 2 no program
Product- or Service- Related Information	6 brochures
Modifications for Consumers	4 yes
Quality Control Policy	4 rigorous programs

<hr>

(continued)

Consumer Regulations Affecting Operations	7 wide range
Reaction to Consumerism	5 increased responsiveness
Evaluation of Consumerism	2 strong support 1 mixed 1 unsure

Clothing Industry

Number of Responses	2
Complaint Policy	2 decentralized
In-House Consumer Advocate	2 no
Education of Consumers	1 broad variety of programs 1 no program
Product- or Service-Related Information	2 labels or enclosures
Modifications for Consumers	2 yes
Quality Control Policy	2 rigorous program
Consumer Regulations Affecting Operations	2 wide range
Reaction to Consumerism	2 increased responsiveness
Evaluation of Consumerism	2 unsure

Household Products Industry

Number of Responses	5
Complaint Policy	3 centralized 2 decentralized
In-House Consumer Advocate	2 yes 3 no
Education of Consumers	1 broad variety of programs 1 brochures 1 no program

(continued)

Table 12.9 (continued)

Product- or Service- Related Information	1 brochures 4 upon request
Modifications for Consumers	3 yes 1 no
Quality Control Policy	4 rigorous program
Consumer Regulations Affecting Operations	1 wide range 1 little effect
Reaction to Consumerism	2 increased responsiveness
Evaluation of Consumerism	1 strong support 2 mixed

Lead, Asbestos, and Fluorocarbons

Number of Responses	6
Complaint Policy	1 centralized 3 decentralized
In-House Consumer Advocate	2 no
Education of Consumers	1 broad variety of programs 4 brochures
Product- or Service- Related Information	5 brochures 1 labels
Modifications for Consumers	5 yes
Quality Control Policy	5 rigorous program
Consumer Regulations Affecting Operations	4 wide range
Reaction to Consumerism	4 increased responsiveness
Evaluation of Consumerism	1 mixed

Mail-Order Industry

Number of Responses	2
Complaint Policy	2 centralized
In-House Consumer Advocate	1 yes 1 no

(continued)

Education of Consumers	1 brochures
	1 no program
Product- or Service- Related Information	1 brochures
	1 no information
Modifications for Consumers	1 yes
	1 no
Quality Control Policy	1 rigorous program
Consumer Regulations Affecting Operations	1 wide range
Reaction to Consumerism	2 increased responsiveness
Evaluation of Consumerism	—

Petroleum Industry

Number of Responses	9
Complaint Policy	3 centralized
	5 decentralized
In-House Consumer Advocate	5 yes
	3 no
Education of Consumers	7 broad variety of programs
	1 brochures
Product- or Service- Related Information	9 brochures
Modifications for Consumers	8 yes
Quality Control Policy	8 rigorous program
Consumer Regulations Affecting Operations	6 wide range
Reaction to Consumerism	7 increased responsiveness
Evaluation of Consumerism	3 strong support
	5 mixed

Pharmaceutical Industry

Number of Responses	4

(continued)

Table 12.9 (continued)

Complaint Policy	3 centralized 1 decentralized
In–House Consumer Advocate	4 no
Education of Consumers	2 broad variety of programs
Product– or Service– Related Information	4 brochures
Modifications for Consumers	2 yes
Quality Control Policy	3 rigorous program
Consumer Regulations Affecting Operations	4 wide range
Reaction to Consumerism	4 increased responsiveness
Evaluation of Consumerism	3 strong support

Professions (Legal and Medical)

Number of Responses	2
Complaint Policy	1 centralized 1 no policy
In–House Consumer Advocate	1 no
Education of Consumers	1 seminars 1 no program
Product– or Service– Related Information	1 broad variety of information 1 no information
Modifications for Consumers	1 yes 1 no
Quality Control Policy	1 rigorous program 1 none
Consumer Regulations Affecting Operations	2 little effect
Reaction to Consumerism	1 increased responsiveness 1 none
Evaluation of Consumerism	1 strong support

(continued)

Retailing

Number of Responses	6
Complaint Policy	2 centralized
	3 decentralized
In-House Consumer Advocate	3 yes
	3 no
Education of Consumers	3 broad variety of programs
	2 no program
Product- or Service-Related Information	2 broad variety of information
	2 brochures
	1 labels
	1 advertising
Modifications for Consumers	4 yes
Quality Control Policy	6 rigorous program
Consumer Regulations Affecting Operations	5 wide range
Reaction to Consumerism	4 increased responsiveness
Evaluation of Consumerism	3 strong support

Totals

Number of Responses	48
Complaint Policy	20 centralized
	23 decentralized
	1 no policy
	4 no response
In-House Consumer Advocate	16 yes
	25 no
	7 no response
Education of Consumers	18 broad variety of programs
	4 seminars
	9 brochures
	1 public relations material
	8 no program
	8 no response

(continued)

Table 12.9 (continued)

Product- or Service- Related Information	6 broad variety of information 29 brochures 4 labels 1 advertising 4 upon request 2 no information 2 no response
Modifications for Consumers	34 yes 3 no 11 no response
Quality Control Policy	39 rigorous programs 1 none 8 no response
Consumer Regulations Affecting Operations	34 wide range 3 little effect 11 no response
Reaction to Consumerism	35 increased responsiveness 1 none 12 no response
Evaluation of Consumerism	14 strong support 12 mixed 4 unsure 18 no response

Source: Compiled by the author from information in Chapters 2 through 11.

IMPACT OF CONSUMERISM

Consumerism has had a significant impact on all the industries examined, with the least effect on the professions and the most effect on banking and pharmaceuticals. As enumerated in Chapter 1, there are a number of consumer groups, government agencies, government legislation, and trade associations that interact on consumer issues. Tables 12.1 to 12.9 show the major consumerism interests and activities in major appliances, banking, clothing, household products, lead, asbestos, and fluorocarbons, mail order, petroleum, pharmaceuticals, professions, and retailing.

During the last decade, consumerism activities have begun to level off, for several reasons:

Consumer groups remain fragmented and disjointed.

The number of consumer groups has stabilized.

A few national concerns (fuel, inflation, and unemployment) obscure other consumer issues.

Consumers have been saturated with warnings and recalls, which do not have the impact of previous such actions.

There is a backlash against big government.

Government agencies have limited resources and many areas to regulate.

Legislation is stabilizing; new consumer legislation is difficult to enact.

Court decisions in class-action suits discourage consumer filings.

Trade associations support their positions well and point out the costs of legislation; many are now consumer-oriented.

Companies are taking the initiative in dealing with consumer issues, lessening the need for consumerism.

EVALUATION OF CONSUMERISM

Regardless of its costs and problems, consumerism has had an extremely positive effect on all industries. When several trade associations and companies state that consumerism has not affected them, they fail to see the implicit contribution of the movement: practices and policies have been improved to avoid government intervention and probing by consumer groups. The success of consumerism should not really lie in the number of laws passed or court cases won, but on the responsible actions of industries and their member companies.

The positive impact of consumerism is reflected in:

Open government proceedings, which encourage participation by all parties.
The growth of municipal consumer affairs departments.
Trade association practices involving self-regulation, consumer education, the use of consumer panels, speeches to consumer groups, and open communication.
Company practices, including employment of in-house consumer advocates, product safety, market research, consumer education, service representative training, credit, honesty in advertising, complaint departments, and so forth.
Participation of consumers and consumer groups in company affairs.
Media coverage of positive and negative business practices.
Industry and company participation in community affairs.
Growing enrollment in business education.
Favorable rating of consumerism by business.
Success of progressive companies.

The influence of consumerism has not been entirely positive; negative payoffs have also occurred:

Excessive regulation of some industries, such as banking and pharmaceuticals, without adequate attempts at self-regulation.
Conflicts among government, business, and consumers.
Premature regulations, such as flammability (Tris required, then recalled).
Aggressive, expensive lobbying by business.
Contradictory rulings by federal, state, and municipal governments.
High costs of government intervention for both government and business.
Time delays in passage of legislation or court decisions.
Growth of unreasonably high demands by consumers and consumer groups.
Industry and company responses to minority views, at the expense of the majority.
Elimination of good products and delays in the introduction of new ones.

As stated at the outset, consumerism is a powerful and positive force, despite its problems.

FUTURE OUTLOOK

The consumer movement will stabilize in the future; in fact, it would be almost impossible to sustain the amount of activity of the 1960s and 1970s. Nonetheless, the influence of the movement will be strong and widespread, since a trend has been established.

Consumer groups will not grow substantially in number. However, they will become more sophisticated, cooperate better, and understand how to use their power. The government will not enact new legislation, but strive to enforce and monitor existing laws. Open hearings and cost-benefit analysis will accompany any new legislative proposals or amendments. The government will continue to come under fire and attempt to delineate clearly the authority of each of its agencies.

Trade associations and companies will continue their move toward a consumer orientation as they implement progressive policies. Self-regulatory efforts will expand. Deceptive and misleading practices will be deplored by responsible associations and companies. Trade associations will still lobby and take opposing stands on sensitive issues, while individual companies fund the associations and remain in the background.

Consumer groups, government, industry, and companies will increase the communication and cooperation among themselves.

RECOMMENDATIONS

Recommendations are offered for consumer groups, government, industry, and companies.

Consumer groups should:

Cooperate with each other.
Set priorities.
Lobby and support proconsumer political candidates.
Specialize in a narrow range of issues.
Encourage national participation.
Educate consumers.
Interact with government and business.
Weed out self-defeating issues.
Propose positive alternatives with all negative statements.
Consider costs and benefits.
Support majority as well as minority issues.
Seek media coverage.

Government should:

Encourage self-regulation.
Hold open hearings on all issues.
Set enforcement priorities.
Interact with business and consumers.
Delineate agency responsibilities.
Evaluate costs and benefits of legislation.
Reassess existing legislation.
Encourage innovations.
Reduce time lags.
Work for uniform regulations among jurisdictions.
Extract meaningful penalties for violations.
Assess the benefits and costs of product recalls.
Provide agencies with adequate resources.

Industries should:

Continue consumer-oriented policies.
Support meaningful government regulations and provide technical expertise.
Maximize self-regulation.
Present the business side to consumer issues.
Educate consumers.
Promote ethics and honesty.
Communicate with government and consumers.
Publicize the accomplishments of business.
Participate in community affairs.
Assess the costs and benefits of business practices.
Encourage and be receptive to consumerism.
Educate member firms.
Discourage poor practices by member firms.

Individual companies should:

Continue consumer-oriented policies.
Adhere to trade association guidelines.
Encourage consumer views.
Support self-regulation.
Follow honest and ethical business practices.
Publicize company viewpoints.
Communicate with government and consumers.
Disseminate a proconsumer attitude to all employees.
Participate in community affairs.
Educate consumers.

Respond promptly to complaints and criticism.
Support meaningful legislation and provide technical expertise.
Adapt or modify products and services as necessary.
Discourage poor practices by fellow firms.

INDEX

ABOUT THE EDITOR
AND CONTRIBUTORS

JOEL R. EVANS is Associate Professor of Marketing and Chairman of the Department of Marketing and International Business at Hofstra University. Dr. Evans has written various articles and consulted for a number of profit and nonprofit institutions. He is coauthor of <u>Retail Management: A Strategic Approach</u>, <u>Applying Retail Management: A Strategic Approach</u>, and the forthcoming <u>Marketing: An Applied Approach</u>.

DONALD E. BONIN has been with Pitney-Bowes since 1964. He is currently an account representative, and was previously a field engineer. He received his MBA in Marketing from Hofstra University.

JOSEPH A. BRAVATE has been in the pharmaceutical industry, performing a variety of activities, for more than ten years. He earned his MBA in Marketing from Hofstra University.

CHARLES A. CASALE has worked in retailing for almost ten years, and is currently an operations officer at Macy's. He completed his MBA in Finance at Hofstra University.

LISA CHIRANKY is presently a market analyst for the Digital Systems Division of Texas Instruments in Houston, Texas. She received her MBA in Marketing from Hofstra University.

KEVIN E. DEMBINSKI is a senior systems analyst in the Material Management Department of Grumman Aerospace Corporation. He received his MBA in Marketing from Hofstra University.

GLORIA J. FENNER is involved with marketing research, and worked previously for a financial institution. She graduated from Hofstra University with an MBA in Marketing.

ALAN D. GAINES is a corporate fixed income rating analyst in the Corporate Finance Department of Standard & Poor's Corporation. He received an MBA in Finance from Hofstra University.

PETER D. HEIN has worked in banking for nearly 20 years, and is now an assistant vice-president at Citibank. He completed an AIB program and an MBA in Finance at Hofstra University.

SUSAN A. LEVEY currently works for American Express, having previously spent over seven years in the direct-marketing industry. She completed her MBA in Management at Hofstra University.

PAUL R. SAUERACKER is manager of market research for the minerals and pigments division of a major U.S. corporation. He pursued graduate studies in geology at Kansas University and received an MBA from Hofstra University.